The Almanac of Online Trading

The Almanac of Online Trading

The Indispensable Reference Guide for Trading Stocks, Bonds, and Futures Online

Terry Wooten

McGraw-Hill

New York   San Francisco   Washington, D.C.   Auckland   Bogotá
Caracas   Lisbon   London   Madrid   Mexico City   Milan
Montreal   New Delhi   San Juan   Singapore
Sydney   Tokyo   Toronto

Library of Congress Cataloging-in-Publication Data

Wooten, Terry.
    The almanac of online trading : the indispensable reference guide for
trading stocks, bonds, and futures online / by Terry Wooten.
      p.   cm.
    ISBN 0-07-135859-5
    1. Investments—Computer network resources.   2. Electronic
trading of securities.   I. Title.

HG4515.95 .W66 2000
025.06'33264—dc21   99-057873

McGraw-Hill

A Division of The **McGraw·Hill** Companies

1 2 3 4 5 6 7 8 9 0 DOC/DOC 0 9 8 7 6 5 4 3 2 1 0

ISBN 0-07-135859-5

*The sponsoring editor for this book was Stephen Isaacs, the editing supervisor was Janice Race, and the production supervisor was Charles Annis. It
was set in Times Ten by North Market Street Graphics.*

Printed and bound by R. R. Donnelley & Sons Company.

McGraw-Hill books are available at special quantity discounts to use as
premiums and sales promotions, or for use in corporate training programs.
For more information, please write to the Director of Special Sales, Professional Publishing, McGraw-Hill, Two Penn Plaza, New York, NY 10121-
2298. Or contact your local bookstore.

This publication is designed to provide accurate and authoritative information in regard to the subject matter covered. It is sold with the understanding that neither the author nor the publisher is engaged in rendering legal,
accounting, or other professional service. If legal advice or other expert
assistance is required, the services of a competent professional person
should be sought.
*—From a Declaration of Principles jointly adopted by a Committee of the
American Bar Association and a Committee of Publishers.*

 This book is printed on recycled, acid-free paper containing a
minimum of 50% recycled, de-inked fiber.

Special thanks to Jimmie Sparks and Margaret Szydlowski for editing, research, and production work well beyond the call of duty. And to Barbara Etzel for her research and editorial contributions.

CONTENTS

ACKNOWLEDGMENTS

The author gratefully acknowledges the cooperation and supply of invaluable information from NFO Interactive (Greenwich, CT), the New York Stock Exchange (NYSE), Nasdaq, the Bond Market Association, the National Futures Association, and all others who contributed to the compilation of this guidebook.

Online Stock Trading
American Capitalism
Storms a New Frontier

Just as it has made a profound change on other segments of American society, the Internet has sparked a revolution in the way the small investor buys and sells stocks, and to a lesser extent, bond and futures contracts. The growth of online trading is a result of the spread of Internet technology, the equity bull market, and lower interest rates, which drove the small investor out of fixed-income instruments in search of greater returns. As small investors flocked to the equity markets, they also sought the most inexpensive way to enter and exit.

As many as 7 million investors now conduct their stock transactions online, bypassing the more expensive full-service brokerage firms and paying only a fraction of their fees. Projections show the volume of online trading rising in coming years. The big brokerage firms are playing catch-up, announcing plans to set up their own electronic trading operations, even though some were denouncing it as recently as late 1998. Alternative trading systems, such as electronic communications networks (ECNs), are not only putting pressure on brokerage firms, they're challenging the traditional securities exchanges as well.

Additional online trading operations are likely to spring up, particularly if the bull market continues its run.

Regulators, such as the Securities Exchange Commission (SEC), have recognized that electronic trading isn't a fad, but is a change in the fundamental way of doing business in financial services that must be accommodated. SEC Chairman Arthur Levitt has emphasized the importance of the changing marketplace. In a September, 1999, speech in New York City, Levitt said:

> Let us not look back at this time as an opportunity not seized, an endeavor not realized, a challenge not taken, or a frontier not explored. We should not indiscriminately jettison the features of yesterday any more than we should allow entrenched interests to stonewall new market entrants and technologies that offer us superior efficiencies. Only by embracing change, renouncing obstructive impediments, and harnessing innovation and competition will we guarantee to our investors, our economy, and our nation the world's most successful capital markets.

PART I

Trading Online

CHAPTER 1

Online Stock Trading

The brochure accompanying the application to open an account with one of the leading online stock brokerage firms portrays a confident, casually dressed man sitting on a mountainside, notebook computer on his lap. He's obviously ready to connect through his cell phone to execute an online stock trade. "Welcome to the future of investing," the brochure says. "Jacket and tie not required."

Farfetched or not, the scene illustrates the sea change taking place in the stock, bond, and futures markets as the new millennium begins, and Internet technology is its standard-bearer. A populist revolution is occurring among American investors, whether they're on a mountaintop or in the basement office at home. By the millions, they are flocking to online trading, turning away from the traditional coat-and-tie attire of full-service brokers to make their own investment decisions and execute their own trades. The Internet has established a virtual frontier impacting all areas of modern life, from consumer shopping to mass communication to business management and beyond. Is it any wonder that the financial world would be caught up in this revolution to push ahead, pioneering new ways of handling commerce? Not since the Industrial Revolution has there been such promise of speed and access to all. It's the wide open field pioneers have always sought—whether the Pilgrims seeking a new world, the Sooners dashing for the land grab, the Forty-Niners rushing to the gold fields, or the Easterners pushing west for a new life.

Although the risks of online trading are to the pocketbook—not life and limb—they still attend the American dream of a better life, a new order. The pioneer traders come from every walk of life. They are doctors, lawyers, teachers, truck drivers, funeral home owners, and farmers. Most

Figure 1

ONLINE INVESTING PROJECTIONS

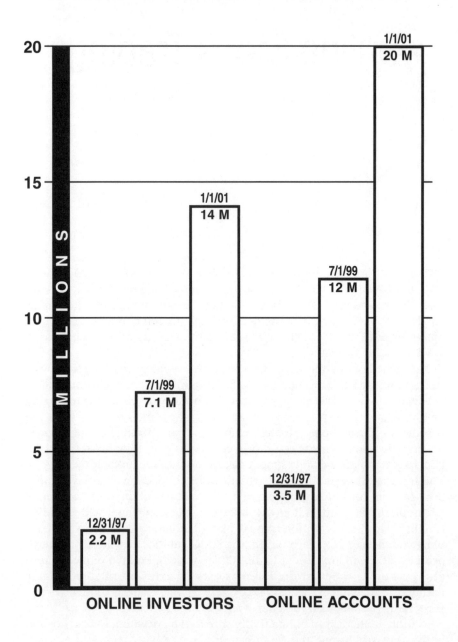

Source: NFO Interactive, Greenwich, CT

work days and trade at night. While Lewis and Clark's frontier was the Louisiana Territory, with its vast mountain ranges to explore and swift rivers to cross, today's online pioneer sits at his or her computer in the basement or spare bedroom in Mount Olive, NC, Stockton, CA, or Stamford, CT. Face glowing from the computer screen, the trader taps in stock orders, checks prices, and looks for investment advice from online newsletters, chat rooms, or news services. In mid-1999, analysts at NFO Research in Greenwich, CT, estimated that as many as 7 million investors were trading as many as 12 million accounts, compared to 2.2 million investors and 3.5 million accounts at the end of 1997. (See Figure 1.) By 2002, NFO predicts there will be as many as 14 million investors with accounts numbering as high as 20 million. Other estimates vary, but all agree the trend is up.

"The ramp has been going up quickly," says Lee Smith, Vice President of Interactive Business Development at NFO, of the growth of online trading. Smith emphasizes that online trading isn't just a fad that will go away. "It's a brand new paradigm," he says. "It's about empowerment, speed, cost, and independence."

"We haven't even scratched the surface yet," echoes James Punishill, an analyst with Forrester Research in Cambridge, MA.

Currently, online investors may be slowing down in some of their activities, reports show, but there remains a large pool of potential online traders. Nevertheless, a recent study by NFO Interactive indicates that online investors continue to be optimistic about the future of online investing, preferring this way of interacting with capital markets. Online investors' activities have just reached a plateau.

"Consequently, online investors will not completely abandon their full-service or discount investing firms," the study notes. NFO emphasizes that the capabilities and attitudes that seduced the current set of online investors may be tugging at the purse strings of offline investors. And since there are six times as many offline investors as online, "the financial community—particularly discount, then full-service firms—should gradually begin to feel investors' transition to the online environment." NFO also notes that both online and offline investors are part of the nearly 42 million—and growing—online households in the United States. Many analysts think that as the comfort level with online investing increases and as Generation X and Baby Busters (the kids who grew up on computers and have never known life without them) take command, online will be the rule, not the exception. Investor attitudes will become more important than demographics or current market positions, according to NFO Interactive.

Online investors have also accelerated changes in the financial marketplace by providing fuel for the electronic communications networks, the most dominant of the alternative trading systems. ECNs handle nearly 20 percent of the more than 12 million securities orders placed online. In addition to posing a threat to broker/dealers by bypassing them, ECNs may evolve into exchanges, challenging such venerable institutions as the New York Stock Exchange. (See Part II, The Players, for more on ECNs.)

CHAPTER 2

Getting Started in Stocks

So with more than 7 million Americans investing online, why shouldn't you? Start by knowing that this is a rapidly changing, ever-expanding field. There are definite pros and cons. It's like the difference between flying with a copilot and flying solo. You may not have enough help or resources if you encounter turbulence. The obvious—and most popular—advantages of trading online are the lower fees and individual freedom, but there's a whole lot more to it than that.

Logging On

If your computer was just delivered last week and you've spent every waking moment surfing the Web, you may think you are ready to connect to the trading world. Yes, you can start trading immediately, without so much as a glance at the rules of the road, but mastering the basics might salvage financial solvency and your survival as an investor in the long run. The novice, blinded by the lure of quick money, is usually headed for trouble.

The National Association of Securities Dealers (NASD) warns that investors should not confuse the procedure for entering an order with making thoughtful investment decisions. Online trading is easy; investing takes time. According to NFO Interactive, the typical online investor has about 20 months of experience.

Even if you are an experienced offline investor and have been buying and selling for years through a broker, having the informational foundation still may not be enough to jump right in. Those minutes spent dialing up the broker, that brief conversation that ensued, that small lapse of time: all represent critical thinking time. It is quite different to push the "Enter" button and have your transaction on record.

Types of Traders

Traders can be divided into several categories. Analysts have their own names for the individual characteristics, but in this discussion, let's stick to basics. Online investors make their own decisions and execute their own trades. Offline investors work through a broker. Most make investment decisions based on their own research and advice from their brokers. Most online and offline traders invest for the longer term.

On the flip side, one group of online investors consists of "day traders." That group differs from most online traders in that they make many more trades, attempting to capture small differentials in stock prices. They are called day traders because they may be in and out of the market several times a day and aren't likely to keep a position open at the end of the day. NFO Interactive says the true day trader transacts 11 times more frequently than the typical online investor does. Day traders are a small minority of online traders, and they are more likely to trade at "day trading" brokerage firms than at home. Day traders have captured a lot of publicity because regulators have been scrutinizing closely the brokerage firms that cater to them.

Give some thought to your trading personality. Determine if you are an aggressive trader, a moderate trader, or a conservative trader. Even if you want to be an aggressive trader, a conservative personality may cause your feet to chill. (See Figure 2.)

Sizes of Portfolios

Trading should come only after planning. What are your short-term and your long-term goals? What strategies do you see helping you accomplish them? The well-ordered portfolio will contain a variety of financial instruments. One of the first steps is to assess your resources. Determine how much money you have available for trading and how you are going to allocate it. Plan what to do if the market turns against you and your resources go down the drain. Although trading stocks online isn't gambling, follow the same rule you would if you were going to a casino: set aside an amount you can afford to lose. Never stretch your resources too thin or get into debt trying to "trade away a loss."

Think about how much you can invest. NFO Interactive says in Q3, 1999, about 23 percent of online investors had a portfolio size above $300,000. That's up from 18 percent at the end of Q1, 1999. Also, because it is now easier to trade, online investors tend to increase the percentage of individual stocks within their portfolios proportionate to mutual funds. Determine the types of stocks you want. Do you want those that show a steady return with little risk? Or do you prefer those that offer high returns

Figure 2

ONLINE TRADING EXPERIENCE

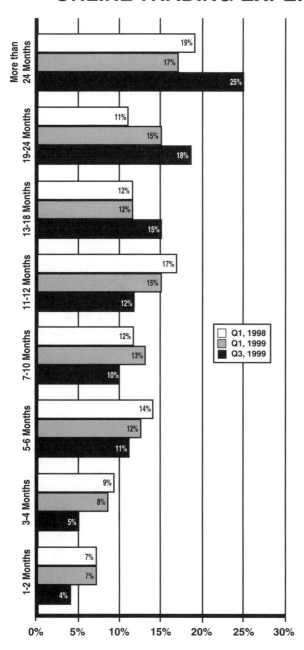

Online Investing Experience

The "typical" online investor has been trading securities online for the past 20 months (up from 18 months in Q1, 1999). The graphic does not reveal a new pattern or dramatic influx of new online investors over the past year–potentially implying a relatively steady growth rate for the online investing industry.

Compared to individuals with less than one year of online investing experience, individuals with one year or more of experience have a more *Aggressive* risk profile, own larger portfolios ($75,000 or larger), manage more than half of their investment portfolio online, are more likely to have switched online trading companies, or are classified as *Heavy* traders.

Source: NFO Interactive, Greenwich, CT

but keep you awake at night? If you don't have an advisor, you'll have to make these decisions yourself.

Types of Accounts

You will also have to decide how to pay for investments. Most investors keep a cash account that requires payment in full for each security purchase, but you can trade a margin account. Buying securities through a margin account means that you can borrow money from the brokerage firm to buy securities. Of course, you pay interest on the loan.

There are disadvantages to margin accounts. If your account falls below the firm's maintenance margin requirement, your broker has the legal right to sell your securities at any time without consulting you first. Some investors have been rudely surprised to learn that "margin calls" are a courtesy, not a requirement.

If the value of your account is less than the amount of the outstanding loan—even if it's because of a one-day market drop—you are liable for the balance. This could be a substantial amount of money, even after your securities are sold. Read your margin agreement carefully and pay attention to the fine print. Make sure you understand it. Even when your broker offers you time to put more cash or securities into your account to meet a margin call, the broker can act without waiting for you to meet the call. In a rapidly declining market your broker can sell your entire margin account at a substantial loss to you, because the securities in the account have declined in value.

Fees

Ask how much deposit you have to make. You might want to avoid companies that charge large deposits. Deposits usually start at about $1000 for a cash account. A margin account deposit likely will be double the amount of a cash deposit.

Question your broker on commission fees. Make sure you know just exactly what charges will be assessed before you start trading. Ask if there are hidden fees. Find out if you're going to be charged extra for different types of trades or for talking to a broker on the telephone. Just as in other sales pitches in the business world, what you see in advertisements may not be quite what you get. Commissions vary. The appeal of online trading is that firms advertise trades for as low as $5 for experienced traders using market orders to $29.95, depending on whom you use and what services you need.

Other Services

Find out what services, if any, you get from the broker. Will you have to pay for extra services? If so, how much? Some online brokerage firms offer few if any extra services. Others offer a wide variety, but you have to pay for them. Before paying for other materials, determine whether you can get your information and research from the Internet for free.

Stock Offerings

What are you buying? Never invest in a product that you don't fully understand, whether online or with a full-service broker. It is not enough to study overall market trends. You must go to the corporate level and track performance and industry changes as well. If your broker does not provide such news, consult print or online business and financial publications. Study annual reports. Get a second opinion from another broker or financial advisor.

Companies that trade on the stock exchanges are known as *public companies*. They have offered their shares to the public to raise capital. *Private companies* are owned by individuals and do not offer their stock for sale to the general public. Know the types of stocks available. *Common stock* is one of two types of stock an investor may purchase in a company. Most stock is common stock. Investors who purchase it have voting rights at the company's annual stockholders' meeting. Common stockholders are not guaranteed dividends, but they may receive higher dividends during the company's prosperous periods. If a company fails or liquidates, common stockholders are paid after bondholders and preferred stockholders.

Preferred stock allows a claim on the company's earnings before payment can be made on common stock and usually entitles the holder to priority over common stockholders if the company fails or liquidates. Preferred stockholders also are entitled to dividends at a specified rate when declared by the company's board of directors, before payment of any dividend on the common stock. Preferred stock normally does not include voting rights.

You should know, too, about initial public offerings (IPOs). These are a company's first sale of stock to the public. A company making an IPO is seeking outside equity capital and a public market for its stock.

Types of Orders and Trades

What kinds of trades do you hope to execute? Most advisors suggest you start with simple trades, buying and selling stocks. Options trading, selling stocks short, and any other complicated trades should be left until you have more experience, or should be made through a seasoned broker.

Ask the broker to explain the difference between market and limit orders and the benefits and risks of each. Firms are required to execute a market order fully and promptly without regard to price. In some market conditions, execution may be at a price significantly different from the current quoted price. Limit orders will be executed only at a specified price or better. Customers using limit orders receive price protection, but there is the possibility that the order will not be executed.

If you are investing in initial public offerings trading in the secondary market, you have to be even more careful. This is particularly true for IPOs that trade at a much higher price than their offering price, or in "hot stocks." Hot stocks are those that have recently traded for a period of time under what is known as "fast market conditions," in which the price of the security changes so quickly that quotes do not keep pace with the trading price of the stock. In these conditions, you are at risk of receiving an execution substantially away from the market price at the time you placed your order. The risk can be reduced significantly by placing a limit order.

You must understand the fast market environment to comprehend the complexity of what can happen and how you can be oblivious and powerless to change the course of your trade if you have not taken precautions ahead of time. As mentioned, the price of some stocks, especially recent hot ones, IPOs, and high tech stocks, can soar and drop suddenly. In these fast markets, when many investors want to trade at the same time and prices change quickly, delays can develop across the board. The situation is literally more than the traffic can bear. Executions and confirmations slow down, while price reports may lag behind actual prices. Online investors are likely to expect instant access to their accounts and near instantaneous executions of their trades. In a fast-moving market, this is not possible. During the past few months, there have been several situations when online brokers had problems handling the volume of trades during volatile market periods.

There are no SEC regulations that require a trade to be executed within a set period of time. However, if firms advertise their speed of execution, they must not exaggerate or fail to inform their investors about the possibility of significant delays.

Remember that to avoid buying or selling a stock at a price higher or lower than you wanted, you need to place a limit order rather than a market order. A market order is a direct buy or sell with no conditions, and it is dependent only on the time the trade is executed. A limit order is an order to buy or sell a security at a specific price. A buy limit order can only be executed at the limit price or lower, and a sell limit order can only be executed at the limit price or higher. When you place a market order, you can't control the price at which your order will be filled.

For example, if you want to buy the stock of a hot IPO that was initially offered at $9 but don't want to end up paying more than $20 for the stock, you can place a limit order to buy the stock at any price up to $20. By entering a limit order rather than a market order, you will not be caught buying the stock at $90 and then suffering immediate losses as the stock drops later in the day or the weeks ahead. Remember that your limit order may never be executed because the market price may quickly surpass your limit before your order can be filled. But by using a limit order, you also protect yourself from buying the stock at too high a price.

Know your options for placing a trade if you are unable to access your account online. Most online trading firms offer alternatives for placing trades. These alternatives may include Touch-tone telephone trades, faxing your order, or doing it the low-tech way—talking to a broker over the phone. Make sure you know whether using these different options can increase your costs. And remember that if you experience delays getting online, you may experience similar delays when you turn to one of these alternatives.

If you place an order, don't assume it didn't go through. Some investors have mistakenly assumed that their orders were not executed and placed another order. They ended up either owning twice as much stock as they could afford or wanted, or in the case of sell orders, selling stock they did not own. Talk with your firm about how you should handle a situation where you are unsure if your original order was executed.

Confirmations and Cancellations

A confirmation is a formal memorandum from a broker to a client giving details of a securities transaction. Make sure you get a confirmation from your broker after you place an order. When a broker acts as a dealer, the confirmation must disclose that fact to the customer.

Cancellations are equally important. When you cancel an online trade, make sure that your original transaction was not executed. Although you may receive an electronic receipt for the cancellation, don't assume that means the trade was canceled. Orders can be canceled only if they have not been executed. Ask your firm about how you should check to see if a cancellation order actually worked.

Broker Selection

By this point in the process, selecting a broker, you should be familiar with the vagaries of the stock market, know the exchanges and their governing bodies, be able to recognize stocks by symbol, routinely perform informational searches, have determined your investment strategy and monetary limits, and understand the basic steps of placing a trade.

To start your selection, log onto the Internet and do a search for online trading firms. They'll pop up like toadstools, and some may be just as deadly to your portfolio as eating toadstools. Mostly, they are just vehicles to execute your order. Some, however, may try to lure you into trading more than you want. (See Knowing the Trading Vehicles in Part II for more information on online brokerages.)

Most full-service brokerage firms will provide limited information even if you aren't a customer. They hope to get your business. They will provide even more if you become a customer. Online trading firms won't provide as much, if any, information. That's why they're charging a lot less for trades. They're executing your orders, not providing research. Don't despair. There's no shortage of stock, bond, and futures information available on the Internet. There are online newsletters, online news agencies, chat rooms, and broker firm sites. Some are free; others can be viewed for a nominal cost. (See Part II, Knowing the Help Sources, for a more extensive listing of places to get financial information.)

The problem, however, is determining who is on the up-and-up and who isn't. On the federal level, the Securities and Exchange Commission (SEC), the watchdog for the securities trading industry, tries to keep up with scams that affect traders. Because of its phenomenal growth during the past few years, the SEC is taking a special interest in online trading. The North American Securities Administrators Association (NASAA), which represents state regulators, also provides information for traders. NASAA last year conducted a study of day-trading firms and concluded that some mislead their investor-customers with promises of quick riches, fail to supervise their operations, and make improper loans to customers to keep them trading. (See Part II, the chapter entitled Knowing the Rules and Regulators, for more details on how to avoid stock scams, both on and off the Internet.)

You wouldn't buy a car without at least kicking the tires and taking a test drive. You might even read some consumer publications to get the lowdown on the make you want to buy. You shouldn't do any less with an online broker, or a full-service broker for that matter. Many online brokers not only let you take a look at their Websites and "kick the tires," they also will let you take it for a test drive. They provide a dummy trading run. Be aware, however, that a dummy trade isn't the real thing any more than a jet simulator is. They're both designed for practice, and the real thing can be a lot scarier and more dangerous. But it's a good idea to check out the sample trading programs of the online firms that offer them. Besides testing out the execution, NASD says an investor should ask some key questions of firms, among them:

1. What about their access and reliability? An investor may suffer market losses during volatility in the price and volume of a stock if there are delays in effecting buy or sell orders. It may be difficult to execute trades because of limitations on system capacity. If you are trading online, you may have difficulty accessing your account due to high Internet traffic. Customers trading through brokers at full-service or discount brokerage firms or through representatives of online firms when online trading has been disabled, or is not available, may have difficulty reaching account representatives on the telephone during periods of high volume. Ask your firm to explain its procedures for responding to these access issues.

2. What about the firm's public communications? The NASD says investors may see a firm using advertisements or sales literature to make claims about the speed and reliability of their trading services. These communications with the public must not exaggerate the broker/dealer's capabilities or omit material information about the risks of trading and the possibilities of delayed executions. Moreover, broker/dealers should have the systems capacity to support any claims they make about their trading

services. Misrepresentations or omissions of material fact in public communications violate NASD rules. You should ask your firm whether it has adequate systems capacity to handle high volume or high volatility days.

Your broker should carefully explain how delays can occur and how they will impact your trade. High trading volumes at market opening or during the trading session may create delays in execution and cause orders to be executed at prices much different from the market price quoted at the time the order was entered. Ask brokers to explain how order executions are handled by market makers, particularly when the market is volatile. NASD says it is extremely important for online investors to inquire about handling, since most expect quick executions at prices at or near the quotes displayed on their computer screens.

3. What about the disciplinary history of a brokerage firm or broker? Your broker's reputation and integrity cannot be assumed. To find out, call (800) 289-9999, a toll-free hotline operated by the National Association of Securities Dealers, Inc. (NASD). Also find out if the brokerage firm is a member of the Securities Investor Protection Corp. (SIPC). SIPC provides limited customer protection if a brokerage firm becomes insolvent. Ask if the firm has other insurance that provides coverage beyond the SIPC limits. Of course, you are not insured against losses attributable to a decline in the market value of your securities when investing with any broker. SIPC can be contacted at 805 15th Street, NW, Suite 800, Washington, D.C. 20005-2207, or by calling (202) 371-8300.

(For more investor information in general, visit the NASDR Website, www.nasdr.com, under "Investors Resources," or visit the NASD's Investor Website at www.investor.nasd.com. Knowing the Rules and Regulators in Part II provides more information on recognizing and avoiding securities scams.)

What if you're not happy with your online broker? It is possible to change, and many investors do. Just as employers, retailers, and others have found, loyalty is no longer a moral imperative. NFO Interactive says that as of mid-1999, about 20 percent of all online investors had switched online brokerage companies. The reasons for switching included transaction fees as well as the availability of new online investing features or capabilities. Lack of customer service was also increasingly cited as a reason to change, the NFO notes. Figure 3 profiles the changing reasons for opening online accounts during 1998 and 1999.

Application

You have made your choice of a broker. Now you're ready to sign on. At the firm's Website, you will be asked to fill out an application. You can either do it online; print it out, sign it, and mail it to the broker with your deposit; or ask for an application to be mailed. The application is similar to any you would fill out for a financial institution. It will require the following:

Figure 3

REASON FOR OPENING AN ONLINE INVESTING ACCOUNT

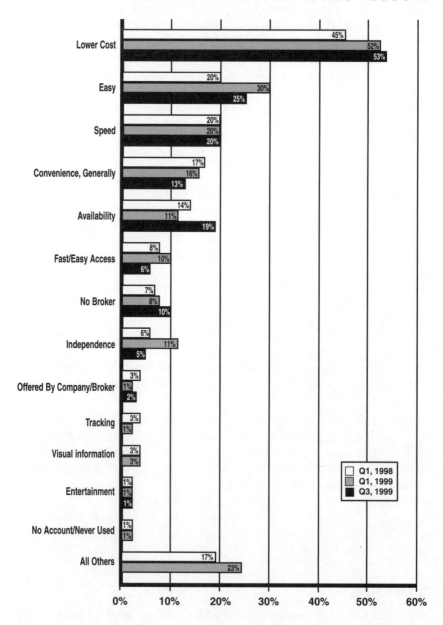

Source: NFO Interactive, Greenwich, CT

- Type of account (individual or joint; cash or margin)
- Deposit option (check, bank transfer, brokerage transfer, mutual fund, securities certificates, etc.)
- Social security number
- Date of birth
- Employment details
- Investment objectives, experience, and knowledge
- Other investment accounts
- Placement of cash distributions between investments (credit interest, money market funds, government securities portfolio, tax-exempt portfolio, etc.)

Stay Smart, Stay Aware, Stay Prepared

Once you've opened your account, you're ready to start trading. You suddenly have the same power as your former broker. You can execute trades. Remember, however, that it is your money on the line; you don't want to spray trades about indiscriminately. Commissions may be cheaper trading online, but investing mistakes can be many times more costly. Unless you have some solid trading experience, use common sense until you get a feel for the online trading system. All that is changed is that you can file your own trades. Being able to trade online doesn't automatically make you the country's next stock guru.

NASD warns investors there is risk in every trade. Besides being prepared before trading online, investors should be smart and aware after they start. The market is an ever-changing environment, making it more important than ever for investors to use tools they understand. It can't be said too often: Know the firm you are dealing with and make sure that when you choose to trade online, you do so in line with your investment objectives and your ability to tolerate investment risk.

Reminder

The NASD lists six points to remember:

1. The higher the expected rate of return, the greater the risk. Depending on market developments, you could lose some or all of your initial investment, or a greater amount.

2. Some investments cannot easily be sold or converted to cash. Check to see if there is any penalty or charge if you have to sell an investment quickly or before its maturity date.

3. Investments in securities issued by a company with little or no operating history or published information may involve greater risk.

4. Securities investments, including mutual funds, are not federally insured against a loss in market value.

5. Securities may be subject to tender offers, mergers, reorganizations, or third-party actions that can affect the value of ownership investments. Pay close attention to public announcements and information sent to you about such transactions. They involve complex investment decisions. You should fully understand the terms of any offer to exchange or sell your shares before you act.

6. The past success of a particular investment is no guarantee of future performance.

CHAPTER 3

Online Futures Trading

The futures market is a different game from either stock trading or bond trading. In the futures markets, traders buy or sell contracts in financial instruments or commodities for future delivery. The trader who buys a December soybean contract for $5.00 a bushel expects it to be worth $5.25 or more by the time he or she sells it. If so, there is a profit. If the price drops to $4.75, the trader suffers a loss.

Although a trader can buy a futures contract with a smaller margin than in the stock markets, there is greater volatility, which can carry with it the increased risk of a novice trader losing money. There are many factors to be aware of in trading the futures markets. On the agricultural commodities side, weather, government policies, and foreign demand all play a part. Most beginning investors would be better served not to include futures in their portfolios until they have become more astute.

Futures traders usually are either hedgers, speculators, or professional traders. Hedgers are mostly farmers, grain elevator operators, processors, and packing plants—those who either grow or use the product. They use the futures markets for price protection, selling contracts to offset the material they are holding. Speculators are the traders who take up that hedge, buying or selling in the hope of making a profit. Professional traders may trade for others or be employed by a large brokerage firm, bank, or other institution. Traditionally, hedgers and professional traders have been seen as having an advantage over the speculator, since they have access to greater resources and information. But the Internet has leveled the playing field between professional traders and hedgers and the typical speculator. Information is available via the Internet at little or no cost that once was available only to the broker or professional trader at a high cost. Delayed price quotes and real-time news are now offered free on many Websites, such as www.futuresource.com. This is a huge leap forward for the individual speculators, who now have timely and useful information at their fingertips.

The online broker may provide up-to-the-minute research and reports, and there are innumerable Websites with free market information. Even if you decide online futures trading is not for you, don't overlook the wealth of free information available on the Web. Everything from real-time news and weather maps to price charts, technical studies, and expert commentary is available, and much of it is free.

Electronic trading has certainly become a cause of worry for the open-outcry traders in the futures pits. More than a few pit traders in Chicago and New York are boning up on their computer skills and are trying the e-trading method, either part-time or full-time. Pit traders still have political clout with U.S. exchange officials, and a complete abandonment of open-outcry trading anytime soon is unlikely. However, pit traders need only look to the European exchanges to see that electronic trading is rapidly growing in popularity, so much so that some exchanges there no longer have open-outcry sessions.

Pros and Cons

Hopefully, if you are even considering futures trading, you are somewhat computer and Internet literate and wary. Even the online trading pros have to be careful. A major financial news service reported this real-life example of e-trading chaos caused by carelessness. A London trader with a major firm inadvertently leaned on his computer keyboard after making a bond futures electronic trade. His computer then sent a wave of 145 separate sell orders for the bonds. His elbow was pressing the "Instant Sell" button!

Knowing the terminology is equally critical. If you don't have futures market orders or other terminology down pat, think twice about executing a trade without other human intervention. Even a discount broker will give guidance on a particular futures trade involving stops or other market orders.

Can you save money by e-trading futures? Maybe. However, there are discount brokers out there fighting for every futures contract they can get. Many don't care if the orders are telephoned in or e-mailed in. The more conventional method of contacting a broker also works well at this point in time. Online may become the cheapest way to trade futures, but presently, the conventional methods are providing tough competition.

As with other forms of e-trading, there are advantages other than lower cost. What value would you put on sitting at your desk in your own home, on your own time, free from distractions or possible pressure from a broker, to trade markets? The appeal of individualism alone is motivation enough for some traders to make the switch to electronic trading. Most successful traders will tell you that much of their success comes from developing a plan and sticking to it, not being swayed during the heat of the battle. Patience and discipline are literally preached in the field of futures trading. Being able to concentrate on trading from your own home will go a long way for some in reaching those dual goals of patience and discipline.

Exchanges

One sign that electronic trading is here to stay is the emphasis the major exchanges have put on after-hours trading. The benchmark after-hours trading medium is GLOBEX, a division of the Chicago Mercantile Exchange. The first "after-hours" futures trading on GLOBEX occurred in June of 1992. Via GLOBEX, the online trader can trade such futures and options markets as the S&P 500 (Standard & Poors), Eurodollars, Japanese yen, Canadian dollar, Swiss franc, and many other currencies, as well as the French CAC 40 stock index on the MATIF Exchange in Paris.

The Chicago Board of Trade's Project A allows the online trader to day-trade corn, soybeans, and wheat, as well as U.S. Treasury bonds, likely the most popular futures contract in the world!

Other U.S. futures exchanges, such as NYMEX (the ACCESS system), also provide after-hours trading in such futures markets as crude oil, heating oil, unleaded gasoline, and natural gas.

To obtain contract specifications on after-hours futures markets and the times those markets trade, go to the exchanges' Websites:

www.cbot.com

www.cme.com

www.nymex.com

Something to consider seriously if you do trade after hours is the liquidity in a market. Make sure the liquidity is adequate to ensure a good fill. You can trade markets that are not open after hours, but you won't get a fill until the open-outcry session opens the next trading day. Volatility is typically less during after-hours trading, but not always. You may want to try some basic trades when beginning. Save the more complicated trades for later, or go the route of the conventional broker.

Brokers

There is certainly no shortage of brokerages offering online futures trading opportunities. As with all e-trading, it's quite another thing to determine which firms are reputable and responsive to consumer needs. You will have to research the field. Many of the well-known and respected brokerages now offer online trading. That is a safe place to start. If you are interested in an online broker that is unfamiliar to you, take the same steps you would in any other situation where the product or service is unknown. A call to the National Futures Association or Commodity Futures Trading

Commission may be prudent. Better yet, e-mail these organizations with your queries.

Even a call to the Better Business Bureau is a start. To find an electronic trading broker via the Web, simply use your favorite Internet search engine and type in the words "electronic futures trading" or some related string. You'll come up with a plethora of sites. When it comes to actual trading and executions, the better electronic brokerages should allow the futures trader to create and transmit orders directly to the floors of the major exchanges, or to after-hours processing centers. Order confirmations, fills, and cancellations are automatically routed to your PC via the Internet in a timely manner. Be aware that some brokerages route the trader's electronic order to a phone clerk, who then processes the order in a conventional way. This should not usually cause worry, however, as this process still occurs quickly.

Fees and Security

Learn what fees are standard and which supplementary services are fee-based with the broker you choose. Online trading commissions per round-turn futures trade range from $15 to the low $30s, not including National Futures Association (NFA) exchange fees and wire transfer fees.

Transferring funds electronically should not be a big concern. Reputable brokerage firms have safeguards in place for your protection during this process and for your account overall. However, these types of risks can never be completely eliminated, and you need to be conversant so you can quiz your broker for assurances regarding security issues.

Application

After much consideration (and learning), you've decided you will try your hand at trading futures. Like the forms traders fill out to trade markets conventionally, be prepared for mountains of e-paperwork. Also, expect to wait until all the paperwork is processed. This can take as little as a few hours, or if the processing is done by snail mail, as long as a few days.

Here are some typical questions asked in the "customer data sheet" that a potential futures trader will need to answer:

Date of birth

Address

Day phone number

Night phone number

Fax number

E-mail address

Bank reference

Bank phone number

Bank contact person

Annual household income

Net worth

Employer

Position held

Social security number

Spouse information

Reminder

All the warnings related to online stock and online bond trading apply to online futures trading—only moreso!

CHAPTER 4

Online Bond Trading

While online bond trading has not received as much attention as online stock trading, that situation likely will change over the next several years. Already, the number of electronic trading options for bonds has doubled. According to the Bond Market Association, an industry trade group, at the end of 1998 there were 26 systems that offered or announced their intention to offer electronic trading of fixed-income instruments. That compares to 11 systems that existed a year earlier. Much of this growth is directed toward systems for institutional clients, banks, corporations, and brokerage firms. Some of that growth, however, is spilling over into online trading services for individuals. Even now, online brokerage activity accounts for approximately 25 percent of all retail stock trades, according to the Securities and Exchange Commission. The number of online brokerage accounts is expected to surpass 10 million by the end of 1999. With the bond and stock markets evenly matched in dollar amounts outstanding, clearly the bond market has much potential for increasing the amount of online trading activity.

Although growth is occurring, the road to online trading hasn't been without its bumps. SEC statistics show complaints about online trading increasing sharply. Some of the issues relate specifically to online trading, whereas others are complaints common to all trading situations. From October 1997 to September 1998, the SEC received 1114 complaints involving online trading firms, a 330 percent increase over the 259 complaints received in the prior year. Since September 1998, the number of complaints has already doubled in comparison to the period of a year earlier. The most common complaint was the difficulty traders had in accessing their accounts. Second came failures or delays in executing orders. The third most common complaint involved errors in processing orders.

The SEC's statistics offer a vivid illustration of the types of problems the online trader should be on the lookout for when selecting an online service. Until the industry develops and refines its system, it's likely that more bumps along the road will be encountered. Until then, online bond traders must arm themselves with information and awareness and be very educated users of online trading systems and methods.

Pros and Cons

For the individual investor, bonds have been something of a hidden world. Why, then, trade bonds online? Even more than with stocks, being online has given the bond trader maximum information and optimal tools. Bonds are the fixed-income instrument many conservative investors prefer. They are a portfolio staple. Despite the difficulties some online traders are experiencing, online bond trading is poised to create more transparency in the market by increasing the amount of information available to the public. While legislation has been on the books for a quarter of a century to integrate and create national markets for both stocks and bonds, the bond market has lagged behind.

Because stocks are traded on an exchange and there is one symbol per stock, it has been much easier to implement online stock and mutual fund trading. But consider: while an investor tends to think of a single 10-year Treasury note, in fact, there are many outstanding 10-year note issues, since the 10-year note is issued quarterly. That complicates the pricing situation. This ongoing issuance produces many older, off-the-run Treasuries that trade infrequently. Attempting to determine a price for them is difficult. Pricing information is more difficult to get for bonds than it is for equities. Even in this day of modern technology, many bond trades are still conducted by brokers calling other brokers to get current prices and to trade. Typically, this technique is even used for online bond trading.

Under competitive pressure, as well as pressure from government authorities, the bond market is beginning to create more transparency. For example, Arthur Levitt, Chairman of the SEC, has called for more transparency in the bond market. And Congress is considering legislation that would direct the SEC to develop rules for collecting data on corporate bonds. Already, some bond pricing information has found its way into the public domain. In 1999, the Bond Market Association began providing pricing data on municipal bonds from the previous day's trade. The information can be searched and organized on the Association's Web page.

Trading bonds online can be fast-paced and exciting. Just don't get so carried away with the act of trading that you forget about the fundamental trading principles. Just because it is easy to trade doesn't mean that it should be done frequently. Even at low commission levels, you still are generating costs that take away from your returns.

Because you are online, it is tempting to get seduced by conversations in chat rooms or postings on message boards. Many times, these tips can be nothing more than unfounded gossip. Don't rely on this information without checking with reliable sources.

Pay attention to the types of prices you are seeing. Are they real-time prices, or does the company need to call another broker to obtain a live quote? If a call has to be made, how long is that quote good for? Are you at risk of the market moving during the time the process is unfolding?

Types of Bond Offerings

When bonds are mentioned, most people immediately think of U.S. government debt and its approximately $450 billion daily market. Within this Treasury category, though, there are many instruments, including government securities such as Treasury bills (T-bills—three- or six-month or 52-week bills), Treasury notes (two-, five-, and 10-year), or the 30-year Treasury bond.

In addition to U.S. Treasury debt, there are municipal bonds, corporate bonds, mortgage- and asset-backed securities, federal agency securities, and foreign government bonds. Besides Treasury bills, there are many other short-maturity options, such as certificates of deposit and commercial paper.

In addition to online trading activity, issuers of Treasury, municipal, and corporate debt have begun to use the Internet to sell debt securities directly to their customers. Doing this provides a convenient way for purchasers to obtain securities and can reduce costs for both the issuer and the purchaser. The U.S. Treasury Department offers investors the chance to buy Treasury securities at its auctions for as little as $1000. Treasuries can be purchased online, or by phone or mail order. To participate, you must set up a TreasuryDirect account. Forms for this can be downloaded from the Bureau of Public Debt's Website or received in the mail.

While the TreasuryDirect program has existed since 1986, it has only been since October 1998 that purchases could be made on the Internet or over the phone. Once the account is set up, traders can purchase Treasury securities at noncompetitive prices when the Treasury auctions its new issues. With a minimum to start of $1000 and in multiples of $1000 thereafter, this online service is particularly well-suited for individuals. Yet the site isn't available for active trading. If the investor decides to sell the security before it matures, the Treasury can do that or the securities can be wired out to the investor's brokerage account. The Treasury also offers the option of reinvesting maturing securities at the next auction.

Corporate and municipal debt issuers are beginning to use the Internet to sell securities as well. However, unlike the Treasury Department's program, this service typically is directed solely at large institutional customers. In the spring of 1999, Ford Credit, a unit of Ford Motor Company, became the first direct issuer to sell commercial paper on the Internet.

Government treasurers and large institutional investors participated and have taken advantage of the speed, convenience, and efficiency of purchasing commercial paper online. The Web allows Ford Credit to benefit from lower operating costs and time savings, and creates a significant competitive advantage over other commercial paper issuers.

A school district in Pennsylvania has used the Internet to sell bonds directly to purchasers. In 1999, the Lancaster, PA, school district sold $29.2 billion of bonds over the Internet. After comparing options and analyzing data from other Pennsylvania bond deals done in the previous year, the school district officials decided that the online auction would provide the lowest expected true interest cost to the school district. Participation in the auction was limited, however, to certified large bidders; individuals were not included.

Broker Selection

When looking for a specific trading firm, the most important principles to keep in mind are the common sense fundamentals of trading. Traders must guard against allowing the ease and speed of online trading to lure them into trading too quickly and without evaluating what they are doing.

Evaluate different trading firms and whether or not they offer the ability to trade bonds online. While it may seem obvious that they would, many online trading firms refer you to a phone number when you want to trade bonds.

Also, not every service offers all options in bond trading. Make certain your potential trading service handles a variety of instruments.

Other factors that should be carefully considered before launching into online bond trading include determining the reliability of the service. Talk to other traders. Pay attention to reports about the difficulties companies experience or the great service they provide. Many publications are running stories comparing and ranking the various online services. Seek out this information before making your choice.

Technology is typically the key to reliability. Because there is great demand for online trading, companies are rushing to update their systems to handle new customers. When they fall behind in this updating, technology constraints arise. The inability to log onto the network to trade is one of the difficulties an online trader faces that a traditional trader doesn't. Also, delay in processing orders is a common complaint among online traders. Judge how your service is going to respond and deal with these situations. Technology also poses other challenges and situations that the trader should understand. For instance, where does the order go once it is sent with the click of the mouse? Does the order need to be seen by another person before it is filled? How long does this process take? Understanding this process and the potential complications will go a long way in helping you protect yourself. Experts also advise using stop-loss orders when placing trades so you don't end up buying a debt security at a significantly worse price than you expected.

Because of technological glitches, it is likely that at some point the online trader will end up being an irritated customer. Find out in advance how the company resolves disputes. Some companies will refund commissions if the trader doesn't think the price received on a trade was as favorable as it should have been. How far will the brokerage you are considering go to make you a satisfied customer?

Discuss with the broker how delays in filling orders are handled. Find out what the procedure is for processing your trade once you click the button. Does it go straight to another computer to be filled? Does someone have to look at it before it can be acted on? Does the trading firm have to make a phone call to get a current quote? Any delay in getting an order filled could result in a less desirable price.

And what about system failure? Is there another way to trade if the system crashes? Ideally, the online trading firm you choose should offer other ways to trade besides online trading, an automated phone system, for instance, or speaking to a broker. This also will provide convenience if you want to make a trade and the computer isn't close by.

Confirmation difficulties can also arise. Without confirmation, you don't know if your order was received or if there was perhaps a technical glitch. Confirmation should be available in a variety of formats for your maximum convenience. These include e-mail, fax, mail, phone call, or pager notification. Nothing is worse than doing a trade, having the market go the right way, and then finding out that the trade was never placed.

You also need to know the broker's bond pricing sources. While stock prices are widely publicized and determined on central exchanges, the situation for the bond market couldn't be more different. There is no dominant, central market location that concentrates a majority of the pricing information. So despite the abundant technology, prices are often determined by brokers phoning other brokers. Ask where the firm gets its pricing information and understand the process. Remember that the prices you see on the screen may not be up-to-date.

News and information services are another item on your comparison checklist when selecting a broker. Online services offer a variety of features, including a large assortment of news and headline services. If it is important that you have a particular news service, does the online company provide it on its Web page?

Having this provided without charge makes your commission dollar go farther—in addition to being very convenient. If you want real-time news headlines, make certain that this is provided by the brokerage Website. Some services provide real-time headlines, and others provide real-time news stories. Some only provide stories on a delayed basis.

The level of research provided by Internet trading sites varies considerably. If there is a research firm that you particularly like, see if it is included on the Websites of companies you are considering. In addition to written research, does the service provide any charts that would be helpful?

Security measures and encryption technology are topics to bring up as well. Make certain that the firm ensures that its site is secure and discusses how it manages that security.

Whether trading stock, futures, or bonds—or having your roof repaired—investigate the history of the firm you are considering. The securities industry, while it is comprised in the majority by honorable firms, does attract its share of fraudulent activity. With the Internet creating an easy and inexpensive entry path for many businesses, beware of the potential for fraud. Look for companies with a solid track record and name recognition. Also, there is nothing wrong with asking for references from existing customers. (For more information on fraud, see Knowing the Rules and Regulators, in Part II.)

Application

Once you've done your homework, it's very easy to begin trading bonds online. Typically, the necessary paperwork can be completed online. Firms ask the standard questions, such as contact information, birth dates, social security numbers, and net worth information. Usually $1000 to $2000 is needed to open an account. Many services allow you to begin trading within the next 24 hours. Another option is to print the form and send it through the mail. In most cases, the paperwork must be processed before trading is allowed. Sometimes, that can take up to a week.

While the forms needed to begin trading often are quite simple, don't let the ease of filling them out lull you into complacency. It is important to understand how to enter trades and how to navigate around the Website. Until you are very familiar with the Website, don't try to trade. To become familiar with the site, use the trading demonstration. Some sites go a few steps further and have a practice trading area where you can enter nonlive trades. Make use of this area in order to avoid expensive mistakes later. If you need to, contact the staff for assistance.

Reminders

Don't ignore the fundamentals.

Be aware of misleading tips and chatter and fraudulent offers.

Know whether you are seeing real-time prices.

Know who to call for alternatives if you encounter system trading problems.

PART II

Toolkits for Trading Online

The Players

The Internet and computer technology and a progressive view of its application by the Securities and Exchange Commission (SEC) have spurred the development of alternative trading systems (ATS) that are now threatening to change permanently the complexion of the securities, bond, and futures industries.

In the forefront of the ATSs are electronic communications networks (ECNs), computerized trading systems that match buy and sell orders without the need for a market maker. ECNs have gained popularity within the securities industry because they also allow investors to remain anonymous and they slash trading costs by bypassing broker-dealer commissions and the fees the exchanges charge investors to access quotes. ECNs also eliminate the need to maintain large numbers of traders, floor brokers, and the costs they entail. Internet trade processing is cheaper than traditional methods. ECN orders are matched electronically so investors get immediate price and transaction confirmation.

Since the SEC, in 1997, adopted more accommodating rules for alternative trading systems, numerous ECNs have been formed. At least nine are playing significant roles in the changes taking place in the securities industry.

ECNs account for nearly a third of the trading of stocks on the Nasdaq Stock Exchange. They are also the preferred method of execution for online brokerage firms, handling nearly 20 percent of those orders. An influx of as many as 7 million individual investors trading online has contributed to this growth.

As the enthusiasm for electronic trading grows, full-service brokerage firms, broker/dealers, and the traditional stock exchanges are feeling the heat. Online brokerage firms, with their cut-rate commissions, have forced the full-service brokers to adjust fees and consider new approaches to keep their customers. ECNs have already pressured broker/dealers in the institutional brokerage sector, but some are now gearing up to take on the stock exchanges.

Some of the leading ECNs, however, are no longer content with just displaying and matching orders and providing after-hours trading. Under the SEC's new regulatory changes designed to create a framework for ECN expansion, some of the electronic firms want to convert to exchanges. Two ECNs—Archipelago and Island—applied in 1999 to the SEC to become stock exchanges. Others may follow. ECN consolidation is seen as likely, particularly when one gains exchange status. However, the process of gaining SEC approval could take as much as 18 months.

If one of the strong ECNs becomes an exchange, the stock market trading field could really experience even greater transformation, analysts say. Besides keeping brokerage fees down, an ECN with exchange status likely would create a more efficient system to narrow the spread between bid and ask prices, which is the most significant investment cost. An electronic exchange would compete with the Nasdaq, the NYSE, and possibly even foreign stock exchanges.

Despite these gathering clouds on the horizon, the NYSE and Nasdaq responded sluggishly during the early part of 1999—reflecting in part their ownership by members. Both NYSE and Nasdaq have considered going public to be in a better position to deal with the ECN onslaught.

James Punishill of Forrester Research says the exchanges in early 1999 were moving at a snail's pace dealing with the ECN threat, and have used every excuse in the book. "Those guys are asleep at the wheel," says Punishill of the reaction of the NYSE and Nasdaq to the ECN challenges.

But by the end of 1999, NYSE and Nasdaq both were moving much quicker to deal not only with ECNs, but to accommodate online traders of every ilk.

One of the results of ECNs and online brokerage firms is the clamor for expanded trading hours. Since the majority of the 7 million online investors work in the day and trade at night, they want greater access to the markets. Several online brokerage firms and ECNs are accepting after-hours trades, making it possible that 24-hour trading will be available for individual investors.

Nasdaq and the NYSE will likely extend trading hours from their traditional 4 p.m. Eastern Time close. If an ECN becomes an exchange, 24-hour trading may come even sooner.

ECNs, although more prevalent in the domestic equities markets because of the increase in individual investors trading online, are moving into the fixed-income sector—but on the institutional side. The Bond Market Association (BMA) said in 1999 that 26 systems were offering, or plan to offer, electronic execution for fixed-income instruments.

ECNs have received strong support from SEC chairman Arthur Levitt, although he has also cautioned them. In a speech in September 1999, Levitt said ECNs "have been one of the most important developments in our markets in years—perhaps decades." He asserted how ECNs present serious competitive challenges to the established market centers and how they "must be able to compete with traditional exchanges and dealer markets in an environment free from unfair advantages or unreasonable barriers." He warned ECNs, too, however: that they have responsibilities and that the SEC would not hesitate to take action against them when they fail to correct capacity deficiencies. He also said the SEC's staff was examining ECNs' quote fees to find a fair and competitive balance.

ECNs and other alternative trading systems are completely changing the playing field in the securities, fixed-income, and futures industries. The impact is greater than just shifting from open-outcry and auction floor trading to the Internet; it will be felt in back offices as well, with processing.

"ECNs will play a significant role in the securities industry and, therefore, in securities processing," Michael T. Reddy, chairman of EDS Global Financial Markets Group, told the Securities Industry Association's Operations Conference in May 1999. "Large firms such as Goldman Sachs and Merrill Lynch are aggressively partnering and investing in multiple ECNs because they realize that the Internet will be a significant delivery channel and ECNs will be a significant executive engine in the future."

Whether they remain ECNs or become exchanges, the new vehicles will play a significant role in the twenty-first century marketplace, and the SEC indicates it will make sure the playing field is level. SEC chairman Levitt has called for greater competition and innovation as markets adapt and respond to new technologies. Speaking at Columbia Law School in New York during the fall of 1999, Levitt said that in meeting these challenges, the principles of integrity, quality, and fairness must not be lost to parochial concerns.

"We have an opportunity today that I don't think we'll have again in our lifetime—to realize the vision for a true national market system—one that embraces our future as much as it honors our past," Levitt said.

Key Electronic Communications Networks

Archipelago

Archipelago filed with the SEC in late summer 1999 to become a stock exchange. Ownership ties with Instinet and other big players make it a formidable force to be watched. Other high-flying investors in Archipelago include the online broker E-Trade Group and investment bankers Goldman Sachs, J.P. Morgan, and American Century. Archipelago handled about 5.5 percent of ECN-executed Nasdaq trades according to early 1999 figures.

Attain

Owned by All-Tech Investment Group, Attain handled less than 1 percent of ECN-executed Nasdaq trades in early 1999.

BRUT (Brass Utility)

Owned by Automated Securities Clearance, BRUT also gets support from Merrill Lynch, Morgan Stanley Dean Witter, and Knight/Trimark Group. BRUT accounted for about 4 percent of Nasdaq ECN trades in early 1999.

Instinet

The granddaddy of ECNs, Instinet has been operating more than 30 years. Owned by the Reuters Group, it also holds 16.4 percent of Archipelago. It had 29 percent of Nasdaq ECN trades in early 1999, down from 52 percent in mid-1998. Establishment of other ECNs has siphoned away market shares from Instinet.

Island ECN

Owned by Datek Online Holdings, the online broker, Island had 48 percent of ECN trades on Nasdaq in early 1999, up from 25 percent in mid-1998. It also has applied to the SEC for exchange status and is expected to slug it out with Archipelago/Instinet in the battle for dominance. Island has partnering arrangements with Waterhouse Group and France's Group Arnault.

NexTrade

Approved as an ECN by the SEC in late 1998, NexTrade is owned by PIM Global Equities/Pro Trade. NexTrade is also a partner in Matchbook FX LLC, an Internet trading platform for spot foreign currency.

REDI

REDI is owned by the brokerage firm of Spear, Leeds & Kellogg, a specialist and market maker on the NYSE, AMEX, and Nasdaq stock exchanges. REDI accounted for about 6 percent of the ECN trades in Nasdaq market in early 1999.

STRIKE

Strike Technologies/Bear Stearns are the owners of STRIKE, with support from DLJ, Salomon Smith Barney, Herzog Heine Geduld, and PaineWebber. Less than 1 percent of ECN Nasdaq trade in early 1999 is attributable to STRIKE.

Tradebook

Bloomberg Tradebook last year linked up with Investment Technology Group, Inc. to form Tradebook SuperECN. ITG includes POSIT, a large electronic equity crossing system. Another venture is with CLSA Global Emerging Markets to form Global Tradebook.

Key Market Makers

Market makers execute trades by buying and selling securities for their own accounts, thus helping to establish prices. Market makers may include institutional investors, investment banks, national and regional brokerage firms—both retail and wholesale—and wire houses. Some analysts think ECNs could force some market makers into niche markets. Listed below are some representative firms in different market-making sectors.

Institutionals

Institutional investors include banks, mutual funds, pension funds, and other corporate entities that trade securities in large volumes.

Goldman Sachs & Co.
85 Broad Street
New York, NY 10004
(212) 902-1000

A global investment banking and securities firm, Goldman Sachs provides a full range of investing, advisory, and financing services worldwide to a substantial and diversified client base, from corporations and financial institutions to governments and high net worth individuals. Founded in 1869, it is one of the oldest and largest investment banking firms.

Lehman Bros.
World Headquarters
3 World Financial Center
New York, NY 10285
(212) 526-7000

Lehman Bros. is a global investment bank and holds leadership positions in fixed income, equities, investment banking, including mergers and acquisitions, as well as private client services. Lehman serves the financial needs of corporations, institutions, governments and municipalities, and high net worth individuals worldwide.

Salomon Smith Barney
388 Greenwich Street
New York, NY 10013-2396
(212) 816-6000

International brokerage firm and investment banker Salomon Smith Barney is a global market maker in foreign exchange.

Morgan Stanley Dean Witter
2 World Trade Center, 73d Floor
New York, NY 10048
(212) 392-7767

Morgan Stanley Dean Witter is a global financial services firm dealing in securities, asset management, and credit services. It also offers investment banking, including underwriting public offerings of securities and mergers and acquisitions.

Wholesalers

Wholesalers sell securities to other brokers, dealers, and institutions.

Herzog Heine Geduld
525 Washington Boulevard, 10th Floor
Jersey City, NJ 07310
(201) 418-4000

Herzog Heine Geduld's primary business is making markets in stocks traded on Nasdaq, EASDAQ, and the London Stock Exchange. Its institutional trading department provides coverage in U.S. equities and stocks listed on the London Stock Exchange and EASDAQ. The international trading desk in New York makes markets in Canadian stocks, South African gold shares, and Latin American ADRs, and the international division in London makes markets in EASDAQ and the London Stock Exchange.

Sherwood Securities Corp.
10 Exchange Place, 15th Floor
Jersey City, NJ 07302-3913
(201) 946-2200

SSC is a proprietary trading firm that makes markets in more than 3500 Nasdaq and OTC securities.

Knight/Trimark Group, Inc.
525 Washington Boulevard
Jersey City, NJ 07310-1607
(201) 222-9400 (Knight Securities)
(914) 251-5800 (Trimark Securities)

The parent company of Knight Securities and Trimark Securities. K/T Group makes markets in more than 7100 equity securities listed on Nasdaq and the OTC bulletin board of the National Association of Securities Dealers (NASD). Trimark trades NYSE- and Amex-listed over the counter stocks and is a leading execution destination for trades originated over the Internet.

M. H. Meyerson & Co., Inc.
525 Washington Boulevard, 34th Floor
Jersey City, NJ 07310
(800) 888-8118

A full-service international financial services firm, Meyerson has divisions specializing in wholesale trading, investment banking, retail services, institutional sales, syndicate, fixed-income, and correspondent service.

Mayer & Schweitzer Incorporated
111 Pavonia Avenue
Jersey City, NJ 07310-1755
(201) 963-3311

One of the largest market makers in over-the-counter stocks, Mayer & Schweitzer makes markets in more than 3000 OTC securities for broker/dealers and institutions.

Investment Banks

Investment banks are also known as underwriters, the "middlemen" between corporations issuing new securities and the public. The usual practice is for one or more investment bankers to buy outright from a corporation a new issue of stocks or bonds. The group forms a syndicate to sell the securities to individuals and institutions. Investment bankers also distribute very large blocks of stocks or bonds.

Chase Securities West
One Bush Street
San Francisco, CA 94104
(415) 439-3000

Bought by Chase Manhattan Corp. in September 1999, Hambrecht & Quist, now Chase Securities West, has been one of the premier providers of investment banking services to companies and investors in high growth companies of the "new economy." This firm gives particular emphasis to technology, life sciences, and information services.

SG Cowen
1 Financial Square
New York, NY 10005
(212) 495-6000

SG Cowen, a full-service, integrated securities and investment banking firm, focuses on emerging growth industries, such as technology, health care, telecommunications, media/entertainment, gaming and lodging, and packaging. It has been a subsidiary since 1998 of the Société Generale Group.

Banc of America Securities
600 Montgomery Street
San Francisco, CA 94111
(415) 627-2000

Banc of America Securities (formerly Montgomery Securities) is a full-service investment bank and brokerage firm. It provides equity underwriting, acquisition financing, private placements, senior loans and loan syndication, municipal finance, and high yield and investment grade debt issuance.

Wire Houses

Wire houses are firms whose branch offices are linked by a communications system that permits the rapid dissemination of prices, information, and research related to financial markets and individual securities.

PaineWebber
1251 Avenue of Americas
New York, NY 10020-1080
(212) 626-8500

PaineWebber is an independent, full-service national securities firm serving the retail investor and capital markets. Its core businesses include private client investment services, asset management, research, investment banking, global fixed income, global equity sales and trading, municipal securities, and transaction services.

Prudential Securities
One Seaport Plaza
New York, NY 10092
(212) 214-1000

Prudential Securities is a full-service broker concentrating on retail sales, mutual funds, institutional sales, investment banking services, and global research.

Regional Firms

These firms provide brokerage and market-making services in their regions, as opposed to national firms. Many are now being absorbed by firms with wider geographical interests.

U.S. Bancorp Piper Jaffray, Inc.
222 South Ninth Street
Minneapolis, MN 55402-3804
(612) 342-5800

U.S. Bancorp Piper Jaffray offers a full range of investment banking services, including IPOs and follow-on offerings, corporate debt underwritings, private placements, and mergers and acquisitions advisory services. Their focus is on the consumer, financial institutions, health care, and industrial growth and technology sectors.

Dain Rauscher Wessels
60 South Sixth Street
Minneapolis, MN 55402-4422
(612) 371-2800

Formerly Dain Bosworth, Dain Rauscher Wessels is a research-driven equity capital markets group that provides investment banking and brokerage services in the consumer, energy, services, health care, and technology sectors.

Southwest Securities, Inc.
1201 Elm Street, Suite 3500
Dallas, TX 75270-2180
(214) 651-1800

Southwest Securities is an investment banking and financial firm engaged in various aspects of the securities business. The company's subsidiaries provide execution, clearing, brokerage, and investment banking and management services to clients mainly, but not exclusively, in the Southwest. Southwest makes markets in about 360 securities.

The Vehicles

Online brokers have multiplied during the last few years, and analysts say there is bound to be some consolidation. Although estimates put the number of online brokers at as many as 150, some may be limited in their offerings. In any event, a recent survey by NFO Interactive indicates that the online brokerage market is dominated by seven firms, representing more than 80 percent of all online accounts (see Figure 4).

Chapter 2 provided tips on how to choose an online broker. To supplement that advice, here are some firms and publications that provide extensive rating services:

www.gomez.com

www.keynote.com

www.kiplinger.com

www.smartmoney.com

Online Brokers

A.B. Watley, Inc.
40 Wall Street
New York, NY 10005
(888) 229-2853
info@abwatley.com (e-mail)
www.abwatley.com

Accutrade
4211 S. 102d Street
Omaha, NE 62127-1031
(800) 494-8939
info@accutrade.com (e-mail)
www.accutrade.com

Figure 4

MARKET SHARE: Q3, 1999

FIRM	Primary Provider Market Share by Customers	Secondary Provider Market Share by Customers	Total Share by Customers	Share by Number of Online Accounts	Share by Number of Online Trades	Share by Number of Online Commission Revenue	Share by Number of Online Assets Online Under Management
Schwab	23.6%	3.8%	27.4%	26.4%	16.5%	27.2%	34.4%
E*TRADE	18.2%	8.0%	26.2%	15.2%	14.4%	16.0%	9.0%
Fidelity	8.8%	6.9%	15.6%	13.8%	8.9%	9.6%	18.1%
Waterhouse	9.9%	1.9%	11.8%	9.9%	15.4%	10.6%	10.1%
DLJ Direct	8.1%	1.6%	9.7%	7.2%	7.6%	8.7%	5.0%
Ameritrade	8.3%	2.4%	10.7%	6.9%	8.6%	5.1%	5.1%
Suretrade	4.7%	0.6%	5.3%	3.1%	2.2%	1.5%	1.2%
DATEK	3.4%	1.4%	4.8%	2.8%	10.7%	7.2%	1.9%
Discover Brokerage Direct	2.3%	0.7%	3.0%	1.9%	2.6%	2.5%	1.9%
Quick & Reilly (Fleet)	1.8%	0.6%	2.3%	1.4%	1.0%	1.2%	1.6%

The table identifies share by primary online brokerage company, secondary online brokerage company, by total customers, and by total accounts. Note that the aggregate "Total Share by Customers" is greater than 100% as a customer can be "owned" by multiple firms.

Source: NFO Interactive, Greenwich, CT

Active Investor
Preferred Capital Markets, Inc.
220 Montgomery Street, Suite 777
San Francisco, CA 94104
(800) 949-0205
info@preftech.com (e-mail)
www.preftech.com

A.F. Trader
415 Madison Avenue, 3d Floor
New York, NY 10017
(212) 644-8520; (888) 682-6973
support@aftrader.com (e-mail)
www.aftrader.com

American Century
4500 Main Street, 4th Floor
Kansas City, MO 64111
(888) 345-2071
www.americancentury.com

American Express
200 Vesey Street
New York, NY 10285
(212) 640-2000
www.my.americanexpress.com

Ameritrade
P.O. Box 2209
Omaha, NE 68103-2209
(800) 454-9272
customerservice@ameritrade.com
(e-mail)
starting@ameritrade.com (e-mail)
www.ameritrade.com

AmeriVest
4211 S. 102d Street
Omaha, NE 68127-1031
(800) 553-9513
info@amerivestinc.com (e-mail)
www.amerivestinc.com

Atlantic Financial
555 Washington Street, Suite 1
Wellesley, MA 02482
(781) 235-5777; (800) 559-2900
service@atlanticfinancial.com (e-mail)
www.atlanticfinancial.com

Bank One
One Invest
300 S. Riverside Plaza, Suite 0860
Chicago, IL 60670
www.oneinvest.com

BCL
303 W. Madison Street, Suite 400
Chicago, IL 60606
(312) 346-8283; (800) 621-0392
www.bclnet.com

Benson York Group, Inc.
One Wall Street
New York, NY 10005
(212) 269-3830
www.bensonyork.com

Bidwell & Co.
209 SW Oak Street
Portland, OR 97204-2791
(503) 790-9000; (800) 547-6337
info@bidwell.com (e-mail)
www.bidwell.com

Brown & Co. Securities Corp.
One Beacon Street, 18th Floor
Boston, MA 02108
(617) 624-6510; (800) 822-2829
www.brownco.com

Bull & Bear Securities, Inc.
1 Liberty Plaza, 5th Floor
New York, NY 10006-1404
(212) 785-0900; (800) 262-5800
www.bullbear.com

Bush Burns Securities
4111-W Andover Road
Bloomfield Hills, MI 48302
(800) 821-4803
service@bushburns.com (e-mail)
www.bushburns.com

Citicorp Investment Services
111 Wall Street, 3d Floor
New York, NY 10005
(800) 275-2484
www.citicorp.com

Comerica Securities
201 W. Fort Street, 3d Floor
Detroit, MI 48226
(800) 232-6983
www.comerica.com/subsid/securities

CompassWeb
P.O. Box 10566
Birmingham, AL 35296
(800) 239-1930; (800) 266-7277
brokerage@compassweb.com (e-mail)
www.compassweb.com

CompuTEL Securities
301 Mission Street, 5th Floor
San Francisco, CA 94015
(800) 432-0327
www.computel.com

Crestar Securities Corp.
11 South 10th Street
Richmond, VA 23219
(800) 343-0300
www.crestar.com/invest/secbrokerage
.stm

Cybercorp.com
1601 Rio Grande, Suite 405
Austin, TX
(512) 320-5444; (888) 762-9237
correspondence@cybercorp.com
(e-mail)
www.cybercorp.com

Datek Online
100 Wood Avenue South
Iselin, NJ 08830-2716
(888) 823-2835
support@datek.com (e-mail)
www.datek.com

Delta Equity Services Corp.
579 Main Street
Bolton, MA 01740-1300
(800) 649-3883
www.deltaequity.com

Discover Brokerage Direct
333 Market Street, 25th Floor
P.O. Box 7037
San Francisco, CA 94120-7037
www.discoverbrokerage.com

DLJdirect, Inc.
P.O. Box 2062
Jersey City, NJ 07303
(800) 825-5723
service@dljdirect.com (e-mail)
www.dljdirect.com

Dreyfus Brokerage Services
P.O. Box 9010
Hicksville, NY 11801-9010
(800) 421-8395
www.edreyfus.com

Empire Financial Group, Inc.
1385 W. State Road
Longwood, FL 32779
(407) 774-1300; (800) 900-8101
www.empirenow.com

E*TRADE Securities, Inc.
4 Embarcadero Plaza
2400 Geng Road
Palo Alto, CA 94303-3317
www.etrade.com

FCNIS
OneInvest
300 S. Riverside Plaza, Suite 0860
Chicago, IL 60670
(888) 843-6382
www.fcnis.com

Fidelity Brokerage Services, Inc.
P.O. Box 770001
Cincinnati, OH 45277-0002
(800) 544-6666
www.fidelity.com

Field Logan
21 Tamal Vista Boulevard, Suite 219
Corte Madera, CA 94925
(415) 927-3007; (888) 353-4353
www.fieldlogan.com

Fifth Third Bank
Fifth Third Securities, Inc.
34 Fountain Square Plaza
Cincinnati, OH 45218
(513) 744-8888; (800) 334-0483
www.fifththird.com

First Charter National Bank
P.O. Box 228
Concord, NC 28026
(800) 601-8471
www.firstcharter.com

First Citizens Bank
c/o Uvest Investment Services, Inc.
(888) 323-4732
www.firstcitizens.com
www.uvest.com

Firstrade Securities, Inc.
136-21 Roosevelt Avenue, 3d Floor
Flushing, NY 11354
(888) 988-6168
www.firstrade.com

Freedom Investments, Inc.
11422 Miracle Hills Drive, Suite 501
Omaha, NE 68154
(402) 431-8500; (800) 944-4033
support@freedominvestments.com
(e-mail)
www.freedominvestments.com

Freeman Welwood & Co., Inc.
1501 4th Avenue, Suite 1700
Seattle, WA 98101-1684
(206) 382-5353; (800) 729-7585
www.freemanwelwood.com

Gay Financial Network, LLC
111 Broadway, 12th Floor
New York, NY 10006
(800) 848-6010
support@gfn.com (e-mail)
www.gfn.com

Investex Securities Group, Inc.
50 Broad Street, Suite 2037
New York, NY 10004
(212) 422-4400; (800) 822-2050
www.investexpress.com

InvestIN.com
1950 Stemmons Freeway, Suite 2016
Dallas, TX 75207
(214) 939-0110; (800) 327-1883
www.investin.com

InvesTrade
950 Milwaukee Avenue, Suite 102
Glenview, IL 60025
(847) 375-6051; (800) 498-7120
support@investrade.com (e-mail)
www.investrade.com

Jack White & Co.
9191 Towne Centre Drive, Suite 220
San Diego, CA 92122
(619) 587-2000; (800) 753-1700
www.jackwhiteco.com
www.investrade.com

JB Oxford & Co.
9665 Wilshire Boulevard, 3d Floor
Beverly Hills, CA 90212
(310) 777-8888; (800) 500-5007
clientserv@jbox.com (e-mail)
www.jboxford.com

Emmett A. Larkin Co., Inc.
c/o Internettrading.com
100 Bush Street, Suite 1000
San Francisco, CA 94104
(800) 696-2811
www.internettrading.com

Lindner Funds
P.O. Box 11208
St. Louis, MO 63105-9838
(800) 995-7777
www.lindnerfunds.com

Main Street Market
ATT: Brokerage Services
26 Broadway, 12th Floor
New York, NY 10004-1798
(800) 710-7160
acuccuru@usclearing.com (e-mail)
www.mainstmarket.com

Mr. Stock, Inc.
220 Bush Street, Suite 360
San Francisco, CA 94104
(800) 467-7865
info@mrstock.com (e-mail)
www.mrstock.com

My Discount Broker
1201 Elm Street, Suite 121
Dallas, TX 75270
(888) 882-5600
info@mydiscountbroker.com (e-mail)
www.mydiscountbroker.com

National Discount Brokers
7 Hanover Square, 4th Floor
New York, NY 10004
(212) 863-4200; (800) 888-3999
service@ndb.com (e-mail)
www.ndb.com

Net.B@ank
Royal Centre 3, Suite 100
11475 Great Oaks Parkway
Alpharetta, GA 30022
customerservice@uvest.com (e-mail)
www.netbank.com

NET Investor
135 S. LaSalle Street, Suite 1500
Chicago, IL 60603
(312) 655-2940; (800) 638-4250
info@netinvestor.com (e-mail)
www.netinvestor.com

net-invest.com
One SE 3d Avenue, 22d Floor
Miami, FL 33131
(305) 925-1051; (800) 548-7796
www.net-ipo.com

Newport Securities Corp.
3151 Airway Avenue, Suite H-1
Costa Mesa, CA 92626
(714) 957-1081
Jeff@newportsecurities.com (e-mail)
www.newportsecurities.com

Norwest
(800) 433-0738
www.norwest.com

Peoples Bank
Bridgeport Center
850 Main Street, 11th Floor
Bridgeport, CT 06604
(203) 338-0800; (800) 772-4400
custserv@peoples.com (e-mail)
www.peoples.com

Peremel & Co., Inc.
1829 Reisterstown Road, Suite 120
Baltimore, MD 21208
(410) 486-4700; (800) 737-3635
info@peremel.com (e-mail)
www.peremel.com

ProTrade
c/o Intertrade Securities
One Hallidie Plaza, Suite 405
San Francisco, CA 94102
(415) 616-5982
www.protrade.com

Quick & Reilly, Inc.
26 Broadway
New York, NY 10004
(212) 747-5000; (800) 925-8395
www.quick-reilly.com

Regal Discount Securities
209 W. Jackson Boulevard, Suite 404
Chicago, IL 60606-6907
(800) 786-9000
support@eregal.com (e-mail)
www.eregal.com

R.J. Forbes
8 Fletcher Place
Melville, NY 11747
(516) 549-7000; (800) 488-0090
www.rjforbes.com

Charles Schwab
MS: 88-03-401
101 Montgomery Street
San Francisco, CA 94104
(800) 225-8570
www.schwab.com

ScoTTrade
(800) 619-7283
www.scudder.com

Muriel Siebert & Co., Inc.
885 Third Avenue, Suite 1720
New York, NY 10022
(800) 872-0711
www.msiebert.com

Sloan Securities Corp.
Two Executive Drive
Ft. Lee, NJ 07024-3308
(201) 592-9901
info@sloansecurities.com (e-mail)
www.sloansecurities.com

State National Bank of West Texas
c/o BHCM, Inc.
1617 Broadway
Lubbock, TX 79401
(806) 749-1850; (800) 658-9895
www.statenationalbank.com

Summit Bank
56 Main Street
Flemington, NJ 08822
(908) 284-4750; (800) 631-1635
call center@summitbank.com (e-mail)
www.summitbank.com

Sunlogic Securities, Inc.
5333 Thornton Avenue
Newark, CA 94560-3237
(800) 556-4600
newaccount@sunlogic.com (e-mail)
www.sunlogic.com

SURETRADE
P.O. Box 862
Lincoln, RI 02865
(401) 642-6900
service@suretrade.com (e-mail)
www.suretrade.com

Swiftrade
c/o West America Securities Corp.
4510 T. Thousand Oaks Boulevard,
Suite 100
Westlake Village, CA 91362
(805) 777-1114
www.swiftrade.com

T. Rowe Price
100 E. Pratt Street, 8th Floor
Baltimore, MD 21202
(301) 547-2308; (800) 225-5132
www.troweprice.com

Trade Options
220 Montgomery Street, Suite 777
San Francisco, CA 94104
(888) 781-0283
tradeoptions@preftech.com (e-mail)
www.tradeoptions.com

Trade4Less
c/o Downstate Discount Brokerage, Inc.
259 Indian Rocks Road North
Belleair Bluffs, FL 33770
(813) 586-3541; (800) 780-3543
www.trade4less.com

Trade-Well Discount Investing
25 Broadway, 7th Floor
New York, NY 10004
(212) 514-4000; (888) 907-9797
clientservice@trade-well.com (e-mail)
www.trade-well.com

Trading Direct
160 Broadway, East Bldg., 10th Floor
New York, NY 10038
(212) 766-0241; (800) 925-8566
info@tradingdirect.com (e-mail)
www.tradingdirect.com

TruTrade
ReCom Securities customers:
142 Northstar West
Minneapolis, MN 55402-1701
(800) 328-8600
Levitt & Levitt customers:
39 S. LaSalle Street, Suite 1415
Chicago, IL 60603
(800) 671-8505
www.trutrade.com

UBOC Investment Services
445 S. Figueroa Street
Los Angeles, CA 90071
(800) 238-4486
www.uboc.com

UMB Bank
1010 Grand Blvd.
Kansas City, MO 64106
(816) 842-2222; (800) 842-9999
www.umbscoutbrokerage.com

US Bank
c/o US Bancorp
US Bank Place
601 Second Avenue South
Minneapolis, MN 55402
(612) 872-2657; (800) 872-2657
www.usbank.com/invest/

US Discount Brokerage
1911 Detroit Road, Suite 203
Rocky River, OH 44116-1740
(440) 356-3160; (800) 257-8625
www.usdb.com

U.S. Rica Financial
1630 Oakland Road, Suite A208
San Jose, CA 95131-2451
(408) 929-2234; (888) 887-7422
info@usrica.com (e-mail)
www.usrica.com

Vanguard
455 Devon Park Drive
Wayne, PA 19087-1815
(610) 669-6696; (800) 992-8327
www.vanguard.com

Vision Trade
310 Central Avenue
Lawrence, NY 11559
(516) 374-2184
info@visiontrade.com (e-mail)
www.visiontrade.com

Wall Street Access
17 Battery Place, 11th Floor
New York, NY 10004
(800) 925-5781
www.wsaccess.com

Wall Street Discount Corp.
100 Wall Street
New York, NY 10005
(888) 492-5578
info@wsdc.com (e-mail)
www.wsdc.com

Wall Street Electronica
7242 SW 42d Terrace
Miami, FL 33155
(305) 669-3026; (800) 925-5783
info@wallstreete.com (e-mail)
www.wallstreete.com

Wang Investment Associates
41-60 Main Street, Suite 209
Flushing, NY 11355-3820
(800) 353-9264
www.wangvest.com

Waterhouse Securities, Inc.
100 Wall Street
New York, NY 10005-3701
www.waterhouse.com

Web Street Securities, Inc.
510 Lake Cook Road, 4th Floor
Deerfield, IL 60015-5271
(800) 932-8723
www.webstreetsecurities.com

Wells Fargo Securities, Inc.
420 Montgomery Street, 8th Floor
MAC 0101-085
San Francisco, CA 94104
www.wellsfargo.com/wellstrade/

White Discount Securities
301 Mission Street, 5th Floor
San Francisco, CA 94105
(415) 597-6800; (800) 669-4483
www.wdsonline.com

Wit Capital
826 Broadway
New York, NY 10003
(212) 253-4400; (800) 452-4340
www.witcapital.com

Wyse Securities
20735 Stevens Creek Boulevard, Suite C
Cupertino, CA 95014
(408) 343-2900; (800) 640-8668
johnh@hooked.net (e-mail)
www.wyse-sec.com

Your Discount Broker
855 S. Federal Highway, #101
Boca Raton, FL 33432-6130
(561) 367-9800; (800) 800-3215
www.ydb.com

Ziegler Thrift Trading, Inc.
733 Marquette Avenue, Suite 106
Minneapolis, MN 55402
(612) 333-4206; (800) 328-4854
ziegler@primenet.com (e-mail)
www.ziegler-thrift.com

Zions Direct Brokerage
c/o Zions Investment Securities, Inc.
One South Main Street, Suite 1340-K3
Salt Lake City, UT 84111
(800) 748-4761
zdbrokerage@zionsbank.com (e-mail)
www3.zionsdirect.com

The Advisors

Finding investing information on the Web isn't a problem; it's sorting through the hundreds of sites and services that provide investment information and products. As you sort through the Websites, you'll learn that the choices aren't really very distinct. Many sites offer the same types of information and services. News from the same vendors typically appears on many of the same sites, which makes choosing online resources and brokerage firms difficult.

There's also quite a bit of variance between sites' billing procedures. Some sites give you access to all of their information without charge. Others share some of the information for free and charge for the rest. Sometimes sites offer a free trial period. One guide to remember is that if you don't want to pay for information, keep looking until you find it where it is free.

The stock and futures exchanges also provide free information on their Websites.

Investment and Research

American Association of Individual Investors
625 Michigan Avenue
Chicago, IL 60611
www.aaii.com

Provides online trading via its Website and publishes the bimonthly newsletter *Computerized Investing.* Has chapters in at least 21 states and Mexico.

Bestcalls.com
www.bestcalls.com

Distributes conference-call schedules and content of the online conference call producers. Good guide for an individual investor seeking information on conference calls. Includes schedules of such providers as Broadcast.com, C-call, CCBN.com, and Vcall.

Bond Market Association
www.investinginbonds.com

This site provides online the *Investors Guide to Bond Basics*. It's a good guide for the beginning bond investor.

Broadcast.com
www.broadcast.com

Provides streaming media content, including financial and business. Carries live and taped press conferences, earnings conference calls, investor conferences, and stockholder meetings. Has a separate business channel.

Business Wire
www.businesswire.com

This site gives access to news releases issued by companies. It also includes a picture file and carries conference calls. You also can search news by company and industry. It provides links to other company Websites.

Hoover's Inc.
www.hoovers.com

This site provides background information on a variety of companies, including access and links to recent news stories.

Investor-Advice
www.investoradvice.com

Asset Advisory Corp. offers financial research material online. Investor-Advice provides custom advice on the stocks you select, using a computer-based expert system that weighs 28 fundamental factors.

Investors Business Daily
www.investors.com

Here's stock, business, economic, and financial news. Check out the charts and graphs, always among this publication's strong points. The investor education page is a gem.

MoneyCentral
www.moneycentral.com

This site gives you a free walk-through on how to trade, as well as providing research on selected stocks. Charges apply.

Morningstar, Inc.
www.morningstar.com

This Chicago-based analytical service provides information for the investor on mutual funds, stocks, and variable insurance investing. It is an independent service and doesn't own, hold, or operate any investment products. There is a mixture of free and subscription information.

Multex.com, Inc.
www.multex.com

Multex.com provides online research and information services to investment professionals and individuals. It offers research reports on companies, with a mix of free and pay materials. Many companies offer free trials.

PR Newswire
www.prnewswire.com

This source provides company and business news releases, including earnings reports. Investors can also listen to company conference calls and other media events by connecting to the Website.

Quicken.com
www.quicken.com

This personal finance Website provides major news and serves as a resource on investment topics. It also offers a free portfolio tracking service along with free price quotes.

SmartMoney
www.smartmoney.com

SmartMoney, the personal finance magazine, has a Website that gives investors news and stock market information along with corporate news.

Stockpoint
www.stockpoint.com

This site provides market index levels and some news along with stock and mutual fund quotes.

StockPower
www.stockpower.com

This Website links individual investors to corporations that offer direct stock purchase plans (DSPP). Open an account for $5 and you can make direct stock purchases in increments as low as $5. Also available are information on SEC filings, shareholder offers, and lists of companies offering discounts on stocks and other services.

Vcall
www.vcall.com

Vcall is an online conference call center that provides company earnings information and other material via the Web for day traders and individual investors.

Wall Street Directory
www.wallstreetdirectory.com

This site provides educational materials. You can order books, audio and video tapes, and financial software. It also lists investment courses and relays special offers for investment services and products.

Yahoo! Finance
http://finance.yahoo.com

This popular Internet reference site provides free news along with some research information. It also offers live events online as well as access to news on other sites.

Zacks Investment Research. Inc.
www.zacks.com

Zacks has a plethora of equity investment material. Some is free, but the best stuff you have to pay for. Zacks is found on a number of news and information Websites.

ZDNet's Inter@ctive Investor
www.zdii.com

This site is targeted at technology investors. It offers a wide selection of brokers' research reports along with an earnings calendar. Price quotes, general market stories, and links to news sites are also given.

News Services

Bridge
www.bridge.com

This site provides a variety of news, charts, and stock, bond, and futures information.

Briefing.com
www.briefing.com

This news service offers financial market comments, quotes, and charts, most of which is free. The analytical material and stock market information generally requires a subscription.

CBS Market Watch
www.cbsmarketwatch.com

This site offers a variety of stock and financial market stories. It includes research reports along with data on the stock market. It also offers other news services, such as Reuters and the Associated Press.

CNBC.com
www.cnbc.com

The Website of CNBC, it provides financial and business news.

Market News International
www.economeister.com

Here you get financial and economic news, both on a real-time and an analytical basis.

Reuters
www.reuters.com

Reuters is one of the leading news agencies in equity and financial news. Unfortunately, you will find only a little of its news on this Website. Much more Reuters news can be found on over 200 other Websites, such as Yahoo! and CBSMarketwatch.com.

The Street.com
www.thestreet.com

This site, which launched an initial public offering in the middle of 1999, provides news on companies and financial markets. Some of this is free, but to see the full range, a subscription is required.

Wall Street Journal Interactive Edition
www.wsj.com

Along with *The Wall Street Journal,* you can get Dow Jones Newswires and Barron's Online. Charges do apply, but there is a free two-week trial period. The site has a search engine that allows you to search over 250 business publications and over 2000 top Websites.

Chat Rooms

These sites all have interactive features.

Avid Trading Company	www.avidtrader.com
Bull Trade	www.bulltrade.com
Excite	www.excite.com
Market Central	www.marketcentral.com
Market Forum	http://forum.ino.com
Momentum Trader Online	www.mtrader.com
The Motley Fool	www.motleyfool.com
Raging Bull	www.ragingbull.com
Silicon Investor	www.techstocks.com
Yahoo! Finance	http://finance.yahoo.com

The Overseers

When you decided to drive a car, you had to study the driver's manual and pass written and operating tests before obtaining a license. A driver's education course may have been required. Unfortunately, investors can and do jump into online stock trading without similar preparation, and those who aren't prepared are in danger of being taken for a ride on the information superhighway. One regulatory group warns that the investment fraud problem could reach epidemic proportions during the next few years as several million unsophisticated new investors surge onto the information superhighway.

A prudent investor, therefore, will identify the regulators and learn some of the rules and regulations of the marketplace before jumping online and committing money. In the stock market, the first place to contact is the Securities and Exchange Commission (SEC), www.sec.gov, the official watchdog of securities trading. The SEC keeps a close eye on online trading and emphasizes that although the Internet has opened up vast new horizons for the individual investor, surfing the Web for investment information can be fraught with peril unless proper precautions are taken.

Although the Internet has become a popular and an excellent tool for investors, it also has provided hucksters the same opportunity, the SEC points out. In 1998, the SEC filed charges against 44 stock promoters involved in Internet fraud. The promoters failed to tell investors that more than 235 companies paid them millions of dollars in cash and shares in exchange for touting their stock on the Internet.

"Not only did they lie about their own independence, some of them lied about the companies they featured, then took advantage of any quick spike in price to sell their shares for a fast and easy profit," says SEC Director of

Enforcement Richard H. Walker. To curb future frauds, the SEC provides alerts to help investors spot different types of Internet shenanigans. The agency also provides information on what the SEC is doing to fight Internet investment scams and on ways to use the Internet to invest wisely.

Where the Frauds Are

Fraudulent activity can be difficult to spot because the hucksters often blend their material with other legitimate material on the Internet. The technology allows individuals and companies to communicate with large audiences without spending a lot of time, effort, or money. It's easy to reach tens of thousands of people by building an Internet Website, posting a message on an online bulletin board, entering a discussion in a live "chat" room, or sending mass e-mails. Fraudsters can make their messages look so real and credible that it can be nearly impossible for investors to distinguish between fact and fiction.

Online Investment Newsletters

Not long after you get on the Internet, you'll find yourself in a traffic jam when it comes to online investment advice. The SEC says hundreds of online investment newsletters have popped up on the Internet in recent years. Many offer investors seemingly unbiased, free information about featured companies, often recommending "stock picks of the month." While legitimate online newsletters can help investors gather valuable information, some online newsletters are tools for fraud, says the SEC. Some companies pay the people who write online newsletters cash or securities to "tout," or recommend their stocks. While this isn't illegal, the federal securities laws require the newsletters to disclose who paid them, the amount, and the type of payment. Many fail to do so, choosing to conceal the payments they receive and to lie about their independence, their so-called research, and their track records. Their newsletters masquerade as sources of unbiased information, when, in fact, they will profit handsomely if they convince investors to buy or sell particular stocks.

The SEC says some online newsletters falsely claim to independently research the stocks they profile. Others spread false information or promote worthless stocks. The most notorious sometimes "scalp" the stocks they hype, driving up the price of the stock with their baseless recommendations and then selling their own holdings at high prices and high profits. The SEC's tips for checking out newsletters can be found on its Web page.

Bulletin Boards and Chat Rooms

Online bulletin boards, whether newsgroups, Usenet, or Web-based bulletin boards, have become an increasingly popular forum for investors to share information. Bulletin boards typically feature "threads," which are made up of numerous messages on various investment opportunities. While some messages may be true, many are bogus—or even scams—says the SEC. Fraudsters often pump up a company or pretend to reveal "inside" information about upcoming announcements, new products, or lucrative contracts.

The SEC emphasizes that it's difficult to know with whom you're dealing—or whether they're credible—because many bulletin boards allow users to hide their identities behind multiple aliases. People claiming to be unbiased observers who have carefully researched a company may actually be company insiders, large shareholders, or paid promoters. A single person can easily create the illusion of widespread interest in a small, thinly traded stock by posting a series of messages under various aliases. The North American Securities Administrators Association (NASAA), another overseer, notes how one online investor marveled that hundreds of thousands of people could be reached with a single message posting: "With a few keystrokes, a couple of accounts, and a macro or two, I can make it appear that many people are posting on many different systems, all talking up a stock. . . . Never before has an individual been able to reach so many people so easily, quickly, or inexpensively."

Internet chat rooms are another gathering spot on the Internet where conversations occur in real time. They have become popular with many day traders as a vehicle to exchange and gather information on stocks and other investments. Now, incidents in which a stock has been pushed higher by comments from the operator of the site or some of his cohorts are on the rise. Chat room operators are, or at least claim to be, knowledgeable about the markets. Many less sophisticated investors subscribe to the chat rooms to see information posted about stocks. They can easily get caught up in the excitement and promise of big gains when an operator starts touting a stock. In one case in the summer of 1999, an Internet stock soared from just over $4 a share to $14 during a week when the chat room operator was pushing it. It closed at the end of the week at $10, causing losses for those who jumped on the bandwagon at the top. That incident, along with other similar ones, has raised regulatory concerns about chat rooms. Regulators urge new investors to "lurk," Internet language for reading the postings on the chat room before getting involved. By lurking, you can follow the personalities in the chat room and determine what their interests are.

As SEC chairman Levitt said,

> Chat rooms, which increasingly have become a source of information and misinformation for many investors, have been compared to a high-tech version of morning gossip or advice at the company water cooler. But at least you knew your co-workers at the water cooler. For the future sake of this medium, I encourage investors to take what they see over chat rooms, not with a grain of salt, but with a rock of salt.

He added,

I've asked the major Internet providers who host these chat rooms to place a link to the SEC's Website where investors can learn more about online investing and file a complaint with us if necessary. I want everyone in a chat room to know that if someone is taking advantage of the technology, you have the opportunity to shine the light on it. Think of it as neighborhood watch on the Internet. With the help of investors, we can get those people who have only one motivation—to ruthlessly make money at the expense of others—out of our communities.

E-Mail Spams

Because "spam," or junk e-mail, is so cheap and easy to create, fraudsters increasingly use it to find investors for bogus investment schemes or to spread false information about a company. Spam allows the unscrupulous to target many more potential investors than cold calling or mass mailing. Using a bulk e-mail program, spammers can send personalized messages to thousands and even millions of Internet users at a time. The North American Securities Administrators Association says that if you combine the circulation of *The Wall Street Journal* (1.8 million) and *USA Today* (1.6 million), you still fall short of the "self-publishing" reach available to someone who joins a few commercial computer bulletin board services.

How to Use the Internet to Invest Wisely

If you got on the freeway before you had driving lessons or had obtained a driver's license, you'd likely encounter trouble. The SEC says the same applies to investing. If you want to invest wisely and steer clear of frauds, it's advisable to get the facts. Obtain at least a "learner's permit," if not a full license, before you begin investing. One of the first rules the SEC suggests is to "never, ever, make an investment based solely on what you read in an online newsletter or bulletin board posting, especially if the investment involves a small, thinly traded company that isn't well known." The SEC also strongly advises against even thinking about investing on your own in small companies that don't file regular reports with the SEC, unless you are willing to investigate each company thoroughly and check the truth of every statement made about the company.

Here, then, is some of what you need to know to conduct your own investigation:

- Get financial statements from the company in question and be able to analyze them.

- Verify the claims about new product developments or lucrative contracts.

- Call every supplier or customer of the company you can and ask if they really do business with the company.

- Check out the people running the company and find out if they've ever made money for investors before.

In addition, the SEC's Web page has a detailed list of questions you need to ask—and have answered—before you invest.

Alternatively, you can start with the SEC's EDGAR database. The federal securities laws require many public companies to register with the SEC and file annual reports containing audited financial statements. For example, the following companies must file reports with the SEC:

- All U.S. companies with more than 500 investors and $10 million in net assets.

- All companies that list their securities on the Nasdaq stock market or a major national stock exchange, such as the New York Stock Exchange.

These reports can be accessed and downloaded from the SEC's EDGAR database for free. So before investing in a company, check to see whether it's registered with the SEC and read its reports.

Remember that some companies don't have to register their securities or file reports on EDGAR. Under a rule known as Regulation A, companies raising less than $5 million in a 12-month period may be exempt from registering the transaction. Instead, these companies must file with the SEC a hard copy of their "offering circular" containing financial statements and other information. Smaller companies raising less than 1 million dollars don't have to register with the SEC, but they must file a *Form D*. Form D is a brief notice that includes the names and addresses of owners and stock promoters—but little other information. If you can't find a company on EDGAR, call the SEC at (202) 942-8090 to find out if the company filed an offering circular under Regulation A or a Form D. Be sure to request a copy.

You can access EDGAR by taking the following steps:

- Go to the SEC's Website at www.sec.gov.

- Click on the EDGAR DATABASE button on the navigational tool bar on the left side of the SEC's home page.

- Click on SEARCH THE EDGAR DATABASE.

- Click on QUICK FORMS LOOKUP.

- Select the type of form you want to view, or use the default ALL to view all forms. If you know what form you want to view but it doesn't appear on the pull-down menu, you can also enter the type of form. For a list of the different forms companies file, click on EDGAR FORM DEFINITIONS from the EDGAR home page.

- Enter the company's name.

- Enter a date range.

- Click on SUBMIT CHOICES.

- Click on the document you would like to view.

The difference between investing in companies that register with the SEC and those that don't is like the difference between driving on a clear sunny day and driving at night without your headlights. You're asking for serious losses if you invest in small, thinly traded companies that are known only by following the signs on Internet bulletin boards or online newsletters.

Contact Your State Securities Regulators

Don't stop with the SEC. You should always check with your state securities regulator to see if they have more information about a company you're interested in and the people behind it. They can check the Central Registration Depository (CRD) and tell you whether the broker touting the stock or the broker's firm has a disciplinary history. They can also tell you whether they've cleared the offering for sale in your state. (State regulators are listed later in this chapter.)

Check with the NASD

The National Association of Securities Dealers, Inc., a self-regulatory organization, can provide a partial disciplinary history on the broker or firm that's touting a stock. Call their toll-free public disclosure hot line at (800) 289-9999, or visit their Website at http://www.nasdr.com.

Online Investment Fraud: New Medium, Same Old Scam

The SEC says the types of investment fraud seen online mirror the frauds perpetrated in the past over the phone or through the mail. But the Internet allows the perpetrators to reach more investors easier. Fraudsters use a variety of Internet tools to spread false information, including bulletin boards, online newsletters, spam, or chat (including Internet Relay Chat or Web Page Chat). They can also build a glitzy, sophisticated Web page. All of these tools cost very little money and can be found at the fingertips of fraudsters. Consider all offers with skepticism, the SEC warns. Investment frauds usually fit one of the following categories.

The "Pump and Dump" Scam

It's common to see messages posted online that urge readers to buy a stock quickly or to sell before the price goes down, the SEC points out. The writers often will claim to have "inside" information about an impending development or to use an "infallible" combination of economic and stock market data to pick stocks. In reality, they may be insiders or paid promoters who stand to gain by selling their shares after the stock price is pumped up by gullible investors. Once these fraudsters sell their shares and stop hyping the stock, the price typically falls and investors lose money. Fraudsters frequently use this ploy with small, thinly traded companies because it's easier to manipulate a stock when there's little or no information available about the company.

The Pyramid

Be wary of messages that read "How to Make Big Money from Your Home Computer!!!" The SEC says one online promoter claimed that investors could "turn $5 into $60,000 in just three to six weeks." In reality, this program was nothing more than an electronic version of the classic pyramid scheme, in which participants attempt to make money solely by recruiting new participants into the program.

The "Risk-Free" Fraud

"Exciting, Low-Risk Investment Opportunities" to participate in exotic-sounding investments—such as wireless cable projects, prime bank securities, and eel farms—have been offered through the Internet. But as the SEC correctly notes, no investment is risk-free. And sometimes the investment products touted do not even exist. They're merely scams. Be wary of opportunities that promise spectacular profits or "guaranteed" returns. If the deal sounds too good to be true, then it probably is.

Off-Shore Frauds

In the past, off-shore schemes targeting U.S. investors cost a great deal of money and were difficult to carry out. Conflicting time zones, differing currencies, and the high cost of international telephone calls and overnight mailings made it difficult for fraudsters to prey on U.S. residents. But the Internet has removed those obstacles. The SEC urges extra caution when considering any investment opportunity from another country because it's difficult for U.S. law enforcement agencies to investigate and prosecute foreign frauds.

Examples of Fraud

The SEC actively investigates allegations of Internet investment fraud and in many cases has taken quick action to stop scams. The agency has also coordinated with federal and state criminal authorities to put Internet fraudsters in jail. Here's a sampling of recent cases in which the SEC took action to fight Internet fraud.

• Two men sent more than 6 million unsolicited e-mails, built bogus Websites, and distributed an online newsletter over a 10-month period to promote two small, thinly traded "microcap" companies. Because they failed to tell investors that the companies they were touting had agreed to pay them in cash and securities, the SEC sued both to stop them from violating the law again and imposed a $15,000 penalty on one. Their massive spamming campaign triggered the largest number of complaints to that point to the SEC's online Enforcement Complaint Center.

• One man and 12 other defendants secretly distributed to friends and family nearly 42 million shares of Systems of Excellence Inc., known by its ticker symbol SEXI. In this classic pump-and-dump scheme, he drove up the price of SEXI shares through false press releases claiming nonexistent multimillion-dollar sales, an acquisition that had not occurred, and revenue projections that had no basis in reality. He also bribed a codefendant to tout SEXI to subscribers of its newsletter. The SEC fined the principal defendant $12.5 million, but he had spent most of his ill-gotten gains so investors did not get their money back. The principal and the online newsletter author were sentenced to federal prison. In addition, four others of the group pled guilty to criminal charges.

- Two men were caught offering "prime bank" securities, a type of security that doesn't even exist. They collected over $3.5 million by promising to double investors' money in four months. The SEC has frozen their assets and stopped them from continuing their activities.

Tips for Investors

Be skeptical of investment opportunities you learn about through the Internet, or anywhere else, for that matter. When you see an offering on the Internet, whether it's on a company's Website, in an online newsletter, on a message board, or in a chat room, you should assume it's a scam until you've done your homework and proven otherwise. Get the facts before you invest, and only invest money you can afford to lose. You can avoid online investment scams by asking, and getting answers to, these three simple questions:

- *Is the investment registered?* To find out, check the SEC's EDGAR database. Some smaller companies don't have to register their securities offerings with the SEC, so always check with your state securities regulator as well. (The telephone numbers and addresses of state securities regulators are listed later in this chapter.) You can also call the North American Securities Administrators Association (NASAA) at (202) 737-0900 or visit www.nasaa.org, NASAA's Website. Many online investment scams involve unregistered securities. One simple phone call can make the difference between investing in a legitimate business or squandering your money on a scam.

- *Is the person licensed and law-abiding?* Find out if the person or firm selling the investment needs to be licensed. Call your state securities regulator and ask whether the person or firm is licensed to do business in your state and whether they have a record of complaints or fraud. You can also get this information by calling NASD Regulation, Inc.'s public disclosure hotline at (800) 289-9999, or by visiting www.nasdr.com, their website.

- *Does the investment sound too good to be true?* If it does, it probably is. High-yield investments tend to involve extremely high risk. Never invest in an opportunity that promises "guaranteed" or "risk-free" returns. Watch out for claims of astronomical yields in a short period of time. Be skeptical of "off-shore" or foreign investments. And beware of exotic or unusual sounding investments, especially those involving so-called prime bank securities. You can find out more about prime bank securities by visiting the Investor Alert section of NASD's Website. Make sure you fully understand the investment before you part with your hard-earned money. Always ask for—and carefully read—the company's prospectus and latest financial statements.

For more tips on avoiding online fraud, read "Internet Fraud: How to Avoid Internet Scams." You can get this brochure by calling the SEC's toll-free publications line at (800) SEC-0330, or by visiting the Internet and Online Trading section of SEC's home Website, www.sec.org. The National Futures Association (NFA) also has a booklet, "Investment Swindles: How They Work and How to Avoid Them." The NFA can be reached at (800) 621-3570. Its home page is www.nfa.org.

Regulatory Agencies and Associations

Stocks

Securities and Exchange Commission (SEC)
450 Fifth Street, NW
Washington, DC 20549
(202) 942-4144; fax (202) 942-4050

Office of Filings, Information Services
(202) 942-8938

Public Reference Branch (for filings by registered companies)
(202) 942-8090
www.sec.gov

National Association of Securities Dealers (NASD)
1735 K Street, NW
Washington, DC 20006
(202) 728-8000
www.nasd.com

NASD is the largest securities industry self-regulatory organization in the U.S. Its subsidiaries are NASD Regulation Inc. and the Nasdaq Stock Market Inc. NASD, with the subsidiaries, develops rules and regulations, conducts regulatory reviews of member activities, and provides a dispute resolution forum. It also designs, operates, and regulates securities markets for investor protection. (See the NASD membership list in Part II, the chapter on Players.)

North American Securities Administrators Association
10 G Street, NE
Washington, DC 20002
(202) 737-0900
www.nasaa.org

Organized in 1919, the North American Securities Administrators Association (NASAA) is the oldest international organization devoted to investor protection. It is a voluntary association whose membership consists of 65 state, provincial, and territorial securities administrators in the 50 states, the District of Columbia, Puerto Rico, Canada, and Mexico. In the United States, NASAA is the voice of the 50 state securities agencies responsible for efficient capital formation and grass-roots investor protection. (See the list of state securities agencies at the end of this chapter.)

Futures

Commodity Futures Trading Commission (CFTC)
Three Lafayette Centre
1155 21st Street, NW
Washington, DC 20581
(202) 418-5498; fax (202) 254-6265
www.cftc.gov

The CFTC, a federal agency, regulates all futures trading in the United States. It has regulatory jurisdiction over currency and financial futures trading as well as traditional commodity futures dealing.

National Futures Association (NFA)
200 W. Madison Street, Suite 1600
Chicago, IL 60606-3447
(312) 781-1300; (800) 621-3570; IL (800) 572-9400; fax (312) 781-1467
www.nfa.futures.org

NFA New York Office
120 Broadway, Suite 1125
New York, NY 10271
(212) 608-8660; fax (212) 964-3913
www.nfa.futures.org

The NFA is the self-regulatory organization of the U.S. futures industry. Authorized by Congress, it came into existence on October 1, 1982.

U.S. State, Canadian and Mexican Regulatory Agencies

ALABAMA

Securities Commission
770 Washington Street, Suite 570
Montgomery, AL 36130-4700
FedEx Zip: 36104
(334) 242-2984; (800) 222-1253;
fax (334) 242-0240
alseccom@dsmd.dsmd.state.al.us

Joseph P. Borg, Esq.
Director
(334) 242-2984
jborg@asc.state.al.us

ALASKA

Department of Community &
Economic Development
Division of Banking, Securities,
& Corporations
State Office Building, 9th Floor
333 Willoughby Avenue
P.O. Box 110807
Juneau, AK 99811-0807
(907) 465-2521; fax (907) 465-2549
http://www.dced.state.ak.us/bsc/
secur.htm

Franklin Terry Elder
Director of Banking, Securities, &
Corporations Division
terry_elder@dced.state.ak.us

ARIZONA

Corporation Commission
1300 West Washington, Third Floor
Phoenix, AZ 85007
(602) 542-4242; fax (602) 594-7470
accsec@ccsd.cc.state.az.us (e-mail)
http://www.ccsd.cc.state.az.us/indexNH.
html

W. Mark Sendrow
Director of Securities
602/542-0643; fax (602) 594-7430
msendrow@ccfd.cc.state.az.us

ARKANSAS

Securities Department
Heritage West Building—Room 300
201 East Markham
Little Rock, AR 72201
(501) 324-9260; fax (501) 324-9268
arsec@ccon.net (e-mail)
http://www.state.ar.us/arsec/

Mac Dodson
Commissioner

CALIFORNIA

Department of Corporations
3700 Wilshire Boulevard
Los Angeles, CA 90010
(213) 736-3481; fax (213) 736-3588
http://www.corp.ca.gov/srd/security.htm

Brian A. Thompson
Acting Chief Deputy Commissioner
Assistant Commissioner, Securities
Regulation Division

COLORADO

Division of Securities
1580 Lincoln, Suite 420
Denver, CO 80203
(303) 894-2320; fax (303) 861-2126
http://www.dora.state.co.us/securities/
home.htm

Fred J. Joseph
Deputy Securities Commissioner

CONNECTICUT

Department of Banking
260 Constitution Plaza
Hartford, CT 06103-1800
(860) 240-8230; (800) 831-7225;
fax (860) 240-8295
http://www.state.ct.us/dob/pages/
secdiv.htm

Ralph A. Lambiase
Director
(860) 240-8231

DELAWARE

Division of Securities
Department of Justice
820 North French Street, 5th Floor
Carvel State Office Building
Wilmington, DE 19801
(302) 577-8424; fax (302) 577-6987
http://www.state.de.us

Charles F. Walker
Securities Commissioner
(302) 577-8925

DISTRICT OF COLUMBIA

The Department of Insurance and
Securities Regulation
810 First Street NE, 6th Floor
Washington, DC 20002
(202) 727-8000; fax (202) 535-1199

Larry Coates
Acting Director of Securities
(202) 442-7845

FLORIDA

Office of Comptroller
Department of Banking & Finance
101 East Gaines Street
Plaza Level, The Capitol
Tallahassee, FL 32399-0350
(850) 488-9805; fax (850) 489-9431
http://www.dbf.state.fl.us/overview.html

Don Saxon
Director, Department of Banking &
Finance
(950) 410-9805; fax (950) 410-9431

GEORGIA

Office of the Secretary of State
Division of Securities & Business
Regulation
Two Martin Luther King, Jr. Drive SE
802 West Tower
Atlanta, GA 30334
(404) 656-3920; fax (404) 651-6451
http://www.sos.state.ga.us/securities/
default.htm

Robert D. Terry
Division Director
Assistant Commissioner of Securities
bterry@sos.state.ga.us

HAWAII

Department of Commerce &
Consumer Affairs
1010 Richards Street
Honolulu, HI 96813

Mailing address:
P.O. Box 40
Honolulu, HI 96810
(808) 586-2744; fax (808) 586-2733
http://www.hawaii.gov/dcca

Ryan S. Ushijima
Commissioner of Securities

IDAHO

Department of Finance
Securities Bureau
700 West State Street, 2d Floor
Boise, ID 83720

Mailing address:
P.O. Box 83720
Boise, ID 83720-0031
(208) 332-8004; fax (208) 332-8099
http://www.state.id.us./finance/sec.htm

Marilyn T. Scanlan
Bureau Chief
(208) 332-8004
mscanlan@fin.state.id.us

ILLINOIS

Office of the Secretary of State
Securities Department
17 North State Street, Suite 1100
Chicago, IL 60601
(312) 793-3384; (800) 628-7937;
fax (312) 793-1202

Springfield office:
Suite 200 Lincoln Tower
520 South Second Street
Springfield, IL 62701
(217) 782-8876; fax (217) 524-9637
http://www.sos.state.il.us/depts/
securities/sec_home.html

William L. Houlihan
Chief Deputy Director
(312) 793-3384

INDIANA

Office of the Secretary of State
Securities Division
302 West Washington, Room E-111
Indianapolis, IN 46204
(317) 232-6681; fax (317) 233-3675
http://www.ai.org/sos/security/

Bradley W. Skolnik
Securities Commissioner
(317) 232-6690
bskolnik@sos.state.in.us

IOWA

Insurance Division
Securities Bureau
340 E. Maple
Des Moines, IA 50319-0066
(515) 281-4441; fax (515) 281-3059;
(515) 281-6467
http://www.sos.state.ia.us/government/
com/ins/security/index.htm

Craig A. Goettsch
Superintendent of Securities

KANSAS

Office of the Securities Commissioner
618 South Kansas Avenue, 2d Floor
Topeka, KS 66603-3804
(785) 296-3307; (800) 232-9580;
fax (785) 296-6872
ksecom@cjnetworks.com (e-mail)
http://www.cjnetworks.com/~ksecom/

David R. Brant
Securities Commissioner
dbrant@cjnetworks.com

Wichita office:
Office of the Securities Commissioner
230 E. William, Suite 7080
Wichita, KS 67202
(316) 337-6280; fax (316) 337-6282
kscict@feist.com (e-mail)

Merilyn Bowman
Senior Examiner-Director of Investor
Education
mbowman@feist.com

KENTUCKY

Department of Financial Institutions
1025 Capital Center Drive, Suite 200
Frankfort, KY 40601
(502) 573-3390; (800) 223-2579;
fax (502) 573-8787
http://www.dfi.state.ky.us/security/
Security.html

Marion Lewis
Director
mlewis@dfi.state.ky.us

LOUISIANA

Securities Commission
3445 North Causeway Boulevard,
Suite 509
Metairie, LA 70002
(504) 846-6970

Harry C. Stansbury
Deputy Securities Commissioner

MAINE

Department of Professional &
Financial Regulation
Bureau of Banking
Securities Division
121 State House Station
Augusta, ME 04333-0121
(207) 624-8551
(207) 624-8590 (fax)

Christine A. Bruenn
Securities Administrator
christine.a.bruenn@state.me.us

MARYLAND

Office of the Attorney General
Division of Securities
200 Saint Paul Place, 20th Floor
Baltimore, MD 21202-2020
(410) 576-6360; fax (410) 576-6532
securities@oag.state.md.us (e-mail)
http://www.oag.state.md.us

Melanie Senter Lubin
Securities Commissioner
(410) 576-6365
mlubin@oag.state.md.us

MASSACHUSETTS

Secretary of the Commonwealth
Securities Division
One Ashburton Place, Room 1701
Boston, MA 02108
(617) 727-3548; fax (617) 248-0177

Matthew Nestor
Director
mnestor@sec.state.ma.us

MICHIGAN

Department of Consumer and Industry Services
Corporation, Securities and Land Development Bureau
6546 Mercantile Way
Lansing, MI 48908

Mailing address:
P.O. Box 30222
Lansing, MI 48909
(517) 334-6213; fax (517) 334-7813
http://www.commerce.state.mi.us/corp/

Julie Croll
Director, Corporation, Securities and Land Development Bureau
julie.croll@cis.state.mi.us

MINNESOTA

Department of Commerce
133 East Seventh Street
St. Paul, MN 55101
(651) 296-4026; fax (651) 296-9434
commerce@state.mn.us (e-mail)
http://www.commerce.state.mn.us/

Scott P. Borchert
Director of Enforcement & Licensing
(651) 296-9431; fax (651) 296-4328

MISSISSIPPI

Secretary of State's Office
Securities Division
202 North Congress Street, Suite 601
Jackson, MS 39201

Mailing address:
P.O. Box 136
Jackson, MS 39205
(601) 359-6371; fax (601) 359-2663

Leslie Scott
Assistant Secretary of State, Business Services
lscott@sos.state.ms.us

MISSOURI

Office of the Secretary of State
600 West Main Street
Jefferson City, MO 65101
(573) 751-4136; fax (573) 526-3124
http://mosl.sos.state.mo.us

Douglas F. Wilburn
Commissioner of Securities
dwilburn@mail.sos.state.mo.us

MONTANA

Office of the State Auditor
Securities Department
126 North Sanders, Room 270
Helena, MT 59604

Mailing address:
P.O. Box 4009
Helena, MT 59604
(406) 444-2040; fax (406) 444-5558

Mark O'Keefe
State Auditor and Securities Commissioner

NEBRASKA

Department of Banking & Finance
Bureau of Securities
1200 N Street, Suite 311
Lincoln, NE 68508

Mailing address:
P.O. Box 95006
Lincoln, NE 68509-5006
(402) 471-3445
http://www.ndbf.org/SEC.HTM

Jack E. Herstein
Assistant Director
jackh@bkg.state.ne.us

NEVADA

Secretary of State
Securities Division
555 E. Washington Avenue
5th Floor, Suite 5200
Las Vegas, NV 89101
(702) 486-2440; fax (702) 486-2452
nvsec@govmail.state.nv.us (e-mail)
http://www.state.nv.us

Donald J. Reis
Chief Deputy Secretary of State
(775) 688-1855; fax (775) 668-1858

Reno office:
Office of the Secretary of State,
Securities Division
1105 Terminal Way, Suite 211
Reno, NV 89502

NEW HAMPSHIRE

Bureau of Securities Regulation
Department of State
State House, Annex—Room 317A
25 Capital Street
Concord, NH 03301

Mailing address:
Room 204, State House
Concord, NH 03301-4989
(603) 271-1463; fax (603) 271-7933

Peter C. Hildreth
Director of Securities Regulation
pch@aol.com

NEW JERSEY

Department of Law & Public Safety
Bureau of Securities
153 Halsey Street, 6th Floor
Newark, NJ 07102

Mailing address:
P.O. Box 47029
Newark, NJ 07101
(973) 504-3600; fax (973) 504-3601

Franklin L. Widmann
Chief, Bureau of Securities
(973) 504-3600; fax (973) 504-3639

NEW MEXICO

Regulation & Licensing Department
Securities Division
725 St. Michaels Drive
Santa Fe, NM 87505-7605
(505) 827-7140; fax (505) 984-0617
http://www.state.nm.us/rld.state.nm.us

Michael J. Vargon
Deputy Director

NEW YORK

Department of Law
Bureau of Investor Protection &
Securities
120 Broadway, 23d Floor
New York, NY 10271
(212) 416-8200; fax (212) 416-8816

Eric R. Dinallo
Assistant Attorney General in Charge

NORTH CAROLINA

Department of the Secretary of State
Securities Division
300 North Salisbury Street, Suite 301
Raleigh, NC 27603-5909
(919) 733-3924; fax (919) 821-0818
http://www.secretary.state.nc.us/sec

David S. Massey
Deputy Securities Administrator
dmassey@mail.secstate.nc.us

NORTH DAKOTA

Securities Commissioner
State Capitol, 5th Floor
600 E. Boulevard
Bismarck, ND 58505-0510
(701) 328-2910; fax (701) 255-3113
http.//www.state.nd.us/securities

Syver Vinje
Commissioner
svinje@pioneer1.state.nd.us

OHIO

Division of Securities
77 South High Street, 22d Floor
Columbus, OH 43215
(614) 644-7381; fax (614) 466-3316
http://www.securities.state.oh.us

Thomas E. Geyer
Commissioner
(614) 644-9530
tom.geyer@com.state.oh.us

OKLAHOMA

Department of Securities
First National Center, Suite 860
120 N. Robinson
Oklahoma City, OK 73102
(405) 280-7700; fax (405) 280-7742
http://www.securities.state.ok.us

Irving L. Faught
Administrator
irving.faught@oklaosf.state.ok.us

OREGON

Department of Consumer &
Business Services
Division of Finance and
Corporate Securities
350 Winter Street NE, Room 410
Salem, OR 97310
(503) 378-4387; fax (503) 947-7862
http://www.cbs.state.or.us/external/dfcs

Richard M. "Dick" Nockelby
Administrator
richard.m.nockleby@state.or.us

James G. Harlan
Deputy Administrator
(503) 947-7478
jame.g.harlan@state.or.us

PENNSYLVANIA

Securities Commission
Eastgate Office Building
1010 North 7th Street, 2d Floor
Harrisburg, PA 17102-1410
(717) 787-8061; fax (717) 783-5122
http://www.psc.state.pa.us/PA_Exec/
Securities/

Robert M. Lam
Chairman
(717) 787-6828

Philadelphia office:
1109 State Office Building
Philadelphia, PA 19130-4088
(215) 560-2088; fax (215) 560-3977

Pittsburgh office:
806 State Office Building
Pittsburgh, PA 15222-1210
(412) 565-5083; fax (412) 565-7647

PUERTO RICO

Commissioner of Financial Institutions
P.O. Box 11855
Fernandez Juncos Station
San Juan, PR 00910-3855
(787) 723-3131; fax (787) 723-4225

Felipe B. Cruz
Securities Commissioner
Ext. 2222 or 2214

RHODE ISLAND

Department of Business Regulation
Securities Division
233 Richmond Street, Suite 232
Providence, RI 02903-4232
(401) 222-3048; fax (401) 222-5629
secdiv@dbr.state.ri.us (e-mail)
http://www.doa.state.ri.us/

Maria D'Alessandro Piccirilli
Associate Director & Superintendent
of Securities
mpicciri@dbr.state.ri.us

SOUTH CAROLINA

Office of the Attorney General
Securities Division
Rembert C. Dennis Office Building
1000 Assembly Street
Columbia, SC 29201

Mailing address:
P.O. Box 11549
Columbia, SC 29211-1549
(803) 734-4731; fax (803) 734-0032
agsecurities@ag.state.sc.us (e-mail)
http://www.scsecurities.com

Charles M. Condon
Attorney General and Securities
Commissioner
(803) 734-4731 or -3970

SOUTH DAKOTA

Division of Securities
118 West Capitol Avenue
Pierre, SD 57501-2017
(605) 773-4823; fax (605) 773-5953
securities@state.sd.us (e-mail)
http://www.state.sd.us/dcr/securities/
security.htm

Debra M. Bollinger
Director
debra.bollinger@state.sd.us

TENNESSEE

Department of Commerce & Insurance
Securities Division
Davy Crockett Tower, Suite 680
500 James Robertson Parkway
Nashville, TN 37243-0575
(615) 741-2947; fax (615) 532-8375
http://www.state.tn.us/commerce/
securdiv.html

Daphne D. Smith
Assistant Commissioner for Securities
dsmith3@mail.state.tn.us

TEXAS

State Securities Board
200 East 10th Street, 5th Floor
Austin, TX 78701

Mailing address:
P.O. Box 13167
Austin, TX 78711-3167
(512) 305-8300; fax (512) 305-8310
http://www.ssb.state.tx.us

Denise Voigt Crawford
Securities Commissioner
(512) 305-8306; fax (512) 305-8336
dcrawford@ssb.state.tx.us

UTAH

Division of Securities
Heber M. Wells Building
160 East 300 South, 2d Floor
Salt Lake City, UT 84111

Mailing address:
P.O. Box 146760
Salt Lake City, UT 84114-6760
(801) 530-6600; fax (801) 530-6980
security@br.state.ut.us (e-mail)
http://www.commerce.state.ut.us

S. Anthony (Tony) Taggart
Director, Securities Division
ttaggart@br.state.ut.us

VERMONT

Department of Banking, Insurance,
Securities & Health Care
Administration
Securities Division
89 Main Street, 2d Floor
Montpelier, VT 05602-3101

Mailing address:
89 Main Street—Drawer 20
Montpelier, VT 05602-3101
(802) 828-3420; fax (802) 828-2896
http://www.state.vt.us/bis

Blythe McLaughlin
Deputy Commissioner
bmclaughlin@bishca.state.vt.us

VIRGINIA

State Corporation Commission
Division of Securities & Retail
Franchising
1300 East Main Street, 9th Floor
Richmond, VA 23219

Mailing address:
P.O. Box 1197
Richmond, VA 23218
(804) 371-9051; fax (804) 371-9911
http://www.state.va.us/scc/division/srf/

Ronald W. Thomas
Director
(804) 371-9006
rthomas@scc.state.va.us

WASHINGTON

Department of Financial Institutions
Securities Division
General Administration Building
210 11th Street
3d Floor West, Room 300
Olympia, WA 98504-1200

Mailing address:
P.O. Box 9033
Olympia, WA 98507-9033
(360) 902-8760; fax (360) 586-5068
http://www.wa.gov/dfi/securities/

Deborah R. Bortner
Director of Securities
(360) 902-8797; fax (360) 704-6997
dbortner@dfi.wa.gov

WEST VIRGINIA

State Auditor's Office
Securities Division
State Capitol Building
Building 1, Room W-114
Charleston, WV 25305
(304) 558-2257; fax (304) 558-4211
http://www.wvauditor.com

Barbara Harmon-Schambarger
Deputy Commissioner of Securities

WISCONSIN

Department of Financial Institutions
Division of Securities
345 W. Washington Avenue, 4th Floor
Madison, WI 53703

Mailing address:
P.O. Box 1768
Madison, WI 53701-1768
(608) 261-9555; fax (608) 256-1259
http://www.wdfi.org

Patricia D. Struck
Administrator
(608) 266-3432
patricia.struck@dfi.state.wi.us

WYOMING

Secretary of State
Securities Division
State Capitol, Room 109
200 W. 24th Street
Cheyenne, WY 82002-0020
(307) 777-7370; fax (307) 777-5339
securities@missc.state.wy.us (e-mail)
http://soswy.state.wy.us

Diana J. Ohman
Secretary of State
dohman@missc.state.wy.us

Canada

ALBERTA

Securities Commission
19th Floor, 10025 Jasper Avenue
Edmonton, Alberta
Canada T5J 3Z5
(780) 427-5201; fax (780) 422-0777

Ron Sczinski
Chief Financial Officer
(780) 422-1490; fax (780) 422-1030
ron.sczinski@seccom.ab.ca

BRITISH COLUMBIA

Securities Commission
200-865 Hornby Street
Vancouver, British Columbia
V6Z 2H4 Canada
(604) 899-6500; fax (604) 899-6506;
(604) 899-6550 (Insider Report fax)
http://www.bcsc.bc.ca

Adrienne Wanstall
Commissioner
(604) 899-6536
awanstall@bcsc.bc.ca

MANITOBA

Securities Commission
1130-405 Broadway
Winnipeg, Manitoba
R3C 3L6 Canada
(204) 945-2548; fax (204) 945-0330

H. Jocelyn Samson, CFA
Chairman
(204) 945-2551
jsamson@cca.gov.mb.ca

NEW BRUNSWICK

Office of the Administrator
Department of Justice
Securities Branch
133 Prince William Street, Suite 606
Harbour Building
Saint John, New Brunswick
E2L 4Y9 Canada

Mailing address:
P.O. Box 5001
Saint John, New Brunswick
E2L 4Y9 Canada
(506) 658-3060; fax (506) 658-3059

Donne W. Smith, Jr.
Administrator
donne.smith@gov.nb.ca

NEWFOUNDLAND AND LABRADOR

Department of Government Services
and Lands
Securities Division
P.O. Box 8700
St. John's, Newfoundland
A1B 4J6 Canada
(709) 729-4189; fax (709) 729-6187

Anthony W. Patey
Director of Securities
(709) 729-4189

NORTHWEST TERRITORIES

Securities Registry
Department of Justice
Government of the Northwest
Territories
4903-49th Street
Yellowknife, Northwest Territories
X1A 2L9 Canada
(867) 873-7490; fax (867) 873-0243

Gary I. MacDougall
Registrar

NOVA SCOTIA

Securities Commission
1690 Hollis Street
2d Floor, Joseph Howe Building
Halifax, Nova Scotia
B3J 3J9 Canada

Mailing address:
P.O. Box 458
Halifax, Nova Scotia
B3H 2P8 Canada
(902) 424-7768; fax (902) 424-4625
hiscocbr@gov.ns.ca (e-mail)

Robert B. MacLellan
Chairman

ONTARIO

Securities Commission
20 Queen Street West, Suite 800
Box 55
Toronto, Ontario
M5H 3S8 Canada
(416) 597-0681; fax (416) 593-8241

Howard I. Wetston, Q.C.
Vice-Chairman
(416) 593-8206; fax (416) 593-8241
hwetston@osc.gov.on.ca

PRINCE EDWARD ISLAND

Department of Community Affairs and
Attorney General
95 Rochford Street, 4th Floor
Charlottetown, Prince Edward Island
C1A 7N8 Canada
(902) 368-4552; fax (902) 368-5283
http://www.gov.pe.ca

Edison Shea
Registrar of Securities
ejshea@gov.pe.ca

QUÉBEC

Commission des valeurs mobilières du
Québec
800 Square Victoria, 17th Floor
P.O. Box 246
Stock Exchange Tower
Montreal, Québec
H4Z 1G3 Canada
(514) 873-5326; fax (514) 873-0711
courrier@cvmq.gouv.qc.ca (e-mail)
http://www.cvmq.com

Jean Martell
Chairman
jean.martel@cvmq.gouv.qc.ca

SASKATCHEWAN

Securities Commission
800 1920 Broad Street
Regina, Saskatchewan
S4P 3V7 Canada
(306) 787-5645; fax (306) 787-5899
ssc@govmail.gov.sk.ca (e-mail)

Marcel de la Gorgendiere, Q.C
Chairman
(306) 787-5630
marcel.de.la.gorgendiere.ssc@govmail.
gov.sk.ca

YUKON TERRITORY

Corporate Affairs
2134 2d Avenue, 3d Floor
Andrew A. Philipsen Law Centre
Whitehorse, Yukon
Y1A 5H3 Canada

Mailing address:
Corporate Affairs J-9
P.O. Box 2703
Whitehorse, Yukon
Y1A 2C6 Canada
(867) 667-5225; fax (867) 393-6251

M. Richard Roberts
Registrar of Securities
rroberts@gov.yk.ca

Mexico

Comisión Nacional Bancaria y de
Valores
International Affairs General Direction
Insergentes Sur 1971
Torre Sur, Piso 11, Plaza Inn
Col. Guadalupe Inn
Mexico, D.F. C.P. 01020
011 525/724-6578, 6589;
fax 011 525/724-6220

Miguel Angel Garza
Director General (International
Affairs)

Other Organizations Dealing with Fraud

National Fraud Information Center
P.O. Box 65868
Washington, DC 20035
(800) 621-3570
www.fraud.org

The Elements

Several years ago a financial wire service reporter was standing on the floor of one of the Chicago exchanges watching the stock ticker scroll the latest prices. A brash young trader from one of the stock index pits walked up, looked at the ticker, and proudly proclaimed that his stock was doing really well. The reporter asked him which stock it was, and the trader answered. The reporter glanced at the ticker and informed the trader that the symbol for that stock showed its price was off sharply. The trader blanched. He had been looking at the wrong symbol for his stock.

Whether you're a beginner, a "middling," or a pro, it helps to know the elements of trading—at least regarding the specific stock you're trading. If you're going to be executing your own trades online, it's even more important to know the companies and their symbols.

The exchanges with which you need to become the most familiar are the New York Stock Exchange (NYSE), the Nasdaq Stock Exchange, and the American Stock Exchange (AMEX), which now is part of Nasdaq. Names and symbols of most of the companies listed on the three exchanges can be found later in this chapter.

Stock and Futures Exchanges

Domestic

American Stock Exchange (AMEX); www.amex.com
Arizona Stock Exchange; www.azx.com
Chicago Board of Trade; www.cbot.com
Chicago Board Options Exchange; www.cboe.com
Chicago Mercantile Exchange; www.cme.com

International Stock Exchange (March 2000); www.iseoptions.com
The Nasdaq Stock Exchange; www.nasdaq.com
New York Stock Exchange (NYSE); www.nyse.com
Pacific Stock Exchange; www.pacificex.com
Philadelphia Stock Exchange; www.phlx.com

Foreign

African Stock Exchange Guide
Amsterdam Stock Exchange (Netherlands); www.aex.nl
Athens Stock Exchange (Greece)
Australian Stock Exchange
Bolsa de Madrid (Spain)
Bombay Stock Exchange (India)
Colombo Stock Exchange (Sri Lanka)
Dhaka Stock Exchange; www.dsebd.org/
Estonian Central Depository for Securities (Estonia)
Frankfurt Stock Exchange (Germany); www.exchange.de
Geneva Stock Exchange (Switzerland)
Jakarta Stock Exchange (Indonesia)
Jamaica Stock Exchange
Kuala Lumpur Stock Exchange (Malaysia)
Lisbon Stock Exchange (Portugal)
Ljubjana Stock Exchange (Slovenia)
London Stock Exchange (UK); www.londonstockexchange.co.uk
London International Financial Futures Exchange; www.liffe.co.uk
Mexico Stock Exchange
Montreal Stock Exchange (Canada)
Moscow Central Stock Exchange (Russia)
Nagoya Stock Exchange (Japan)
National Stock Exchange of India (India)
Milan Stock Exchange (Italy)
New Zealand Investment Center
Oslo Stock Exchange (Norway)
Philippine Stock Watch
Russian Trading System (Russia)
São Paulo Stock Exchange (Brazil)
SBF Bourse de Paris (France)
Stockholm Stock Exchange (Sweden)
Stock Exchange of Singapore
Stock Exchange of Thailand
Taiwan Stock Exchange
Tel Aviv Stock Exchange (Israel)
Toronto Stock Exchange (Canada)
Vancouver Stock Exchange (Canada)
Vienna Stock Exchange (Austria)
Warsaw Stock Exchange (Poland)

Zagreb Stock Exchange (Croatia)

For more details and easy access to stock exchange Websites, see http://dir.yahoo.com/Business_and_Economy/Finance_and_Investment/ Exchanges/Stock_Exchanges/.

Stock Indexes

Dow Jones Industrial Average

COMPANY (SYMBOL)

Alcoa Inc. (AA)
American Express Co. (AXP)
AT&T Corp. (T)
Boeing Co. (BA)
Caterpillar, Inc. (CAT)
Citigroup, Inc. (C)
Coca-Cola Co. (KO)
DuPont (E.I.) de Nemours (DD)
Eastman Kodak Co. (EK)
Exxon Corp. (XON)
General Electric Co. (GE)
General Motors (GM)
Hewlett-Packard Co. (HWP)
Home Depot Inc. (HD)
Honeywell International Inc. (HON)
International Bus. Mach. (IBM)

COMPANY (SYMBOL)

International Paper Co. (IP)
J. P. Morgan & Co. (JPM)
Johnson & Johnson (JNJ)
McDonald's Corp. (MCD)
Merck & Co. Inc. (MRK)
Microsoft Corp. (MSFT)
Minnesota Mining & Mfg. (MMM)
Philip Morris (MO)
Procter & Gamble Co. (PG)
SBC Communications Inc. (SBC)
Union Carbide Corp. (UK)
United Technologies Corp. (UTX)
Wal-Mart Stores, Inc. (WMT)
Walt Disney Co. (DIS)
(As of November 1, 1999)

S&P 100 Index Companies

COMPANY (SYMBOL)

Alcoa Inc. (AA)
Allegheny Teledyne Inc. (ALT)
American Electric Power (AEP)
American Express Co. (AXP)
American General Corp. (AGC)
American International Group (AIG)
Ameritech Corp. (AIT)
AMP, Inc. (AMP)
AT&T Corp. (T)
Atlantic Richfield (ARC)
Avon Products (AVP)
Baker Hughes Inc. (BHI)
Bank One Corp. (ONE)
BankAmerica Corp. (BAC)
Baxter International, Inc. (BAX)
Bell Atlantic Corp. (BEL)
Bethlehem Steel Corp. (BS)
Black & Decker Corp. (BDK)
Boeing Co. (BA)
Boise Cascade Corp. (BCC)
Bristol-Myers Squibb (BMY)
Brunswick Corp. (BC)

COMPANY (SYMBOL)

Burlington Northern Santa Fe (BNI)
Campbell Soup Co. (CPB)
CBS Corp. (CBS)
Ceridian Corp. (CEN)
Champion International (CHA)
CIGNA Corp. (CI)
Cisco Systems Inc. (CSCO)
Citigroup Inc. (C)
Coastal Corp. (CGP)
Coca-Cola Co. (KO)
Colgate-Palmolive (CL)
Columbia/HCA Healthcare (COL)
Computer Sciences Corp. (CSC)
Delta Air Lines Inc. (DAL)
Dow Chemical Co. (DOW)
Du Pont (E.I.) deNemours (DD)
Eastman Kodak Co. (EK)
Entergy Corp. (ETR)
Exxon Corp. (XON)
FDX Holding Corp. (FDX)
Fluor Corp. (FLR)
Ford Motor Co. (F)

COMPANY (SYMBOL)	COMPANY (SYMBOL)
General Dynamics Corp. (GD)	Norfolk Southern Corp. (NSC)
General Electric Co. (GE)	Northern Telecom, Ltd. (NT)
General Motors (GM)	Occidental Petroleum Corp. (OXY)
H. J. Heinz Co. (HNZ)	Oracle Corp. (ORCL)
Haliburton Co. (HAL)	PepsiCo Inc. (PEP)
Harrah's Entertainment (HET)	Pharmacia & Upjohn, Inc. (PNU)
Harris Corp. (HRS)	Polaroid Corp. (PRD)
Hartford Financial (HIG)	Procter & Gamble Co. (PG)
Hewlett-Packard Co. (HWP)	Ralston Purina Group (RAL)
Homestake Mining Co. (HM)	Raytheon Co. "B" (RTNB)
Honeywell Inc. (HON)	Rockwell International Corp. (ROK)
Intel Corp. (INTC)	Schlumberger Limited (SLB)
International Business Machines (IBM)	Sears, Roebuck and Co. (S)
International Flav./Frag. (IFF)	Southern Co. (SO)
International Paper Co. (IP)	Tandy Corp. (TAN)
Johnson & Johnson (JNJ)	Tektronix, Inc. (TEK)
Kmart Corp. (KM)	Texas Instruments, Inc. (TXN)
Limited Inc. (LTD)	Toys R Us Inc. (TOY)
Mallinckrodt Inc. (MKG)	Unicorn Corp. (UCM)
May Dept. Stores Co. (MAY)	Unisys Corp. (UIS)
McDonald's Corp. (MCD)	United Technologies Corp. (UTX)
Merck & Co. Inc. (MRK)	U.S. Bancorp, Inc. (USB)
Merrill Lynch & Co. Inc. (MER)	Wal-Mart Stores, Inc. (WMT)
Microsoft Corp. (MSFT)	Walt Disney Co. (DIS)
Minnesota Mining & Mfg. (MMM)	Wells Fargo (WFC)
Mobil Corp. (MOB)	Weyerhaeuser Co. (WY)
Monsanto Co. (MTC)	Williams Cos. Inc. (WMB)
National Semiconductor (NSM)	Xerox Corp. (XRX)

S&P 500 Index Companies

COMPANY (SYMBOL)	COMPANY (SYMBOL)
3Com Corp. (COMS)	Ameren Corp. (AEE)
Abbott Labs (ABT)	America Online (AOL)
ADC Telecommunications (ADCT)	American Electric Power (AEP)
Adobe Systems (ADBE)	American Express (AXP)
Advanced Micro Devices (AMD)	American General (AGC)
AES Corp. (AES)	American Greetings Corp. (AM)
Aetna Inc. (AET)	American Home Products (AHP)
AFLAC Corporation (AFL)	American International Group (AIG)
Air Products & Chemicals (APD)	Ameritech (AIT)
Alberto-Culver (ACV)	Amgen (AMGN)
Albertson's (ABS)	AMR Corp. (AMR)
Alcan Aluminum Ltd. (AL)	AmSouth Bancorporation (ASO)
Alcoa Inc. (AA)	Anadarko Petroleum (APC)
Allegheny Teledyne Inc. (ALT)	Andrew Corp. (ANDW)
Allergan, Inc. (AGN)	Anheuser-Busch (BUD)
Allied Waste Industries (AW)	Aon Corp. (AOC)
AlliedSignal (ALD)	Apache Corp. (APA)
Allstate Corp. (ALL)	Apple Computer (AAPL)
ALLTEL Corp. (AT)	Applied Materials (AMAT)
ALZA Corp. (AZA)	Archer-Daniels-Midland (ADM)
Amerada Hess (AHC)	Armstrong World (ACK)

COMPANY (SYMBOL)	COMPANY (SYMBOL)
ASARCO Inc. (AR)	Central & South West (CSR)
Ashland Inc. (ASH)	CenturyTel, Inc. (CTL)
Associates First Capital (AFS)	Ceridian Corp. (CEN)
AT&T Corp. (T)	Champion International (CHA)
Atlantic Richfield (ARC)	Charles Schwab (SCH)
Autodesk, Inc. (ADSK)	Chase Manhattan (CMB)
Automatic Data Processing Inc. (AUD)	Chevron Corp. (CHV)
AutoZone Inc. (AZO)	Chubb Corp. (CB)
Avery Dennison Corp. (AVY)	CIGNA Corp. (CI)
Avon Products (AVP)	Cincinnati Financial (CINF)
Baker Hughes (BHI)	Cinergy Corp. (CIN)
Ball Corp. (BLL)	Circuit City Group (CC)
Bank of America Corp. (BAC)	Cisco Systems (CSCO)
Bank of New York (BK)	Citigroup Inc. (C)
Bank One Corp. (ONE)	Clear Channel Communications (CCU)
BankBoston Corp. (BKB)	Clorox Co. (CLX)
Bard (C.R.) Inc. (BCR)	CMS Energy (CMS)
Barrick Gold Corp. (ABX)	Coastal Corp. (CGP)
Bausch & Lomb (BOL)	Coca Cola Co. (KO)
Baxter International Inc. (BAX)	Coca-Cola Enterprises (CCE)
BB&T Corporation (BBT)	Colgate-Palmolive (CL)
Bear Stearns Cos. (BSC)	Columbia Energy Group (CG)
Becton, Dickinson (BDX)	Columbia/HCA Healthcare Corp. (COL)
Bell Atlantic (BEL)	Comcast Class A Special (CMCSK)
BellSouth (BLS)	Comerica Inc. (CMA)
Bemis Company (BMS)	COMPAQ Computer (CPQ)
Best Buy Co., Inc. (BBY)	Computer Associates Intl. (CA)
BestFoods Inc. (BFO)	Computer Sciences Corp. (CSC)
Bethlehem Steel (BS)	Compuware Corp. (CPWR)
Biomet, Inc. (BMET)	ConAgra Inc. (CAG)
Black & Decker Corp. (BDK)	Conoco Inc. (COC.B)
Block, H&R (HRB)	Conseco Inc. (CNC)
BMC Software (BMCS)	Consolidated Edison Hldgs. (ED)
Boeing Company (BA)	Consolidated Natural Gas (CNG)
Boise Cascade (BCC)	Consolidated Stores (CNS)
Boston Scientific (BSX)	Constellation Energy Group (CEG)
Briggs & Stratton (BGG)	Cooper Industries (CBE)
Bristol-Myers Squibb (BMY)	Cooper Tire & Rubber (CTB)
Brown-Forman Corp. (BFB)	Coors (Adolph) (RKY)
Brunswick Corp. (BC)	Corning Inc. (GLW)
Burlington Northern Santa Fe Corp. (BNI)	Costco Wholesale Corp. (COST)
Burlington Resources (BR)	Countrywide Credit Industries (CCR)
Cabletron Systems (CS)	Crane Company (CR)
Campbell Soup (CPB)	Crown Cork & Seal (CCK)
Capital One Financial (COF)	CSX Corp. (CSX)
Cardinal Health, Inc. (CAH)	Cummins Engine Co., Inc. (CUM)
Carnival Corp. (CCL)	CVS Corp. (CVS)
Carolina Power & Light (CPL)	Cyprus Amax Minerals Co. (CYM)
Case Corp. (CSE)	Dana Corp. (DCN)
Caterpillar Inc. (CAT)	Danaher Corp. (DHR)
CBS Corp. (CBS)	Darden Restaurants (DRI)
Cendant Corporation (CD)	Data General (DGN)
Centex Corp. (CTX)	Dayton Hudson (DH)

COMPANY (SYMBOL)

Deere & Co. (DE)
Dell Computer (DELL)
Delphi Automotive Systems (DPH)
Delta Air Lines (DAL)
Deluxe Corp. (DLX)
Dillard Inc. (DDS)
Dollar General (DG)
Dominion Resources (D)
Donnelley (R.R.) & Sons (DNY)
Dover Corp. (DOV)
Dow Chemical (DOW)
Dow Jones & Co. (DJ)
DTE Energy Co. (DTE)
Du Pont (E.I.) (DD)
Duke Energy (DUK)
Dun & Bradstreet Corp. (New) (DNB)
E G & G Inc. (EGG)
Eastern Enterprises (EFU)
Eastman Chemical (EMN)
Eastman Kodak (EK)
Eaton Corp. (ETN)
Ecolab Inc. (ECL)
Edison Int'l. (EIX)
Electronic Data Systems (EDS)
EMC Corp. (EMC)
Emerson Electric (EMR)
Engelhard Corp. (EC)
Enron Corp. (ENE)
Entergy Corp. (ETR)
Equifax Inc. (EFX)
Exxon Corp. (XON)
Fannie Mae (FNM)
FDX Holding Corp. (FDX)
Federal Home Loan Mtg. (FRE)
Federated Dept. Stores (FD)
Fifth Third Bancorp (FITB)
First Data (FDC)
First Union Corp. (FTU)
Firstar Corporation (FSR)
FirstEnergy Corp. (FE)
Fleet Financial Group (FLT)
Fleetwood Enterprises (FLE)
Florida Progress (FPC)
Fluor Corp. (FLR)
FMC Corp. (FMC)
Ford Motor (F)
Fort James Corp. (FJ)
Fortune Brands, Inc. (FO)
Foster Wheeler (FWC)
FPL Group (FPL)
Franklin Resources Inc. (BEN)
Freeport-McMoran Copper & Gold (FCX)
Frontier Corp. (FRO)
Fruit of the Loom Ltd. Hldg. Co. (FTL)

COMPANY (SYMBOL)

Gannett Co. (GCI)
Gap (The) (GPS)
Gateway, Inc. (GTW)
General Dynamics (GD)
General Electric (GE)
General Instrument Corp. (GIC)
General Mills (GIS)
General Motors (GM)
Genuine Parts (GPC)
Georgia-Pacific Group (GP)
Gillette Co. (G)
Golden West Financial (GDW)
Goodrich (B.F.) (GR)
Goodyear Tire & Rubber (GT)
GPU Inc. (GPU)
Grace (W.R.) & Co. (New) (GRA)
Grainger (W.W.) Inc. (GWW)
Great A & P (GAP)
Great Lakes Chemical (GLK)
GTE Corp. (GTE)
Guidant Corp. (GDT)
Halliburton Co. (HAL)
Harcourt General Inc. (H)
Harrah's Entertainment (HET)
Harris Corp. (HRS)
Hartford Financial Svc. Gp. (HIG)
Hasbro Inc. (HAS)
HCR Manor Care (HCR)
HEALTHSOUTH Corp. (HRC)
Heinz (H.J.) (HNZ)
Helmerich & Payne (HP)
Hercules, Inc. (HPC)
Hershey Foods (HSY)
Hewlett-Packard (HWP)
Hilton Hotels (HLT)
Home Depot (HD)
Homestake Mining (HM)
Honeywell (HON)
Household International (HI)
Humana Inc. (HUM)
Huntington Bancshares (HBAN)
IKON Office Solutions (IKN)
Illinois Tool Works (ITW)
IMS Health Inc. (RX)
Inco, Ltd. (N)
Ingersoll-Rand (IR)
Intel Corp. (INTC)
International Business Machines (IBM)
International Flav./Frag. (IFF)
International Paper (IP)
Interpublic Group (IPG)
ITT Industries, Inc. (IIN)
Jefferson-Pilot (JP)
Johnson & Johnson (JNJ)

COMPANY (SYMBOL)

Johnson Controls (JCI)
Jostens Inc. (JOS)
Kansas City Southern Ind. (KSU)
Kaufman & Broad Home Corp. (KBH)
Kellogg Co. (K)
Kerr-McGee (KMG)
KeyCorp (KEY)
Kimberly-Clark (KMB)
King World Productions (KWP)
KLA-Tencor Corp. (KLAC)
Kmart Corp. (KM)
Knight-Ridder Inc. (KRI)
Kohl's Corp. (KSS)
Kroger Co. (KR)
Laidlaw Inc. (LDW)
Lehman Bros. Hldgs. (LEH)
Lexmark Int'l. Group A (LXK)
Lilly (Eli) & Co. (LLY)
Limited, Inc. (LTD)
Lincoln National (LNC)
Liz Claiborne, Inc. (LIZ)
Lockheed Martin Corp. (LMT)
Loews Corp. (LTR)
Longs Drug Stores (LDG)
Louisiana Pacific (LPX)
Lowe's Cos. (LOW)
LSI Logic (LSI)
Lucent Technologies (LU)
Mallinckrodt Inc. (MKG)
Marriott Int'l. (New) (MAR)
Marsh & McLennan (MMC)
Masco Corp. (MAS)
Mattel, Inc. (MAT)
May Dept. Stores (MAY)
Maytag Corp. (MYG)
MBIA Inc. (MBI)
MBNA Corp. (KRB)
McDermott International (MDR)
McDonald's Corp. (MCD)
McGraw-Hill (MHP)
MCI WorldCom (WCOM)
McKesson HBOC Inc. (MCK)
Mead Corp. (MEA)
MediaOne Group Inc. (UMG)
Medtronic Inc. (MDT)
Mellon Bank Corp. (MEL)
Merck & Co. (MRK)
Meredith Corp. (MDP)
Merrill Lynch (MER)
MGIC Investment (MTG)
Micron Technology (MU)
Microsoft Corp. (MSFT)
Milacron Inc. (MZ)
Millipore Corp. (MIL)

COMPANY (SYMBOL)

Minnesota Mining & Mfg. (MMM)
Mirage Resorts (MIR)
Mobil Corp. (MOB)
Monsanto Company (MTC)
Morgan (J.P.) & Co. (JPM)
Morgan Stanley Dean Witter (MWD)
Motorola Inc. (MOT)
Nabisco Group Hldgs. (NGH)
NACCO Ind. Cl. A (NC)
National City Corp. (NCC)
National Semiconductor (NSM)
National Service Ind. (NSI)
Navistar International Corp. (NAV)
Network Appliance (NTAP)
New Century Energies (NCE)
New York Times Cl. A (NYT)
Newell Rubbermaid Inc. (NWL)
Newmont Mining (NEM)
NEXTEL Communications (NXTL)
Niagara Mohawk Hldgs. Inc. (NMK)
NICOR Inc. (GAS)
NIKE Inc. (NKE)
Nordstrom (JWN)
Norfolk Southern Corp. (NSC)
Nortel Networks Corp. (NT)
Northern States Power (NSP)
Northern Trust Corp. (NTRS)
Northrop Grumman Corp. (NOC)
Novell Inc. (NOVL)
Nucor Corp. (NUE)
Occidental Petroleum (OXY)
Office Depot (ODP)
Omnicom Group (OMC)
ONEOK Inc. (OKE)
Oracle Corp. (ORCL)
Owens Corning (OWC)
Owens-Illinois (OI)
PACCAR Inc. (PCAR)
PacifiCorp (PPW)
PaineWebber Group (PWJ)
Pall Corp. (PLL)
Parametric Technology (PMTC)
Parker-Hannifin (PH)
Paychex Inc. (PAYX)
PE Corp.-PE Biosystems Group (PEB)
PECO Energy Co. (PE)
Penney (J.C.) (JCP)
Peoples Energy (PGL)
PeopleSoft Inc. (PSFT)
Pep Boys (PBY)
PepsiCo Inc. (PEP)
Pfizer, Inc. (PFE)
PG&E Corp. (PCG)
Pharmacia & Upjohn, Inc. (PNU)

COMPANY (SYMBOL)

Phelps Dodge (PD)
Philip Morris (MO)
Phillips Petroleum (P)
Pioneer Hi-Bred Int'l. (PHB)
Pitney-Bowes (PBI)
Placer Dome Inc. (PDG)
PNC Bank Corp. (PNC)
Polaroid Corp. (PRD)
Potlatch Corp. (PCH)
PP & L Resources (PPL)
PPG Industries (PPG)
Praxair, Inc. (PX)
Procter & Gamble (PG)
Progressive Corp. (PGR)
Providian Financial Corp. (PVN)
Public Serv. Enterprise Inc. (PEG)
Pulte Corp. (PHM)
Quaker Oats (OAT)
QUALCOMM Inc. (QCOM)
Ralston Purina Gp (RAL)
Raytheon Co. (RTNB)
Reebok International (RBK)
Regions Financial Corp. (RGBK)
Reliant Energy (REI)
Republic New York (RNB)
Reynolds Metals (RLM)
Rite Aid (RAD)
Rockwell International (ROK)
Rohm & Haas (ROH)
Rowan Cos. (RDC)
Royal Dutch Petroleum (RD)
Russell Corp. (RML)
Ryder System (R)
SAFECO Corp. (SAFC)
Safeway Inc. (SWY)
Sara Lee Corp. (SLE)
SBC Communications Inc. (SBC)
Schering-Plough (SGP)
Schlumberger Ltd. (SLB)
Scientific-Atlanta (SFA)
Seagate Technology (SEG)
Seagram Co. Ltd. (VO)
Sealed Air Corp. (New) (SEE)
Sears, Roebuck & Co. (S)
Sempra Energy (SRE)
Service Corp. International (SRV)
Shared Medical Systems (SMS)
Sherwin-Williams (SHW)
Sigma-Aldrich (SIAL)
Silicon Graphics (SGI)
SLM Holding Corp. (SLM)
Snap-On Inc. (SNA)
Solectron Corp. (SLR)
Sonat Inc. (SNT)

COMPANY (SYMBOL)

Southern Co. (SO)
SouthTrust Corp. (SOTR)
Southwest Airlines (LUV)
Springs Industries Inc. (SMI)
Sprint Corp. FON Group (FON)
Sprint Corp. PCS Group (PCS)
St. Jude Medical (STJ)
St. Paul Cos. (SPC)
Stanley Works (SWK)
Staples Inc. (SPLS)
State Street Corp. (STT)
Summit Bancorp (SUB)
Sun Microsystems (SUNW)
Sunoco Inc. (SUN)
SunTrust Banks (STI)
Supervalu Inc. (SVU)
Synovus Financial (SNV)
Sysco Corp. (SYY)
Tandy Corp. (TAN)
Tektronix Inc. (TEK)
Tellabs, Inc. (TLAB)
Temple-Inland (TIN)
Tenet Healthcare Corp. (THC)
Tenneco Inc. (TEN)
Texaco Inc. (TX)
Texas Instruments (TXN)
Texas Utilities Hldg. Cos. (TXU)
Textron Inc. (TXT)
Thermo Electron (TMO)
Thomas & Betts (TNB)
Time Warner Inc. (TWX)
Times Mirror (TMC)
Timken Co. (TKR)
TJX Companies Inc. (TJX)
Torchmark Corp. (TMK)
Tosco Corp. (TOS)
Toys R Us Hldg. Cos. (TOY)
Tribune Co. (TRB)
TRICON Global Restaurants (YUM)
TRW Inc. (TRW)
Tupperware Corp. (TUP)
Tyco International (TYC)
Unicom Corp. (UCM)
Unilever N.V. (UN)
Union Carbide (UK)
Union Pacific (UNP)
Union Pacific Resources Group (UPR)
Union Planters (UPC)
Unisys Corp. (UIS)
United HealthCare Corp. (UNH)
United Technologies (UTX)
Unocal Corp. (UCL)
UNUMProvident Corp. (UNM)
U.S. Bancorp (USB)

COMPANY (SYMBOL)

US West Inc. (USW)
USAirways Group Inc. (U)
UST Inc. (UST)
USX-Marathon Group (MRO)
USX-U.S. Steel Group (X)
V.F. Corp. (VFC)
Viacom Inc. (VIAB)
Vulcan Materials (VMC)
Wachovia Corp. (WB)
Walgreen Co. (WAG)
Wal-Mart Stores (WMT)
Walt Disney Co. (DIS)
Warner-Lambert (WLA)
Washington Mutual, Inc. (WM)

COMPANY (SYMBOL)

Waste Management (New) (WMI)
Watson Pharmaceuticals (WPI)
WellPoint Health Networks (WLP)
Wells Fargo & Co. (New) (WFC)
Wendy's International (WEN)
Westvaco Corp. (W)
Weyerhaeuser Corp. (WY)
Whirlpool Corp. (WHR)
Willamette Industries (WLL)
Williams Cos. (WMB)
Winn-Dixie (WIN)
Worthington Ind. (WTHG)
Wrigley (Wm.) Jr. (WWY)
Xerox Corp. (XRX)

Nasdaq-100 Component Securities

COMPANY (SYMBOL)

3Com Corporation (COMS)
Adaptec Inc. (ADPT)
ADC Telecommunications Inc. (ADCT)
Adelphia Communications Corp. (ADLAC)
Adobe Systems Incorporated (ADBE)
ADTRAN Inc. (ADTN)
Altera Corporation (ALTR)
American Greetings Corp. (AGREA)
American Power Conversion Corp. (APCC)
Amgen Inc. (AMGN)
Apple Computer Inc. (AAPL)
Applied Materials Inc. (AMAT)
Applied Micro Circuits Corp. (AMCC)
Ascend Communications Inc. (ASND)
Atmel Corp. (ATML)
Bed Bath & Beyond Inc. (BBBY)
Biogen Inc. (BGEN)
Biomet Inc. (BMET)
BMC Software Inc. (BMCS)
Boston Chicken Inc. (BOST)
BroadVision Inc. (BVSN)
Centocor Inc. (CNTO)
Chiron Corporation (CHIR)
Cintas Corporation (CTAS)
Cirrus Logic Inc. (CRUS)
Cisco Systems Inc. (CSCO)
Comcast Corp. (CMCSK)
Compuware Corp. (CPWR)
Concord EFS Inc. (CEFT)
Corporate Express Inc. (CEXP)
Costco Companies Inc. (COST)
Cracker Barrel Old Ctry. Store (CBRL)
Dell Computer Corporation (DELL)
DSC Communications Corp. (DIGI)
EchoStar Communications Corp. (DISH)
Electronic Arts Inc. (ERTS)

COMPANY (SYMBOL)

Fiserv Inc. (FISV)
Food Lion Inc. (FDLNB)
FORE Systems Inc. (FORE)
Gartner Group (GART)
General Nutrition Companies (GNCI)
Genzyme Corporation (GENZ)
Glenayre Technologies Inc. (GEMS)
HBO & Company (HBOC)
Herman Miller Inc. (MLHR)
IDEXX Laboratories Inc. (IDXX)
i2 Technologies Inc. (ITWO)
Informix Corp. (IFMX)
Intel Corporation (INTC)
Intuit Inc. (INTU)
Jefferson Smurfit Corp. (JJSC)
KLA-Tencor Corporation (KLAC)
Komag Incorporated (KMAG)
Legato Systems Inc. (LGTO)
Linear Technology Corporation (LLTC)
Maxim Integrated Products Inc. (MXIM)
McCormick & Company Inc. (MCCRK)
MCI Communications Corp. (MCIC)
Medimmune Inc. (MEDI)
Metromedia Fiber Network Inc. (MFNX)
Microchip Technology Inc. (MCHP)
Microsoft Corporation (MSFT)
Molex Inc. (MOLX)
Netscape Communications Corp. (NSCP)
Network Appliance Inc. (NTAP)
Network Associates Inc. (NETA)
Networks Solutions Inc. (NSOL)
Nextel Communications Inc. (NXTL)
NEXTLINK Communications Inc. (NXLK)
Nordstrom Inc. (NOBE)
Northwest Airlines Corp. (NWAC)
Novell Inc. (NOVL)

COMPANY (SYMBOL)	COMPANY (SYMBOL)
Oracle Systems Corporation (ORCL)	Quintiles Transnational Corp. (QTRN)
Outback Steakhouse Inc. (OSSI)	RF Micro Devices Inc. (RFMD)
Oxford Health Plans Inc. (OXHP)	RPM Inc. (RPOW)
PACCAR Inc. (PCAR)	SDL Inc. (SDLI)
PacifiCare Health Sys. (PHSYB)	Sigma-Aldrich Corporation (SIAL)
Paging Network Inc. (PAGE)	Staples Inc. (SPLS)
PairGain Technologies Inc. (PAIR)	Starbucks Corp. (SBUX)
PanAmSat Corporation (SPOT)	Sun Microsystems Inc. (SUNW)
Parametric Technology Corp. (PMTC)	Sybase Inc. (SYBS)
Paychex Inc. (PAYX)	Synopsys Inc. (SNPS)
PeopleSoft Inc. (PSFT)	Tele-Communications Inc. (TCOMA)
PETsMART Inc. (PETM)	Tellabs Inc. (TLAB)
PhyCor Inc. (PHYC)	U.S. Office Products Company (OFIS)
PMC Sierra Inc. (PMCS)	Viking Office Products Inc. (VKNG)
Qlogic Corp. (QLGC)	Wisconsin Central Transport (WCLX)
QUALCOMM Inc. (QCOM)	WorldCom Inc. (WCOM)
Quantum Corporation (QNTM)	Xilinx Inc. (XLNX)

Russell 2000 Index

The Russell 2000 Index measures the performance of the 2000 smallest companies in the Russell 3000 Index, which represent about 98 percent of the total U.S. equity market. Considered by many to be the premier measure of small-capitalization stocks, the Russell 2000 is designed to be a comprehensive representation of the U.S. small-capitalization equity market that is qualified for investment. The index is value-weighted and includes only common stocks belonging to corporations domiciled in the U.S.

Wilshire 5000 Stock Index

The Wilshire 5000 Stock Index is probably the broadest index measuring the performance of U.S. stocks. Created in 1974, the index was originally composed of about 5000 stocks. There are now more than 7000 stocks in the index. Stocks included in the Wilshire 5000 must have headquarters in the U.S. and have readily available pricing data.

Types of Stock and Their Symbols

In the stock and symbols table herein, some companies may have more than one listing. That is because they may issue different types of stocks. The two stock types are common and preferred. Common stocks are securities that provide voting rights and entitle the holder to a share of the company's profits through dividends and/or capital appreciation. Should a liquidation occur, common stockholders have rights to a company's assets only after bondholders, other debtholders and preferred stockholders have been satisfied. Preferred stock is a capital stock which provides a specific dividend that is paid before any dividends are paid to common stockholders. Some companies also issue different classes of stock, such as Class A and Class B. Investors should be familiar with the different categories.

New York Stock Exchange Listed Companies

COMPANY (SYMBOL)

A

Aames Financial Corporation (AAM)
AAR Corp. (AIR)
Aaron Rents, Inc. (RNT)
Aaron Rents, Inc. (RNTA)
Abbey National PLC (ANBPRA)
A. G. Edwards, Inc. (AGE)
A. H. Belo Corporation (BLC)
A. O. Smith Corporation (AOS)
A. O. Tatneft (TNT)
Abbott Laboratories (ABT)
Abercrombie & Fitch Co. (ANF)
Abitibi-Consolidated Inc. (ABY)
ABM Industries Incorporated (ABM)
ABN AMRO Capital Funding Trust I
(AANPRA)
ABN AMRO Capital Funding Trust II
(AANPRB)
ABN AMRO Holding N.V. (AAN)
Acadia Realty Trust (AKR)
Acceptance Insurance Companies Inc. (AIF)
ACE Limited (ACL)
Ackerley Group, Inc. (The) (AK)
ACM Government Income Fund, Inc.
(ACG)
ACM Government Opportunity Fund, Inc.
(AOF)
ACM Government Securities Fund, Inc.
(GSF)
ACM Government Spectrum Fund, Inc. (SI)
ACM Managed Dollar Income Fund, Inc.
(ADF)
ACM Managed Income Fund, Inc. (AMF)
ACM Municipal Securities Income Fund,
Inc. (AMU)
Acme Electric Corporation (ACE)
Acme Metal Inc. (AMI)
ACNielsen Corporation (ART)
Acuson Corporation (ACN)
ACX Technologies, Inc. (ACX)
Adams Express Company (ADX)
Administaff, Inc. (ASF)
Administradora de Fondos de Pensiones
Provida S.A. (PVD)
Adolph Coors Company (RKY)
Advanced Communications Group, Inc.
(ADG)
Advanced Micro Devices, Inc. (AMD)
Advest Group, Inc. (The) (ADV)
ADVO, Inc. (AD)
Advocat Inc. (AVC)
AEGON N.V. (AEG)
AeroFlex Incorporated (ARX)

COMPANY (SYMBOL)

AES Corporation (The) (AES)
AES Trust I (AESPRT)
Aetna Capital L.L.C. (AETPRA)
Aetna Inc. (AET)
Aetna Inc. (AETPRC)
Affiliated Computer Services, Inc. (ACS)
Affiliated Managers Group, Inc. (AMG)
AFLAC Incorporated (AFL)
Ag Services of America, Inc. (ASV)
AGCO Corporation (AG)
AGL Resources Inc. (ATG)
Agnico-Eagle Mines Limited (AEM)
Agree Realty Corporation (ADC)
Agribrands International, Inc. (AGX)
Agrium Inc. (AGU)
Agrium Inc. (AGUPR)
AICI Capital Trust (AIFPRT)
Air Products and Chemicals, Inc. (APD)
Airborne Freight Corporation (ABF)
Airgas, Inc. (ARG)
Airlease Ltd., A California Limited
Partnership (FLY)
AirNet Systems, Inc. (ANS)
AirTouch Communications, Inc. (ATIPRC)
AK Steel Holding Corporation (AKS)
Aktiebolaget Svensk Exportkredit (SEPPR)
Aktiebolaget Svensk Exportkredit
(SEPPRA)
Alabama Power Capital Trust I (ALPPRQ)
Alabama Power Capital Trust II (ALPPRR)
Alabama Power Company (ABJ)
Alabama Power Company (ACA)
Alabama Power Company (ALPPRN)
Alabama Power Company (ALPPRO)
Alabama Power Company (ALZ)
Alamo Group Inc. (ALG)
Alaska Air Group, Inc. (ALK)
Albany International Corp. (AIN)
Albemarle Corporation (ALB)
Alberta Energy Company Ltd. (AOG)
Alberto-Culver Company (ACV)
Alberto-Culver Company (ACVA)
Albertson's, Inc. (ABS)
Alcan Aluminium Limited (AL)
Alcatel (ALA)
Alcoa, Inc. (AA)
Alexander's, Inc. (ALX)
Alexandria Real Estate Equities, Inc. (ARE)
All-American Term Trust Inc. (AAT)
Alleghany Corporation (Y)
Allegheny Energy, Inc. (AYE)
Allegheny Teledyne Incorporated (ALT)
Allen Telecom Inc. (ALN)

COMPANY (SYMBOL)

Allergan, Inc. (AGN)
Allfirst Financial Inc. (FMBPR)
Alliance All-Market Advantage Fund, Inc.
  (AMO)
Alliance Capital Management L.P. (AC)
Alliance Forest Products Inc. (PFA)
Alliance World Dollar Government Fund II
  (AWF)
Alliance World Dollar Government Fund,
  Inc. (AWG)
Alliant Energy Corporation (LNT)
Alliant Techsystems Inc. (ATK)
Allied Holdings, Inc. (AHI)
Allied Irish Banks, P.L.C. (AIB)
Allied Products Corporation (ADP)
Allied Waste Industries Inc. (AW)
AlliedSignal Inc. (ALD)
Allmerica Financial Corporation (AFC)
Allmerica Securities Trust (ALM)
Allstate Corporation (The) (ALJ)
Allstate Corporation (The) (ALL)
Allstate Financing I (ALLPRA)
Alltel Corporation (AT)
Alltel Corporation (ATPR)
Alltrista Corporation (ALC)
ALPHARMA Inc. (ALO)
Alpine Group, Inc. (The) (AGI)
Alstom (ALS)
Altos Hornos de Mexico S.A. de C.V. (IAM)
ALZA Corporation (AZA)
AMB Property Corporation (AMB)
AMB Property Corporation (AMBPRA)
Ambac Financial Group, Inc. (ABK)
Ambac Financial Group, Inc. (AKB)
Amcast Industrial Corporation (AIZ)
Amcol International Corporation (ACO)
Amdocs Limited (DOX)
Amerada Hess Corporation (AHC)
AMERCO (AOPRA)
Ameren Corporation (AEE)
America First Mortgage Investments, Inc.
  (MFA)
America Online, Inc. (AOL)
America West Airlines, Inc. (AWAWS)
America West Holdings Corporation (AWA)
American Annuity Group Capital Trust I
  (AAGPRT)
American Annuity Group, Inc. (AAG)
American Axle & Manufacturing Holdings,
  Inc. (AXL)
American Business Products, Inc. (ABP)
American Electric Power Company, Inc.
  (AEP)
American Express Company (AXP)

COMPANY (SYMBOL)

American Express Company Capital Trust I
  (AXPPRA)
American Financial Capital Trust I
  (AFGPRT)
American Financial Group, Inc. (AFG)
American General Capital, L.L.C.
  (AGCPRM)
American General Capital, L.L.C.
  (AGCPRN)
American General Corporation (AGC)
American General Corporation (AGCPRD)
American General Delaware, L.L.C.
  (AGCPRC)
American Greetings Corporation (AM)
American Health Properties, Inc. (AHE)
American Health Properties, Inc.
  (AHEPRB)
American Heritage Life Investment
  Corporation (AHL)
American Heritage Life Investment
  Corporation (AHLPRI)
American Home Products Corporation
  (AHP)
American Home Products Corporation
  (AHPPR)
American Industrial Properties REIT (IND)
American International Group, Inc. (AIG)
American Italian Pasta Company (PLB)
American Medical Security Group, Inc.
  (AMZ)
American Municipal Income Portfolio Inc.
  (XAA)
American Municipal Term Trust Inc. (AXT)
American Municipal Term Trust Inc. - II
  (BXT)
American Municipal Term Trust Inc. - III
  (CXT)
American National Can Group, Inc. (CAN)
American Precision Industries Inc. (APR)
American Re Capital (ARNPRA)
American Real Estate Partners, L.P. (ACP)
American Real Estate Partners, L.P.
  (ACPPR)
American Realty Trust, Inc. (ARB)
American Residential Investment Trust, Inc.
  (INV)
American Retirement Corporation (ACR)
American Safety Insurance Group, LTD.
  (ASI)
American Select Portfolio, Inc. (SLA)
American Skiing Company (SKI)
American Standard Companies Inc. (ASD)
American States Water Company (Holding
  Co.) (AWR)

COMPANY (SYMBOL)

American Stores Company (ASC)
American Strategic Income Portfolio Inc.
 (ASP)
American Strategic Income Portfolio Inc. - II
 (BSP)
American Strategic Income Portfolio Inc. -
 III (CSP)
American Tower Corporation (AMT)
American Water Works Company, Inc. (AWK)
American Water Works Company, Inc.
 (AWKPRA)
American Water Works Company, Inc.
 (AWKPRB)
AmeriCredit Corp. (ACF)
AmeriGas Partners, L.P. (APU)
AmeriSource Health Corporation (AAS)
Ameritech Corporation (AIT)
Ameron International Corporation (AMN)
AmerUs Life Holdings, Inc. (AHB)
AmerUs Life Holdings, Inc. (AMH)
AMETEK, Inc. (AME)
AMF Bowling, Inc. (PIN)
AMFM Inc. (AFM)
Amli Residential Properties Trust (AML)
Ampco-Pittsburgh Corporation (AP)
Amphenol Corporation (APH)
AMR Corporation (AMR)
AMREP Corporation (AXR)
AmSouth Bancorporation (ASO)
AMVESCAP PLC (AVZ)
Amway Asia Pacific Ltd. (AAP)
Amway Japan Limited (AJL)
Anadarko Petroleum Corporation (APC)
Analog Devices, Inc. (ADI)
Angelica Corporation (AGL)
Anglogold Limited (AU)
Anheuser-Busch Companies, Inc. (BUD)
Anixter International Inc. (AXE)
Ann Taylor Stores Corporation (ANN)
Annaly Mortgage Management, Inc. (NLY)
Anthracite Capital, Inc. (AHR)
ANZ Exchangeable Preferred Trust
 (ANUPR)
ANZ Exchangeable Preferred Trust II
 (ANJPR)
Aon Corporation (AOC)
Apache Corporation (APA)
Apache Corporation (APAPRC)
Apartment Investment and Management
 Company (AIV)
Apartment Investment and Management
 Company (AIVPRC)
Apartment Investment and Management
 Company (AIVPRD)

COMPANY (SYMBOL)

Apartment Investment and Management
 Company (AIVPRG)
Apartment Investment and Management
 Company (AIVPRH)
Apartment Investment and Management
 Company (AIVPRK)
Apex Mortgage Capital, Inc. (AXM)
Apex Municipal Fund, Inc. (APX)
Appalachian Power Company (AJA)
Appalachian Power Company (AJB)
Appalachian Power Company (AJC)
Appalachian Power Company (APJ)
Applied Industrial Technologies, Inc. (APZ)
Applied Magnetics Corporation (APM)
Applied Power Inc. (APW)
Apria Healthcare Group Inc. (AHG)
APT Satellite Holdings Limited (ATS)
AptarGroup, Inc. (ATR)
Aquarion Company (WTR)
Aracruz Celulose S.A. (ARA)
Arcadia Financial Ltd. (AAC)
Arch Chemicals, Inc. (ARJ)
Arch Coal, Inc. (ACI)
Archer-Daniels-Midland Company (ADM)
Archstone Communities Trust (ASN)
Archstone Communities Trust (ASNPRA)
Archstone Communities Trust (ASNPRB)
Archstone Communities Trust (ASNPRC)
Arden Realty, Inc. (ARI)
Argentaria, Caja Postal Y Banco
 Hipotecario, S.A. (AGR)
Argentaria Preferred Capital Limited
 (AGRPRA)
Argentina Fund, Inc. (The) (AF)
Argosy Gaming Company (AGY)
Arizona Public Service Company (AZD)
ARM Financial Group, Inc. (ARM)
Armco Inc. (AS)
Armco Inc. (ASPR)
Armco Inc. (ASPRA)
Armco Inc. (ASPRB)
Armor Holdings, Inc. (AH)
Armstrong World Industries, Inc. (ACK)
Armstrong World Industries, Inc. (AKK)
Arrow Electronics, Inc. (ARW)
Arthur J. Gallagher & Co. (AJG)
Artra Group Incorporated (ATA)
Arvin Industries, Inc. (ARV)
A/S Eksportfinans (EKPPR)
ASA Limited (ASA)
ASARCO Incorporated (AR)
Ashanti Goldfields Company Limited
 (ASL)
Ashland Inc. (ASH)

COMPANY (SYMBOL)

Asia Pacific Fund, Inc. (The) (APB)
Asia Pacific Resources International
   Holdings Ltd. (ARH)
Asia Pacific Wire & Cable Corporation
   Limited (AWC)
Asia Pulp & Paper Company Ltd (PAP)
Asia Pulp & Paper Company Ltd (PAPWS)
Asia Satellite Telecommunications Holdings
   Limited (SAT)
Asia Tigers Fund, Inc. (The) (GRR)
Asset Investors Corporation (AIC)
Associated Estates Realty Corporation
   (AEC)
Associated Estates Realty Corporation
   (AECPRA)
Associates First Capital Corporation (AFS)
AstraZeneca PLC (AZN)
Atalanta/Sosnoff Capital Corporation
   (ATL)
Atchison Casting Corporation (FDY)
Atlantic Capital I (CIVPRB)
Atlantic Capital II (CIVPRC)
Atlantic Richfield Company (ARC)
Atlantic Richfield Company (ARCPRA)
Atlantic Richfield Company (ARCPRC)
Atlas Air, Inc. (CGO)
Atmos Energy Corporation (ATO)
Atwood Oceanics, Inc. (ATW)
AT&T Capital Corporation (NCD)
AT&T Capital Corporation (NCF)
AT&T Corp. (LMGA)
AT&T Corp. (LMGB)
AT&T Corp. (T)
Aurora Foods Inc. (AOR)
Australia and New Zealand Banking Group
   Limited (ANZ)
Australia and New Zealand Banking Group
   Limited (ANZPR)
Austria Fund, Inc. (The) (OST)
Authentic Fitness Corporation (ASM)
Autoliv, Inc. (ALV)
Automatic Common Exchange Security
   Trust II (RTR)
Automatic Data Processing, Inc. (AUD)
AutoNation, Inc. (AN)
AutoZone, Inc. (AZO)
AvalonBay Communities Inc. (AVB)
AvalonBay Communities Inc. (AVBPRC)
AvalonBay Communities Inc. (AVBPRD)
AvalonBay Communities Inc. (AVBPRF)
AvalonBay Communities Inc. (AVBPRG)
AvalonBay Communities Inc. (AVBPRH)
Avery Dennison Corporation (AVY)
Aviall, Inc. (AVL)
Aviation Sales Company (AVS)

COMPANY (SYMBOL)

Avis Rent A Car Inc. (AVI)
Avista Capital I (AVAPRA)
Avista Corporation (AVA)
Avista Corporation (AVAPRL)
Avnet, Inc. (AVT)
Avon Products Inc. (AVP)
AVX Corporation (AVX)
AXA (AXA)
Aztar Corporation (AZR)
Aztec Manufacturing Co. (AZZ)
Azurix Corp. (AZX)

B

B. F. Goodrich Company (The) (GR)
Bacou USA, Inc. (BAU)
Bairnco Corporation (BZ)
Baker Fentress & Company (BKF)
Baker Hughes Incorporated (BHI)
Baldor Electric Company (BEZ)
Ball Corporation (BLL)
Ballantyne of Omaha, Inc. (BTN)
Ballard Medical Products (BMP)
Bally Total Fitness Holding Corporation
   (BFT)
Banco BHIF (BB)
Banco Bilbao Vizcaya International
   (Gibraltar) Limited (BVGPR)
Banco Bilbao Vizcaya International
   (Gibraltar) Limited (BVGPRB)
Banco Bilbao Vizcaya International
   (Gibraltar) Limited (BVGPRC)
Banco Bilbao Vizcaya International
   (Gibraltar) Limited (BVGPRE)
Banco Bilbao Vizcaya, S.A. (BBV)
Banco Comercial Portugues, S.A. (BPC)
Banco de A. Edwards (AED)
Banco Frances del Rio de La Plata S.A.
   (BFR)
Banco Ganadero S.A. (BGA)
Banco Ganadero S.A. (BGAPR)
Banco Latinoamericano de Exportaciones,
   S.A. (BLX)
Banco Rio de la Plata S.A. (BRS)
Banco Santander Central Hispano S.A.
   (STD)
Banco Santander - Chile (BSB)
Banco Santander Puerto Rico (SBP)
Banco Santander Puerto Rico (SBPPRA)
Banco Santiago (SAN)
Banco Wiese Limitado (BWP)
BanColombia (CIB)
BancorpSouth, Inc. (BXS)
BancWest Corporation (BWE)
Bandag, Incorporated (BDG)
Bandag, Incorporated (BDGA)

COMPANY (SYMBOL)

Bangor Hydro-Electric Company (BGR)
Bank of America Corporation (BAC)
Bank of Montreal (BMO)
Bank of New York Inc. (BK)
Bank of Tokyo - Mitsubishi, Limited (The)
 (MBK)
Bank One Corporation (ONE)
Bank One Corporation (ONEPRB)
Bank One Corporation (ONEPRC)
Bank One Corporation (ONEPRU)
Bank United (BKUPRA)
Bank United (BKUPRB)
BankAmerica Capital I (BACPRZ)
BankAmerica Capital IV (BACPRY)
BankAtlantic Bancorp, Inc. (BBX)
BankBoston Corporation (BKB)
Bankers Trust Corporation (BT)
Bankers Trust Corporation (BTPRQ)
Bankers Trust Corporation (BTPRR)
Bankers Trust Corporation (BTPRS)
BankUnited Capital III (BUFPRC)
Banta Corporation (BN)
Barclays Bank PLC (BCBPR)
Barclays Bank PLC (BCBPRC)
Barclays Bank PLC (BCBPRD)
Barclays PLC (BCS)
Barnes & Noble, Inc. (BKS)
Barnes Group Inc. (B)
Barr Laboratories, Inc. (BRL)
Barrett Resources Corporation (BRR)
Barrick Gold Corporation (ABX)
Bass PLC (BAS)
Battle Mountain Gold Company (BMG)
Battle Mountain Gold Company (BMGPR)
Bausch & Lomb Incorporated (BOL)
Baxter International Inc. (BAX)
Bay View Capital I (BVS)
Bay View Capital Corporation (BVC)
BB&T Corporation (BBT)
BCE Inc. (BCE)
BCE Mobile Communications Inc. (BCX)
BCH Capital Limited (CTHPR)
BCH Capital Limited (CTHPRB)
BCH International - Puerto Rico, Inc.
 (HPNPR)
BCP International Bank Limited
 (BPCPRA)
Bear Stearns Capital Trust II (BSCPRY)
Bear Stearns Companies Inc. (The) (BSC)
Bear Stearns Companies Inc. (The)
 (BSCPRA)
Bear Stearns Companies Inc. (The)
 (BSCPRE)
Bear Stearns Companies Inc. (The)
 (BSCPRF)

COMPANY (SYMBOL)

Bear Stearns Companies Inc. (The)
 (BSCPRG)
Beazer Homes USA, Inc. (BZH)
Beckman Coulter, Inc. (BEC)
Becton, Dickinson and Company (BDX)
Bedford Property Investors, Inc. (BED)
Beijing Yanhua Petrochemical Company
 Limited (BYH)
Belco Oil & Gas Corp. (BOG)
Belco Oil & Gas Corp. (BOGPR)
Belden, Inc (BWC)
Bell & Howell Company (BHW)
Bell Atlantic Corporation (BEL)
Bell Industries, Inc. (BI)
BellSouth Corporation (BLS)
Bemis Company, Inc. (BMS)
Benchmark Electronics, Inc. (BHE)
Benckiser N.V. (BNV)
Benetton Group S.P.A. (BNG)
Benguet Corporation (BE)
Benton Oil and Gas Company (BNO)
Bergen Brunswig Corporation (BBC)
Berkshire Hathaway Inc. (BRKA)
Berkshire Hathaway Inc. (BRKB)
Berkshire Realty Company, Inc. (BRI)
Berlitz International, Inc. (BTZ)
Bernard Chaus, Inc. (CHS)
Berry Petroleum Company (BRY)
Best Buy Co., Inc. (BBY)
Bestfoods (BFO)
Bethlehem Steel Corporation (BS)
Bethlehem Steel Corporation (BSPR)
Bethlehem Steel Corporation (BSPRB)
Beverly Enterprises, Inc. (BEV)
BFGoodrich Capital (GRPRA)
BG plc (BRG)
BGE Capital Trust I (BGEPRA)
Big Flower Holdings, Inc. (BGF)
Bindley Western Industries, Inc. (BDY)
Biomatrix, Inc. (BXM)
Biovail Corporation International (BVF)
Birmingham Steel Corporation (BIR)
BJ Services Company (BJS)
BJ Services Company (BJSWS)
BJ's Wholesale Club, Inc. (BJ)
Black & Decker Corp. (BDK)
Black Hills Corporation (BKH)
BlackRock 1999 Term Trust Inc. (The)
 (BNN)
BlackRock 2001 Term Trust Inc. (The)
 (BLK)
BlackRock Advantage Term Trust Inc. (The)
 (BAT)
BlackRock California Insured Municipal
 2008 Term Trust Inc. (The) (BFC)

COMPANY (SYMBOL)

BlackRock Florida Insured Municipal 2008
  Term Trust (The) (BRF)
BlackRock High Yield Trust (The) (BHY)
BlackRock Income Trust Inc. (The) (BKT)
BlackRock Insured Municipal 2008 Term
  Trust Inc. (The) (BRM)
BlackRock Insured Municipal Term Trust
  (The) (BMT)
BlackRock Investment Quality Municipal
  Trust (The) (BKN)
BlackRock Investment Quality Term Trust
  Inc. (The) (BQT)
BlackRock Municipal Target Term Trust Inc.
  (The) (BMN)
BlackRock New York Insured Municipal
  2008 Term Trust Inc. (The) (BLN)
BlackRock North American Government
  Income Trust (The) (BNA)
BlackRock Strategic Term Trust, Inc. (The)
  (BGT)
BlackRock Target Term Trust Inc. (The)
  (BTT)
Blockbuster Inc. (BBI)
Blount International, Inc. (BLT)
Blount International, Inc. (BLTB)
Blue Chip Value Fund, Inc. (BLU)
Blue Square-Israel Ltd. (BSI)
Bluegreen Corporation (BXG)
Blyth Industries, Inc. (BTH)
BMC Industries, Inc. (BMC)
BNY Capital II (BKPRC)
BNY Capital III (BKPRD)
BNY Capital IV (BKPRE)
BOC Group plc (The) (BOX)
Boeing Company (The) (BA)
Boise Cascade Corporation (BCC)
Boise Cascade Office Products Corporation
  (BOP)
Bombay Company (The) (BBA)
Bord Telecom Éireann PLC (EIR)
Borden Chemicals and Plastics Limited
  Partnership (BCU)
Borders Group, Inc. (BGP)
Borg-Warner Automotive, Inc. (BWA)
Boston Beer Company, Inc. (The) (SAM)
Boston Celtics Limited Partnership (Holding
  Co.) (BOS)
Boston Properties, Inc. (BXP)
Boston Scientific Corporation (BSX)
Bouygues Offshore S.A. (BWG)
Bowater Incorporated (BOW)
Bowne & Co., Inc. (BNE)
Boyd Gaming Corporation (BYD)
Boyds Collection, LTD. (The) (FOB)
Boykin Lodging Company (BOY)

COMPANY (SYMBOL)

BP Amoco P.L.C. (BPA)
BP Prudhoe Bay Royalty Trust (BPT)
Bradley Real Estate, Inc. (BTR)
Bradley Real Estate, Inc. (BTRPRA)
Brady Corporation (BRC)
Brandywine Realty Trust (BDN)
Brazil Fund, Inc. (The) (BZF)
Brazilian Equity Fund, Inc. (The) (BZL)
BRE Properties, Inc. (BRE)
BRE Properties, Inc. (BREPRA)
Breed Technologies, Inc. (BDT)
Briggs & Stratton Corporation (BGG)
Brilliance China Automotive Holdings
  Limited (CBA)
Brinker International, Inc. (EAT)
Bristol Hotel & Resorts, Inc. (BH)
Bristol-Myers Squibb Company (BMY)
Bristol-Myers Squibb Company (BMYPR)
British Airways PLC (BAB)
British Sky Broadcasting Group plc (BSY)
British Steel PLC (BST)
British Telecommunications PLC (BTY)
Broadway Stores, Inc. (BWYWS)
Broken Hill Proprietary Company Limited
  (The) (BHP)
Brooke Group Ltd. (BGL)
Brookfield Properties Corp. (BPO)
Brown & Brown, Inc. (BRO)
Brown & Sharpe Manufacturing Company
  (BNS)
Brown Group, Inc. (BG)
Brown Shoe Company, Inc. (BWS)
Brown-Forman Corporation (BFA)
Brown-Forman Corporation (BFB)
BRT Realty Trust (BRT)
Brunswick Corporation (BC)
Brush Wellman Inc. (BW)
BSCH Finance Limited (BSFPRA)
BSCH Finance Limited (BSFPRB)
BSCH Finance Limited (BSFPRC)
BSCH Finance Limited (BSFPRD)
BSCH Finance Limited (BSFPRE)
BSCH Finance Limited (BSFPRF)
BSCH Finance Limited (BSFPRG)
BSCH Finance Limited (BSFPRH)
BSCH Finance Limited (BSFPRJ)
BT Preferred Capital Trust I (BTPRA)
Buckeye Partners, L.P. (BPL)
Buckeye Technologies Inc. (BKI)
Buckle, Inc. (The) (BKE)
Budget Group, Inc. (BD)
Bufete Industrial, S.A. (GBI)
BUNZL PLC (BNL)
Burlington Coat Factory Warehouse
  Corporation (BCF)

COMPANY (SYMBOL)

Burlington Industries, Inc. (BUR)
Burlington Northern Santa Fe Corporation
  (BNI)
Burlington Resources Inc. (BR)
Burnham Pacific Properties, Inc. (BPP)
Bush Boake Allen Inc. (BOA)
Bush Industries, Inc. (BSH)
Butler Manufacturing Company (BBR)
BWAY Corporation (BY)

C

C&D Technologies, Inc. (CHP)
C. R. Bard, Inc. (BCR)
Cable and Wireless Plc (CWP)
Cable & Wireless Communications PLC
  (CWZ)
Cable & Wireless HKT (HKT)
Cable Design Technologies Corporation
  (CDT)
Cabletron Systems, Inc. (CS)
Cabot Corporation (CBT)
Cabot Industrial Trust (CTR)
Cabot Oil & Gas Corporation (COG)
Cadbury Schweppes Delaware, L.P.
  (CSDPRA)
Cadbury Schweppes Public Limited
  Company (CSG)
Cadence Design Systems, Inc. (CDN)
Cadillac Fairview Corporation (CDF)
Calgon Carbon Corporation (CCC)
California Federal Bank, a Federal Savings
  Bank (CFPPRC)
California Federal Preferred Capital
  Corporation (CFP)
California Water Service Group (CWT)
Callaway Golf Company (ELY)
Callon Petroleum Company (CPE)
Callon Petroleum Company (CPEPRA)
Calpine Corporation (CPN)
Cambrex Corporation (CBM)
Camden Property Trust (CPT)
Camden Property Trust (CPTPRA)
Cameco Corporation (CCJ)
Cameco Corporation (CCJPR)
Cameron Ashley Building Products, Inc.
  (CAB)
Campbell Resources Inc. (CCH)
Campbell Soup Company (CPB)
Canadian General Capital (CGGPRT)
Canadian Imperial Bank of Commerce (BCM)
Canadian National Railway Company (CNI)
Canadian Occidental Petroleum Ltd.
  (CZXPR)
Canadian Occidental Petroleum Ltd.
  (CZXPRA)

COMPANY (SYMBOL)

Canadian Pacific Limited (CP)
CanWest Global Communications Corp.
  (CWG)
Capital One Financial Corporation (COF)
Capital Re Corporation (KRE)
Capital Re LLC (KREPRL)
Capital Senior Living Corporation (CSU)
Capital Trust, Inc.(Maryland) (CT)
Capstead Mortgage Corporation (CMO)
Capstead Mortgage Corporation
  (CMOPRA)
Capstead Mortgage Corporation
  (CMOPRB)
Cardinal Health, Inc. (CAH)
Carey Diversified LLC (CDC)
Caribiner International, Inc. (CWC)
Carlisle Companies Incorporated (CSL)
Carlton Communications PLC (CCMPR)
Carmike Cinemas Inc. (CKE)
Carnival Corporation (CCL)
Carolina Power & Light Company (CPD)
Carolina Power & Light Company (CPL)
Carpenter Technology Corporation (CRS)
CarrAmerica Realty Corporation (CRE)
CarrAmerica Realty Corporation
  (CREPRB)
CarrAmerica Realty Corporation
  (CREPRC)
CarrAmerica Realty Corporation
  (CREPRD)
Carriage Services, Inc. (CSV)
Carson, Inc. (CIC)
Carter-Wallace, Inc. (CAR)
Cascade Corporation (CAE)
Cascade Natural Gas Corporation (CGC)
Case Corporation (CSE)
Cash America International, Inc. (PWN)
Castle & Cooke Inc. (CCS)
Catalina Lighting, Inc. (LTG)
Catalina Marketing Corporation (POS)
Catellus Development Corporation (CDX)
Caterpillar Inc. (CAT)
Cavalier Homes, Inc. (CAV)
Cavanaughs Hospitality Corporation (CVH)
CB Richard Ellis Services, Inc. (CBG)
CBL & Associates Properties, Inc. (CBL)
CBL & Associates Properties, Inc.
  (CBLPRA)
CBS Corporation (CBS)
CCB Financial Corporation (CCB)
CDI Corp. (CDI)
CEC Entertainment, Inc. (CEC)
Cedar Fair, L.P. (FUN)
Celestica Inc. (CLS)
Cendant Corporation (CD)

COMPANY (SYMBOL)

Cendant Corporation (CDPRG)
Cendant Corporation (CDPRI)
CenterPoint Properties Trust (CNT)
CenterPoint Properties Trust (CNTPRA)
CenterTrust Retail Properties, Inc. (CTA)
Centex Construction Products, Inc. (CXP)
Centex Corporation (CTX)
Central and South West Corporation (CSR)
Central European Equity Fund, Inc. (The)
  (CEE)
Central European Value Fund, Inc. (The)
  (CRF)
Central Hudson Gas & Electric Corporation
  (CNH)
Central Illinois Light Company (CERPR)
Central Newspapers, Inc. (ECP)
Central Parking Corporation (CPC)
Central Vermont Public Service Corporation
  (CV)
Centris Group, Inc. (The) (CGE)
Centura Banks, Inc. (CBC)
CenturyTel, Inc. (CTL)
Ceridian Corporation (CEN)
CFC Preferred Trust (CFBPR)
CGI Group Inc. (GIB)
Champion Enterprises, Inc. (CHB)
Champion International Corporation
  (CHA)
Championship Auto Racing Teams, Inc.
  (MPH)
Charles E. Smith Residential Realty, Inc.
  (SRW)
Charles Schwab Corporation (The) (SCH)
Chart House Enterprises, Inc. (CHT)
Chart Industries, Inc. (CTI)
Chartwell Dividend and Income Fund, Inc.
  (CWF)
Chartwell Re Corporation (CWL)
Chase Capital IV (CMV)
Chase Capital V (CBF)
Chase Industries Inc. (CSI)
Chase Manhattan Corporation (The) (CMB)
Chase Manhattan Corporation (The)
  (CMBPRB)
Chase Manhattan Corporation (The)
  (CMBPRC)
Chase Manhattan Corporation (The)
  (CMBPRG)
Chase Manhattan Corporation (The)
  (CMBPRL)
Chase Manhattan Corporation (The)
  (CMBPRN)
Chase Preferred Capital Corporation (The)
  (CMBPR)
Chateau Communities, Inc. (CPJ)

COMPANY (SYMBOL)

Checkpoint Systems, Inc. (CKP)
Chelsea GCA Realty, Inc. (CCG)
Chemed Corporation (CHE)
CHEMFAB Corporation (CFA)
ChemFirst Inc. (CEM)
Chesapeake Corporation (CSK)
Chesapeake Energy Corporation (CHK)
Chesapeake Energy Corporation (CHKPR)
Chesapeake Utilities Corporation (CPK)
Chevron Corporation (CHV)
Chevy Chase Preferred Capital Corporation
  (CCPPRA)
Chic By H.I.S., Inc. (JNS)
Chicago Bridge & Iron Company N.V.
  (CBI)
Chicago Title Corporation (CTZ)
Chile Fund, Inc. (The) (CH)
China Eastern Airlines Corporation Limited
  (CEA)
China Fund, Inc. (The) (CHN)
China Southern Airlines Company Limited
  (ZNH)
China Telecom (Hong Kong) Limited (CHL)
China Tire Holdings Limited (TIR)
China Yuchai International Limited (CYD)
Chiquita Brands International, Inc. (CQB)
Chiquita Brands International, Inc.
  (CQBPRA)
Chiquita Brands International, Inc.
  (CQBPRB)
Chittenden Corporation (CHZ)
Chock Full O'Nuts Corporation (CHF)
Choice Hotels International, Inc. (CHH)
ChoicePoint Inc. (CPS)
Chris-Craft Industries, Inc. (CCN)
Chris-Craft Industries, Inc. (CCNPRA)
Chris-Craft Industries, Inc. (CCNPRB)
Chromcraft Revington, Inc. (CRC)
CHS Electronics, Inc. (HS)
Chubb Corporation (CB)
Church & Dwight Co., Inc. (CHD)
Chyron Corporation (CHY)
CIBER, Inc. (CBR)
CIGNA Corporation (CI)
CIGNA High Income Shares (HIS)
Cigna Investment Securities, Inc. (IIS)
CILCORP Inc. (CER)
Cincinnati Bell Inc. (CSN)
Cincinnati Gas & Electric Company (The)
  (CINPRA)
Cincinnati Gas & Electric Company (The)
  (JRL)
Cinergy Corp. (CIN)
Circuit City Stores, Inc. - CarMax Group
  (KMX)

COMPANY (SYMBOL)

Circuit City Stores, Inc. - Circuit City Group (CC)
Circus Circus Enterprises, Inc. (CIR)
CIT Group, Inc. (The) (CIT)
Citicorp Capital III (CIHPRA)
Citigroup Capital I (CPRE)
Citigroup Capital IV (CPRN)
Citigroup Capital V (CPRW)
Citigroup Capital VI (CPRX)
Citigroup Inc. (C)
Citigroup Inc. (CPRF)
Citigroup Inc. (CPRG)
Citigroup Inc. (CPRH)
Citigroup Inc. (CPRM)
Citigroup Inc. (CPRQ)
Citigroup Inc. (CPRR)
Citigroup Inc. (CPRS)
Citigroup Inc. (CPRU)
Citigroup Inc. (CCIPRK)
Citigroup Inc. (CCIPRT)
Citizens Utilities Company (CZN)
Citizens Utilities Trust (CZNPR)
City National Corporation (CYN)
CKE Restaurants, Inc. (CKR)
CL&P Capital, L.P. (CPMPRA)
Claire's Stores, Inc. (CLE)
CLARCOR Inc. (CLC)
Clarion Commercial Holdings, Inc. (CLR)
Clayton Homes, Inc. (CMH)
Clear Channel Communications, Inc. (CCU)
CLECO Corporation (CNL)
Clemente Strategic Value Fund, Inc. (CLM)
Cleveland Electric Illuminating Company (The) (CVXPR)
Cleveland Electric Illuminating Company (The) (CVXPRB)
Cleveland Electric Illuminating Company (The) (CVXPRL)
Cleveland Electric Illuminating Company (The) (CVXPRT)
Cleveland-Cliffs Inc. (CLF)
Clorox Company (The) (CLX)
CMAC Investment Corporation (CMT)
CMI Corporation (CMI)
CMP Group, Inc. (Holding Co.) (CTP)
CMS Energy Corp. (CMS)
CMS Energy Corp. (CPG)
CNA Financial Corp. (CNA)
CNA Income Shares, Inc. (CNN)
CNA Surety Corporation (SUR)
CNB Bancshares, Inc. (BNK)
CNB Capital Trust I (BNKPRA)
CNF Transportation Inc. (CNF)
CNF Trust I (CNFPRT)

COMPANY (SYMBOL)

Coach USA, Inc. (CUI)
Coachmen Industries, Inc. (COA)
Coastal Corporation (The) (CGP)
Coastal Corporation (The) (CGPPRA)
Coastal Corporation (The) (CGPPRB)
Coastal Finance I (CGPPRT)
Coastcast Corporation (PAR)
Coca-Cola Company (The) (KO)
Coca-Cola Enterprises Inc. (CCE)
Coca-Cola FEMSA, S.A. de C.V. (KOF)
Coeur d'Alene Mines Corporation (CDE)
Coeur d'Alene Mines Corporation (CDEPR)
Cohen & Steers Total Return Realty Fund, Inc. (RFI)
Cold Metal Products, Inc. (CLQ)
Cole National Corporation (CNJ)
Coleman Company, Inc. (The) (CLN)
Coles Myer Ltd. (CM)
Colgate-Palmolive Company (CL)
Colgate-Palmolive Company (CLPR)
Collins & Aikman Corporation (CKC)
Colonial BancGroup, Inc. (The) (CNB)
Colonial High Income Municipal Trust (CXE)
Colonial Intermarket Income Trust I (CMK)
Colonial Intermediate High Income Fund (CIF)
Colonial Investment Grade Municipal Trust (CXH)
Colonial Municipal Income Trust (CMU)
Colonial Properties Trust (CLP)
Colonial Properties Trust (CLPPRA)
Columbia Energy Group (CG)
Columbia/HCA Healthcare Corporation (COL)
Columbus Southern Power Company (CJA)
Columbus Southern Power Company (CSJ)
Comdisco, Inc. (CDO)
ComEd Financing I (CWEPRT)
Comerica Incorporated (CMA)
Comfort Systems USA, Inc. (FIX)
Commerce Bancorp, Inc. (CBH)
Commerce Capital Trust I (CBHPRT)
Commerce Group, Inc. (The) (CGI)
Commercial Federal Corporation (CFB)
Commercial Intertech Corp. (TEC)
Commercial Metals Company (CMC)
Commercial Net Lease Realty, Inc. (NNN)
Commonwealth Edison Company (CWEPRK)
Commonwealth General LLC (COHPRMCL)
CommScope, Inc. (CTV)

COMPANY (SYMBOL)

Community Bank System, Inc. (CBU)
Compagnie Generale de Geophysique
  (GGY)
Companhia Brasileira de Distribuicao
  (CBD)
Companhia Cervejaria Brahma (BRH)
Companhia Cervejaria Brahma (BRHC)
Companhia Paranaense de Energia-COPEL
  (ELP)
Companhia Siderurgica Nacional (SID)
Compania Anonima Nacional Telefonos de
  Venezuela (CANTV) (VNT)
Compania Cervecerias Unidas S.A. (CU)
Compania de Minas Buenaventura S.A.
  (BVN)
Compania de Telecomunicaciones de Chile
  S.A. (CTC)
Compaq Computer Corporation (CPQ)
CompUSA Inc. (CPU)
Computer Associates International, Inc.
  (CA)
Computer Sciences Corporation (CSC)
Computer Task Group, Incorporated (TSK)
CompX International Inc. (CIX)
COMSAT Capital I, L.P. (CQPRA)
COMSAT Corporation (CQ)
Comstock Resources, Inc. (CRK)
ConAgra Capital, L.C. (CAGPRA)
ConAgra Capital, L.C. (CAGPRB)
ConAgra Capital, L.C. (CAGPRC)
ConAgra, Inc. (CAG)
Cone Mills Corporation (COE)
Conectiv (CIV)
Conectiv (CIVA)
Congoleum Corporation (CGM)
Connecticut Energy Corporation (CNE)
Conoco Inc. (COC)
Conseco Financing Trust I (CNCPRT)
Conseco Financing Trust V (CNCPRV)
Conseco Financing Trust VI (CNCPRG)
Conseco, Inc. (CNC)
Conseco, Inc. (CNCPRF)
Conseco Strategic Income Fund (CFD)
CONSOL Energy, Inc. (CNX)
Consolidated Edison Company of New
  York, Inc. (EDL)
Consolidated Edison Company of New
  York, Inc. (EDPRA)
Consolidated Edison Company of New
  York, Inc. (EDPRC)
Consolidated Edison, Inc. (ED)
Consolidated Graphics, Inc. (CGX)
Consolidated Natural Gas Company (CNG)
Consolidated Papers, Inc. (CDP)

COMPANY (SYMBOL)

Consolidated Products, Inc. (COP)
Consolidated Stores Corporation (CNS)
Consorcio G Grupo Dina, S.A. de C.V.
  (DIN)
Consorcio G Grupo Dina, S.A. de C.V.
  (DINL)
Constellation Energy Group Inc. (CEG)
Consumers Energy Company (CMSPRA)
Consumers Energy Company (CMSPRB)
Consumers Energy Company Financing I
  (CMSPRJ)
Consumers Energy Company Financing II
  (CMSPRK)
ContiFinancial Corporation (CFN)
Continental Airlines, Inc. (CAL)
Continental Airlines, Inc. (CALA)
Controladora Comercial Mexicana, S.A. de
  C.V. (MCM)
Convergys Corporation (CVG)
Converse Inc. (CVE)
Cooker Restaurant Corporation (CGR)
Cooper Cameron Corporation (CAM)
Cooper Companies, Inc. (The) (COO)
Cooper Industries, Inc. (CBE)
Cooper Tire & Rubber Company (CTB)
Copene-Petroquimica do Nordeste S.A.
  (PNE)
Coram Healthcare Corporation (CRH)
Cordant Technologies Inc. (CDD)
Cordiant Communications Group PLC
  (CDA)
Core Laboratories N.V. (CLB)
Corimon C.A. (CRM)
Corn Products International, Inc. (CPO)
Cornell Corrections, Inc. (CRN)
Cornerstone Propane Partners, L.P. (CNO)
Cornerstone Properties Inc. (CPP)
Cornerstone Realty Income Trust, Inc.
  (TCR)
Corning Incorporated (GLW)
Corporate Asset Backed Corporation (PFH)
Corporate High Yield Fund II, Inc. (KYT)
Corporate High Yield Fund III, Inc. (CYE)
Corporate High Yield Fund, Inc. (COY)
Corporate Office Properties Trust (OFC)
Correctional Properties Trust (CPV)
Corrpro Companies, Inc. (CO)
CORT Business Services Corporation
  (CBZ)
Cotelligent Inc. (CGZ)
Countrywide Credit Industries, Inc. (CCR)
Cousins Properties Incorporated (CUZ)
Covance Inc. (CVD)
Cox Communications, Inc. (COX)

COMPANY (SYMBOL)

Cox Radio, Inc. (CXR)
CPI Corp. (CPY)
CPL Capital I (CPZPRA)
Craig Corporation (CRG)
Craig Corporation (CRGPR)
Crane Co. (CR)
Crawford & Company (CRDA)
Crawford & Company (CRDB)
Credicorp Ltd. (BAP)
Credit Suisse Asset Management Income
   Fund, Inc. (FBF)
Credit Suisse Asset Management Strategic
   Global Income Fund, Inc. (FBI)
Crescent Real Estate Equities Company
   (CEI)
Crescent Real Estate Equities Company
   (CEIPRA)
Crestline Capital Corporation (CLJ)
CRIIMI MAE Inc. (QCMM)
CRIIMI MAE Inc. (QCMMPRB)
Cristalerias de Chile S.A. (CGW)
Crompton & Knowles Corporation (CNK)
Cross Timbers Oil Company (XTO)
Cross Timbers Oil Company (XTOPRA)
Cross Timbers Royalty Trust (CRT)
Crown American Realty Trust (CWN)
Crown American Realty Trust (CWNPRA)
Crown Cork & Seal Company, Inc. (CCK)
Crown Cork & Seal Company, Inc.
   (CCKPR)
Crown Crafts, Inc. (CRW)
Crown Pacific Partners, L.P. (CRO)
CryoLife, Inc. (CRY)
CSK Auto Corporation (CAO)
CSS Industries, Inc. (CSS)
CSX Corporation (CSX)
CTG Resources, Inc. (CTG)
CTS Corporation (CTS)
Cullen/Frost Bankers, Inc. (CFR)
Culp, Inc. (CFI)
Cummins Engine Company, Inc. (CUM)
Current Income Shares, Inc. (CUR)
Curtiss-Wright Corporation (CW)
CV Reit, Inc. (CVI)
CVS Automatic Common Exchange Security
   Trust (CTF)
CVS Corporation (CVS)
Cypress Semiconductor Corporation (CY)
Cyprus Amax Minerals Company (CYM)
Cytec Industries Inc. (CYT)

D

D. R. Horton, Inc. (DHI)
Daimler-Benz AG (DAJ)

COMPANY (SYMBOL)

DaimlerChrysler AG (DCX)
Dain Rauscher Corporation (DRC)
Dallas Semiconductor Corporation (DS)
Dal-Tile International Inc. (DTL)
Dames & Moore Group (DM)
Dan River Inc. (DRF)
Dana Corporation (DCN)
Danaher Corporation (DHR)
Daniel Industries, Inc. (DAN)
Darden Restaurants, Inc. (DRI)
Data General Corporation (DGN)
Dayton Hudson Corporation (DH)
Dayton Superior Corporation (DSD)
DBT Online, Inc. (DBT)
De Rigo S.P.A. (DER)
Dean Foods Company (DF)
Debt Strategies Fund II, Inc. (DSU)
Debt Strategies Fund III, Inc. (DBU)
Debt Strategies Fund, Inc. (DBS)
DECS Trust (DET)
DECS Trust II (RYD)
Deere & Company (DE)
Del Monte Foods Company (DLM)
Del Webb Corporation (WBB)
Delaware Group Dividend & Income Fund,
   Inc. (DDF)
Delaware Group Global Dividend and
   Income Fund, Inc. (DGF)
Delco Remy International, Inc. (RMY)
Delmarva Power Financing I (CIVPRD)
Delphi Automotive Systems Corporation
   (DPH)
Delphi Financial Group, Inc. (DFG)
Delta Air Lines, Inc. (DAL)
Delta and Pine Land Company (DLP)
Delta Financial Corporation (DFC)
Delta Woodside Industries, Inc. (DLW)
Deltic Timber Corporation (DEL)
Deluxe Corporation (DLX)
Denbury Resources Inc. (DNR)
Department 56, Inc. (DFS)
Desc, S.A. de C.V. (DES)
Designer Finance Trust (DSHPRA)
Detroit Diesel Corporation (DDC)
Detroit Edison Company (DTA)
Detroit Edison Company (DTB)
Detroit Edison Company (DTH)
Deutsche Telekom AG (DT)
Developers Diversified Realty Corporation
   (DDR)
Developers Diversified Realty Corporation
   (DDRPRA)
Developers Diversified Realty Corporation
   (DDRPRB)

COMPANY (SYMBOL)

Developers Diversified Realty Corporation (DDRPRC)
Developers Diversified Realty Corporation (DDRPRD)
DeVry Inc. (DV)
Dexter Corporation (DEX)
DIAGEO PLC (DEO)
Diagnostic Products Corporation (DP)
Dial Corporation (The) (DL)
Diamond Offshore Drilling, Inc. (DO)
Diebold, Incorporated (DBD)
Dillard's Capital Trust I (DDT)
Dillard's Inc. (DDS)
Dime Bancorp, Inc. (DME)
DiMon Incorporated (DMN)
Discount Auto Parts, Inc. (DAP)
Distribucion y Servicio D & S S.A. (DYS)
DLJ Capital Trust I (DLJPRT)
DLJ High Yield Bond Fund (DHY)
Dole Food Company, Inc. (DOL)
Dollar General Corporation (DG)
Dollar General STRYPES Trust (DGS)
Dollar Thrifty Automotive Group, Inc. (DTG)
Dominion Resources Black Warrior Trust (DOM)
Dominion Resources, Inc. (D)
Domtar Inc. (DTC)
Donaldson Company, Inc. (DCI)
Donaldson, Lufkin & Jenrette, Inc. (DLJ)
Donaldson, Lufkin & Jenrette, Inc. (DLJPRA)
Donaldson, Lufkin & Jenrette, Inc. (DLJPRB)
DONCASTERS PLC (DCS)
Donna Karan International Inc. (DK)
Donnelly Corporation (DON)
Dot Hill Systems Corp. (HIL)
Dover Corporation (DOV)
Dover Downs Entertainment, Inc. (DVD)
Dow Chemical Company (The) (DOW)
Dow Jones & Company, Inc. (DJ)
Downey Financial Corp. (DSL)
DPL Inc. (DPL)
DQE, Inc. (DQE)
Dreyfus High Yield Strategies Fund (DHF)
Dreyfus Strategic Governments Income, Inc. (DSI)
Dreyfus Strategic Municipal Bond Fund, Inc. (DSM)
Dreyfus Strategic Municipals, Inc. (LEO)
Dril-Quip, Inc. (DRQ)
DSP Communications, Inc. (DSP)
DST Systems, Inc. (DST)
DTE Energy Company (DTE)

COMPANY (SYMBOL)

Duane Reade Inc. (DRD)
Ducati Motor Holding S.P.A. (DMH)
Ducommun Incorporated (DCO)
Duff & Phelps Credit Rating Co. (DCR)
Duff & Phelps Utilities Income Inc. (DNP)
Duff & Phelps Utilities Tax-Free Income Inc. (DTF)
Duff & Phelps Utility & Corporate Bond Trust (DUC)
Duke-Weeks Realty Corporation (DRE)
Duke-Weeks Realty Corporation (DREPRA)
Duke-Weeks Realty Corporation (DREPRD)
Duke-Weeks Realty Corporation (DREPRE)
Duke Capital Financing Trust I (DUKPRT)
Duke Capital Financing Trust II (DUKPRU)
Duke Energy Capital Trust I (DUKPRQ)
Duke Energy Corporation (DUK)
Duke Energy Corporation (DUKPRA)
Duke Energy Corporation (DUT)
Dun & Bradstreet Corporation (The) (DNB)
Duquesne Capital L.P. (DQPRA)
Duquesne Light Company (DQUPRA)
Duquesne Light Company (DQUPRB)
Duquesne Light Company (DQUPRC)
Duquesne Light Company (DQUPRD)
Duquesne Light Company (DQUPRE)
Duquesne Light Company (DQUPRG)
Duquesne Light Company (DQZ)
DVI, Inc. (DVI)
Dycom Industries, Inc. (DY)
Dyersburg Corporation (DBG)
DYNEGY INC. (DYN)

E

Earthgrains Company (The) (EGR)
E. I. du Pont de Nemours and Company (DD)
E. I. du Pont de Nemours and Company (DDPRA)
E. I. du Pont de Nemours and Company (DDPRB)
E. W. Blanch Holdings, Inc. (EWB)
E. W. Scripps Company (The) (SSP)
Eastern American Natural Gas Trust (NGT)
Eastern Enterprises (EFU)
Eastern Utilities Associates (EUA)
EastGroup Properties Inc. (EGP)
EastGroup Properties Inc. (EGPPRA)
Eastman Chemical Company (EMN)
Eastman Kodak Company (EK)
Eaton Corporation (ETN)

COMPANY (SYMBOL)

Eaton Vance Corp. (EV)
Eaton Vance Municipal Income Trust (EVN)
Eaton Vance Senior Income Trust (EVF)
ECC International Corp. (ECC)
Echelon International Corporation (EIN)
Ecolab Inc. (ECL)
EDF London Capital L.P. (ELOPRA)
Edison International (EIX)
EDO Corporation (EDO)
EDP-Electricidade de Portugal, S.A. (EDP)
EEX Corporation (EEX)
EG&G, Inc. (EGG)
Ek Chor China Motorcycle Co. Ltd. (EKC)
El Paso Energy Capital Trust I (EPGPRC)
El Paso Energy Corporation (EPG)
El Paso Tennessee Pipeline Company
  (EPGPR)
Elan Corporation, PLC (ELN)
Elan Corporation, PLC (ELNWSA)
Elcor Corporation (ELK)
ElderTrust (ETT)
Electronic Data Systems Corporation (EDS)
Elf Aquitaine (ELF)
Eli Lilly and Company (LLY)
Elscint Limited (ELT)
Elsevier NV (ENL)
Embotelladora Andina S.A. (AKOA)
Embotelladora Andina S.A. (AKOB)
Embratel Participacoes S.A. (EMT)
EMC Corporation (EMC)
Emerging Markets Floating Rate Fund Inc.
  (The) (EFL)
Emerging Markets Income Fund II, Inc.
  (EDF)
Emerging Markets Income Fund Inc.
  (EMD)
Emerging Markets Infrastructure Fund, Inc.
  (The) (EMG)
Emerging Markets Telecommunications
  Fund, Inc. (The) (ETF)
Emerson Electric Co. (EMR)
Empire District Electric Company (EDE)
Empire District Electric Company
  (EDEPRA)
Empire District Electric Company
  (EDEPRB)
Empire District Electric Company
  (EDEPRC)
Empresa Nacional de Electricidad S.A.
  (Chile) (ENDESA) (EOC)
Empresas ICA Sociedad Controladora, S.A.
  de C.V. (ICA)
Encal Energy Ltd. (ECA)
ENDESA S.A. (ELE)
Energen Corporation (EGN)

COMPANY (SYMBOL)

Energy East Corporation (NEG)
EnergyNorth, Inc. (EI)
Enersis S.A. (ENI)
Enesco Group, Inc. (ENC)
Engelhard Corporation (EC)
Enhance Financial Services Group Inc.
  (EFS)
ENI S.P.A. (E)
Ennis Business Forms, Inc. (EBF)
Enron Capital LLC (ENEPRC)
Enron Capital Resources, L.P. (ENEPRA)
Enron Capital Trust I (ENEPRT)
Enron Capital Trust II (ENEPRR)
Enron Corp. (ENE)
Enron Corp. (ENEPRJ)
Enron Oil & Gas Company (EOG)
ENSCO International Incorporated (ESV)
Enserch Corporation (ENSPRF)
Entercom Communications Corp. (ETM)
Entergy Arkansas Capital I (EAIPRA)
Entergy Corporation (ETR)
Entergy Gulf States Capital I (EGSPRA)
Entergy Gulf States, Inc. (GSUPR)
Entergy Gulf States, Inc. (GSUPRB)
Entergy Gulf States, Inc. (GSUPRD)
Entergy Gulf States, Inc. (GSUPRE)
Entergy Gulf States, Inc. (GSUPRG)
Entergy Louisiana Capital I (LPLPRB)
Enterprise Capital Trust I (PEGPRS)
Enterprise Capital Trust III (PEGPRR)
Enterprise Oil PLC (ETP)
Enterprise Oil PLC (ETPPRB)
Enterprise Products Partners L.P. (EPD)
Entertainment Properties Trust (EPR)
Environmental Elements Corporation (EEC)
EOTT Energy Partners, L.P. (EOT)
EQUANT N.V. (ENT)
Equifax Inc. (EFX)
Equitable Companies, Inc. (The) (EQ)
Equitable Resources Capital Trust I (ERE)
Equitable Resources, Inc. (EQT)
Equity Inns, Inc. (ENN)
Equity Inns, Inc. (ENNPRA)
Equity Office Properties Trust (EOP)
Equity Office Properties Trust (EOPPRA)
Equity Office Properties Trust (EOPPRB)
Equity Office Properties Trust (EOPPRC)
Equity One, Inc. (EQY)
Equity Residential Properties Trust (EQR)
Equity Residential Properties Trust
  (EQRPRA)
Equity Residential Properties Trust
  (EQRPRB)
Equity Residential Properties Trust
  (EQRPRC)

COMPANY (SYMBOL)

Equity Residential Properties Trust (EQRPRD)
Equity Residential Properties Trust (EQRPRE)
Equity Residential Properties Trust (EQRPRF)
Equity Residential Properties Trust (EQRPRG)
Equity Residential Properties Trust (EQRPRH)
Equity Residential Properties Trust (EQRPRJ)
Equity Residential Properties Trust (EQRPRL)
Equus II Incorporated (EQS)
ESCO Electronics Corporation (ESE)
Espirito Santo Financial Group S.A. (ESF)
Espirito Santo Overseas Limited (ESBPRA)
Essex Property Trust, Inc. (ESS)
Estee Lauder Automatic Common Exchange Security Trust (ECT)
Estee Lauder Automatic Common Exchange Security Trust II (ECJ)
Estee Lauder Companies Inc. (The) (EL)
Esterline Technologies Corporation (ESL)
Ethan Allen Interiors Inc. (ETH)
Ethyl Corporation (EY)
Europe Fund, Inc. (The) (EF)
European Warrant Fund, Inc. (The) (EWF)
EVEREN Capital Corporation (EVR)
Everest Reinsurance Holdings, Inc. (RE)
Excelsior Income Shares, Inc. (EIS)
Exide Corporation (EX)
Extended Stay America Inc. (ESA)
Extendicare Inc. (EXEA)
Exxon Corporation (XON)

F

Fairchild Corporation (The) (FA)
FINOVA Group Inc. (The) (FNV)
First Commonwealth Fund, Inc. (The) (FCO)
First Israel Fund, Inc. (The) (ISL)
First Philippine Fund Inc. (The) (FPF)
Ford Motor Company (F)
Ford Motor Company (FPRB)
Ford Motor Company Capital Trust I (FPRT)
Foreign & Colonial Emerging Middle East Fund, Inc. (The) (EME)
Foremost Corporation of America (FOM)
Forest City Enterprises, Inc. (FCEA)
Forest City Enterprises, Inc. (FCEB)
Forest Oil Corporation (FST)
Fort Dearborn Income Securities, Inc. (FTD)

COMPANY (SYMBOL)

Fort James Corporation (FJ)
Fortis Securities, Inc. (FOR)
Fortune Brands, Inc. (FO)
Fortune Brands, Inc. (FOPRA)
Foster Wheeler Corporation (FWC)
Foundation Health Systems, Inc. (FHS)
Four Seasons Hotels Inc. (FS)
Fox Entertainment Group, Inc. (FOX)
FPC Capital I (FPCPRA)
FPL Group, Inc. (FPL)
France Growth Fund, Inc. (The) (FRF)
France Telecom (FTE)
Franchise Finance Corporation of America (FFA)
Franklin Covey Co. (FC)
Franklin Electronic Publishers, Incorporated (FEP)
Franklin Multi-Income Trust (FMI)
Franklin Resources, Inc. (BEN)
Franklin Universal Trust (FT)
Fred Meyer, Inc. (FMY)
Freedom Securities Corporation (FSI)
Freeport-McMoRan Copper & Gold Inc. (FCX)
Freeport-McMoRan Copper & Gold Inc. (FCXA)
Freeport-McMoRan Copper & Gold Inc. (FCXPRA)
Freeport-McMoRan Copper & Gold Inc. (FCXPRB)
Freeport-McMoRan Copper & Gold Inc. (FCXPRC)
Freeport-McMoRan Copper & Gold Inc. (FCXPRD)
Fremont General Corporation (FMT)
Fremont General Financing I (FMTPR)
Fresenius Medical Care AG (FMS)
Fresenius Medical Care AG (FMSPR)
Fresh Del Monte Produce Inc. (FDP)
Friede Goldman International Inc. (FGI)
Friedman, Billings, Ramsey Group, Inc. (FBG)
Frontier Corporation (FRO)
Frontier Insurance Group, Inc. (FTR)
Frontier Oil Corporation (FTO)
Fruit of the Loom, LTD. (FTL)
Fund American Enterprises Holdings, Inc. (FFC)
Furniture Brands International Inc. (FBN)
Furon Company (FCY)
Furr's/Bishop's, Incorporated (CHI)
FW Preferred Capital Trust I (FWCPRA)

G

G & L Realty Corp (GLR)

COMPANY (SYMBOL)

G & L Realty Corp (GLRPRA)
G & L Realty Corp (GLRPRB)
Gabelli Asset Management Inc. (GBL)
Gabelli Convertible Securities Fund, Inc.
  (The) (GCV)
Gabelli Convertible Securities Fund, Inc.
  (The) (GCVPR)
Gabelli Equity Trust Inc. (The) (GAB)
Gabelli Equity Trust Inc. (The) (GABPR)
Gabelli Global Multimedia Trust Inc. (The)
  (GGT)
Gabelli Global Multimedia Trust Inc. (The)
  (GGTPR)
Gabelli Utility Trust (The) (GUT)
Gables Residential Trust (GBP)
Gables Residential Trust (GBPPRA)
GAINSCO, INC. (GNA)
Galey & Lord, Inc. (GNL)
Galileo International, Inc. (GLC)
Gallaher Group PLC (GLH)
Gannett Co., Inc. (GCI)
Gap, Inc. (The) (GPS)
Gardner Denver, Inc. (GDI)
Gartner Group, Inc. (IT)
Gateway Inc. (GTW)
GATX Corporation (GMT)
GATX Corporation (GMTPR)
Gaylord Entertainment Company (GET)
GC Companies, Inc. (GCX)
GenCorp Inc. (GY)
Genentech, Inc. (DNA)
Gener S.A. (CHR)
General American Investors Company, Inc.
  (GAM)
General American Investors Company, Inc.
  (GAMPR)
General Cable Corporation (BGC)
General Chemical Group Inc. (The) (GCG)
General Cigar Holdings, Inc. (MPP)
General DataComm Industries, Inc. (GDC)
General Dynamics Corporation (GD)
General Electric Company (GE)
General Growth Properties, Inc. (GGP)
General Growth Properties, Inc. (GGPPRA)
General Housewares Corp. (GHW)
General Instrument Corporation (GIC)
General Mills, Inc. (GIS)
General Motors Capital Trust D (GMPRX)
General Motors Capital Trust G (GMPRY)
General Motors Corporation (GM)
General Motors Corporation (GMH)
General Motors Corporation (GMPRD)
General Motors Corporation (GMPRG)
General Semiconductor, Inc. (SEM)
GENESCO Inc. (GCO)

COMPANY (SYMBOL)

Genesis Energy L.P. (GEL)
Genesis Health Ventures, Inc. (GHV)
GenRad, Inc. (GEN)
GenTek Inc. (GK)
Genuine Parts Company (GPC)
Geon Company (The) (GON)
Georgia Gulf Corporation (GGC)
Georgia Power Capital, L.P. (GPEPRM)
Georgia Power Capital Trust I (GPEPRT)
Georgia Power Capital Trust II (GPEPRU)
Georgia Power Capital Trust III (GPEPRV)
Georgia Power Capital Trust IV (GPEPRA)
Georgia Power Company (GPB)
Georgia Power Company (GPD)
Georgia Power Company (GPF)
Georgia-Pacific Corporation (GP)
Georgia-Pacific Corporation (TGP)
Gerber Childrenswear, Inc. (GCW)
Gerber Scientific, Inc. (GRB)
Gerdau S.A. (GGB)
Germany Fund, Inc. (The) (GER)
Getty Petroleum Marketing Inc. (GPM)
Getty Realty Corp. (New) (GTY)
Getty Realty Corp. (New) (GTYPRA)
GIANT GROUP, LTD. (GPO)
Giant Industries, Inc. (GI)
Gillette Company (The) (G)
Glamis Gold Ltd. (GLG)
Glaxo Wellcome PLC (GLX)
Gleason Corporation (GLE)
Glenborough Realty Trust Incorporated
  (GLB)
Glenborough Realty Trust Incorporated
  (GLBPRA)
Glimcher Realty Trust (GRT)
Glimcher Realty Trust (GRTPRB)
Global High Income Dollar Fund, Inc.
  (GHI)
Global Industrial Technologies, Inc. (GIX)
Global Marine Inc. (GLM)
Global Partners Income Fund Inc. (GDF)
Global Vacation Group, Inc. (GVG)
Global-Tech Appliances Inc. (GAI)
Goldcorp Inc. (GG)
Goldcorp Inc. (GGA)
Golden State Bancorp Inc. (GSB)
Golden West Financial Corporation (GDW)
Goldman Sachs Group, Inc. (The) (GS)
Goodrich Petroleum Corporation (GDP)
Goodyear Tire & Rubber Company (GT)
Gottschalks Inc. (GOT)
Governor and Company of the Bank of
  Ireland (The) (IRE)
GP Strategies Corporation (GPX)
GPU, Inc. (GPU)

COMPANY (SYMBOL)

Graco Inc. (GGG)
Grand Metropolitan Delaware, L.P. (GRMPRA)
Granite Construction Incorporated (GVA)
Gray Communications Systems, Inc. (GCS)
Gray Communications Systems, Inc. (GCSB)
GRC International, Inc. (GRH)
Great Atlantic & Pacific Tea Company, Inc. (The) (GAP)
Great Lakes Chemical Corporation (GLK)
Great Lakes REIT (GL)
Great Lakes REIT (GLPRA)
Great Northern Iron Ore Properties (GNI)
Great Western Financial Trust I (GWFPRT)
Greater China Fund, Inc. (The) (GCH)
Green Mountain Power Corporation (GMP)
Greenbrier Companies, Inc. (The) (GBX)
GreenPoint Financial Corp. (GPT)
Greenwich Street Municipal Fund Inc. (GSI)
Griffon Corporation (GFF)
Group 1 Automotive, Inc. (GPI)
Group Maintenance America Corp. (MAK)
Groupe AB SA (ABG)
Groupe Danone (DA)
Grubb & Ellis Company (GBE)
Gruma S.A. de C.V. (GMK)
Grupo Casa Autrey, S.A. de C.V. (ATY)
Grupo Elektra, S.A. de C.V. (EKT)
Grupo Imsa, S.A. de C.V. (IMY)
Grupo Industrial Durango, S.A. de C.V. (GID)
Grupo Industrial Maseca, S.A. de C.V. (MSK)
Grupo Mexicano de Desarrollo, S.A. de C.V. (GMD)
Grupo Mexicano de Desarrollo, S.A. de C.V. (GMDB)
Grupo Radio Centro, S.A. de C.V. (RC)
Grupo Televisa, S.A. (TV)
Grupo Tribasa, S.A. de C.V. (GTR)
GS Financial Products U.S., L.P. (GSA)
GTE Corporation (GTE)
GTE Delaware, L.P. (GTEPRY)
GTE Delaware, L.P. (GTEPRZ)
GTE Florida Inc. (GLFPRA)
GTE Florida Inc. (GLFPRB)
GTECH Holdings Corporation (GTK)
Guangshen Railway Company Limited (GSH)
Gucci Group N.V. (GUC)
Guess ?, Inc. (GES)
Guest Supply, Inc. (GSY)
Guidant Corporation (GDT)
Guilford Mills, Inc. (GFD)

COMPANY (SYMBOL)

Gulf Canada Resources Limited (GOU)
Gulf Canada Resources Limited (GOUPRA)
Gulf Indonesia Resources Limited (GRL)
Gulf Power Capital Trust I (GUPPRA)
Gulf Power Capital Trust II (GUPPRB)
Gundle/SLT Environmental, Inc. (GSE)

H

H&Q Healthcare Investors (HQH)
H&Q Life Sciences Investors (HQL)
H&R Block, Inc. (HRB)
H. J. Heinz Company (HNZ)
H. J. Heinz Company (HNZPR)
Haemonetics Corporation (HAE)
Halliburton Company (HAL)
Hallwood Group Incorporated (The) (HWG)
HA-LO Industries, Inc. (HMK)
Hambrecht & Quist Group (HQ)
Hancock Fabrics, Inc. (HKF)
Handleman Company (HDL)
Hanger Orthopedic Group, Inc. (HGR)
Hannaford Bros. Co. (HRD)
Hanover Compressor Company (HC)
Hanson PLC (HAN)
Harcourt General, Inc. (H)
Harcourt General, Inc. (HPRA)
Harley-Davidson, Inc. (HDI)
Harman International Industries, Incorporated (HAR)
Harrah's Entertainment, Inc. (HET)
Harris Corporation (HRS)
Harris Preferred Capital Corporation (HBCPR)
Harsco Corporation (HSC)
Harte-Hanks, Inc. (HHS)
Hartford Capital I (HIGPRQ)
Hartford Capital II (HIGPRB)
Hartford Financial Services Group, Inc. (The) (HIG)
Hartford Life Capital I (HLIPRA)
Hartford Life, Inc. (HLI)
Hartmarx Corporation (HMX)
Hatteras Income Securities, Inc. (HAT)
Haverty Furniture Companies, Inc. (HVT)
Haverty Furniture Companies, Inc. (HVTA)
Hawaiian Electric Industries Capital Trust I (HEPRS)
Hawaiian Electric Industries, Inc. (HE)
Hawk Corporation (HWK)
Hayes Lemmerz International, Inc. (HAZ)
HCC Insurance Holdings, Inc. (HCC)
HCI Direct, Inc. (HCD)

COMPANY (SYMBOL)

HCR Manor Care Inc. (HCR)
Health Care Property Investors, Inc. (HCP)
Health Care Property Investors, Inc.
  (HCPPRA)
Health Care Property Investors, Inc.
  (HCPPRB)
Health Care REIT, Inc. (HCN)
Health Care REIT, Inc. (HCNPRB)
Health Management Associates, Inc. (HMA)
Healthcare Realty Trust Incorporated (HR)
Healthcare Realty Trust Incorporated
  (HRPRA)
HealthPlan Services Corporation (HPS)
HEALTHSOUTH Corporation (HRC)
Hearst-Argyle Television, Inc. (HTV)
Hecla Mining Company (HL)
Hecla Mining Company (HLPRB)
HECO Capital Trust I (HEPRQ)
HECO Capital Trust II (HEPRT)
Heico Corporation (HEI)
Heico Corporation (HEIA)
Heilig-Meyers Company (HMY)
Hellenic Telecommunications Organization
  S.A. (OTE)
Heller Financial, Inc. (HF)
Heller Financial, Inc. (HFPRA)
Helmerich & Payne, Inc. (HP)
Hercules Incorporated (HPC)
Hercules Trust I (HPCPRA)
Heritage Propane Partners, L.P. (HPG)
Heritage U.S. Government Income Fund
  (HGA)
Hershey Foods Corporation (HSY)
Hertz Corporation (The) (HRZ)
Hewlett-Packard Company (HWP)
Hexcel Corporation (HXL)
Hibernia Corporation (HIB)
High Income Opportunity Fund, Inc. (HIO)
High Yield Income Fund, Inc. (The) (HYI)
High Yield Plus Fund, Inc. (The) (HYP)
Highlands Insurance Group, Inc. (HIC)
Highwoods Properties, Inc. (HIW)
Highwoods Properties, Inc. (HIWPRB)
Highwoods Properties, Inc. (HIWPRD)
Hilb, Rogal and Hamilton Company (HRH)
Hillenbrand Industries, Inc. (HB)
Hilton Hotels Corporation (HLT)
Hitachi, Ltd. (HIT)
HL&P Capital Trust I (REIPRA)
Hoechst Aktiengesellschaft (HOE)
Hollinger International Inc. (HLR)
Hollinger International Inc. (HLRPRP)
Hollywood Park, Inc. (HPK)
Home Depot, Inc. (The) (HD)

COMPANY (SYMBOL)

Home Properties of New York, Inc. (HME)
HomeBase Inc. (HBI)
Homestake Mining Company (HM)
Homestead Village Incorporated (HSD)
Hon Industries Inc. (HNI)
Honda Motor Co., Ltd. (HMC)
Honeywell Inc. (HON)
Horace Mann Educators Corporation
  (HMN)
Hormel Foods Corporation (HRL)
Hospitality Properties Trust (HPT)
Hospitality Properties Trust (HPTPRA)
Host Marriott Corporation (REIT) (HMT)
Host Marriott Services Corporation
  (HMS)
Houghton Mifflin Company (HTN)
Household Capital Trust I (HIPRT)
Household Capital Trust II (HIPRY)
Household Capital Trust IV (HIPRP)
Household International, Inc. (HI)
Household International, Inc. (HIPRM)
Household International, Inc. (HIPRN)
Household International, Inc. (HIPRO)
Household International, Inc. (HIPRZ)
Houston Exploration Company (The)
  (THX)
Houston Industries, Inc. (HXT)
Howell Corporation (HWL)
Howmet International Inc. (HWM)
HRPT Properties Trust (HRP)
HS Resources, Inc. (HSE)
HSB Group, Inc. (HSB)
HSBC Holdings plc (HBC)
Huaneng Power International, Inc. (HNP)
Hubbell Incorporated (HUBA)
Hubbell Incorporated (HUBB)
Hudson United Bancorp (HU)
Huffy Corporation (HUF)
Hughes Supply, Inc. (HUG)
Hugoton Royalty Trust (HGT)
Humana Inc. (HUM)
Hunt Corporation (HUN)
Huntco Inc. (HCO)
Huntingdon Life Sciences Group PLC
  (HTD)
Huntway Refining Company (HWY)
Hussmann International, Inc. (HSM)
Hypercom Corporation (HYC)
Hyperion 1999 Term Trust, Inc. (HIT)
Hyperion 2002 Term Trust, Inc. (HTB)
Hyperion 2005 Investment Grade
  Opportunity Term Trust, Inc. (HTO)
Hyperion Total Return Fund, Inc. (The)
  (HTR)

COMPANY (SYMBOL)

I

IAC Capital Trust (IACPRA)
IBP, Inc. (IBP)
ICF Kaiser International, Inc. (ICF)
ICN Pharmaceuticals, Inc. (ICN)
Idacorp Inc. (Holding Company) (IDA)
IDEX Corporation (IEX)
IES Utilities Inc. (IEU)
IKON Office Solutions, Inc. (IKN)
Illinois Power Capital, L.P. (IPCPRM)
Illinois Power Company (IPCPRA)
Illinois Power Company (IPCPRB)
Illinois Power Company (IPCPRC)
Illinois Power Company (IPCPRD)
Illinois Power Company (IPCPRE)
Illinois Power Financing I (IPCPRT)
Illinois Tool Works Inc. (ITW)
Illinova Corporation (ILN)
Imation Corp. (IMN)
IMC Global Inc. (IGL)
IMC Global Inc. (IGLWS)
IMCO Recycling Inc. (IMR)
Imperial Bancorp (IMP)
Imperial Chemical Industries PLC (ICI)
Imperial Tobacco Group PLC (ITY)
IMS Health Incorporated (RX)
InaCom Corp. (ICO)
INCO Limited (N)
INCO Limited (NPRE)
INCO Limited (NVB)
Income Opportunities Fund 1999, Inc. (IOF)
Income Opportunities Fund 2000, Inc. (IFT)
India Fund, Inc. (The) (IFN)
India Growth Fund Inc. (The) (IGF)
Indiana Energy, Inc. (IEI)
Indiana Michigan Power Company (IMJ)
Indiana Michigan Power Company (IMK)
Indonesia Fund, Inc. (The) (IF)
Industrial Distribution Group, Inc. (IDG)
Industrias Bachoco, S.A. de C.V. (IBA)
Industrie Natuzzi S.p.A. (NTZ)
IndyMac Mortgage Holdings, Inc. (NDE)
Infinity Broadcasting Corporation (INF)
Information Holdings Inc. (IHI)
ING GROEP N.V. (ING)
Ingersoll-Rand Company (IR)
Ingersoll-Rand Company (IRPRG)
Ingersoll-Rand Company (IRPRI)
Ingram Micro Inc. (IM)
Innkeepers USA Trust (KPA)
Innkeepers USA Trust (KPAPRA)
Input/Output, Inc. (IO)
Insignia Financial Group, Inc. (IFS)
Insteel Industries, Inc. (III)

COMPANY (SYMBOL)

Insured Municipal Income Fund (PIF)
Integrated Electrical Services, Inc. (IEE)
Integrated Health Services, Inc. (IHS)
Interim Services Inc. (IS)
Internacional de Ceramica, S.A. de C.V.
  (ICM)
International Aluminum Corporation (IAL)
International Business Machines
  Corporation (IBM)
International Business Machines
  Corporation (IBMPRA)
International Flavors & Fragrances Inc.
  (IFF)
International Game Technology (IGT)
International Home Foods, Inc. (IHF)
International Multifoods Corporation (IMC)
International Paper Capital Trust III (IPP)
International Paper Company (IP)
International Rectifier Corporation (IRF)
International Shipholding Corporation
  (ISH)
International Specialty Products Inc. (ISP)
Interpool, Inc. (IPX)
Interpublic Group of Companies, Inc. (The)
  (IPG)
Interstate Bakeries Corporation (IBC)
InterTAN Inc. (ITN)
Intertape Polymer Group (ITP)
Intimate Brands, Inc. (IBI)
Intrawest Corporation (IDR)
Inversiones y Representaciones S.A. (IRS)
INVESCO Global Health Sciences Fund
  (GHS)
Investment Grade Municipal Income Fund
  (PPM)
Investment Technology Group, Inc. (ITG)
Iomega Corporation (IOM)
Ionics, Incorporated (ION)
IPALCO Enterprises, Inc. (IPL)
IPSCO Inc. (IPS)
IRI International Corporation (IIR)
Irish Investment Fund, Inc. (The) (IRL)
Iron Mountain Incorporated (IRM)
IRT Property Company (IRT)
Irvine Apartment Communities, Inc. (IAC)
Ispat International N.V. (IST)
Istituto Bancario San Paolo di Torino S.p.A.
  (IMI)
Istituto Nazionale delle Assicurazioni S.p.A.
  (INZ)
IT Group, Inc. (ITX)
IT Group, Inc. (ITXPR)
Italy Fund Inc. (The) (ITA)
ITT Educational Services, Inc. (ESI)

COMPANY (SYMBOL)

ITT Industries, Inc. (IIN)
Ivex Packaging Corporation (IXX)

J

J. Alexander's Corporation (JAX)
J. C. Penney Company, Inc. (JCP)
J. M. Smucker Company (The) (SJMA)
J. M. Smucker Company (The) (SJMB)
J. P. Morgan & Co. Incorporated (JPM)
J. P. Morgan & Co. Incorporated (JPMPRA)
J. P. Morgan & Co. Incorporated (JPMPRH)
Jabil Circuit, Inc. (JBL)
Jackpot Enterprises, Inc. (J)
Jacobs Engineering Group Inc. (JEC)
Jakarta Growth Fund, Inc. (JGF)
Japan Equity Fund, Inc. (The) (JEQ)
Japan OTC Equity Fund, Inc. (JOF)
Jardine Fleming China Region Fund, Inc.
  (JFC)
Jardine Fleming India Fund, Inc. (JFI)
JCP&L Capital, L.P. (JYPPRZ)
JDN Realty Corporation (JDN)
JDN Realty Corporation (JDNPRA)
Jefferies Group, Inc.(NEW) (JEF)
Jefferson-Pilot Corporation (JP)
Jefferson-Pilot Corporation (NBX)
Jefferson Smurfit Group PLC (JS)
Jenny Craig, Inc. (JC)
Jersey Central Power & Light Company
  (JYPPR)
Jersey Central Power & Light Company
  (JYPPRE)
Jilin Chemical Industrial Company Limited
  (JCC)
JLG Industries, Inc. (JLG)
JLK Direct Distribution Inc. (JLK)
Jo-Ann Stores, Inc. (JASA)
Jo-Ann Stores, Inc. (JASB)
John H. Harland Company (JH)
John Q. Hammons Hotels, Inc. (JQH)
John Hancock Bank and Thrift Opportunity
  Fund (BTO)
John Hancock Income Securities Trust (JHS)
John Hancock Investors Trust (JHI)
John Hancock Patriot Global Dividend
  Fund (PGD)
John Hancock Patriot Preferred Dividend
  Fund (PPF)
John Hancock Patriot Premium Dividend
  Fund I (PDF)
John Hancock Patriot Premium Dividend
  Fund II (PDT)
John Hancock Patriot Select Dividend Trust
  (DIV)

COMPANY (SYMBOL)

John Nuveen Company (The) (JNC)
John Wiley & Sons, Inc. (JWA)
John Wiley & Sons, Inc. (JWB)
Johns Manville Corporation (JM)
Johnson & Johnson (JNJ)
Johnson Controls, Inc. (JCI)
Johnston Industries, Inc. (JII)
Jones Apparel Group, Inc. (JNY)
Jones Lang Lasalle Incorporated (JLL)
Joseph E Seagrams & Sons Ltd (VOS)
Jostens, Inc. (JOS)
Journal Register Company (JRC)
JP Realty, Inc. (JPR)
JSB Financial, Inc. (JSB)

K

K2 Inc. (KTO)
Kaiser Aluminum Corporation (KLU)
Kaneb Pipe Line Partners, L.P. (KPP)
Kaneb Services, Inc. (KAB)
Kaneb Services, Inc. (KABPRA)
Kansas City Power & Light Company (KLT)
Kansas City Power & Light Company
  (KLTPRA)
Kansas City Power & Light Company
  (KLTPRD)
Kansas City Power & Light Company
  (KLTPRE)
Kansas City Southern Industries, Inc. (KSU)
Kansas City Southern Industries, Inc.
  (KSUPR)
Katy Industries, Inc. (KT)
Kaufman and Broad Home Corporation
  (KBH)
Kaufman and Broad Home Corporation
  (KBHPRG)
Kaufman and Broad Home Corporation
  (KBHPRI)
Kaydon Corporation (KDN)
KCPL Financing I (KLTPRT)
KCS Energy, Inc. (KCS)
Keebler Foods Company (KBL)
Keithley Instruments, Inc. (KEI)
Kellogg Company (K)
Kellwood Company (KWD)
Kemper High Income Trust (KHI)
Kemper Intermediate Government Trust
  (KGT)
Kemper Multi-Market Income Trust (KMM)
Kemper Municipal Income Trust (KTF)
Kemper Strategic Income Trust (KST)
Kemper Strategic Municipal Income Trust
  (KSM)
Kennametal Inc. (KMT)

COMPANY (SYMBOL)

Kenneth Cole Productions, Inc. (KCP)
Kent Electronics Corporation (KNT)
Kentucky Power Company (KPC)
Kerr-McGee Corporation (KMG)
Key Energy Services, Inc. (KEG)
Key Production Company, Inc. (KP)
KeyCorp (KEY)
KeySpan Energy (KSE)
KeySpan Energy (KSEPRA)
Keystone Consolidated Industries, Inc.
  (KES)
Kilroy Realty Corporation (KRC)
Kimberly-Clark Corporation (KMB)
Kimco Realty Corporation (KIM)
Kimco Realty Corporation (KIMPRA)
Kimco Realty Corporation (KIMPRB)
Kimco Realty Corporation (KIMPRC)
Kimco Realty Corporation (KIMPRD)
Kinam Gold Inc. (KGCPRB)
Kinder Morgan Energy Partners, L.P. (ENP)
King World Productions, Inc. (KWP)
Kinross Gold Corporation (KGC)
Kirby Corporation (KEX)
Kleinwort Benson Australian Income Fund,
  Inc. (KBA)
KLM Royal Dutch Airlines (KLM)
Kmart Corporation (KM)
Kmart Financing I (KMPRT)
KN Energy, Inc. (KNE)
KN Energy, Inc. (KNP)
Knight-Ridder, Inc. (KRI)
Knoll, Inc. (KNL)
Kohl's Corporation (KSS)
Kollmorgen Corporation (KOL)
Koninklijke Ahold NV (AHO)
Koninklijke Philips Electronics N.V. (PHG)
Konover Property Trust, Inc. (KPT)
Koor Industries Limited (KOR)
Korea Electric Power Corporation (KEP)
Korea Equity Fund, Inc. (KEF)
Korea Fund, Inc. (The) (KF)
Korea Telecommunications (KTC)
Korean Investment Fund, Inc. (The) (KIF)
Korn/Ferry International (KFY)
Kranzco Realty Trust (KRT)
Kranzco Realty Trust (KRTPR)
Kranzco Realty Trust (KRTPRD)
Kroger Co. (The) (KR)
Kubota Corporation (KUB)
K-V Pharmaceutical Company (KVA)
K-V Pharmaceutical Company (KVB)
Kyocera Corporation (KYO)

L
L. S. Starrett Company (The) (SCX)

COMPANY (SYMBOL)

L-3 Communications Holdings, Inc. (LLL)
Labor Ready, Inc. (LRW)
Laboratorio Chile S.A. (LBC)
Laboratory Corporation of America
  Holdings (LH)
Laboratory Corporation of America
  Holdings (LHPRA)
Laboratory Corporation of America
  Holdings (LHPRB)
LaBranche & Co. Inc. (LAB)
Laclede Gas Company (LG)
Lafarge Corporation (LAF)
Laidlaw Inc. (LDW)
Laidlaw One, Inc. (UXL)
Lakehead Pipe Line Partners, L.P. (LHP)
Lamson & Sessions Co. (The) (LMS)
Lan Chile S.A. (LFL)
LandAmerica Financial Group, Inc. (LFG)
Lands' End, Inc. (LE)
LaSalle Hotel Properties (LHO)
LaSalle Re Holdings Limited (LSH)
LaSalle Re Holdings Limited (LSHPRA)
LASER Mortgage Management, Inc.
  (LMM)
LASMO PLC (LSO)
LASMO PLC (LSOPRA)
Latin America Equity Fund, Inc. (The)
  (LAQ)
Latin America Investment Fund, Inc. (The)
  (LAM)
Latin American Discovery Fund, Inc. (The)
  (LDF)
Lawter International, Inc. (LAW)
La-Z-Boy Incorporated (LZB)
Lear Corporation (LEA)
Leasing Solutions, Inc. (LSN)
Lee Enterprises, Incorporated (LEE)
Legg Mason, Inc. (LM)
Leggett & Platt, Incorporated (LEG)
Lehman Brothers Holdings Capital Trust I
  (LEHPRI)
Lehman Brothers Holdings Capital Trust II
  (LEHPRJ)
Lehman Brothers Holdings Inc. (LEH)
Lehman Brothers Holdings Inc. (LEHPRC)
Lehman Brothers Holdings Inc. (LEHPRD)
Lehman Brothers Holdings Inc. (LEQ)
Lennar Corporation (LEN)
Lennox International Inc. (LII)
Leucadia National Corporation (LUK)
Leviathan Gas Pipeline Partners, L.P. (LEV)
Leviathan Gas Pipeline Partners, L.P.
  (LEVP)
Lexford Residential Trust (LFT)
Lexington Corporate Properties Trust (LXP)

COMPANY (SYMBOL)

Lexmark International Group, Inc. (LXK)
LG&E Energy Corp. (LGE)
Libbey Inc. (LBY)
Liberte Investors Inc. (LBI)
Liberty All-Star Equity Fund (USA)
Liberty All-Star Growth Fund, Inc. (ASG)
Liberty Corporation (The) (LC)
Liberty Financial Companies, Inc. (L)
Liberty Property Trust (LRY)
Liberty Property Trust (LRYPRA)
Liberty Term Trust, Inc. - 1999 (LTT)
Lilly Industries, Inc. (LI)
Limited, Inc. (The) (LTD)
Lincoln National Capital I (LNCPRX)
Lincoln National Capital II (LNCPRY)
Lincoln National Capital III (LNCPRZ)
Lincoln National Convertible Securities
    Fund, Inc. (LNV)
Lincoln National Corporation (LNC)
Lincoln National Corporation (LNCPR)
Lincoln National Corporation (LNCPRG)
Lincoln National Corporation (LNCPRI)
Lincoln National Income Fund, Inc. (LND)
Lindsay Manufacturing Co. (LNN)
Linens'N Things, Inc. (LIN)
Lithia Motors, Inc. (LAD)
Litton Industries, Inc. (LIT)
Litton Industries, Inc. (LITPRB)
Liz Claiborne, Inc. (LIZ)
LL&E Royalty Trust (LRT)
LNR Property Corporation (LNR)
Lockheed Martin Corporation (LMT)
Lodgian, Inc. (LOD)
Loewen Group Inc. (The) (LWN)
Loews Cineplex Entertainment Corporation
    (LCP)
Loews Corporation (LTR)
Lone Star Industries, Inc. (LCE)
Lone Star Industries, Inc. (LCEWS)
Lone Star Technologies, Inc. (LSS)
Longs Drug Stores Corporation (LDG)
Longview Fibre Company (LFB)
Loral Space & Communications Ltd. (LOR)
Louis Dreyfus Natural Gas Corp. (LD)
Louisiana-Pacific Corporation (LPX)
Lowe's Companies, Inc. (LOW)
LSI Logic Corporation (LSI)
LTC Properties, Inc. (LTC)
LTC Properties, Inc. (LTCPRA)
LTC Properties, Inc. (LTCPRB)
LTV Corporation (The) (LTV)
Lubrizol Corporation (The) (LZ)
Luby's, Inc. (LUB)
Lucent Technologies Inc. (LU)
Luxottica Group S.P.A. (LUX)

COMPANY (SYMBOL)

Lydall, Inc. (LDL)
Lyondell Chemical Company (LYO)

M

M. A. Hanna Company (MAH)
M. D. C. Holdings, Inc. (MDC)
M & F Worldwide Corp. (MFW)
M & T Bank Corporation (MTB)
Macerich Company (The) (MAC)
MacDermid, Incorporated (MRD)
Mac-Gray Corporation (TUC)
Mack-Cali Realty Corporation (CLI)
MacNeal-Schwendler Corporation (The)
    (MNS)
Madeco S.A. (MAD)
Magellan Health Services, Inc. (MGL)
Magna International Inc. (MGA)
MagneTek, Inc. (MAG)
Magyar Tavkozlesi Rt. (MTA)
Mail-Well, Inc. (MWL)
Malan Realty Investors, Inc. (MAL)
Malaysia Fund, Inc. (The) (MF)
Mallinckrodt Inc. (MKG)
Mallinckrodt Inc. (MKGPR)
Managed High Income Portfolio Inc. (MHY)
Managed High Yield Fund (PHT)
Managed High Yield Plus Fund Inc. (HYF)
Managed Municipals Portfolio II Inc. (MTU)
Managed Municipals Portfolio Inc. (MMU)
Manitowoc Company, Inc. (The) (MTW)
Manpower Inc. (MAN)
Manufactured Home Communities, Inc.
    (MHC)
Marcus Corporation (The) (MCS)
Marine Drilling Companies, Inc. (MRL)
MarineMax, Inc. (HZO)
Mariner Post-Acute Network, Inc. (MPN)
Maritrans Inc. (TUG)
Mark IV Industries, Inc. (IV)
Markel Corporation (MKL)
Marriott International, Inc. (MAR)
Marsh & McLennan Companies, Inc. (MMC)
Marshall Industries (MI)
Martin Marietta Materials Inc. (MLM)
Marvel Enterprises Inc. (MVL)
Masco Corporation (MAS)
MascoTech, Inc. (MSX)
Masisa S.A. (MYS)
MassMutual Corporate Investors (MCI)
MassMutual Participation Investors (MPV)
MasTec, Inc. (MTZ)
Material Sciences Corporation (MSC)
Matlack Systems, Inc. (MLK)
Matsushita Electric Industrial Co., Ltd.
    (MC)

COMPANY (SYMBOL)

Mattel, Inc. (MAT)
Mattel, Inc. (MATPRC)
Mavesa, S.A. (MAV)
Maxim Group, Inc. (The) (MXG)
MAXIMUS, Inc. (MMS)
Maxxim Medical, Inc. (MAM)
May Department Stores Company (The)
 (MAY)
Maytag Corporation (MYG)
MBIA Inc. (MBD)
MBIA Inc. (MBI)
MBNA Capital C (KRBPRC)
MBNA Corporation (KRB)
MBNA Corporation (KRBPRA)
MBNA Corporation (KRBPRB)
McClatchy Company (The) (MNI)
McDermott International, Inc. (MDR)
McDonald's Corporation (MCD)
McDonald's Corporation (MCJ)
McDonald's Corporation (MCW)
McGraw-Hill Companies, Inc. (The) (MHP)
McKesson HBOC, Inc. (MCK)
McMoRan Exploration Co. (MMR)
MCN Energy Group Inc. (MCN)
MCN Energy Group Inc. (MCNPRI)
MCN Financing I (MCNPRA)
MCN Financing II (MCNPRS)
MCN Michigan Limited Partnership
 (MCNPRT)
McWhorter Technologies, Inc. (MWT)
MDU Resources Group, Inc. (MDU)
Mead Corporation (The) (MEA)
Meadowbrook Insurance Group, Inc. (MIG)
Medco Research, Inc. (MRE)
Medeva PLC (MDV)
Media Arts Group, Inc. (MDA)
MediaOne Finance Trust I (UMGPRA)
MediaOne Finance Trust II (UMGPRB)
MediaOne Finance Trust III (UMGPRC)
MediaOne Financing A (UMGPRX)
MediaOne Financing B (UMGPRY)
MediaOne Group, Inc. (UMG)
MediaOne Group, Inc. (UMGPRD)
MediaOne Group, Inc. (UMX)
Medical Assurance, Inc. (MAI)
Medicis Pharmaceutical Corporation (MRX)
Meditrust Corporation (MT)
Meditrust Corporation (MTPR)
MedPartners, Inc. (MDM)
MedPartners, Inc. (MDX)
Medtronic, Inc. (MDT)
Mellon Bank Corporation (MEL)
MEMC Electronic Materials, Inc. (WFR)
Mentor Income Fund, Inc. (MRF)

COMPANY (SYMBOL)

MEPC International Capital, L.P.
 (MUKPRA)
Mercantile Bancorporation Inc. (MTL)
Merck & Co., Inc. (MRK)
Mercury General Corporation (MCY)
Meredith Corporation (MDP)
Meridian Gold Inc. (MDG)
Meridian Resource Corporation (The)
 (TMR)
MeriStar Hospitality Corporation (MHX)
MeriStar Hotels & Resorts, Inc. (MMH)
Meritage Corporation (MTH)
Meritor Automotive Inc. (MRA)
Merrill Lynch Depositor, Inc. (FWJ)
Merrill Lynch Preferred Capital Trust I
 (MERPRB)
Merrill Lynch Preferred Capital Trust II
 (MERPRC)
Merrill Lynch Preferred Capital Trust III
 (MERPRD)
Merrill Lynch Preferred Capital Trust IV
 (MERPRE)
Merrill Lynch Preferred Capital Trust V
 (MERPRF)
Merrill Lynch & Co., Inc. (BOB)
Merrill Lynch & Co., Inc. (DJM)
Merrill Lynch & Co., Inc. (IEM)
Merrill Lynch & Co., Inc. (IML)
Merrill Lynch & Co., Inc. (JEM)
Merrill Lynch & Co., Inc. (MCO)
Merrill Lynch & Co., Inc. (MEE)
Merrill Lynch & Co., Inc. (MER)
Merrill Lynch & Co., Inc. (MERPRA)
Merrill Lynch & Co., Inc. (MIJ)
Merrill Lynch & Co., Inc. (MIM)
Merrill Lynch & Co., Inc. (MIX)
Merrill Lynch & Co., Inc. (MLBCL)
Merrill Lynch & Co., Inc. (TKM)
Mesa Royalty Trust (MTR)
Mesabi Trust (MSB)
Mestek, Inc. (MCC)
Metals USA, Inc. (MUI)
Met-Ed Capital, L.P. (MTTPRZ)
Met-Pro Corporation (MPR)
Metris Companies Inc. (MXT)
MetroGas S.A. (MGS)
Metro-Goldwyn-Mayer Inc. (MGM)
Mettler-Toledo International Inc. (MTD)
Mexico Equity and Income Fund, Inc. (The)
 (MXE)
Mexico Fund, Inc. (The) (MXF)
MFS Charter Income Trust (MCR)
MFS Government Markets Income Trust
 (MGF)

COMPANY (SYMBOL)

MFS Intermediate Income Trust (MIN)
MFS Multimarket Income Trust (MMT)
MFS Municipal Income Trust (MFM)
MFS Special Value Trust (MFV)
MGI Properties (MGI)
MGIC Investment Corporation (MTG)
MGM Grand, Inc. (MGG)
M/I Schottenstein Homes, Inc. (MHO)
MicroFinancial Incorporated (MFI)
Micron Technology, Inc. (MU)
Mid Atlantic Medical Services, Inc. (MME)
Mid-America Apartment Communities, Inc.
   (MAA)
Mid-America Apartment Communities, Inc.
   (MAAPRA)
Mid-America Apartment Communities, Inc.
   (MAAPRB)
Mid-America Apartment Communities, Inc.
   (MAAPRC)
MidAmerican Energy Financing I
   (MECPRA)
MidAmerican Energy Holdings Company
   (MEC)
Midas, Inc. (MDS)
Mid-Atlantic Realty Trust (MRR)
Midland Bank PLC (MIBPRA)
Midland Bank PLC (MIBPRB)
Midland Bank PLC (MIBPRC)
Midland Bank PLC (MIBPRD)
Midway Games Inc. (MWY)
Midwest Express Holdings, Inc. (MEH)
MIIX Group, Incorporated (The) (MHU)
Mikasa, Inc. (MKS)
Milacron Inc. (MZ)
Millennium Chemicals Inc. (MCH)
Miller Industries, Inc. (MLR)
Millipore Corporation (MIL)
Mills Corporation (The) (MLS)
Minerals Technologies Inc. (MTX)
Minnesota Mining and Manufacturing
   Company (MMM)
Minnesota Municipal Term Trust Inc. (MNA)
Minnesota Power, Inc. (MPL)
Mirage Resorts, Incorporated (MIR)
Mission Capital, L.P. (MEPRA)
Mission Capital, L.P. (MEPRB)
Mississippi Chemical Corporation (GRO)
Mississippi Power Capital Trust I (MPPRD)
Mississippi Power Company (MPPRB)
Mississippi Power Company (MPPRC)
Mitchell Energy & Development Corp.
   (MNDA)
Mitchell Energy & Development Corp.
   (MNDB)

COMPANY (SYMBOL)

Mitel Corporation (MLT)
ML Macadamia Orchards L.P. (NUT)
MMI Companies, Inc. (MMI)
Mobil Corporation (MOB)
Modis Professional Services Inc. (MPS)
Mohawk Industries, Inc. (MHK)
Molecular Biosystems, Inc. (MB)
Monaco Coach Corporation (MNC)
Monarch Machine Tool Company (The)
   (MMO)
Monongahela Power Company (WVQ)
Monsanto Company (MCT)
Monsanto Company (MTC)
Montana Power Capital I (MTPPRA)
Montana Power Company (The) (MTP)
Montedison S.P.A. (MNT)
Montedison S.P.A. (MNTPR)
Montgomery Street Income Securities, Inc.
   (MTS)
MONY Group Inc. (THE) (MNY)
Moore Corporation Limited (MCL)
Morgan Grenfell Smallcap Fund, Inc. (MGC)
Morgan Stanley High Yield Fund, Inc. (The)
   (MSY)
Morgan Keegan, Inc. (MOR)
Morgan Stanley Dean Witter (GVT)
Morgan Stanley Dean Witter (ICB)
Morgan Stanley Dean Witter (ICS)
Morgan Stanley Dean Witter (IIC)
Morgan Stanley Dean Witter (IIM)
Morgan Stanley Dean Witter (IMB)
Morgan Stanley Dean Witter (IMS)
Morgan Stanley Dean Witter (IMT)
Morgan Stanley Dean Witter (IQC)
Morgan Stanley Dean Witter (IQI)
Morgan Stanley Dean Witter (IQM)
Morgan Stanley Dean Witter (IQN)
Morgan Stanley Dean Witter (IQT)
Morgan Stanley Dean Witter (OIA)
Morgan Stanley Dean Witter (OIB)
Morgan Stanley Dean Witter (OIC)
Morgan Stanley Dean Witter (PIA)
Morgan Stanley Dean Witter (TFA)
Morgan Stanley Dean Witter (TFB)
Morgan Stanley Dean Witter (TFC)
Morgan Stanley Dean Witter (YLD)
Morgan Stanley Dean Witter (YLH)
Morgan Stanley Dean Witter (YLT)
Morgan Stanley Dean Witter (BDJ)
Morgan Stanley Dean Witter (BGS)
Morgan Stanley Dean Witter (BRX)
Morgan Stanley Dean Witter (MWD)
Morgan Stanley Dean Witter & Co.
   (MWDPRE)

COMPANY (SYMBOL)

Morgan Stanley Dean Witter & Co. (MWDPRF)

Morgan Stanley Dean Witter (RBT)

Morgan Stanley Dean Witter Africa Investment Fund Inc. (AFF)

Morgan Stanley Dean Witter Asia-Pacific Fund, Inc. (APF)

Morgan Stanley Dean Witter Eastern Europe Fund, Inc. (RNE)

Morgan Stanley Dean Witter Emerging Markets Debt Fund, Inc. (MSD)

Morgan Stanley Dean Witter Emerging Markets Fund, Inc. (MSF)

Morgan Stanley Dean Witter Global Opportunity Bond Fund, Inc. (MGB)

Morgan Stanley Dean Witter India Investment Fund, Inc. (IIF)

Morgan Stanley Finance PLC (MSE)

Morgan Stanley Finance PLC (MSP)

Morgan Stanley Finance PLC (MSV)

Morrison Health Care, Inc. (MHI)

Morrison Knudsen Corporation (MK)

Morrison Knudsen Corporation (MKWS)

Morton International, Inc. (MII)

Morton's Restaurant Group, Inc. (MRG)

Mossimo, Inc. (MGX)

MotivePower Industries, Inc. (MPO)

Motorola Capital Trust I (MOTPRA)

Motorola, Inc. (MOT)

MP&L Capital I (MPLPR)

MSC Industrial Direct Co., Inc. (MSM)

MSDW Capital Trust I (MWC)

Mueller Industries, Inc. (MLI)

MuniAssets Fund, Inc. (MUA)

Municipal Advantage Fund Inc. (MAF)

Municipal High Income Fund Inc. (MHF)

Municipal Mortgage & Equity, LLC (MMA)

Municipal Partners Fund II Inc. (MPT)

Municipal Partners Fund Inc. (MNP)

MuniEnhanced Fund, Inc. (MEN)

MuniHoldings California Insured Fund II, Inc. (MUC)

MuniHoldings California Insured Fund III, Inc. (MCF)

MuniHoldings California Insured Fund IV, Inc. (CIL)

MuniHoldings California Insured Fund, Inc. (CLH)

MuniHoldings Florida Insured Fund (MFL)

MuniHoldings Florida Insured Fund II (MUF)

MuniHoldings Florida Insured Fund III (MFD)

COMPANY (SYMBOL)

MuniHoldings Florida Insured Fund IV (MFR)

MuniHoldings Fund II, Inc. (MUH)

MuniHoldings Fund, Inc. (MHD)

MuniHoldings Insured Fund II, Inc. (MUE)

MuniHoldings Insured Fund, Inc. (MUS)

MuniHoldings Michigan Insured Fund, Inc. (MCG)

MuniHoldings New Jersey Insured Fund II, Inc. (MWJ)

MuniHoldings New Jersey Insured Fund III, Inc. (MNJ)

MuniHoldings New Jersey Insured Fund, Inc. (MUJ)

MuniHoldings New York Fund, Inc. (MUN)

MuniHoldings New York Insured Fund II, Inc. (MNU)

MuniHoldings New York Insured Fund III, Inc. (MNK)

MuniHoldings New York Insured Fund, Inc. (MHN)

MuniVest Florida Fund (MVS)

MuniVest Fund II, Inc. (MVT)

MuniVest Michigan Insured Fund, Inc. (MVM)

MuniVest New Jersey Fund, Inc. (MVJ)

MuniVest Pennsylvania Insured Fund (MVP)

MuniYield California Fund, Inc. (MYC)

MuniYield California Insured Fund II, Inc. (MCA)

MuniYield California Insured Fund, Inc. (MIC)

MuniYield Florida Fund, Inc. (MYF)

MuniYield Florida Insured Fund (MFT)

MuniYield Fund, Inc. (MYD)

MuniYield Insured Fund, Inc. (MYI)

MuniYield Michigan Fund, Inc. (MYM)

MuniYield Michigan Insured Fund, Inc. (MIY)

MuniYield New Jersey Fund, Inc. (MYJ)

MuniYield New Jersey Insured Fund, Inc. (MJI)

MuniYield New York Insured Fund II, Inc. (MYT)

MuniYield New York Insured Fund, Inc. (MYN)

MuniYield Pennsylvania Fund (MPA)

MuniYield Quality Fund II, Inc. (MQT)

MuniYield Quality Fund, Inc. (MQY)

Murphy Oil Corporation (MUR)

Musicland Stores Corporation (MLG)

Mutual Risk Management Ltd. (MM)

COMPANY (SYMBOL)

Mylan Laboratories Inc. (MYL)
MYR Group Inc. (MYR)

N
NAB Exchangeable Preferred Trust
(NARPR)
Nabisco Holdings Corp. (NA)
NAC Re Corp. (NRC)
NACCO Industries, Inc. (NC)
Nalco Chemical Company (NLC)
Nashua Corporation (NSH)
National Australia Bank Limited (NAB)
National Australia Bank Limited (NAU)
National City Corporation (NCC)
National Data Corporation (NDC)
National Discount Brokers Group, Inc.
(NDB)
National Equipment Services, Inc. (NSV)
National Fuel Gas Company (NFG)
National Golf Properties, Inc. (TEE)
National Health Investors, Inc. (NHI)
National Health Investors, Inc. (NHIPR)
National Power PLC (NP)
National Presto Industries, Inc. (NPK)
National Processing, Inc. (NAP)
National R.V. Holdings, Inc. (NVH)
National Rural Utilities Cooperative
Finance Corporation (NRU)
National Rural Utilities Cooperative
Finance Corporation (NRV)
National Rural Utilities Cooperative
Finance Corporation (NRX)
National Semiconductor Corporation (NSM)
National Service Industries, Inc. (NSI)
National Steel Corporation (NS)
National Westminster Bank PLC (NW)
National Westminster Bank PLC (NWPRB)
National Westminster Bank PLC (NWPRC)
National Westminster Bank PLC
(NWXPRA)
National-Oilwell, Inc. (NOI)
National-Standard Company (NSD)
Nations Balanced Target Maturity Fund, Inc.
(NBM)
Nations Government Income Term Trust
2003, Inc. (NGI)
Nations Government Income Term Trust
2004, Inc. (NGF)
NationsRent, Inc. (NRI)
Nationwide Financial Services Capital Trust
II (NFSPRA)
Nationwide Financial Services, Inc. (NFS)
Nationwide Health Properties, Inc. (NHP)
Navigant Consulting, Inc. (NCI)

COMPANY (SYMBOL)

Navistar International Corporation (NAV)
Navistar International Corporation (Pfd's
Only) (NAVPRD)
NB Capital Corporation (NBD)
NB Capital Trust I (NBPRA)
NCH Corporation (NCH)
NCI Building Systems, Inc. (NCS)
NCL Holding ASA (NRW)
NCR Corporation (NCR)
Neff Corp. (NFF)
Neiman Marcus Group, Inc. (The) (NMG)
Network Equipment Technologies, Inc.
(NWK)
Nevada Power Company (NVP)
New America High Income Fund, Inc. (The)
(HYB)
New American Healthcare Corporation
(NAH)
New Century Energies, Inc. (NCE)
New England Business Service, Inc. (NEB)
New England Electric System (NES)
New Germany Fund, Inc. (The) (GF)
New Holland N.V. (NH)
New Jersey Economic Development
Authority (NJP)
New Jersey Resources Corporation (NJR)
New Plan Excel Realty Trust Inc. (NXL)
New Plan Excel Realty Trust Inc. (NXLPRA)
New Plan Excel Realty Trust Inc. (NXLPRB)
New South Africa Fund Inc. (The) (NSA)
New York Times Company (The) (NYT)
Newbridge Networks Corporation (NN)
Newcourt Credit Group Inc. (NCT)
Newell Rubbermaid Inc. (NWL)
Newfield Exploration Company (NFX)
Newhall Land and Farming Company (The)
(NHL)
Newmont Mining Corporation (NEM)
Newpark Resources, Inc. (NR)
Newport News Shipbuilding Inc. (NNS)
News Corporation Limited (The) (NWS)
News Corporation Limited (The) (NWSA)
Newscorp Overseas Limited (NOPPRA)
Newscorp Overseas Limited (NOPPRB)
NFO Worldwide, Inc. (NFO)
Niagara Mohawk Holdings, Inc. (NMK)
Niagara Mohawk Power Corporation
(NMKPR)
Niagara Mohawk Power Corporation
(NMKPRA)
Niagara Mohawk Power Corporation
(NMKPRB)
Niagara Mohawk Power Corporation
(NMKPRC)

COMPANY (SYMBOL)

Niagara Mohawk Power Corporation (NMKPRD)
Niagara Mohawk Power Corporation (NMKPRE)
Niagara Mohawk Power Corporation (NMKPRG)
Niagara Mohawk Power Corporation (NMKPRH)
Niagara Mohawk Power Corporation (NMKPRI)
Niagara Mohawk Power Corporation (NMKPRK)
Niagara Mohawk Power Corporation (NMKPRM)
NICOR Inc. (GAS)
Nielsen Media Research, Inc. (NMR)
NIKE, Inc. (NKE)
Nine West Group Inc. (NIN)
Nippon Telegraph and Telephone Corporation (NTT)
NIPSCO Capital Markets, Inc. (NIC)
NiSource Inc. (NI)
NiSource Inc. (NIPRB)
NL Industries, Inc. (NL)
Noble Affiliates, Inc. (NBL)
Noble Drilling Corporation (NE)
Nokia Corporation (NOK)
NorAm Financing I (NAEPRT)
Nord Resources Corporation (NRD)
Norfolk Southern Corporation (NSC)
Norfolk Southern Railway Company (NSRPR)
Norsk Hydro ASA (NHY)
Nortek, Inc. (NTK)
NORTEL INVERSORA S.A. (NRT)
NORTEL INVERSORA S.A. (NTL)
Nortel Networks Corporation (NT)
North European Oil Royalty Trust (NET)
North Fork Bancorporation, Inc. (NFB)
Northeast Utilities (NU)
Northern Border Partners, L.P. (NBP)
Northern Indiana Public Service Company (NIPRA)
Northern States Power Company (NSP)
Northern States Power Company (NSPPRA)
Northern States Power Company (NSPPRB)
Northern States Power Company (NSPPRC)
Northern States Power Company (NSPPRD)
Northern States Power Company (NSPPRE)
Northern States Power Company (NSPPRG)
Northrop Grumman Corporation (NOC)

COMPANY (SYMBOL)

NorthWestern Capital Financing I (NORPRB)
NorthWestern Corporation (NOR)
NOVA Chemicals Corporation (NCX)
NOVA Chemicals Corporation (NCXPR)
NOVA Chemicals Corporation (NCXPRA)
NOVA Corporation (Georgia) (NIS)
NovaCare, Inc. (NOV)
NovaStar Financial, Inc. (NFI)
Novo-Nordisk A/S (NVO)
NS Group, Inc. (NSS)
NSP Financing I (NSPPRT)
NSTAR (NST)
Nu Skin Enterprises, Inc. (NUS)
Nucor Corporation (NUE)
Nuevo Energy Company (NEV)
Nuevo Financing I (NEVPRT)
Nuevo Grupo Iusacell, S.A. de C.V. (Series V) (CEL)
NUI Corporation (NUI)
Nuveen Arizona Premium Income Municipal Fund, Inc. (NAZ)
Nuveen California Investment Quality Municipal Fund Inc. (NQC)
Nuveen California Municipal Market Opportunity Fund Inc. (NCO)
Nuveen California Municipal Value Fund, Inc. (NCA)
Nuveen California Performance Plus Municipal Fund, Inc. (NCP)
Nuveen California Quality Income Municipal Fund, Inc. (NUC)
Nuveen California Select Quality Municipal Fund, Inc. (NVC)
Nuveen Connecticut Premium Income Municipal Fund (NTC)
Nuveen Florida Investment Quality Municipal Fund (NUF)
Nuveen Insured California Premium Income Municipal Fund 2 (NCL)
Nuveen Insured California Premium Income Municipal Fund, Inc. (NPC)
Nuveen Insured California Select Tax-Free Income Portfolio (NXC)
Nuveen Insured Florida Premium Income Municipal Fund (NFL)
Nuveen Insured Municipal Opportunity Fund, Inc. (NIO)
Nuveen Insured New York Premium Income Municipal Fund, Inc. (NNF)
Nuveen Insured New York Select Tax-Free Income Portfolio (NXN)
Nuveen Insured Premium Income Municipal Fund 2 (NPX)

COMPANY (SYMBOL)

Nuveen Insured Quality Municipal Fund, Inc. (NQI)

Nuveen Investment Quality Municipal Fund, Inc. (NQM)

Nuveen Maryland Premium Income Municipal Fund (NMY)

Nuveen Massachusetts Premium Income Municipal Fund (NMT)

Nuveen Michigan Premium Income Municipal Fund, Inc. (NMP)

Nuveen Michigan Quality Income Municipal Fund, Inc. (NUM)

Nuveen Municipal Advantage Fund, Inc. (NMA)

Nuveen Municipal Income Fund, Inc. (NMI)

Nuveen Municipal Market Opportunity Fund, Inc. (NMO)

Nuveen Municipal Value Fund, Inc. (NUV)

Nuveen New Jersey Investment Quality Municipal Fund, Inc. (NQJ)

Nuveen New Jersey Premium Income Municipal Fund, Inc. (NNJ)

Nuveen New York Investment Quality Municipal Fund, Inc. (NQN)

Nuveen New York Municipal Value Fund, Inc. (NNY)

Nuveen New York Performance Plus Municipal Fund, Inc. (NNP)

Nuveen New York Quality Income Municipal Fund, Inc. (NUN)

Nuveen New York Select Quality Municipal Fund, Inc. (NVN)

Nuveen North Carolina Premium Income Municipal Fund (NNC)

Nuveen Ohio Quality Income Municipal Fund, Inc. (NUO)

Nuveen Pennsylvania Investment Quality Municipal Fund (NQP)

Nuveen Pennsylvania Premium Income Municipal Fund 2 (NPY)

Nuveen Performance Plus Municipal Fund, Inc. (NPP)

Nuveen Premier Insured Municipal Income Fund, Inc. (NIF)

Nuveen Premier Municipal Income Fund, Inc. (NPF)

Nuveen Premium Income Municipal Fund 2, Inc. (NPM)

Nuveen Premium Income Municipal Fund 4, Inc. (NPT)

Nuveen Premium Income Municipal Fund, Inc. (NPI)

Nuveen Quality Income Municipal Fund, Inc. (NQU)

COMPANY (SYMBOL)

Nuveen Select Maturities Municipal Fund (NIM)

Nuveen Select Quality Municipal Fund, Inc. (NQS)

Nuveen Select Tax-Free Income Portfolio (NXP)

Nuveen Select Tax-Free Income Portfolio 2 (NXQ)

Nuveen Select Tax-Free Income Portfolio 3 (NXR)

Nuveen Texas Quality Income Municipal Fund (NTX)

Nuveen Virginia Premium Income Municipal Fund (NPV)

Nvest, L.P. (NEW)

NVP Capital I (NVPPR)

NVP Capital III (NVPPRB)

NWPS Capital Financing I (NORPRA)

Nycomed Amersham PLC (NYE)

NYMAGIC, Inc. (NYM)

O

Oak Industries, Inc. (OAK)

Oakley, Inc. (OO)

Oakwood Homes Corporation (OH)

Occidental Petroleum Corporation (OXY)

Occidental Petroleum Corporation (OXYPRA)

Ocean Energy, Inc. (OEI)

Oceaneering International, Inc. (OII)

Octel Corporation (OTL)

Ocwen Asset Investment Corp. (OAC)

Ocwen Financial Corporation (OCN)

OEA, Inc. (OEA)

OEC Medical Systems, Inc. (OXE)

Office Depot, Inc. (ODP)

OfficeMax, Inc. (OMX)

Ogden Corporation (OG)

Ogden Corporation (OGPR)

OGE Energy Corp. (OGE)

Ohio Edison Company (OECPRA)

Ohio Edison Company (OECPRB)

Ohio Edison Company (OECPRC)

Ohio Edison Company (OECPRD)

Ohio Edison Company (OECPRM)

Ohio Edison Financing Trust (OECPRT)

Ohio Power Company (OJA)

Ohio Power Company (OJB)

Ohio Power Company (OPJ)

Oil-Dri Corporation of America (ODC)

Old Kent Financial Corporation (OK)

Old Republic International Corporation (ORI)

COMPANY (SYMBOL)

Olin Corporation (OLN)
Olsten Corporation (The) (OLS)
OM Group Inc. (OMP)
Omega Healthcare Investors, Inc. (OHI)
Omega Healthcare Investors, Inc. (OHIPRA)
Omega Healthcare Investors, Inc. (OHIPRB)
Omega Protein Corporation (OME)
OMI Corporation (OMM)
Omnicare, Inc. (OCR)
Omnicom Group Inc. (OMC)
One Valley Bancorp, Inc. (OV)
Oneida Ltd. (OCQ)
ONEOK Inc. (OKE)
Open Joint Stock Company Vimpel-Communications (VIP)
Oppenheimer Multi-Sector Income Trust (OMS)
Orange-co Inc. (OJ)
Orbital Engine Corporation Limited (OE)
Orbital Sciences Corporation (ORB)
Oregon Steel Mills, Inc. (OS)
Oriental Financial Group, Inc. (OFG)
Orion Capital Corporation (OC)
ORIX Corporation (IX)
Orthodontic Centers of America, Inc. (OCA)
Osmonics, Inc. (OSM)
O'Sullivan Industries Holdings, Inc. (OSU)
Outdoor Systems, Inc. (OSI)
Overseas Shipholding Group, Inc. (OSG)
Owens & Minor, Inc. (OMI)
Owens Corning (OWC)
Owens Corning (OWC)
Owens-Illinois, Inc. (OI)
Owens-Illinois, Inc. (OIPRA)
Oxford Industries, Inc. (OXM)
Oxy Capital Trust I (OXYPRB)

P

P. H. Glatfelter Company (GLT)
P. T. Tri Polyta Indonesia (TPI)
Pacific American Income Shares, Inc. (PAI)
Pacific Century Financial Corporation (BOH)
Pacific Gulf Properties Inc. (PAG)
Pacific Telesis Financing I (PACPRT)
Pacific Telesis Financing II (PACPRU)
PacifiCorp (PCQ)
PacifiCorp (PCX)
PacifiCorp (PPW)
PacifiCorp Capital I (PPWPRA)
PacifiCorp Capital II (PPWPRB)
Paine Webber Group Inc. (PWJ)

COMPANY (SYMBOL)

Pakistan Investment Fund, Inc. (PKF)
Pall Corporation (PLL)
Pameco Corporation (PCN)
Pan Pacific Retail Properties, Inc. (PNP)
Panamerican Beverages, Inc. (PB)
Panavision Inc. (PVI)
Par Technology Corporation (PTC)
Paracelsus Healthcare Corporation (PLS)
Park Electrochemical Corp. (PKE)
Park Place Entertainment Corporation (PPE)
Parker Drilling Company (PKD)
Parker-Hannifin Corporation (PH)
Parkway Properties, Inc. (PKY)
Parkway Properties, Inc. (PKYPRA)
PartnerRe Ltd. (PRE)
PartnerRe Ltd. (PREPRA)
Patina Oil & Gas Corporation (POG)
Patina Oil & Gas Corporation (POGPR)
Patina Oil & Gas Corporation (POGWS)
Patriot American Hospitality, Inc. (PAH)
Patriot American Hospitality, Inc. (PAHPRB)
Paxar Corporation (PXR)
Payless ShoeSource, Inc. (PSS)
PE Corporation (CRA)
PE Corporation (PEB)
PEC Israel Economic Corporation (IEC)
Pechiney (PY)
PECO Energy Capital, L.P. (PEPRZ)
PECO Energy Capital Trust II (PEPRX)
PECO Energy Company (PE)
PECO Energy Company (PEPRA)
PECO Energy Company (PEPRB)
PECO Energy Company (PEPRC)
PECO Energy Company (PEPRD)
Pediatrix Medical Group, Inc. (PDX)
Penelec Capital, L.P. (PECPRZ)
Penn Engineering & Manufacturing Corp. (PNN)
Penn Engineering & Manufacturing Corp. (PNNA)
Penn Treaty American Corporation (PTA)
Penn Virginia Corporation (PVA)
Penn-America Group, Inc. (PNG)
PennCorp Financial Group, Inc. (PFG)
PennCorp Financial Group, Inc. (PFGPR)
Pennsylvania Enterprises, Inc. (PNT)
Pennsylvania Real Estate Investment Trust (PEI)
Pennzoil-Quaker State Company (PZL)
Pentacon, Inc. (JIT)
Pentair, Inc. (PNR)
Penton Media, Inc. (PME)
Peoples Energy Corporation (PGL)

COMPANY (SYMBOL)

Pep Boys-Manny, Moe & Jack (The) (PBY)
Pepsi Bottling Group, Inc. (The) (PBG)
PepsiCo, Inc. (PEP)
Pepsi-Cola Puerto Rico Bottling Company (PPO)
Pepsi-Gemex, S.A. de C.V. (GEM)
Permian Basin Royalty Trust (PBT)
Perot Systems Corporation (PER)
Personnel Group of America, Inc. (PGA)
Perusahaan Perseroan (Persero) P.T. Indonesian Satellite Corporation (IIT)
Perusahaan Perseroan (Persero) P.T. Telekomunikasi Indonesia (TLK)
Petro-Canada (PCZ)
Petroleum & Resources Corporation (PEO)
Petroleum Geo-Services ASA (PGO)
Petsec Energy Ltd (PSJ)
Pfeiffer Vacuum Technology AG (PV)
Pfizer Inc (PFE)
PG&E Corporation (PCG)
Pharmaceutical Resources, Inc. (PRX)
Pharmacia & Upjohn, Inc. (PNU)
Phelps Dodge Corporation (PD)
Philadelphia Authority for Industrial Development (POB)
Philadelphia Suburban Corporation (PSC)
Philip Morris Companies Inc. (MO)
Philippine Long Distance Telephone Company (PHI)
Philippine Long Distance Telephone Company (PHIPRA)
Philips International Realty Corp. (PHR)
Phillips 66 Capital I (PPRC)
Phillips Petroleum Company (P)
Phillips-Van Heusen Corporation (PVH)
Phoenix Investment Partners, Ltd. (PXP)
Phosphate Resource Partners Limited Partnership (PLP)
Piccadilly Cafeterias, Inc. (PIC)
Piedmont Natural Gas Company, Inc. (PNY)
Pier 1 Imports, Inc. (PIR)
Pierce Leahy Corp. (PLH)
Pilgrim America Capital Corporation (PFX)
Pilgrim Prime Rate Trust (PPR)
Pilgrim's Pride Corporation (CHX)
Pillowtex Corporation (PTX)
PIMCO Advisors Holdings L.P. (PA)
PIMCO Commercial Mortgage Securities Trust, Inc. (PCM)
Pinnacle West Capital Corporation (PNW)
Pioneer Corporation (PIO)
Pioneer Hi-Bred International, Inc. (PHB)
Pioneer Interest Shares (MUO)
Pioneer Natural Resources Company (PXD)
Pitney Bowes Inc. (PBI)

COMPANY (SYMBOL)

Pitney Bowes Inc. (PBIPR)
Pittston BAX Group (PZX)
Pittston Company (The) (PZB)
Pittston Company (The) (PZM)
Pittway Corporation (PRY)
Pittway Corporation (PRYA)
Placer Dome Inc. (PDG)
Placer Dome Inc. (PDGPRA)
Plains All American Pipeline, L.P. (PAA)
Plantronics, Inc. (PLT)
Playboy Enterprises, Inc. (PLA)
Playboy Enterprises, Inc. (PLAA)
Playtex Products, Inc. (PYX)
PLC Capital L.L.C. (PLPRM)
PLC Capital Trust I (PLPRT)
Plum Creek Timber Company, L.P. (PCL)
PMI Group, Inc. (The) (PMA)
PNC Bank Corp (PNC)
PNC Bank Corp (PNCPRC)
PNC Bank Corp (PNCPRD)
Pogo Producing Company (PPP)
Pohang Iron & Steel Co., Ltd. (PKX)
Polaris Industries Inc. (PII)
Polaroid Corporation (PRD)
Policy Management Systems Corporation (PMS)
Polo Ralph Lauren Corporation (RL)
Polymer Group, Inc. (PGI)
Pope & Talbot, Inc. (POP)
Portland General Electric Company (PGB)
Portugal Fund, Inc. (The) (PGF)
Portugal Telecom, S.A. (PT)
Post Properties, Inc. (PPS)
Post Properties, Inc. (PPSPRA)
Post Properties, Inc. (PPSPRB)
Post Properties, Inc. (PPSPRC)
Potash Corporation of Saskatchewan Inc. (POT)
Potlatch Corporation (PCH)
Potomac Edison Company (The) (PEQ)
Potomac Electric Power Company (POM)
Potomac Electric Power Company Trust I (POMPRT)
PowerGen PLC (PWG)
PP&L Capital Trust II (PPLPRD)
PP&L, Inc. (PPLPRA)
PP&L, Inc. (PPLPRB)
PP&L Resources, Inc. (PPL)
PPG Industries, Inc. (PPG)
Praxair, Inc. (PX)
Precision Castparts Corp. (PCP)
Precision Drilling Corporation (PDS)
Preferred Income Fund Incorporated (PFD)
Preferred Income Management Fund, Inc. (PFM)

COMPANY (SYMBOL)

Preferred Income Opportunity Fund
Incorporated (PFO)
Premark International, Inc. (PMI)
Premdor Inc. (PI)
Premier Farnell PLC (PFP)
Premier Farnell PLC (PFPPR)
Premier Parks Inc. (PKS)
Premier Parks Inc. (PKSPRA)
PremiumWear, Inc. (PWA)
Prentiss Properties Trust (PP)
Pre-Paid Legal Services, Inc. (PPD)
Presley Companies (The) (PDC)
Pride International Inc. (PDE)
Primark Corporation (PMK)
Prime Group Realty Trust (PGE)
Prime Group Realty Trust (PGEPRB)
Prime Hospitality Corp. (PDQ)
Prime Retail, Inc. (PRT)
Prime Retail, Inc. (PRTPRA)
Prime Retail, Inc. (PRTPRB)
PRIMEDIA Inc. (PRM)
Prison Realty Trust Inc. (PZN)
Prison Realty Trust Inc. (PZNPRA)
Procter & Gamble Company (The) (PG)
Progressive Corporation (The) (PGR)
ProLogis Trust (PLD)
ProLogis Trust (PLDPRA)
ProLogis Trust (PLDPRB)
ProLogis Trust (PLDPRD)
ProLogis Trust (PLDPRE)
Promus Hotel Corporation (PRH)
Prospect Street High Income Portfolio Inc.
(PHY)
Protection One Inc. (POI)
Protective Life Corporation (PL)
Protective Life Corporation (PLPRP)
ProVantage Health Services, Inc. (PHS)
Providence Energy Corporation (PVY)
Provident Companies, Inc. (PVT)
Providian Financial Corporation (PVN)
PS Group Holdings, Inc. (PSG)
PSCO Capital Trust I (PSRPRC)
PSE&G Capital Trust I (PEGPRU)
PSE&G Capital Trust II (PEGPRT)
PSI Energy, Inc. (CINPRB)
PSI Energy, Inc. (CINPRC)
PSI Energy, Inc. (CINPRJ)
PSO Capital I (PSTPRA)
Public Service Company of New Mexico
(PNM)
Public Service Company of North Carolina,
Incorporated (PGS)
Public Service Electric and Gas Capital, L.P.
(PEGPRX)

COMPANY (SYMBOL)

Public Service Electric and Gas Capital, L.P.
(PEGPRZ)
Public Service Electric and Gas Company
(PEGPRA)
Public Service Electric and Gas Company
(PEGPRB)
Public Service Electric and Gas Company
(PEGPRC)
Public Service Electric and Gas Company
(PEGPRD)
Public Service Electric and Gas Company
(PEGPRE)
Public Service Electric and Gas Company
(PEGPRW)
Public Service Electric and Gas Company
(PEGPRY)
Public Service Enterprise Group
Incorporated (PEG)
Public Storage, Inc. (PSA)
Public Storage, Inc. (PSAPRA)
Public Storage, Inc. (PSAPRB)
Public Storage, Inc. (PSAPRC)
Public Storage, Inc. (PSAPRD)
Public Storage, Inc. (PSAPRE)
Public Storage, Inc. (PSAPRF)
Public Storage, Inc. (PSAPRG)
Public Storage, Inc. (PSAPRH)
Public Storage, Inc. (PSAPRI)
Public Storage, Inc. (PSAPRJ)
Public Storage, Inc. (PSAPRK)
Public Storage, Inc. (PSAPRL)
Puerto Rican Cement Company, Inc.
(PRN)
Puget Sound Energy, Inc. (PSD)
Puget Sound Energy, Inc. (PSDPRA)
Puget Sound Energy, Inc. (PSDPRC)
Pulitzer Inc. (PTZ)
Pulte Corporation (PHM)
Putnam Convertible Opportunities and
Income Trust (PCV)
Putnam Dividend Income Fund (PDI)
Putnam High Income Convertible and Bond
Fund (PCF)
Putnam High Yield Municipal Trust (PYM)
Putnam Investment Grade Municipal Trust
(PGM)
Putnam Investment Grade Municipal Trust
II (PMG)
Putnam Managed High Yield Trust (PTM)
Putnam Managed Municipal Income Trust
(PMM)
Putnam Master Income Trust (PMT)
Putnam Master Intermediate Income Trust
(PIM)

COMPANY (SYMBOL)

Putnam Municipal Opportunities Trust (PMO)
Putnam Premier Income Trust (PPT)
Putnam Tax-Free Health Care Fund (PMH)
PWG Capital Trust I (PWJPRA)
PWG Capital Trust II (PWJPRB)
PXRE Corporation (PXT)

Q

QMS, Inc. (AQM)
Quaker Chemical Corporation (KWR)
Quaker Oats Company (The) (OAT)
Quanex Corporation (NX)
Quanta Services, Inc. (PWR)
Quantum Corporation (DSS)
Quantum Corporation (HDD)
Quebecor Printing Inc. (PRW)
Quest Diagnostics Incorporated (DGX)
Questar Corporation (STR)
Quiksilver, Inc. (ZQK)
Quilmes Industrial (Quinsa), Societe Anonyme (LQU)
QUINENCO S.A. (LQ)

R

R & B Falcon Corporation (FLC)
R. G. Barry Corporation (RGB)
R. H. Donnelley Corporation (RHD)
R.O.C. Taiwan Fund (The) (ROC)
R. R. Donnelley & Sons Company (DNY)
Ragen MacKenzie Group Incorporated (RMG)
Ralcorp Holdings, Inc. (RAH)
Ralston-Ralston Purina Group (IBX)
Ralston-Ralston Purina Group (RAL)
Ramco-Gershenson Properties Trust (RPT)
Range Resources Corporation (RRC)
Ranger Oil Limited (RGO)
Raymond James Financial, Inc. (RJF)
Rayonier, Inc. (RYN)
Rayovac Corporation (ROV)
Raytech Corporation (QRAY)
Raytheon Company (RTNA)
Raytheon Company (RTNB)
RCM Strategic Global Government Fund, Inc. (RCS)
RDO Equipment Co. (RDO)
Reader's Digest Association, Inc. (The) (RDA)
Reader's Digest Association, Inc. (The) (RDB)
Reader's Digest Automatic Common Exchange Security Trust (RDT)
Realty Income Corporation (O)

COMPANY (SYMBOL)

Realty Income Corporation (OUI)
Reckson Associates Realty Corp. (RA)
Reckson Associates Realty Corp. (RAPRA)
Redwood Trust, Inc. (RWT)
Redwood Trust, Inc. (RWTPRB)
Reebok International Ltd. (RBK)
Reed International P.L.C. (RUK)
Regency Realty Corporation (REG)
RehabCare Group, Inc. (RHB)
REI Trust I (REIPRC)
Reinsurance Group of America, Incorporated (RGA)
Reinsurance Group of America, Incorporated (RGAA)
Reliance Group Holdings, Inc. (REL)
Reliance Steel & Aluminum Co. (RS)
Reliant Energy Incorporated (REI)
ReliaStar Financial Corp. (RLR)
ReliaStar Financing I (RLRPRA)
ReliaStar Financing II (RLRPRB)
RenaissanceRe Holdings Ltd. (RNR)
Rent-Way Inc. (RWY)
Repsol International Capital Limited (REPPRA)
Repsol, S.A. (REP)
Republic Group Incorporated (RGC)
Republic New York Corporation (RNB)
Republic New York Corporation (RNBPRD)
Republic New York Corporation (RNBPRE)
Republic New York Corporation (RNBPRF)
Republic Services, Inc. (RSG)
ResortQuest International, Inc. (RZT)
Revlon, Inc. (REV)
REX Stores Corporation (RSC)
Reynolds and Reynolds Company (The) (REY)
Reynolds Metals Company (RLM)
RFS Hotel Investors, Inc. (RFS)
Rhodia (RHA)
Rhone-Poulenc Overseas Limited (RPOPRA)
Rhone-Poulenc S.A. (RP)
Rhone-Poulenc S.A. (RPPR)
Rhone-Poulenc S.A. (RPWS)
Richfood Holdings, Inc. (RFH)
RightCHOICE Managed Care, Inc. (RIT)
Rio Algom Limited (ROMPR)
Rio Tinto PLC (RTP)
Ritchie Bros. Auctioneers Incorporated (RBA)
Rite Aid Corporation (RAD)

COMPANY (SYMBOL)

RJR Nabisco Holdings Capital Trust I (RNPRTCL)
RJR Nabisco Holdings Capital Trust II (RNPRU)
RJR Nabisco Holdings Corp. (RN)
RLI Corp. (RLI)
Robbins & Myers, Inc. (RBN)
Robert Half International Inc. (RHI)
Robertson-Ceco Corporation (RHH)
Rochester Gas and Electric Corporation (RGS)
Rock-Tenn Company (RKT)
Rockwell International Corporation (ROK)
Rogers Cantel Mobile Communications Inc. (RCN)
Rogers Communications Inc. (RG)
Rohm and Haas Company (ROH)
Rollins, Inc. (ROL)
Rollins Truck Leasing Corp. (RLC)
Roper Industries, Inc. (ROP)
Rostelecom Open Joint Stock Company of Long Distance and International Telecommunications (ROS)
Rouge Industries, Inc. (ROU)
Rouse Capital (RSEPRZ)
Rouse Company (The) (RSE)
Rouse Company (The) (RSEPRB)
Rowan Companies, Inc. (RDC)
Rowe Companies (The) (ROW)
Royal Appliance Mfg. Co. (RAM)
Royal Bank of Canada (RY)
Royal Bank of Scotland Group PLC (The) (RBSPRB)
Royal Bank of Scotland Group PLC (The) (RBSPRC)
Royal Bank of Scotland Group PLC (The) (RBSPRD)
Royal Bank of Scotland Group PLC (The) (RBSPRE)
Royal Bank of Scotland Group PLC (The) (RBSPRF)
Royal Bank of Scotland Group PLC (The) (RBSPRG)
Royal Bank of Scotland Group PLC (The) (RBSPRH)
Royal Bank of Scotland Group PLC (The) (RBSPRX)
Royal Caribbean Cruises Ltd. (RCL)
Royal Caribbean Cruises Ltd. (RCLPR)
Royal Dutch Petroleum Company (RD)
Royal Group Technologies Limited (RYG)
Royal PTT Nederland NV (KPN)
Royce Value Trust, Inc. (RVT)
Royce Value Trust, Inc. (RVTPR)
Royce Value Trust, Inc. (RVTPRA)

COMPANY (SYMBOL)

RPC, Inc. (RES)
RPM, Inc. (RPM)
RTI International Metals Inc. (Holding Company) (RTI)
Ruby Tuesday, Inc. (RI)
Ruddick Corporation (RDK)
Russ Berrie and Company, Inc. (RUS)
Russell Corporation (RML)
Ryder System, Inc. (R)
Ryerson Tull, Inc. (NEW) (RT)
Ryland Group, Inc. (The) (RYL)

S

Saatchi & Saatchi PLC (SSA)
Sabine Royalty Trust (SBR)
SABRE Group Holdings, Inc. (The) (TSG)
Safeguard Scientifics, Inc. (SFE)
Safety-Kleen Corp (SK)
Safeway Inc. (SWY)
Saks Incorporated (SKS)
Salomon Brothers 2008 Worldwide Dollar Government Term Trust Inc. (SBG)
Salomon Brothers Fund Inc. (The) (SBF)
Salomon Brothers High Income Fund II Inc. (HIX)
Salomon Brothers High Income Fund Inc. (HIF)
Salomon Brothers Worldwide Income Fund, Inc. (SBW)
Salomon Smith Barney Holdings Inc. (CXB)
Salomon Smith Barney Holdings Inc. (NXS)
Salomon Smith Barney Holdings Inc. (XSB)
Salton, Inc. (SFP)
San Juan Basin Royalty Trust (SJT)
Santa Fe Energy Trust (SFF)
Santa Fe International Corporation (SDC)
Santa Fe Snyder Corporation (SFS)
Santa Isabel S.A. (ISA)
Santander Overseas Bank, Inc. (OPRPRD)
SAP Aktiengesellschaft (SAP)
Sappi Limited (SPP)
Sara Lee Corporation (SLE)
Sauer Inc. (SHS)
Saul Centers, Inc. (BFS)
Savannah Electric Capital Trust I (SVAPR)
Savia S.A. de C.V. (VAI)
Sbarro, Inc. (SBA)
SBC Communications Inc. (SBC)
SBC Communications Inc. (XTS)
Scana Corporation (SCG)
Scania AB (SCVA)
Scania AB (SCVB)
SCE&G Trust I (SACPRT)
Schawk, Inc. (SGK)
Schein Pharmaceutical, Inc. (SHP)

COMPANY (SYMBOL)

Schering-Plough Corporation (SGP)
Schlumberger Limited (SLB)
Schweitzer-Mauduit International, Inc.
    (SWM)
SCI Systems, Inc. (SCI)
Scientific Games Holdings Corp. (SG)
Scientific-Atlanta, Inc. (SFA)
SCOR (SCO)
Scottish Power PLC (SPI)
Scotts Company (The) (SMG)
Scott's Liquid Gold Inc. (SGD)
SCPIE Holdings Inc. (SKP)
Scudder Global High Income Fund, Inc.
    (LBF)
Scudder New Asia Fund, Inc. (SAF)
Scudder New Europe Fund, Inc. (NEF)
Sea Containers Ltd. (SCRA)
Sea Containers Ltd. (SCRB)
SEACOR SMIT Inc. (CKH)
Seagate Technology, Inc. (SEG)
Seagram Company Ltd. (The) (VO)
Sealed Air Corporation (SEE)
Sealed Air Corporation (SEEPRA)
Sears Roebuck Acceptance Corp. (SRF)
Sears Roebuck Acceptance Corp. (SRH)
Sears, Roebuck and Co. (S)
Security Capital Group Incorporated (SCZ)
Security Capital Group Incorporated
    (SCZA)
Security Capital U.S. Realty (RTY)
Seitel, Inc. (SEI)
Seligman Quality Municipal Fund, Inc.
    (SQF)
Seligman Select Municipal Fund, Inc. (SEL)
Sempra Energy (SRE)
Senior High Income Portfolio, Inc. (ARK)
Sensormatic Electronics Corporation (SRM)
Sequa Corporation (SQAA)
Sequa Corporation (SQAB)
Sequa Corporation (SQAPR)
Service Corporation International (SRV)
Service Experts, Inc. (SVE)
Service Merchandise Company, Inc.
    (QSME)
ServiceMaster Company (The) (SVM)
SFX Entertainment, Inc. (SFX)
SGL CARBON Aktiengesellschaft (SGG)
Shandong Huaneng Power Development Co.
    Ltd. (SH)
Shanghai Petrochemical Company Limited
    (SHI)
Shared Medical Systems Corporation (SMS)
Shaw Communications Inc. (SJR)
Shaw Communications Inc. (SJRPRA)
Shaw Communications Inc. (SJRPRB)

COMPANY (SYMBOL)

Shaw Group Inc. (The) (SGR)
Shaw Industries, Inc. (SHX)
Shell Transport and Trading Company,
    Public Limited Company (The) (SC)
Sherwin-Williams Company (The) (SHW)
Shoney's, Inc. (SHN)
Shopko Stores, Inc. (SKO)
Shorewood Packaging Corporation (SWD)
Shurgard Storage Centers, Inc. (SHU)
Shurgard Storage Centers, Inc. (SHUPRB)
Shurgard Storage Centers, Inc. (SHUPRC)
SI Financing Trust I (SBPRG)
Sierra Health Services, Inc. (SIE)
Sierra Pacific Power Capital I (SRPPRT)
Sierra Pacific Resources (SRP)
SIGCORP, Inc. (SIG)
Signal Apparel Company, Inc. (SIA)
Silicon Graphics, Inc. (SGI)
Silverleaf Resorts, Inc. (SVR)
Simon Property Group Inc. (SPG)
Simon Property Group Inc. (SPGPRB)
Simpson Manufacturing Co., Inc. (SSD)
Simula, Inc. (SMU)
Singapore Fund, Inc. (The) (SGF)
Singer Company N.V. (The) (SEW)
SITEL Corporation (SWW)
Sizeler Property Investors, Inc. (SIZ)
Sizzler International, Inc. (SZ)
SJG Capital Trust (SJIPRT)
SK Telecom Co., Ltd. (SKM)
Sketchers USA, Inc. (SKX)
Skyline Corporation (SKY)
SL Green Realty Corp. (SLG)
SL Green Realty Corp. (SLGPRA)
SL Industries, Inc. (SL)
SLI, Inc. (SLI)
SLM Holding Corporation (SLM)
Smart & Final Inc. (SMF)
Smart & Final Inc. (SMFRT)
Smedvig asa (SMVA)
Smedvig asa (SMVB)
Smith International, Inc. (SII)
SmithKline Beecham PLC (SBH)
Snap-On Incorporated (SNA)
Snyder Communications, Inc. (SNC)
Snyder STRYPES Trust (STX)
Sociedad Quimica y Minera de Chile S.A.
    (SQM)
Sociedad Quimica y Minera de Chile S.A.
    (SQMA)
Sodexho Marriott Services Inc. (SDH)
Software AG Systems, Inc. (AGS)
Sola International Inc. (SOL)
Solectron Corporation (SLR)
Solutia Inc. (SOI)

COMPANY (SYMBOL)

Sonat Inc. (SNT)
Sonic Automotive, Inc. (SAH)
Sonoco Products Company (SON)
Sony Corporation (SNE)
Sotheby's Holdings, Inc. (BID)
Source Capital, Inc. (SOR)
Source Capital, Inc. (SORPR)
Source One Mortgage Corporation
  (SMQCL)
South Carolina Electric & Gas Co. (SACPR)
South Jersey Industries, Inc. (SJI)
Southdown, Inc. (SDW)
Southern Africa Fund, Inc. (The) (SOA)
Southern Company (The) (SO)
Southern Company Capital Trust III
  (SOPRA)
Southern Company Capital Trust IV
  (SOPRB)
Southern Company Capital Trust V
  (SOPRC)
Southern Peru Copper Corporation (PCU)
Southern Union Company (SUG)
Southern Union Financing I (SUGPRA)
Southwest Airlines Co. (LUV)
Southwest Gas Capital I (SWXPRA)
Southwest Gas Corporation (SWX)
Southwest Securities Group, Inc. (SWS)
Southwestern Bell Telephone Company
  (DSW)
Southwestern Energy Company (SWN)
Southwestern Public Service Capital I
  (SPSPRT)
Sovran Self Storage, Inc. (SSS)
Spain Fund, Inc. (The) (SNF)
Spartech Corporation (SEH)
Sparton Corporation (SPA)
Specialty Equipment Companies, Inc. (SEC)
Speedway Motorsports, Inc. (TRK)
Spelling Entertainment Group Inc. (SP)
SPG Properties Inc. (SGVPRB)
Spieker Properties, Inc. (SPK)
Spieker Properties, Inc. (SPKPRB)
Spieker Properties, Inc. (SPKPRC)
Spieker Properties, Inc. (SPKPRE)
Sport Supply Group, Inc. (GYM)
Sports Authority, Inc. (The) (TSA)
Springs Industries, Inc. (SMI)
Sprint Corporation (FON)
Sprint Corporation (FONPR)
Sprint Corporation (FONPRA)
Sprint Corporation (FXN)
Sprint Corporation (PCS)
SPS Technologies, Inc. (ST)
SPX Corporation (SPW)
SSBH Capital I (SSR)

COMPANY (SYMBOL)

Stage Stores, Inc. (SGE)
Stancorp Financial Group, Inc. (SFG)
Standard Commercial Corporation (STW)
Standard Motor Products, Inc. (SMP)
Standard Pacific Corp. (SPF)
Standard Products Company (The) (SPD)
Standard Register Company (The) (SR)
Standex International Corporation (SXI)
Stanley Works (The) (SWK)
Star Gas Partners, L.P. (SGH)
Star Gas Partners, L.P. (SGU)
StarTek, Inc. (SRT)
Starwood Hotels & Resorts Worldwide, Inc.
  (HOT)
State Street Corporation (STT)
Staten Island Bancorp, Inc. (SIB)
Station Casinos, Inc. (STN)
Station Casinos, Inc. (STNPRCL)
Steelcase Inc. (SCS)
Steinway Musical Instruments, Inc. (LVB)
Stepan Company (SCL)
Stepan Company (SCLPR)
STERIS Corporation (STE)
Sterling Bancorp (STL)
Sterling Commerce, Inc. (SE)
Sterling Software, Inc. (SSW)
Stewart Information Services Corporation
  (STC)
Stifel Financial Corp. (SF)
STMicroelectronics N.V. (STM)
Stokely Van Camp Inc. (SVCPR)
Stone & Webster, Incorporated (SW)
Stone Container Corporation (STOPRE)
Stone Energy Corporation (SGY)
Stoneridge, Inc. (SRI)
Storage Technology Corporation (STK)
Storage USA, Inc. (SUS)
Strategic Global Income Fund, Inc. (SGL)
Stride Rite Corporation (The) (SRR)
Stryker Corporation (SYK)
Student Loan Corporation (The) (STU)
Student Loan Marketing Association
  (SLMPRA)
Sturm, Ruger & Company, Inc. (RGR)
St. Joe Company (The) (JOE)
St. John Knits, Inc. (SJK)
St. Joseph Light & Power Company (SAJ)
St. Jude Medical, Inc. (STJ)
St. Laurent Paperboard (SLW)
St. Paul Capital L.L.C. (SPCPRM)
St. Paul Companies, Inc. (The) (SPC)
Suburban Propane Partners, L.P. (SPH)
Suiza Foods Corporation (SZA)
Sulzer Medica Ltd. (SM)
Summit Bancorp (SUB)

COMPANY (SYMBOL)

Summit Properties Inc. (SMT)
Sun Communities, Inc. (SUI)
Sun Energy Partners, L.P. (SLP)
Sun International Hotels Limited (SIH)
SunAmerica Capital Trust II (SAIPRV)
SunAmerica Capital Trust III (SAIPRW)
Sunbeam Corporation (SOC)
Sunburst Hospitality Corporation (SNB)
Suncor Energy Inc. (SU)
Suncor Energy Inc. (SUPRA)
Sundstrand Corporation (SNS)
SunGard Data Systems Inc. (SDS)
Sunoco, Inc. (SUN)
Sunrise Medical, Inc. (SMD)
Sunshine Mining and Refining Company
  (SCC)
SunSource Capital Trust (SDPPR)
SunSource, Inc. (SDP)
Sunstone Hotel Investors, Inc. (SSI)
Sunterra Corporation (OWN)
SunTrust Banks, Inc. (STI)
Superior Industries International, Inc. (SUP)
Superior TeleCom Inc. (SUT)
Superior Trust I (SUTPRA)
Supermercados Unimarc S.A. (UNR)
Super-Sol Ltd. (SAE)
Supervalu Inc. (SVU)
SWEPCO Capital I (SWOPRA)
Swift Energy Company (SFY)
Swisher International Group Inc. (SWR)
Swiss Helvetia Fund, Inc. (The) (SWZ)
Swisscom AG (SCM)
Sybron International Corporation (SYB)
Symbol Technologies, Inc. (SBL)
Syms Corp. (SYM)
Synovus Financial Corp. (SNV)
Sysco Corporation (SYY)
Systemax Inc. (SYX)

T
TAG Heuer International SA (THW)
Taiwan Equity Fund, Inc. (The) (TYW)
Taiwan Fund, Inc. (The) (TWN)
Taiwan Semiconductor Manufacturing
  Company Ltd. (TSM)
Talbots, Inc. (The) (TLB)
Talisman Energy Inc. (TLM)
Talisman Energy Inc. (TLMPRA)
Tandy Corporation (TAN)
Tandycrafts, Inc. (TAC)
Tanger Factory Outlet Centers (SKT)
Tanger Factory Outlet Centers (SKTPRA)
Tasty Baking Company (TBC)
Taubman Centers, Inc. (TCO)
Taubman Centers, Inc. (TCOPRA)

COMPANY (SYMBOL)

TB Wood's Corporation (TBW)
TCBY Enterprises, Inc. (TBY)
TCF Financial Corporation (TCB)
TCI Communications Financing I (TFIPR)
TCI Communications Financing II
  (TFIPRA)
TCI Communications Financing IV
  (TFIPRB)
TCW Convertible Securities Fund, Inc.
  (CVT)
TCW/DW Term Trust 2000 (TDT)
TCW/DW Term Trust 2002 (TRM)
TCW/DW Term Trust 2003 (TMT)
TD Waterhouse Group, Inc. (TWE)
TDK Corporation (TDK)
Technitrol, Inc. (TNL)
Tech-Sym Corporation (TSY)
TECO Energy, Inc. (TE)
Teekay Shipping Corporation (TK)
Tefron Ltd (TFR)
Tejon Ranch Co. (TRC)
Tektronix, Inc. (TEK)
Tele Celular Sul Participacoes S.A. (TSU)
Tele Centro Oeste Celular Participacoes
  S.A. (TRO)
Tele Centro Sul Participacoes S.A. (TCS)
Tele Danmark A/S (TLD)
Tele Leste Celular Participacoes S.A.
  (TBE)
Tele Nordeste Celular Participacoes S.A.
  (TND)
Tele Norte Celular Participacoes S.A. (TCN)
Tele Norte Leste Participacoes S.A. (TNE)
Tele Sudeste Celular Participacoes S.A.
  (TSD)
TELECOM ARGENTINA STET - France
  Telecom S.A. (TEO)
Telecom Corporation of New Zealand
  Limited (NZT)
Telecom Italia S.P.A. (TI)
Telecom Italia S.P.A. (TIA)
Telecomunicacoes Brasileiras S.A.-Telebras
  (TBH)
Telecomunicacoes Brasileiras S.A.-Telebras
  (TBR)
Telecomunicacoes Brasileiras S.A.-Telebras
  (RTB)
Teleflex Incorporated (TFX)
Telefonica de Argentina S.A. (TAR)
Telefonica del Peru S.A. (TDP)
Telefonica S.A. (TEF)
Telefonos de Mexico, S.A. de C.V. (TMX)
Teleglobe Inc. (TGO)
Telemig Celular Participacoes S.A. (TMB)
Telesp Celular Participacoes S.A. (TCP)

COMPANY (SYMBOL)	COMPANY (SYMBOL)
Telesp Participacoes S.A. (TSP)	Thomas Industries, Inc. (TII)
Telex-Chile S.A. (TL)	Thomas Nelson, Inc. (TNM)
Telstra Corporation Limited (TLS)	Thomas Nelson, Inc. (TNMB)
Temple-Inland Inc. (TIN)	Thor Industries, Inc. (THO)
Templeton China World Fund, Inc. (TCH)	Thornburg Mortgage Asset Corp. (TMA)
Templeton Dragon Fund, Inc. (TDF)	Thornburg Mortgage Asset Corp. (TMAPRA)
Templeton Emerging Markets Appreciation Fund, Inc. (TEA)	Three-Five Systems, Inc. (TFS)
Templeton Emerging Markets Fund, Inc. (EMF)	Tidewater Inc. (TDW)
Templeton Emerging Markets Income Fund, Inc. (TEI)	Tiffany & Co. (TIF)
Templeton Global Governments Income Trust (TGG)	Timberland Company (The) (TBL)
Templeton Global Income Fund, Inc. (GIM)	Time Warner Capital I (TWXPRT)
Templeton Russia Fund, Inc. (TRF)	Time Warner Inc. (TWX)
Templeton Vietnam and Southeast Asia Fund, Inc. (TVF)	Times Mirror Company (The) (TMC)
Tenet Healthcare Corporation (THC)	Times Mirror Company (The) (TME)
Tenneco Inc. (TEN)	Timken Company (The) (TKR)
Tennessee Valley Authority (TVA)	Titan Corporation (The) (TTN)
Tennessee Valley Authority (TVB)	Titan Corporation (The) (TTNPR)
Tennessee Valley Authority (TVC)	Titan International, Inc. (TWI)
Tennessee Valley Authority (TVE)	Titanium Metals Corporation (TIE)
TEPPCO Partners, L.P. (TPP)	TJX Companies, Inc. (The) (TJX)
Teradyne, Inc. (TER)	TNP Enterprises, Inc. (TNP)
Terex Corporation (TEX)	TNT Post Group N.V. (TP)
Terra Industries, Inc. (TRA)	Todd Shipyards Corporation (TOD)
Terra Nitrogen Company, L.P. (TNH)	Tokheim Corporation (TOK)
Terra Nova (Bermuda) Holdings Ltd. (TNA)	Toledo Edison Co. (TEDPRE)
Tesoro Petroleum Corporation (TSO)	Toledo Edison Co. (TEDPRF)
Tesoro Petroleum Corporation (TSOPRA)	Toledo Edison Co. (TEDPRK)
Tetra Technologies, Inc. (TTI)	Toledo Edison Co. (TEDPRL)
Texaco Capital LLC (TXCPRA)	Toll Brothers, Inc. (TOL)
Texaco Capital LLC (TXCPRB)	Tomkins PLC (TKS)
Texaco Inc. (TX)	Tommy Hilfiger Corporation (TOM)
Texas Industries, Inc. (TXI)	Too, Inc. (TOO)
Texas Instruments Incorporated (TXN)	Tootsie Roll Industries, Inc. (TR)
Texas Pacific Land Trust (TPL)	Torch Energy Royalty Trust (TRU)
Texas Utilities Company (TXU)	Torchmark Capital L.L.C. (TMKPRM)
Texas Utilities Company (TXUPRG)	Torchmark Corporation (TMK)
Texas Utilities Company (TXUPRI)	Toro Company (The) (TTC)
Texas Utilities Electric Company (TUEPRA)	Toronto-Dominion Bank (The) (TD)
Texas Utilities Electric Company (TUEPRB)	Tosco Corporation (TOS)
Textron Capital I (TXTPRT)	TOTAL (TOT)
Textron Inc. (TXT)	Total Renal Care Holdings, Inc. (TRL)
Textron Inc. (TXTPRA)	Total System Services, Inc. (TSS)
Textron Inc. (TXTPRB)	Totta & Acores Financing, Ltd. (BTAPRA)
Thai Capital Fund, Inc. (The) (TC)	Tower Automotive, Inc. (TWR)
Thai Fund, Inc. (The) (TTF)	Tower Realty Trust, Inc (TOW)
Theragenics Corporation (TGX)	Town and Country Trust (The) (TCT)
Thermo Electron Corporation (TMO)	Toys 'R' Us, Inc. (TOY)
Thomas & Betts Corporation (TNB)	Trammell Crow Company (TCC)
	Transaction Network Services, Inc. (TNI)
	Transamerica Delaware, L.P. (TAPRA)
	Transamerica Finance Corporation (TFD)
	Transamerica Income Shares, Inc. (TAI)
	Transatlantic Holdings, Inc. (TRH)
	TransCanada Capital (TCLPR)

COMPANY (SYMBOL)

TransCanada PipeLines Limited (TRP)
TransCanada PipeLines Limited (TRPPR)
TransCanada PipeLines Limited (TRPPRC)
Transcontinental Realty Investors, Inc.
  (TCI)
Transmedia Network Inc. (TMN)
Transocean Offshore Inc. (RIG)
Transportacion Maritima Mexicana, S.A. de
  C.V. (TMM)
Transportacion Maritima Mexicana, S.A. de
  C.V. (TMMA)
Transportadora de Gas del Sur S.A. (TGS)
Transportation Components, Inc. (TUI)
TransPro, Inc. (TPR)
TransTechnology Corporation (TT)
Travelers Corporate Loan Fund Inc. (TLI)
Travelers P&C Capital I (TAPPRA)
Travelers P&C Capital II (TAPPRB)
Travelers Property Casualty Corp. (TAP)
TRC Companies, Inc. (TRR)
Tredegar Corporation (TG)
Tremont Corporation (TRE)
Trex Company, Inc. (TWP)
Triangle Bancorp, Inc. (TGL)
Triarc Companies, Inc. (TRY)
Tribune Company (TRB)
Tribune Company (TRD)
TRICOM, S.A. (TDR)
Tricon Global Restaurants, Inc. (YUM)
Tri-Continental Corporation (TY)
Tri-Continental Corporation (TYPR)
Trigen Energy Corporation (TGN)
Trigon Healthcare, Inc. (TGH)
TriNet Corporate Realty Trust, Inc. (TRI)
TriNet Corporate Realty Trust, Inc.
  (TRIPRA)
TriNet Corporate Realty Trust, Inc.
  (TRIPRB)
TriNet Corporate Realty Trust, Inc.
  (TRIPRC)
Trinity Industries, Inc. (TRN)
TriStar Aerospace Co. (TSX)
Triton Energy Limited (Cayman Islands)
  (OIL)
Triumph Group, Inc. (TGI)
TrizecHahn Corporation (TZH)
TrizecHahn Corporation (TZHWS)
True North Communications Inc. (TNO)
Trump Hotels & Casino Resorts, Inc. (DJT)
TRW Inc. (TRW)
TRW Inc. (TRWPRB)
TRW Inc. (TRWPRD)
TU Electric Capital I (TUEPRM)
TU Electric Capital III (TUEPRO)
Tuboscope Inc. (TBI)

COMPANY (SYMBOL)

Tultex Corporation (TTX)
Tupperware Corporation (TUP)
Turkish Investment Fund, Inc. (The) (TKF)
Turner Corporation (The) (TUR)
TV Azteca, S.A. de C.V. (TZA)
TVX Gold Inc. (TVX)
Twin Disc, Incorporated (TDI)
TXI Capital Trust I (TXIPRS)
TXU Capital I (TXUPRA)
Tyco International Ltd. (TYC)
Tyler Technologies, Inc. (TYL)
Tyson Foods, Inc. (TSN)

U

U S WEST, Inc. (USW)
UAL Corporation (UAL)
UAL Corporation (UALPRB)
UAL Corporation Capital Trust I
  (UALPRT)
UCAR International Inc. (UCR)
UDS Capital I (UDSPRA)
UGI Corporation (UGI)
UICI (UCI)
Ultramar Diamond Shamrock Corporation
  (UDS)
Unibanco-Uniao de Bancos Brasileiros S.A.
  (UBB)
UniCapital Corporation (UCP)
Unicom Corporation (UCM)
Unifi, Inc. (UFI)
Unifirst Corporation (UNF)
Unigraphics Solutions Inc. (UGS)
Unilever N.V. (UN)
Unilever PLC (UL)
Union Carbide Corporation (UK)
Union Electric Company (UEPPRA)
Union Electric Company (UEPPRC)
Union Electric Company (UEPPRD)
Union Electric Company (UEPPRE)
Union Pacific Corporation (UNP)
Union Pacific Resources Group Inc. (UPR)
Union Planters Corporation (UPC)
UnionBancal Finance Trust I (UBT)
UniSource Energy Corporation (UNS)
Unisource Worldwide, Inc. (UWW)
Unisys Corporation (UIS)
Unisys Corporation (UISPRA)
Unit Corporation (UNT)
United American Healthcare Corporation
  (UAH)
United Asset Management Corporation
  (UAM)
United Auto Group, Inc. (UAG)
United Capital Funding Partnership L.P.
  (UILPRA)

COMPANY (SYMBOL)

United Dominion Industries Limited (UDI)
United Dominion Realty Trust, Inc. (UDM)
United Dominion Realty Trust, Inc. (UDR)
United Dominion Realty Trust, Inc. (UDRPRA)
United Dominion Realty Trust, Inc. (UDRPRB)
United Healthcare Corporation (UNH)
United Illuminating Company (The) (UIL)
United Industrial Corporation (UIC)
United Park City Mines Company (UPK)
United Rentals, Inc. (URI)
United Technologies Corporation (UTX)
United Utilities PLC (UU)
United Water Resources Inc. (UWR)
United Wisconsin Services, Inc. (NEW) (UWZ)
Unitrode Corporation (UTR)
Universal Corporation (UVV)
Universal Foods Corporation (UFC)
Universal Health Realty Income Trust (UHT)
Universal Health Services, Inc. (UHS)
Univision Communications, Inc. (UVN)
Uno Restaurant Corporation (UNO)
Unocal Corporation (UCL)
UNOVA, Inc. (UNA)
UNUM Corporation (UND)
UNUM Corporation (UNM)
UPM-Kymmene (UPM)
Urban Shopping Centers, Inc. (URB)
URS Corporation (URS)
Urstadt Biddle Properties Inc. (UBP)
Urstadt Biddle Properties Inc. (UBPA)
US Airways Group, Inc. (U)
U.S. Bancorp (USB)
U.S. Can Corporation (USC)
U.S. Foodservice (UFS)
U.S. Home Corporation (UH)
U.S. Industries, Inc. (USI)
U.S. Restaurant Properties, Inc. (USV)
U.S. Restaurant Properties, Inc. (USVPRA)
U.S. Trust Corporation (UTC)
USB Capital II (USBPRA)
USEC Inc. (USU)
USG Corporation (USG)
USLIFE Income Fund, Inc. (UIF)
UST Inc. (UST)
USX Capital LLC (XLCPR)
USX Capital Trust I (XPRZ)
USX-Marathon Group (MRO)
USX-Marathon Group (XPRA)
USX-U.S. Steel Group (X)
Utah Medical Products, Inc. (UM)

COMPANY (SYMBOL)

UtiliCorp Capital, L.P. (UCUPRC)
UtiliCorp United Inc. (UCU)

V

Vail Resorts, Inc. (MTN)
Valassis Communications, Inc. (VCI)
Valero Energy Corporation (VLO)
Valhi, Inc. (VHI)
Valley National Bancorp (VLY)
Valmet Oy (MX)
Valspar Corporation (The) (VAL)
Value City Department Stores, Inc. (VCD)
Van Kampen Advantage Municipal Income Trust (VKA)
Van Kampen Advantage Pennsylvania Municipal Income Trust (VAP)
Van Kampen Bond Fund (VBF)
Van Kampen California Quality Municipal Trust (VQC)
Van Kampen California Value Municipal Income Trust (VCV)
Van Kampen Convertible Securities Fund (VXS)
Van Kampen Florida Quality Municipal Trust (VFM)
Van Kampen High Income Trust (VIT)
Van Kampen High Income Trust II (VLT)
Van Kampen Income Trust (VIN)
Van Kampen Investment Grade Municipal Trust (VIG)
Van Kampen Municipal Income Trust (VMT)
Van Kampen Municipal Opportunity Trust (VMO)
Van Kampen Municipal Opportunity Trust II (VOT)
Van Kampen Municipal Trust (VKQ)
Van Kampen New York Quality Municipal Trust (VNM)
Van Kampen New York Value Municipal Income Trust (VNV)
Van Kampen Ohio Quality Municipal Trust (VOQ)
Van Kampen Pennsylvania Quality Municipal Trust (VPQ)
Van Kampen Pennsylvania Value Municipal Income Trust (VPV)
Van Kampen Senior Income Trust (VVR)
Van Kampen Strategic Sector Municipal Trust (VKS)
Van Kampen Trust for Insured Municipals (VIM)
Van Kampen Trust for Investment Grade California Municipals (VIC)

COMPANY (SYMBOL)

Van Kampen Trust for Investment Grade
  Florida Municipals (VTF)
Van Kampen Trust for Investment Grade
  Municipals (VGM)
Van Kampen Trust for Investment Grade
  New Jersey Municipals (VTJ)
Van Kampen Trust for Investment Grade
  New York Municipals (VTN)
Van Kampen Trust for Investment Grade
  Pennsylvania Municipals (VTP)
Van Kampen Value Municipal Income Trust
  (VKV)
Varco International, Inc. (VRC)
Varian Medical Systems, Inc. (VAR)
Vastar Resources, Inc. (VRI)
VEBA Aktiengesellschaft (VEB)
Venator Group, Inc. (Z)
Ventas, Inc. (VTR)
Veritas DGC Inc. (VTS)
Vertex Communications Corporation (VTX)
Vesta Insurance Group, Inc. (VTA)
Vestaur Securities, Inc. (VES)
VF Corporation (VFC)
Viacom Inc. (VIA)
Viacom Inc. (VIAB)
Viad Corp (VVI)
Viad Corp (VVIPR)
Vina Concha y Toro S.A. (VCO)
Vintage Petroleum, Inc. (VPI)
Virginia Electric and Power Company
  (VEA)
Virginia Electric and Power Company
  (VELPRE)
Virginia Power Capital Trust I (VELPRT)
Vishay Intertechnology, Inc. (VSH)
Vitro, Sociedad Anonima (VTO)
Vlasic Foods International Inc. (VL)
Vodafone AirTouch PLC (VOD)
Volt Information Sciences, Inc. (VOL)
Vornado Realty Trust (VNO)
Vornado Realty Trust (VNOPRA)
Vornado Realty Trust (VNOPRB)
Vulcan Materials Company (VMC)

W
W. R. Grace & Co. (GRA)
W. W. Grainger, Inc. (GWW)
Wabash National Corporation (WNC)
Wachovia Corporation (WB)
Wackenhut Corporation (The) (WAK)
Wackenhut Corporation (The) (WAKB)
Wackenhut Corrections Corporation
  (WHC)
Waddell & Reed Financial, Inc. (WDR)

COMPANY (SYMBOL)

Waddell & Reed Financial, Inc. (WDRB)
Walden Residential Properties Inc. (WDN)
Walden Residential Properties Inc.
  (WDNPRB)
Walden Residential Properties Inc.
  (WDNPRD)
Walden Residential Properties Inc.
  (WDNPRS)
Walgreen Co. (WAG)
Wallace Computer Services, Inc. (WCS)
Wal-Mart Stores, Inc. (WMT)
Walt Disney Company (The) (DIS)
Walter Industries, Inc. (WLT)
Warnaco Group, Inc. (The) (WAC)
Warner-Lambert Company (WLA)
Washington Gas Light Company (WGL)
Washington Homes, Inc. (WHI)
Washington Mutual Inc. (WM)
Washington Post Company (The) (WPO)
Washington Real Estate Investment Trust
  (WRE)
Waste Management, Inc. (WMI)
Waterlink, Inc. (WLK)
Waters Corporation (WAT)
Watkins-Johnson Company (WJ)
Watsco, Inc. (WSO)
Watson Pharmaceuticals, Inc. (WPI)
Watts Industries, Inc. (WTS)
Wausau-Mosinee Paper Corporation
  (WMO)
WBK STRYPES Trust (WPK)
Weatherford International Inc. (WFT)
WEC Capital Trust I (WECPRA)
Weeks Corporation (WKS)
Weeks Corporation (WKSPRA)
Weider Nutrition International, Inc. (WNI)
Weingarten Realty Investors (WRI)
Weingarten Realty Investors (WRIPRA)
Weingarten Realty Investors (WRIPRC)
Weirton Steel Corporation (WS)
Weis Markets, Inc. (WMK)
Wellman, Inc. (WLM)
WellPoint Health Networks Inc. (WLP)
Wells Fargo & Company (New) (WFC)
Wells Fargo & Company (New) (WFCPRB)
Wendy's Financing I (WENPRT)
Wendy's International, Inc. (WEN)
Wesco International, Inc. (WCC)
West Penn Power Company (WQP)
West Penn Power Company (WSPPR)
West Pharmaceutical Services, Inc. (WST)
Westcoast Energy Inc. (WE)
Westcorp (WES)
Western Digital Corporation (WDC)

COMPANY (SYMBOL)

Western Gas Resources, Inc. (WGR)
Western Gas Resources, Inc. (WGRPR)
Western Gas Resources, Inc. (WGRPRA)
Western Resources Capital I (WRPRA)
Western Resources Capital II (WRPRB)
Western Resources, Inc. (WR)
Westfield America, Inc. (WEA)
Westpac Banking Corporation (WBK)
Westvaco Corporation (W)
Westwood One, Inc. (WON)
Weyerhaeuser Company (WY)
Whirlpool Corporation (WHR)
White Mountains Insurance Group, Inc.
　(WTM)
Whitman Corporation (WH)
WHX Corporation (WHX)
WHX Corporation (WHXPR)
WHX Corporation (WHXPRB)
WICOR Inc. (WIC)
Willamette Industries, Inc. (WLL)
Willbros Group, Inc. (WG)
Williams Coal Seam Gas Royalty Trust
　(WTU)
Williams Companies, Inc. (The) (WMB)
Williams-Sonoma, Inc. (WSM)
Wilmington Trust Corporation (WL)
Wilshire Oil Company of Texas (WOC)
Windmere-Durable Holdings, Inc. (WND)
Winn-Dixie Stores, Inc. (WIN)
Winnebago Industries, Inc. (WGO)
Winston Hotels, Inc. (WXH)
Winston Hotels, Inc. (WXHPRA)
Wisconsin Energy Corporation (WEC)
Wiser Oil Company (The) (WZR)
Wm. Wrigley Jr. Company (WWY)
WMC Limited (WMC)

COMPANY (SYMBOL)

WMS Industries Inc. (WMS)
Wolverine Tube, Inc. (WLV)
Wolverine World Wide, Inc. (WWW)
World Color Press, Inc. (WRC)
World Fuel Services Corporation (INT)
Worldtex, Inc. (WTX)
Worldwide DollarVest Fund, Inc. (WDV)
WPS Resources Corporation (WPS)
WPSR Capital Trust I (WPSPRA)
Wyman-Gordon Company (WYG)
Wynn's International, Inc. (WN)

X
Xerox Corporation (XRX)
XL Capital LTD. (XL)
Xtra Corporation (XTR)

Y
Yankee Energy System, Inc. (YES)
Yanzhou Coal Mining Company Limited
　(YZC)
York International Corporation (YRK)
Yorkshire Capital Trust I (YCT)
Young & Rubicam Inc. (YNR)
YPF Sociedad Anonima (YPF)

Z
Zale Corporation (ZLC)
Zapata Corporation (ZAP)
Zemex Corporation (ZMX)
Zenith National Insurance Corp. (ZNT)
Zenix Income Fund Inc. (ZIF)
Ziff-Davis Inc. (ZD)
ZDNET (ZDZ)
Zweig Fund, Inc. (The) (ZF)
Zweig Total Return Fund, Inc. (The) (ZTR)

American Stock Exchange

COMPANY (SYMBOL)

A
Acadiana Bancshares, Inc. (ANA)
Acme United Corporation (ACW)
Adrien Arpel, Inc. (RPL)
Advanced Magnetics, Inc. (AVM)
Advanced Photonix, Inc. (API)
Aegis Realty, Inc. (AER)
AeroCentury Corp. (ACY)
Aerosonic Corporation (AIM)
Air & Water Technologies Corporation
　(AWT)
Air & Water Technologies Corporation
　(AWT/WS)
Alarmguard Holdings, Inc. (AGD)

COMPANY (SYMBOL)

Alba-Waldensian, Inc. (AWS)
Alliance Bancorp of New England, Inc.
　(ANE)
Allied Digital Technologies Corp. (ADK)
Allied Research Corp. (ALR)
Allou Health & Beauty Care, Inc. (ALU)
Alternative Living Services, Inc. (ALI)
Aluminum Company of America (AA)
American Bank of Connecticut (BKC)
American Biltrite Inc. (ABL)
American Insured Mortgage Investors
　(AIA)
American Insured Mortgage Series 85 (AII)
American Insured Mortgage Series 86 (AIJ)

COMPANY (SYMBOL)

American Insured Mortgage Series 88 (AIK)
American Real Estate Investment Corp. (REA)
American Shared Hospital Services (AMS)
American Technical Ceramics Corp. (AMK)
American Vanguard Corporation (AVD)
Ampal American Israel Corporation (AIS)
Ampex Corporation (AXC)
AMTEC, Inc. (ATC)
Amwest Insurance Group, Inc. (AMW)
Andrea Electronics Corporation (AND)
Angeles Mortgage Investment Trust (ANM)
Anworth Asset Mortgage Corporation (ANH)
Apex Silver Mines Limited (SIL)
Apple Orthodontix, Inc. (AOI)
ARC International Corporation (ATV)
Arizona Land Income Corporation (AZL)
Arm Financial Group (ARM)
Armor Holdings, Inc. (ABE)
Arrhythmia Research Technology Inc. (HRT)
ARV Assisted Living, Inc. (SRS)
Assisted Living Concepts, Inc. (ALF)
AT Plastics Inc. (ATJ)
Atlantic Premium Brands Ltd (ABR)
Atlantic Tele-Network, Inc. (ANK)
Atlantis Plastics, Inc. (AGH)
Audio Book Club, Inc. (KLB)
Audio Communications Network, Inc. (ANI)
Audiovox Corporation (VOX)
Audits and Surveys Worldwide, Inc. (ASW)
AutoBond Acceptance Corporation (ABD)
Autotote Corporation (TTE)
Avalon Holdings Corporation (AWX)
Avenue Entertainment Group, Inc. (PIX)
Aviva Petroleum, Inc. (AVV)
Axogen Limited (AXG/U)
Azco Mining Inc. (AZC)

B

Badger Meter, Inc. (BMI)
Baker (Michael) Corporation (BKR)
Balanced Care Corporation (BAL)
Balchem Corporation (BCP)
Baldwin Technology Company, Inc. (BLD)
Bar Harbor Bankshares, Inc. (BHB)
Barnwell Industries, Inc. (BRN)
Barrister Information Systems Corp. (BIS)
Bay State Bancorp (BYS)
Bayard Drilling Technologies, Inc. (BDI)
Baycorp Holdings, Ltd. (MWH)
Bayou Steel Corporation (BYX)
Beard Company (BOC)
Bema Gold Corporation (BGO)

COMPANY (SYMBOL)

Bentley Pharmaceuticals, Inc. (BNT)
Bergstrom Capital Corporation (BEM)
Besicorp Group, Inc. (BGI/EC)
Bethlehem Corporation (The) (BET)
BFC Construction Corporation (BNC)
BFX Hospitality Group, Inc. (BFX)
BHC Communications, Inc. (BHC)
Bibb Company (The) (BIB)
Big City Radio, Inc. (YFM)
Binks Sames Corporation (BIN)
Bio-Rad Laboratories, Inc. (BIO)
Bio-Rad Laboratories, Inc. (BIO/B)
Biscayne Apparel, Inc. (BHA)
Blair Corporation (BL)
BLC Financial Services, Inc. (BCL)
Blimpie International, Inc. (BLM)
Blonder Tongue Laboratories, Inc. (BDR)
Boddie-Noell Properties, Inc. (BNP)
Bolt Technology Corporation (BTJ)
Boots and Coots International Well (WEL)
Bowl America, Inc. (WWL/A)
Bowlin Outdoor Advertising & Travel (BWN)
Bowmar Instrument Corp. (BOM)
Bowne & Co., Inc. (BNE)
Brad Ragan, Inc. (BRD)
Bridge View Bancorp (BVD)
Brilliant Digital Entertainment, Inc. (BDE)
British American Tobacco Industries (BTI)
Bull & Bear U.S. Govt. Securities, Fund (BBG)

C

Coast Distribution System, Inc. (The) (CRV)
Crystallex International Corporation (KRY)
Cubic Corporation (CUB)
CVB Financial Corp. (CVB)
CVF Corporation (CNV)

D

Dairy Mart Convenience Stores, Inc. (DMC/A)
Dairy Mart Convenience Stores, Inc. (DMC/B)
Dallas Gold & Silver Exchange, Inc. (DLS)
Danielson Holding Corporation (DHC)
Darling International Inc. (DAR)
Dataram Corporation (DTM)
Daxor Corporation (DXR)
Dayton Mining Corporation (DAY)
Decorator Industries, Inc. (DII)
Del Laboratories, Inc. (DLI)
DenAmerica Corp. (DEN)
Devon Energy Corporation (DVN)
DeWolfe Companies, Inc. (The) (DWL)
Dia Met Minerals Ltd. (DMM/A)

COMPANY (SYMBOL)

Dia Met Minerals Ltd. (DMM/B)
Digital Power Corporation (DPW)
Digital Power Corporation (DPW/WS)
Diodes Incorporated (DIO)
Diversified Corporate Resources, Inc. (HIR)
Dixon Ticonderoga Co. (DXT)

E

Earl Scheib, Inc. (ESH)
Eastern Company (The) (EML)
Echo Bay Mines Ltd. (ECO)
Ecology and Environment, Inc. (EEI)
Edperbrascan Corporation (EBC)
EFC Bancorp, Inc. (EFC)
El Paso Electric Company (EE)
Electrochemical Industries (1952) Ltd. (EIL)
Ellsworth Convertible Growth and Income
  Fund (ECF)
Emerging Communications, Inc. (ECM)
Emeritus Corporation (ESC)
Emerson Radio Corporation (MSN)
Empire of Carolina, Inc. (EMP)
Emultek, Ltd (EMU)
Endorex Corporation (DOR)
Energy Research Corporation (ERC)
Environmental Safeguards, Inc. (EVV)
Environmental Tectonics Corp. (ETC)
Envirotest Systems Corp. (ENR)
Enzo Biochem, Inc. (ENZ)
Equality Bancorp (EBI)
Equity Income Fund, 1St Exchange (ATF)
Espey Manufacturing & Electronics (ESP)
Essex Bancorp Inc. (ESX)
ETZ Lavuad Limited (ETZ)
ETZ Lavuad Limited (ETZ/A)
EXX, Inc. (EXX/A)
EXX, Inc. (EXX/B)
E-Z-EM, Inc. (EZM/A)
E-Z-EM, Inc. (EZM/B)

F

FAB Industries, Inc. (FIT)
Fall River Gas Company (FAL)
Falmouth Bancorp, Inc. (FCB)
Female Health Company (The) (FHC)
FFP Marketing Company, Inc. (FMM)
FFP Partners, LP (FFP)
First National Corporation of Orangeburg
  (FNC)
First Philson Financial Corporation (FPB)
First West Virginia Bancorp, Inc. (FWV)
Firstfed America Bancorp, Inc. (FAB)
Flanigan's Enterprises, Inc. (BDL)
Florida Public Utilities Company (FPU)

COMPANY (SYMBOL)

Foodarama Supermarkets, Inc. (FSM)
Forest Laboratories, Inc. (FRX)
Fortune Natural Resources Corporation
  (FPX)
Franklin Capital Corporation (FKL)
Franklin Select Realty Trust (FSN)
Frequency Electronics, Inc. (FEI)
Friedman Industries Inc. (FRD)
Frisch's Restaurants, Inc. (FRS)
Frontier Adjusters of America, Inc.
  (FAJ)

G

G.A. Financial (GAF)
Gamma Biologicals, Inc. (GBL)
Garan, Incorporated (GAN)
Gaylord Container Corporation (GCR)
Gencor Industries Inc. (GX)
General Automation, Inc. (GA)
General Employment Enterprises, Inc.
  (JOB)
General Microwave Corporation (GMW)
Genovese Drug Stores, Inc. (GDX/A)
Getchell Gold Corporation (GGO)
Giant Food, Inc. (GFS/A)
Gildan Activeware, Inc. (GIL)
GK Intelligent Systems, Inc. (GKI)
Glacier Water Services, Inc. (HOO)
Glacier Water Services, Inc. (HOOA)
Glatfelter (P.H.) Company (GLT)
Global Ocean Carriers Limited (GLO)
Globalink, Inc. (GNK)
Golden Star Resources, Ltd (GSR)
Goldfield Corporation (The) (GV)
Golf Trust of America, Inc. (GTA)
Gorman-Rupp Company (The) (GRC)
Go-Video, Inc. (VCR)
Graham Corporation (GHM)
Greenbriar Corporation (The) (GBR)
Grey Wolf, Inc. (GW)
Greyhound Lines, Inc. (BUS)
Gristede's Sloan's, Inc. (GRI)
Grove Property Trust (GVE)
Grupo Simec, S.A. De CV. (SIM)
Gull Laboratories, Inc (GUL)

H

Halifax Corporation (HX)
Hallmark Financial Services, Inc. (HAF)
Hallwood Energy Partners, L.P. (HEP)
Hallwood Energy Partners, L.P. (HEP/C)
Hallwood Realty Partners, L.P. (Units)
  (HRY)
Halsey Drug Co., Inc. (HDG)

COMPANY (SYMBOL)

Halter Marine Group, Inc. (HLX)
Hampton Industries, Inc. (HAI)
Hanger Orthopedic Group, Inc. (HGR)
Hanover Capital Mortgage Holdings, Inc.
 (HCM)
Hanover Capital Mortgage Holdings, Inc.
 (HCM/WS)
Hanover Direct, Inc. (HNV)
Harold's Stores, Inc. (HLD)
Hasbro, Inc. (HAS)
Hastings Manufacturing Company (HMF)
Hawaiian Airlines, Inc. (HA)
Haywood Bancshares, Inc. (HBS)
Health-Chem Corporation (HCH)
Healthy Planet Products Inc. (HPP)
Heartland Partners, L.P. (HTL)
HEARx Ltd. (EAR)
Hector Communications Corporation
 (HCT)
HEICO Corporation (HEI)
Heist (C.H.) Corp. (HST)
Helm Capital Group, Inc. (HHH)
Helmstar Group, Inc. (HLM)
Hi-Shear Technology Corp. (HSR)
HMG/Courtland Properties, Inc. (HMG)
Holly Corporation (HOC)
Home Security International, Inc. (HIS)
Hooper Holmes, Inc. (HH)
Horizon Pharmacies, Inc. (HZP)
Hospitality Worldwide Services Inc. (HWS)
Host Funding, Inc. (HFD)
Hovnanian Enterprises, Inc. (HOV)
Howard B. Wolf, Inc. (HBW)
Hudson General Corporation (HGC)
Hungarian Telephone & Cable Corp. (HTC)

I

IGI, Inc. (IG)
ILX Resorts, Incorporated (ILX)
Impac Commercial Holdings, Inc. (ICH)
Impac Mortgage Holdings, Inc. (IMH)
Imperial Holly Corporation (IHK)
Imperial Oil Limited (IMO)
Income Opportunity Realty Trust (IOT)
Independent Bankshares, Inc. (IBK)
Infocure Corporation (INC)
InSite Vision Incorporated (ISV)
Instron Corporation (ISN)
Integra, Inc. (IGR)
Integrated Technology USA, Inc. (ITH)
Integrated Technology USA, Inc. (ITH/WS)
Intelligent Controls, Inc. (ITC/EC)
Intelligent Polymers Limited (IXP/U)
Intelligent Systems Corporation (INS)

COMPANY (SYMBOL)

InterCept Group, Inc. (The) (ICG)
Interchange Financial Services Corp. (ISB)
InterDigital Communications Corp. (IDC)
Interlott Technologies, Inc. (ILI)
Intermagnetics General Corporation (IMG)
International Airline Support Group, Inc.
 (YLF)
International Comfort Products Corp. (ICP)
International Remote Imaging Systems, Inc.
 (IRI)
Interstate General Company L.P. (IGC)
InterSystems, Inc. (II)
Intertape Polymer Group Inc. (ITP)
Iomed, Inc. (IOX)
IPC Information Systems, Inc. (IPI)
IVAX Corporation (IVX)

J

Jaclyn, Inc. (JLN)
Jalate, Ltd. (JLT)
Jan Bell Marketing, Inc. (JBM)
Jetronic Industries, Inc. (JET)
Jinpan International Limited (JST)
Joule' Inc. (JOL)
JWGenesis Financial Corp. (JWG)

K

Kafus Environmental Industries Ltd. (KS)
Kankakee Bancorp, Inc. (KNK)
Katz Digital Technologies, Inc. (KTZ)
KBK Capital Corporation (KBK)
Keane, Inc. (KEA)
Kentucky First Bancorp Inc. (KYF)
KFX Inc. (KFX)
Killearn Properties, Inc. (KPI)
Kinark Corporation (KIN)
King Power International Group Co., LTD.
 (KPG)
Kit Manufacturing Company (KIT)
Koger Equity, Inc. (KE)
Krause's Furniture, Inc. (KFI)
KRUG International Corp. (KRG)
KV Pharmaceutical Company (KV/A)
KV Pharmaceutical Company (KV/B)

L

LaBarge, Inc. (LB)
Lancer Corporation (LAN)
Landauer, Inc. (LDR)
Laser Technology Inc. (LSR)
Lazare Kaplan International, Inc. (LKI)
Leather Factory, Inc. (The) (TLF)
Lillian Vernon Corporation (LVC)
Local Financial Corporation (LO)

COMPANY (SYMBOL)

LXR Biotechnology Inc. (LXR)
Lynch Corporation (LGL)

M

Magicworks Entertainment, Inc. (MJK)
Magnum Hunter Resources, Inc. (MHR)
MAI Systems Corporation (NOW)
Maine Public Service Company (MAP)
Malibu Entertainment International Inc.
  (MBE)
Marlton Technologies, Inc. (MTY)
Marquee Group, Inc. (The) (MRT)
Massachusetts Health and Education
  (MHE)
MATEC Corporation (MXC)
Maui Land & Pineapple Company, Inc.
  (MLP)
Maxim Pharmaceuticals, Inc. (MMP)
Maxim Pharmaceuticals, Inc. (MMP/WS)
Maxx Petroleum Ltd. (MMX)
MAXXAM Inc. (MXM)
MC Shipping Inc. (MCX)
McRae Industries, Inc. (MRI/A)
McRae Industries, Inc. (MRI/B)
Measurement Specialties, Inc. (MSS)
Medco Research, Inc. (MRE)
Media General, Inc. (MEG/A)
Media Logic, Inc. (TST)
Medtox Scientific, Inc. (TOX)
Merchants Group, Inc. (MGP)
Mercury Air Group, Inc. (MAX)
Meridian Industrial Trust, Inc. (MDN/WS)
Merrimac Industries, Inc. (MRM)
Metrika Systems, Inc. (MKA)
Metromedia International Group, Inc.
  (MMG)
Michael Anthony Jewelers, Inc. (MAJ)
Mid Penn Bancorp (MBP)
Mid-America Bancorp (MAB)
Midcoast Energy Resources, Inc. (MRS)
Midland Company (The) (MLA)
Midland Resources, Inc. (MLD)
Midland Resources, Inc. (MLD/WS)
MidSouth Bancorp (MSL)
Milestone Scientific, Inc. (MS)
Minnesota Power & Light Company (MPLA)
Mission West Properties (MSW)
Monongahela Power Company (MPNA)
Monongahela Power Company (MPNC)
Moog Inc. (MOG/A)
Moog Inc. (MOG/B)
Moore Medical Corp. (MMD)
Morgan Group, Inc. (The) (MG)
Morgan's Foods, Inc. (MR)
Movie Star, Inc. (MSI)

COMPANY (SYMBOL)

Msr Exploration Limited (MSR)
Multigraphics, Inc. (MTI)
Myers Industries, Inc. (MYE)

N

National Bancshares Corp. of Texas (NBT)
National Beverage Corp. (FIZ)
National Gas & Oil Company (NLG)
National Health Realty, Inc. (NHR)
National Healthcare Corp. (NHC)
National Realty, L.P. (Units) (NLP)
NeoPharm, Inc. (NEO)
New Mexico and Arizona Land Co. (NZ)
NFC Public Limited Company (NFC)
Noble International, Ltd. (NIL)
Nordic American Tanker Shipping Ltd
  (NAT)
North American Vaccine, Inc. (NVX)
Northeast Bancorp (NBN)
Novavax, Inc. (NOX)
nStor Technologies, Inc. (NSO)
NTN Communications, Inc. (NTN)
NTN Communications, Inc. (NTN/WS)
Numac Energy Inc. (NMC)
NVR, Inc (NVR)

O

Oncor, Inc. (ONM)
OncorMed, Inc. (ONC)
One Liberty Properties, Inc. (OLP)
O'Okiep Copper Company Limited (OKP)
Organogenesis Inc. (ORG)
Oriole Homes Corp. (OHC/A)
Oriole Homes Corp. (OHC/B)
Orleans Homebuilders, Inc. (OHB)
Oshman's Sporting Goods, Inc. (OSH)
O'Sullivan Corporation (OSL)

P

PAB Bankshares (PAB)
Pacific Enterprises (PETA)
Pacific Enterprises (PETB)
Pacific Enterprises (PETC)
Pacific Enterprises (PETD)
Pacific Gas & Electric Co. (PCGA)
Pacific Gas & Electric Co. (PCGB)
Pacific Gas & Electric Co. (PCGC)
Pacific Gas & Electric Co. (PCGD)
Pacific Gas & Electric Co. (PCGE)
Pacific Gas & Electric Co. (PCGG)
Pacific Gas & Electric Co. (PCGH)
Pacific Gas & Electric Co. (PCGI)
Pacific Gas & Electric Co. (PCGU)
Pacific Gas & Electric Co. (PCGX)
Pacific Gas & Electric Co. (PCGY)

COMPANY (SYMBOL)

Pacific Gas & Electric Co. (PCGZ)
Pacific Gateway Properties, Inc. (PGP)
Pacific Pharmaceuticals, Inc. (PHA)
Pacific Research & Engineering Corp.
 (PXE)
Pacific Research & Engineering Corp.
 (PXE/WS)
Pamida Holdings Corporation (PAM)
Park National Corporation (PRK)
Paxson Communications Corporation
 (PAX)
PC Quote, Inc. (PQT)
Pentegra Dental Group, Inc. (PEN)
Peoples Holding Company (The) (PHC)
Peoples Telephone Company, Inc. (PHO)
Perini Corporation (PCR)
Phonetel Technologies, Inc. (PHN)
Pico Products, Inc. (PPI)
Piedmont Bancorp, Inc. (PDB)
Pinnacle Bancshares, Inc. (PLE)
Pitt-Des Moines, Inc. (PDM)
Pittsburgh & West Virginia Railroad (PW)
Plains Resources, Inc. (PLX)
Playcore, Inc. (PCO)
PLC Systems Inc. (PLC)
PLM International, Inc. (PLM)
Plymouth Rubber Company, Inc. (PLR/A)
Plymouth Rubber Company, Inc. (PLR/B)
PMC Capital, Inc. (PMC)
PMC Commercial Trust (PCC)
Polk Audio, Inc. (PKA)
PolyMedica Corporation (PM)
Polyphase Corporation (PLY)
PolyVision Corporation (PLI)
Porta Systems Corp. (PSI)
Premier Bancshares, Inc. (PMB)
Pre-Paid Legal Services, Inc. (PPD)
Presidential Realty Corporation (PDL/A)
Presidential Realty Corporation (PDL/B)
Price Communications Corporation (PR)
Proactive Technologies, Inc. (PTE)
Professional Bancorp (MDB)
Professional Dental Technologies, Inc.
 (PRO/EC)
Property Capital Trust (PCT)
Provena Foods, Inc. (PZA)
Providence and Worcester Railroad Co.
 (PWX)
PS Business Parks, Inc. (PSB)
Psychemedics Corporation (PMD)

Q

QC Optics, Inc. (OPC)
QC Optics, Inc. (OPC/WS)
Quebecor Inc. (PQB)

COMPANY (SYMBOL)

R

Ramco Energy PLC (RCO)
Randers Group Incorporated (The)
 (RGI/EC)
Redwood Empire Bancorp (REB)
Reeds Jewelers, Inc. (RJI)
REFAC Technology Development Corp.
 (REF)
Regal-Beloit Corporation (RBC)
Resource Bankshares Corporation (RBV)
Resources Asset Investment Trust (RAS)
Rexx Environmental Corporation (REX)
RF Power Products, Inc. (RFP)
Ribogene, Inc. (RBO)
Richmont Mines, Inc. (RIC)
Richton International Corporation (RHT)
Rio Algom Ltd. (ROM)
Riveria Tool Company (RTC)
Riviera Holdings Corporation (RIV)
Roberts Pharmaceutical Corporation (RPC)
Roberts Realty Investors, Inc. (RPI)
Rogers Corporation (ROG)
Rotonics Manufacturing, Inc. (RMI)
Rottlund Company, Inc. (The) (RH)
Royal Oak Mines Inc. (RYO)

S

S. Y. Bancorp, Inc. (SYI)
Saba Petroleum Company (SAB)
Saga Communications, Inc. (SGA)
San Diego Gas & Electric Company
 (SDOA)
San Diego Gas & Electric Company
 (SDOB)
San Diego Gas & Electric Company
 (SDOC)
San Diego Gas & Electric Company
 (SDOH)
Santa Fe Gaming Corporation (SGM)
SBM Industries, Inc. (SBM)
Scandinavia Company, Inc. (The) (SCF)
Scope Industries (SCP)
Scotland Bancorp (SSB)
Seaboard Corporation (SEB)
Security Associates International, Inc. (IDL)
Selas Corporation of America (SLS)
Selfcare, Inc. (SLF)
Sentry Technology Corporation (SKV)
Seracare, Inc. (SRK)
Servotronics, Inc. (SVT)
Seven Seas Petroleum Inc. (SEV)
Sheffield Pharmaceuticals, Inc. (SHM)
Sherwood Brands, Inc. (SHD)
Sherwood Brands, Inc. (SHD/WS)
Showpower, Inc. (SHO)

COMPANY (SYMBOL)

Siem Industries Inc. (NXA)
SIFCO Industries, Inc. (SIF)
Signal Technology Corporation (STZ)
Silverado Foods, Inc. (SLV)
SJW Corporation (SJW)
Smith (A.O.) Corporation (SMC/A)
Softnet Systems, Inc. (SOF)
Soligen Technologies, Inc. (SGT/EC)
Sonic Foundry, Inc. (SFO)
Sonus Corporation (SSN)
Southern Banc Company, Inc. (The) (SRN)
Southern California Edison Company
  (SCEB)
Southern California Edison Company
  (SCEC)
Southern California Edison Company
  (SCED)
Southern California Edison Company
  (SCEE)
Southern California Edison Company
  (SCE/Q)
SouthFirst Bancshares, Inc. (SZB)
Southwest Georgia Financial Corp. (SGB)
Spatial Technology, Inc. (STY)
Specialty Chemical Resources, Inc. (CHM)
Spinnaker Industries, Inc. (SKK)
Spinnaker Industries, Inc. (SKK/A)
Sports Club Company, Inc. (The) (SCY)
Stage II Apparel Corp. (SA)
Standard Automotive Corporation (AJX)
Starwood Financial Trust (APT)
Stephan Company (The) (TSC)
Sterling Capital Corporation (SPR)
Stevens International, Inc. (SVG/A)
Stevens International, Inc. (SVG/B)
Stillwater Mining Company (SWC)
Stone Street Bancorp, Inc. (SSM)
Storage Computer Corporation (SOS)
Strategia Corporation (SAA)
Stratesec, Incorporated (SFT)
Sulcus Hospitality Technologies Corp. (SUL)
Sunair Electronics, Inc. (SNR)
Superior Uniform Group, Inc. (SGC)
Supreme Industries, Inc. (STS)
Surety Capital Corporation (SRY)
Sussex Bancorp (SBB)
SVI Holdings, Inc. (SVI)
Sybron Chemicals Inc. (SYC)

T
Tab Products, Co. (TBP)
Tag-it Pacific, Inc. (TAG)
Team, Inc. (TMI)
Teche Holding Company (TSH)

COMPANY (SYMBOL)

Tech/Ops Sevcon, Inc. (TO)
Tejon Ranch Company (TRC)
Telephone and Data Systems, Inc. (TDS)
Telephone and Data Systems, Inc. (TDSA)
Telephone and Data Systems, Inc. (TDSB)
Teletouch Communications, Inc. (TLL)
Teletouch Communications, Inc. (TLL/WS)
Tenera, L.P. (TNR)
Texarkana First Financial Corporation
  (FTF)
Texas Biotechnology Corporation (TXB)
Texas Biotechnology Corporation
  (TXB/WS)
Thackeray Corporation (THK)
Thermedics Detection, Inc. (TDX)
Thermedics Inc. (TMD)
Thermo Bioanalysis Corp. (TBA)
Thermo Cardiosystems, Inc. (TCA)
Thermo Ecotek Corporation (TCK)
Thermo Fibergen, Inc. (TFG)
Thermo Fibertek, Inc. (TFT)
Thermo Instrument Systems Inc. (THI)
Thermo Optek Corporation (TOC)
Thermo Power Corporation (THP)
Thermo Process Systems, Inc. (TTT)
Thermo Remediation Inc. (THN)
Thermo Sentron Inc. (TSR)
Thermo Vision Corporation (VIZ)
Thermo Voltek Corp. (TVL)
ThermoLase Corporation (TLZ)
ThermoLase Corporation (TLZ.U)
ThermoQuest Corporation (TMQ)
ThermoSpectra Corporation (THS)
ThermoTrex Corporation (TKN)
Thermwood Corporation (THM)
Three Rivers Financial Corporation (THR)
Tipperary Corporation (TPY)
Todhunter International, Inc. (THT)
Tofutti Brands Inc. (TOF)
Toledo Edison Company (TEDA)
Toledo Edison Company (TEDB)
Toledo Edison Company (TEDC)
Toledo Edison Company (TEDD)
Tompkins County Trustco, Inc. (TMP)
Top Air Manufacturing, Inc. (TPC)
Top Source Technologies, Inc. (TPS)
Torotel, Inc. (TTL)
Trans World Airlines, Inc. (TWA)
Trans World Airlines, Inc. (TWA/WS)
Transfinancial Holdings, Inc. (TFH)
Trans-Lux Corporation (TLX)
Transmontaigne Inc. (TMG)
Transnational Financial Corporation (TFN)
Trex Medical Corporation (TXM)

COMPANY (SYMBOL)

Trinitech Systems, Inc. (TSI)
Tubos de Acero de Mexico (TAM)
Turner Corporation (The) (TUR)

U

U. S. B. Holding Company, Inc. (UBH)
Unapix Entertainment, Inc. (UPX)
Uniflex, Inc. (UFX)
Unilab Corporation (ULB)
Unimar Company (UMR)
Uni-Marts, Inc. (UNI)
Unique Mobility, Inc. (UQM)
United Capital Corporation (AFP)
United Foods, Inc. (UFD/A)
United Foods, Inc. (UFD/B)
United Mobile Homes, Inc. (UMH)
United States Cellular Corporation (USM)
United States Exploration, Inc. (UXP)
UNITED-GUARDIAN, INC. (UG)
Unitel Video, Inc. (UNV)
UNITIL Corporation (UTL)
U.S. Bioscience, Inc. (UBS)
U.S. Liquids Inc. (USL)
UTI Energy Corp. (UTI)

V

Valley Forge Corporation (VF)
Valley Resources, Inc. (VR)
Versar, Inc. (VSR)
Viacom Inc. (VIA)
Viacom Inc. (VIA/B)
Viacom Inc. (VIA/WS/E)
Vicon Industries, Inc. (VII)
Video Services Corporation (VS)
Virco Manufacturing Corporation (VIR)

COMPANY (SYMBOL)

Vita Food Products, Inc. (VSF)
Vita Food Products, Inc. (VSF/WS)
Vulcan International Corp. (VUL)

W

Washington Real Estate Investment
  (WRE)
Washington Savings Bank (The) (WSB)
Watsco, Inc. (WSO/B)
Webco Industries, Inc. (WEB)
Wellco Enterprises, Inc. (WLC)
Wellsford Real Properties Inc. (WRP)
Wells-Gardner Electronics Corporation
  (WGA)
Wendt-Bristol Health Services (WMD)
Wendt-Bristol Health Services (WMD/WS)
Wesco Financial Corporation (WSC)
Western Investment Real Estate Trust
  (WIR)
Western Star Trucks Holdings, Ltd. (WSH)
Westower Corporation (WTW)
Westower Corporation (WTW/WS)
Whitman Education Group, Inc. (WIX)
Windsor Energy Corporation (WNS)
Winston Resources, Inc. (WRS)
Winton Financial Corporation (WFI)
Wireless Telecom Group, Inc. (WTT)
Wisconsin Power & Light Co. (WIS)

X

XCL Ltd. (XCL)

Z

Zevex International, Inc. (ZVX)
Ziegler Companies, Inc. (The) (ZCO)

NASDAQ

COMPANY (SYMBOL)

A

@plan.Inc. (APLN)
1-800 Contacts, Inc. (CTAV)
1-800-FLOWERS.COM, Inc. (FLWS)
1st Bancorp (FBCV)
1st Source Corporation (SRCE)
1st Source Corporation (SRCEP)
1st State Bancorp, Inc. (FSBC)
21st Century Holding Company (TCHC)
24/7 Media, Inc. (TFSM)
3CI Complete Compliance (TCCC)
3D Systems Corporation (TDSC)
3DX Technologies, Inc. (TDXT)
4 Kids Entertainment, Inc. (KIDE)

COMPANY (SYMBOL)

4Health, Inc. (HHHHW)
AAON, Inc. (AAON)
ABC Bancorp (ABCB)
ABC Dispensing Technologies (ABCC)
Aber Resources Ltd. (ABERF)
Abgenix, Inc. (ABGX)
ABIOMED, Inc. (ABMD)
AboveNet Communications, Inc. (ABOV)
Accel International (ACLE)
Access Anytime Bancorp, Inc. (AABC)
Access Solutions (ASICW)
Accredo Health, Inc. (ACDO)
Accrue Software, Inc. (ACRU)
Ace Cash Express, Inc. (AACE)

COMPANY (SYMBOL)

ACMAT Corporation (ACMTA)
Acorn Holding Corp. (AVCC)
Acrodyne Communications, Inc. (ACRO)
A.C.S. Electronics Limited (ACSEF)
Action Products International (APII)
Active Apparel Group, Inc. (AAGP)
Active Software, Inc. (ASWX)
Adams Golf, Inc. (ADGO)
Adaptec, Inc. (ADPT)
Adaptive Solutions, Inc. (ADSOW)
ADDvantage Media Group, Inc. (ADDM)
AdForce, Inc. (ADFC)
ADM Tronics Unlimited, Inc. (ADMT)
Admiralty Bancorp, Inc. (AAABB)
Advanced Aerodynamics & Structures, Inc.
  (AASI)
Advanced Environmental (AERTZ)
Advantage Bancorp, Inc. (AADV)
AEP Industries, Inc. (AEPI)
AES Corporation (The) (AESCW)
AFSALA Bancorp, Inc. (AFED)
Ag-Chem Equipment Co., Inc. (AGCH)
Agile Software Corporation (AGIL)
Agritope, Inc. (AGTOV)
Aid Auto Stores, Inc. (AIDAW)
Air Canada Corporation (ACNGF)
Aironet Wireless Communications (AIRO)
Ajay Sports, Inc. (AJAJU)
Ajay Sports, Inc. (AJAYP)
ALARIS Medical, Inc. (ALRS)
Albany Molecular Research, Inc. (AMRI)
Albion Banc Corp. (ALBC)
Alcohol Sensors International (ASIL)
Alcohol Sensors International (ASILZ)
Alexion Pharmaceuticals, Inc. (ALXN)
Allaire Corp. (ALLR)
Allegiance Telecom, Inc. (ALGX)
Allen Organ Company (AORGB)
Allergan Specialty Therapeutics, Inc.
  (ASTIV)
Alliance Financial Corp. (ALNC)
Alliance Resource Partners (ARLP)
Allied Holdings, Inc. (HAUL)
ALLIED Life Financial (ALFC)
Alloy Online, Inc. (ALOY)
Allscripts, Inc. (MDRX)
Allstate Financial Corporation (ASFN)
Aloette Cosmetics, Inc. (ALET)
Alpha Hospitality Corporation (ALHYW)
Alpha Industries, Inc. (ALHAA)
Alpha Microsystems (ALMI)
AlphaNet Solutions, Inc. (ALPH)
Altera Corporation (ALTR)
Alternate Postal Delivery (ALTD)
Amazon.com, Inc. (AMZN)

COMPANY (SYMBOL)

AMB Financial Group (AMFC)
AMBANC Corp. (AMBK)
AMCOL International (ACOL)
AMCON Distributing Company (DIST)
AMCOR Capital Corporation (ACAP)
Amcor Limited (AMCPF)
AMEDISYS, INC. (AMED)
AmerAlia, Inc. (AALA)
America First Apartment (APROZ)
American Aircarriers Support, Inc. (AIRS)
American Bio Medica Corp. (ABMC)
American Business Financial (ABFI)
American Champion (ACEI)
American Claims Evaluation (AMCE)
American Craft Brewing (ABREF)
American Dental Partners, Inc. (ADPI)
American Eagle Outfitters (AEOS)
American First Participating (AFPFZ)
American Growth Fund, Inc. (AGRO)
American Locker Group, Inc. (ALGI)
American National Bankshares, Inc.
  (AMNB)
American National Financial, Inc. (ANFI)
American Pacific Bank (AMPBB)
American Physician Partners (APPM)
American Software, Inc. (AMSWA)
American Technology Corporation (ATCO)
American United Global, Inc. (AUGIW)
American Xtai Technology, Inc. (AXTI)
AmerisSoft Corporation (AREM)
AmeriVest Properties, Inc. (AMVP)
AmerTranz Worldwide Holding (AMTZ)
AmerTranz Worldwide Holding (AMTZW)
Amgen, Inc. (AMGN)
Ampace Corporation (PACE)
Amplicon, Inc. (AMPI)
Amplidyne, Inc. (AMPDW)
AMRESCO Capital Trust (AMCT)
AMRESCO INC. (AMMB)
Amsurg Corp. (AMSGA)
Amsurg Corp. (AMSGB)
AmTrust Capital Corp. (ATSB)
ANACOMP, Inc. (ANCOW)
Andean Development Corporation (ADCC)
Andean Development Corporation
  (ADCCW)
Anderson Group, Inc. (ANDR)
Andyne Computing Limited (ADYNF)
Annuity and Life Re (Holdings), Ltd.
  (ALREF)
AnswerThink Consulting Group, Inc.
  (ANSR)
Antenna TV S.A. (ANTV)
Apollo Group Inc. Cl A (APOL)
Apollo International of Delaware (AIOD)

COMPANY (SYMBOL)

Apollo International of Delaware (AIODW)
Apparel Technologies, Inc. (APTXW)
Apple Computer, Inc. (AAPL)
Applied Films Corporation (AFCO)
Applied Intelligence Group (IQIQ)
Applied Materials, Inc. (AMAT)
Applied Micro Circuits (AMCC)
AppliedTheory Corp. (ATHY)
AppNet Systems, Inc. (APNT)
APS Holding Corporation (APSI)
Aqua Care Systems, Inc. (AQCRU)
Aquila Biopharmaceuticals, Inc. (AQLA)
Arbor Software Corporation (ARSW)
Area Bancshares Corporation (AREA)
Argosy Education Group, Inc. (ARGY)
Arguss Holdings, Inc. (ARGX)
ARI Network Services, Inc. (ARIS)
ARIAD Pharmaceuticals, Inc. (ARIAW)
Ariba, Inc. (ARBA)
Ariely Advertising, Limited (RELEF)
Arista Investors Corp. (ARINA)
Aristotle Corporation (The) (ARTL)
Arizona Instrument Corporation (AZIC)
Ark Restaurants Corp. (ARKR)
Arkansas Best Corporation (ABFSP)
ARM Holdings PLC (ARMY)
Arrow-Magnolia International (ARWM)
Art Technology Group, Inc. (ARTG)
Artisan Components, Inc. (ARTI)
Art's-Way Manufacturing Co. (ARTW)
ASAHI/America, Inc. (ASAM)
ASB Financial Corp. (ASBP)
Aseco Corporation (ASEC)
ASHA Corporation (ASHA)
Asia Pacific Resources, Ltd. (APQCF)
Ask Jeeves, Inc. (ASKJ)
A.S.V., Inc. (ASVI)
Aspec Technology, Inc. (ASPC)
Associated Materials Incorporated (SIDE)
Asta Funding, Inc. (ASFI)
Astro-Med, Inc. (ALOT)
Astronics Corporation (ATRO)
Astropower, Inc. (APWR)
Asymetrix Learning Systems, Inc. (ASYM)
At Home Corporation (ATHM)
ATC Group Services, Inc. (ATCSL)
ATEC Group Inc. (ATECW)
ATG Inc. (ATGC)
Athey Products Corporation (ATPC)
ATI Technologies Inc. (ATYTF)
Atlantic Bank and Trust (ATLB)
Atlantic Pharmaceuticals, Inc. (ATLCU)
Atlantic Preferred Capital Corp. (ATLPP)
Atlantic Realty Trust (ATLRS)

COMPANY (SYMBOL)

Atlas Pacific Limited (APCFY)
Atmel Corporation (ATML)
ATMI Inc. (ATMI)
ATRION Corporation (ATRI)
Auburn National (AUBN)
Audible, Inc. (ADBL)
AudioCodes Ltd. (AUDC)
Augment Systems, Inc. (AUGSW)
AutoBond Acceptance (ABND)
Autobytel.com, Inc. (ABTL)
Autologic Information (AIII)
Autoweb.com, Inc. (AWEB)
Avalon Capital, Inc. (MIST)
Avalon Community Services, (CITY)
Aviation Group, Inc. (AVGPW)
Avondale Financial Corp. (AVND)
Axsys Technologies, Inc. (AXYS)
Azurel Ltd. (AZURW)

B

Back Yard Burgers, Inc. (BYBI)
BackWeb Technologies Ltd. (BWEB)
Balance Bar Company (BBAR)
Baldwin & Lyons, Inc. (BWINA)
Baldwin & Lyons, Inc. (BWINB)
Baldwin Piano & Organ Company (BPAO)
Bally Total Fitness Holding (BFIT)
Bally's Grand, Inc. (BGLV)
Bally's Grand, Inc. (BGLVW)
Baltek Corporation (BTEK)
Baltic International USA, Inc. (BISA)
Baltic International USA, Inc. (BISAW)
bamboo.com, Inc. (BAMB)
BancFirst Corporation (BANF)
BancFirst Ohio Corp. (BFOH)
Bancinsurance Corporation (BCIS)
Bando McGlocklin Capital (BMCC)
Bank Corporation (The) (TBNC)
Bank of Essex (BSXT)
Bank of Granite Corporation (GRAN)
Bank of Santa Clara (BNSC)
Bank of South Carolina Corp. (BKSC)
Bank of the Ozarks (OZRK)
Bank of the Sierra (BSRR)
Bank Rhode Island (BARI)
BankAtlantic Bancorp, Inc. (BANCP)
BankFirst Corporation (BKFR)
BankUnited Financial (BKUNO)
BankUnited Financial (BKUNP)
BankUnited Financial (BKUNZ)
Banyan Strategic Realty Trust (VLANS)
Barbeques Galore Limited (BBQZY)
barnesandnoble.com, inc. (BNBN)
Base Ten Systems, Inc. (BASEB)
Batteries Batteries, Inc. (BATSW)

COMPANY (SYMBOL)

Bay Bancshares, Inc. (BAYB)
BCAM International Inc. (BCAML)
BCAM International Inc. (BCAMZ)
BCB Financial Services (BCBF)
BCSB Bankcorp, Inc. (BCSB)
BCT International Inc. (BCTI)
Be Incorporated (BEOS)
BeautiControl Cosmetics, Inc. (BUTI)
bebe stores, inc. (BEBE)
Bedford Bancshares, Inc. (BFSB)
Benihana Inc. (BNHN)
Benton Oil and Gas Company (BNTNW)
Beringer Wine Estates (BERW)
Berkshire Gas Company (The) (BGAS)
Bernard Haldane Associates, Inc. (BHAL)
BGS Systems, Inc. (BGSS)
B.H.I. Corporation (BHIKF)
Biacore International AB (BCOR)
Bid.Com International, Inc. (BIDS)
Big Buck Brewery & Steakhouse (BBUC)
Big Buck Brewery & Steakhouse (BBUCU)
Big Buck Brewery & Steakhouse (BBUCW)
Big Dog Holding, Inc. (BDOG)
Big Foot Financial Corp. (BFFC)
Big Star Entertainment, Inc. (BGST)
BindView Development Corp. (BVEW)
Bioanalytical Systems, Inc. (BASI)
Biocircuits Corporation (BIOC)
Biocontrol Technology, Inc. (BICO)
Bio-Imaging Technologies, Inc. (BITI)
BioMarin Pharmaceutical, Inc. (BMRN)
Biomune Systems, Inc. (BIME)
Bionutrics, Inc. (BNRX)
Biopure Corporation (BPUR)
Biora AB (BIORY)
Bio-Reference Laboratories (BRLIZ)
Biper SA de CV (BIPRY)
Bird Corporation (BIRDP)
Birmingham Utilities, Inc. (BIRM)
Birner Dental Management Services, Inc.
   (BDMS)
Biznessonline.com, Inc. (BIZZ)
BKC Semiconductors (BKCS)
Black Rock Golf Corporation (BLRK)
Block Drug Company, Inc. (BLOCA)
Blowout Entertainment, Inc. (BLWT)
Blue Dolphin Energy Company (BDCOD)
Blue Rhino Corporation (RINO)
BMJ Medical Management, Inc. (BONS)
BNC Mortgage, Inc. (BNCM)
Bogen Communications International
   (BOGNW)
BOK Financial Corporation (BOKF)
Bolle Inc. (BEYE)
Bonded Motors, Inc. (BMTR)

COMPANY (SYMBOL)

Bontex Inc. (BOTX)
Borel Bank & Trust Company (BLCA)
Boron, LePore & Associates (BLPG)
B.O.S. Better Online Solutions (BOSWF)
Boston Acoustics, Inc. (BOSA)
Boston Biomedica, Inc. (BBII)
Boston Private Bancorp, Inc. (BPBC)
Bottomline Technologies, Inc. (EPAY)
BPI Packaging Technologies (BPIEP)
Brake Headquarters U.S.A. (BHQUW)
Brass Eagle, Inc. (XTRM)
Braun Consulting, Inc. (BRNC)
Brazil Fast Food Corporation (BOBSZ)
Brazos Sportswear, Inc. (BRZS)
Brenton Banks, Inc. (BRBK)
BridgeStreet Accommodations (BEDS)
Bridgford Foods Corporation (BRID)
BrightStar Information Technology Group
   (BTSR)
Britton & Koontz Capital (BKBK)
Broadcom Corporation (BRCM)
Broadway & Seymour, Inc. (BSIS)
Broadway Financial Corporation (BYFC)
Brocade Communications Systems (BRCD)
Brookline Bancorp, Inc. (BRKL)
Brooks Automation, Inc. (BRKS)
Brunswick Technologies, Inc. (BTIC)
Bryn Mawr Bank Corporation (BMTC)
BT Financial Corporation (BTFC)
Buca, Inc. (BUCA)
Builders Transport (TRUKH)
Building Materials Holding (BMHC)
Bull & Bear Group, Inc. (BNBGA)
Burke Mills, Inc. (BMLS)
Business Objects S.A. (BOBJY)
BYL Bancorp (BOYL)

C

C. Brewer Homes, Inc. (CBHI)
C3, Inc. (CTHR)
Cable Michigan, Inc. (CABL)
Cade Industries, Inc. (CADE)
CAIS Internet, Inc. (CAIS)
Caliber Learning Network, Inc. (CLBR)
California Federal Bank, FSB (CALGL)
California Independent Bancorp (CIBN)
California Micro Devices (CAMD)
California Microwave, Inc. (CMICG)
California State Bank (CSTB)
Callon Petroleum Company (CLNP)
Callon Petroleum Company (CLNPP)
Calloway's Nursery, Inc. (CLWY)
Cal-Maine Foods, Inc. (CALM)
CAM Designs, Inc. (CMDAW)
Cambridge Technology Partners (CATP)

COMPANY (SYMBOL)

Campo Electronics, Appliances (CMPOQ)
Canandaigua Brands, Inc. (CBRNB)
Candela Corporation (CLZR)
Canisco Resources Inc. (DE) (CANR)
Cannon Express, Inc. (CANX)
Cannon Inc. (CANNY)
Cantab Pharmaceuticals PLC (CNTBY)
Cantel Industries, Inc. (CNTL)
Canterbury Information (XCEL)
Canterbury Park Holding (TRAKW)
Cape Cod Bank and Trust (CCBT)
Capital Automotive REIT (CARS)
Capital Bancorp (CBCP)
Capital Bank (CBKN)
Capital City Bank Group (CCBG)
Capital Corp of the West (CCOW)
Capital Environmental Resource (CERI)
Capital Factors Holding, Inc. (CAPF)
Capital Savings Bancorp, Inc. (CAPS)
Capital Southwest (CSWC)
Capitol Bancorp Ltd. (CBCL)
Capitol Federal Financial (CFFN)
CardioDynamics International (CDIC)
Cardiovascular Dynamics, Inc. (CCVD)
Career Education Corporation (CECO)
Careerbuilder, Inc. (CBDR)
CareInsite, Inc. (CARI)
Carematrix Corporation (CMDC)
Caribbean Cigar Company (CIGRW)
Caring Products International (BDRYU)
Carolina Fincorp, Inc. (CFNC)
Carolina First Bancshare, Inc. (CFBI)
Carolina Southern Bank (CSBK)
Carollton Bancorp (CRRB)
Carreker-Antinori, Inc. (CANI)
Carrier Access Corp. (CACS)
Carver Corporation (CAVR)
Casa Olé Restaurants, Inc. (CASA)
Cascade Financial Corp. (CASB)
Casco International Inc. (CASCW)
Casino Magic Corp. (CMAG)
Cass Commercial Corporation (CASS)
Castelle (CSTL)
Catapult Communications Corp. (CATT)
Cathay Bancorp, Inc. (CATY)
Cavalry Bancorp, Inc. (CAVB)
CB Bancshares, Inc. (CBBI)
CBES Bancorp, Inc. (CBES)
CBT Corporation (CBTC)
Cdnow, Inc. (CDNW)
CE Software Holdings, Inc. (CESH)
Celeritek, Inc. (CLTK)
Cellegy Pharmaceuticals, Inc. (CLGYW)
CEM Corporation (CEMX)
Centocor, Inc. (CNTO)

COMPANY (SYMBOL)

Central Coast Bancorp (CCBN)
Central Co-Operative Bank (CEBK)
Central Reserve Life (CRLC)
Central Virginia Bankshares (CVBK)
Centurion Mines Corporation (CTMC)
Century Bancshares, Inc. (CTRY)
Century Financial Corporation (CYFN)
CERBCO, Inc. (CERB)
Certron Corporation (CRTN)
CFC International, Inc. (CFCI)
CFS Bancorp, Inc. (CITZ)
CFW Communications Company (CFWC)
Chalone Wine Group, Ltd. (The) (CHLN)
Chancellor Media Corporation (ANFM)
Channell Commercial (CHNL)
Chapman Capital Management Holdings (CMGT)
Charles River Associates, Inc. (CRAI)
Charter Financial, Inc. (CBSB)
Chastain Capital Corporation (CHAS)
CHC Helicopter Corporation (FLYAF)
Cheap Tickets, Inc. (CTIX)
Chefs International, Inc. (CHEF)
Chem International, Inc. (CXILW)
Chemdex Corporation (CMDX)
Chemical Financial Corporation (CHFC)
Chemi-Trol Chemical Co. (CTRL)
Cherry Corporation (The) (CHERB)
Chester Bancorp, Inc. (CNBA)
China.com Corporation (CHINA)
Chiron Corporation (CHIR)
Chittenden Corporation (CNDN)
ChoiceTel Communications, Inc. (PHONW)
Chroma Vision Medical Systems (CVSN)
Chronimed Inc. (CHMD)
Churchill Downs, Incorporated (CHDN)
CIENA Corp. (CIEN)
Cimatron, Limited (CIMTF)
Cincinnati Financial (CINFG)
Cinemastar Luxury Theaters, (LUXYZ)
Cinram International, Inc. (CNRMF)
Cirque Energy Ltd. (CIRQF)
Citadel Communications Corp. (CITC)
Citizens Bancshares, Inc. (CICS)
Citizens Financial Corporation (CNFL)
CNBT Bancshares, Inc. (CNBT)
Citrix Systems, Inc. (CTXS)
City Holding Company Trust II (CHCOP)
CKF Bancorp, Inc. (CKFB)
Claimsnet.com, Inc. (CLAI)
Clarent Corporation (CLRN)
Clark/Bardes Holdings, Inc. (CLKB)
Classic Bancshares, Inc. (CLAS)
Clayton Williams Energy, Inc. (CWEI)

COMPANY (SYMBOL)

Clean Diesel Technologies, Inc. (CDTI)
Clean Harbors, Inc. (CLHB)
Cleveland Indians Baseball Company, Inc. (CLEV)
CleveTrust Realty Investors (CTRIS)
ClinTrials Research Inc. (CCRO)
CMGI, Inc. (CMGI)
CNB Financial Corporation (CCNE)
CNET, Inc. (CNET)
CNS Bancorp, Inc. (CNSB)
CNY Financial Corporation (CBIC)
Coast Bancorp (CTBP)
Coast Federal Litigation Contingent Payment (CCPRZ)
Cobalt Group, Inc. (The) (CBLT)
CoBancorp, Inc. (COBI)
Coda Music Technology, Inc. (COMT)
Coflexip (CXIPY)
Cognicase Inc. (COGIF)
Cognizant Technology Solutions Corporation (CTSH)
Cohesant Technologies Inc. (COHT)
Cohoes Bancorp, Incorporated (COHB)
Coinmach Laundry Corporation (WDRY)
CollaGenex Pharmaceuticals (CGPI)
Collateral Therapeutics, Inc. (CLTX)
Colonial Commercial Corp. (CCOM)
Colonial Commercial Corp. (CCOMP)
Colony Bankcorp, Inc. (CBAN)
Colorado Business Bankshares, Inc. (COBZ)
Columbia Bancorp (CBBO)
Columbia Bancorp (CBMD)
Columbia Banking System, Inc. (COLB)
Columbia Financial of Kentucky, Inc. (CFKY)
Columbia Sportswear Company (COLM)
Columbus McKinnon Corporation (CMCO)
Com21, Inc. (CMTO)
Comair Holdings, Inc. (COMR)
CombiChem, Inc. (CCHM)
Comm Bancorp, Inc. (CCBP)
Command Systems, Inc. (CMND)
Commander Aircraft Company (CMDR)
Commerce Bank/Harrisburg (COBH)
Commerce One, Inc. (CMRC)
Commercial Bank of New York (CBNY)
Commercial National Financial (CNAF)
Commonwealth Bancorp, Inc. (CMSB)
Commtouch Software Ltd. (CTCH)
Communications World (CWII)
Community Bank Shares of Indiana (CBIN)
Community Financial Holding (CMFH)
Community First Banking (CFBC)
Community Medical Transport (CMTI)
Community Savings Bancshares (CMSV)

COMPANY (SYMBOL)

Community Trust Bancorp, Inc. (CTBI)
Community Trust Bancorp, Inc. (CTBIP)
Community West Bancshares (GLTB)
COMPS.COM, Inc. (CDOT)
CompScript Inc. (CPRX)
CompuCredit Corporation (CCRT)
CompuDyne Corporation (CDCY)
CompuMed, Inc. (CMPD)
Computer Language Research (CLRI)
Computer Literacy, Inc. (CMPL)
Computone Corporation (CMPT)
Comtrex Systems Corporation (COMX)
Comverse Technology, Inc. (CMVT)
Concepts Direct, Inc. (CDIR)
Concur Technologies, Inc. (CNQR)
Condor Technology Solutions, Inc. (CNDR)
Conductus, Inc. (CDTS)
Conexant Systems, Inc. (CNXT)
CONMED Corporation (CNMD)
Conning Corporation (CNNG)
Conrad Industries, Inc. (CNRD)
Consolidated Mercantile Corp. (CSLMF)
Consulier Engineering, Inc. (CSLR)
Consumers Financial (CFINP)
Continental Choice Care, Inc. (CCCI)
Continental Health Affiliates (CTHL)
Continental Information (CISC)
Continental Mortgage (CMETS)
Continental Natural Gas, Inc. (CNGL)
Continuous Software Corp. (CNSW)
Contour Medical, Inc. (CTMI)
Control Chief Holdings, Inc. (DIGM)
Convergent Communications, Inc. (CONV)
Conversion Technologies (CTIXW)
Cooperative Bankshares, Inc. (COOP)
Copper Mountain Networks, Inc. (CMTN)
CoreComm Limited (BKFRF)
Corinthian Colleges, Inc. (COCO)
Corixa Corporation (CRXA)
Corporate Executive Board Company (EXBD)
Corporate Office Properties (RLIN)
Corporate Renaissance Group, Inc. (CREN)
Correctional Services (CSCQ)
Cortech, Inc. (CRTQ)
Cortecs PLC (DLVRY)
CORUS Bankshares, Inc. (CORS)
CorVel Corporation (CRVL)
Cosmetic Center, Inc. (The) (COSC)
Cost-U-Less, Inc. (CULS)
Cotton States Life Insurance (CSLI)
Covad Communications Group, Inc. (COVD)
Covalent Group, Inc. (CVGR)
Covenant Bancorp, Inc. (CNSK)

COMPANY (SYMBOL)

Covenant Bancorp, Inc. (CNSKO)
Covenant Transport, Inc. (CVTI)
CoVest Bancshares, Inc. (COVB)
Covol Technologies, Inc. (CVOL)
Cowlitz Bancorporation (CWLZ)
Coyote Network Systems, Inc. (CYOE)
CPAC, Inc. (CPAK)
CPB, Inc. (CPBI)
Cragar Industries, Inc. (CRGRW)
Crazy Woman Creek Bancorp (CRZY)
Creative Host Services, Inc. (CHST)
Creative Master International, Inc. (CMST)
Credit Depot Corporation (LEND)
Creditrust Corp. (CRDT)
Credo Petroleum Corporation (CRED)
Creo Products, Inc. (CREOV)
Crescendo Pharmaceuticals (CNDO)
Crescent Operating, Inc. (COPI)
Cresud S.A.C.I.F. y A. (CRESY)
CRH, public limited company (CRHCY)
Critical Path, Inc. (CPTH)
Cronos Group (The) (CRNSF)
Crown Andersen Inc. (CRAN)
Crown Castle International Corp. (TWRS)
Crusader Holding Corp. (CRSB)
Cryomedical Sciences, Inc. (CMSI)
Crystal Systems Solutions (CRYSF)
CSK Corporation (CSKKY)
CTB International Corp. (CTBC)
CTI Industries Corporation (CTIB)
CulturalAccess Worldwide, Inc. (CAWW)
Cumberland Technologies, Inc. (CUMB)
Cumulus Media, Inc. (CMLS)
Cunningham Graphics International, Inc.
  (CGII)
CuraGen Corporation (CRGN)
Curtis International Ltd. (CURTF)
Cusac Gold Mines, Limited (CUSWF)
Cutco Industries, Inc. (CUTC)
CyBear, Inc. (CYBA)
Cyberian Outpost, Inc. (COOL)
CyberSource Corporation (CYBS)
Cytoclonal Pharmaceutics Inc. (CYPH)

D

D & E Communications, Inc. (DECC)
D. G. Jewellery of Canada Ltd. (DGJLF)
D. G. Jewellery of Canada Ltd. (DGJWF)
DA Consulting Group, Inc. (DACG)
Dai'ei, Inc. (DAIEY)
Dakotah, Incorporated (DKTH)
Daktronics, Inc. (DAKT)
Daniel Green Company (DAGR)
Dart Group Corporation (DARTA)

COMPANY (SYMBOL)

Data Translation Inc. (DATX)
Datalink Corporation (DTLK)
Datamark Holding, Inc. (DTAM)
Datum, Inc. (DATM)
Davel Communications Group (DAVL)
David's Bridal, Inc. (DABR)
Deb Shops, Inc. (DEBS)
Decoma International, Inc. (DECF)
DECS Trust V (TWDE)
Dell Computer Corporation (DELL)
Delta Petroleum Corporation (DPTR)
Delta-Galil Industries Ltd. (DELT)
Deltek Systems, Inc. (DLTK)
Denali Incorporated (DNLI)
Dental/Medical Diagnostic (DMDS)
Dental/Medical Diagnostic (DMDSW)
DENTSPLY International Inc. (XRAY)
DepoMed, Inc. (DPMD)
DepoMed, Inc. (DPMDW)
Descartes Systems Group Inc. (DSGXF)
Desert Community Bank (DCBK)
Designs, Inc. (DESI)
Destia Communications, Inc. (DEST)
DHB Capital Group (DHBT)
dick clark productions, inc. (DCPI)
Didax, Inc. (AMEN)
Diehl Graphsoft, Inc. (DIEG)
Digex, Inc. (DIGX)
Digital Island, Inc. (ISLD)
Digital Recorders, Inc. (TBUS)
Digital River, Inc. (DRIV)
Digital Transmission Systems (DTSXW)
Digitale Telekabel AG (DTAGY)
Diplomat Corporation (DIPLW)
Direct Focus, Inc. (DFXI)
Disc Graphics, Inc. (DSGR)
Disc Graphics, Inc. (DSGRW)
Discovery Laboratories Inc. (DSCOU)
Discovery Laboratories Inc. (DSCOW)
Ditech Communications Corp. (DITC)
DLB Oil & Gas, Inc. (DLBI)
DNAP Holding Corporation (DNAP)
DOCdata N.V. (DOCDF)
DocuCorp International, Inc. (DOCCR)
Dollar Tree Stores, Inc. (DLTR)
Dominguez Services Corporation (DOMZ)
Donegal Group, Inc. (DGIC)
Doral Financial Corp. (DORLP)
Dorel Industries, Inc. (DIIBF)
Double Eagle Petroleum and Mining Co.
  (DBLE)
Double Eagle Petroleum and Mining Co.
  (DBLEW)
DoubleClick, Inc. (DCLK)

COMPANY (SYMBOL)

drkoop.com, Inc. (KOOP)
Drug Emporium, Inc. (DEMPG)
Drugstore.com, Inc. (DSCM)
DSET Corporation (DSET)
DSG International Limited (DSGIF)
DT Industries, Inc. (DTII)
DTM Corporation (DTMC)
Dura Pharmaceuticals, Inc. (DURAH)
Dyna Group International, Inc. (DGIX)
DynaGen, Inc. (CYGNW)
Dynamic Oil Limited (DYOLF)
Dynamics Research Corporation (DRCO)
Dynatec International, Inc. (DYNX)
Dynex Capital Inc. (DXCPO)
Dynex Capital Inc. (DXCPP)

E

Eagle BancGroup, Inc. (EGLB)
EarthCare Company (ECCO)
EarthShell Container Corporation (ERTH)
EarthWeb Inc. (EWBX)
East West Bancorp, Inc. (EWBC)
Eastco Industrial Safety Corp. (ESTOW)
Eastco Industrial Safety Corp. (ESTOZ)
eBay, Inc. (EVAY)
Echelon Corp. (ELON)
EchoCath, Inc. (ECHTA)
EchoStar Communications (DISHP)
Eclipsys Corporation (ECLP)
Ecomat, Inc. (ECMT)
EcoScience Corporation (ECSC)
EcoTyre Technologies, Inc. (ETTIW)
Edac Technologies Corporation (EDAC)
Edelbrock Corporation (EDEL)
Edgar Online, Inc. (EDGR)
Edison Control Corporation (EDCO)
Education Management (EDMC)
Educational Insights, Inc. (EDIN)
Effective Management Systems (EMSI)
Effective Management Systems (EMSIW)
Efficient Networks, Inc. (EFNT)
EFI Electronics Corporation (EFIC)
EFTC Corporation (EFTC)
Elder-Beerman Stores Corp. (The) (EBSCV)
Electronic Boutique Holdings Corp.
  (ELBO)
Electronic Designs, Inc. (EDIXW)
Electronica Tele-Communications (ETCIA)
Electro-Sensors, Inc. (ELSE)
Elmer's Restaurants, Inc. (ELMS)
Elmira Savings Bank, FSB (The) (ESBK)
E-Loan, Inc. (EELN)
ELXSI Corporation (ELXS)
EMC Insurance Group, Inc. (EMCI)
EMCEE Broadcast Products (ECIN)

COMPANY (SYMBOL)

EMCORE Corporation (EMKR)
Emerald Isle Bancorp, Inc. (EIRE)
Emons Transporation Group (EMON)
Empire Federal Bancorp, Inc. (EFBC)
Encore Wire Corporation (WIRE)
Energy Search, Incorporated (EGAS)
Energy Search, Incorporated (EGASW)
Energy West, Inc. (EWST)
e-Net, Inc. (ETELW)
Enex Resources Corporation (ENEX)
Engage Technologies, Inc. (ENGA)
Engel General Developers Ltd. (ENGEF)
Engineering Measurements (EMCO)
Enhanced Services Company (ESVS)
Ensec International, Inc. (ENSC)
ENStar, Inc. (ENSR)
Entrust Technologies, Inc. (ENTU)
Envirodyne Industries, Inc. (EDYN)
Envirogen, Inc. (ENVGU)
Enzon, Inc. (ENZN)
Equitable Federal Savings Bank (EQSB)
Equity Marketing, Inc. (EMAK)
ErgoBilt, Inc. (ERGB)
ESELCO, Inc. (EDSE)
Eskimo Pie Corporation (EPIE)
ESPS, Inc. (ESPS)
Esquire Communications Ltd. (ESQSW)
E-Tek Dynamics, Inc. (ETEK)
eToys, Inc. (ETYS)
Euro Tech Holdings Company (CLWWF)
Europa Cruises Corporation (KRUZ)
European Micro Holdings, Inc. (EMCC)
Evans & Sutherland Computer (ESCC)
Evans & Sutherland Computer (ESCCG)
Evans, Inc. (EVAN)
Evans Systems, Inc. (EVSI)
Evolving Systems, Inc. (EVOL)
Excalibur Technologies (EXCA)
Excel Switching Corporation (XLSW)
Excel Technology, Inc. (XLTC)
Exchange Applications, Inc. (EXAP)
Executive TeleCard, Ltd. (EXTL)
EXECUTONE Information Systems
  (XTON)
Exigent International, Inc. (XGNT)
Exodus Communications, Inc. (EXDS)
Expeditors International of Washington, Inc.
  (EXPD)
Extended Systems Incorporated (XTND)
Extreme Networks, Inc. (EXTR)
Ezcony Interamerica Inc. (EZCOF)

F

F & M Bancorp (FMBN)
F & M Bancorporation, Inc. (FMBK)

COMPANY (SYMBOL)

F5 Networks, Inc. (FFIV)
Failure Group, Inc. (The) (FAIL)
Fantom Technologies Inc. (FTMTF)
Farmer Brothers Company (FARM)
Farmers Capital Bank (FFKT)
Farr Company (FARC)
Farrel Corporation (FARL)
Fashionmall.com, Inc. (FASH)
FCNB Corporate Trust (FCNBP)
Featherlite Mg., Inc. (FTHR)
Federal Screw Works (FSCR)
FFD Financial Corporation (FFDF)
FFLC Bancorp, Inc. (FFLC)
FFVA Financial Corporation (FFFC)
FFW Corporation (FFWC)
Fiberstars, Inc. (FBST)
Fidelity Bancorp, Inc. (FSBI)
Fidelity Financial of Ohio (FFOH)
Fidelity Holdings, Inc. (FDHG)
Fieldcrest Cannon, Inc. (FLDCP)
Fields Aircraft Spares, Inc. (FASI)
Financial Industries (FNIN)
Financial Institutions, Inc. (FISI)
FinishMaster, Inc. (FMST)
First Albany Companies, Inc. (FACT)
First Bancorp of Indiana, Inc. (FBEI)
First Banks, Inc. (FBNKO)
First Bell Bancorp, Inc. (FBBC)
First Charter Corporation (FCTR)
First Coastal Corporation (FCME)
First Colonial Group, Inc. (FTCG)
First Commerce Bancshares (FCBIA)
First Community Financial Corp. (FCFN)
First Consulting Group, Inc. (FCGI)
First Corporation of Long Island (FLIC)
First Dynasty Mines Ltd. (FDYMF)
First Enterprise Financial (FENT)
First Federal Bancorp, Inc. (FFBZ)
First Federal Bancorporation (BDJI)
First Federal Capital Corp. (FTFC)
First Federal Savings and Loan (FFES)
First Financial Bancorp. (FFBC)
First Financial Bancorp, Inc. (FFBI)
First Financial Bankshares (FFIN)
First Financial Corp. (FTFN)
First Home Bancorp, Inc. (FSPG)
First Kansas Financial Corporation (FKAN)
First Keystone Financial, Inc. (FKFS)
First Liberty Financial Corp. (FLFC)
First Mariner Bancorp (FMAR)
First Merchants Corporation (FRME)
First Midwest Financial, Inc. (CASH)
First Mutual Savings Bank (FMSB)
First National Lincoln Corp. (FNLC)
First Northern Capital (FNGB)

COMPANY (SYMBOL)

First Oak Brook Bancshares (FOBBA)
First Place Financial Corporation (FPFC)
First Savings Bancorp Inc. (SOPN)
First South Africa Corp., Ltd. (FSAUF)
First Southern Bancshares, Inc. (FSTH)
First Sterling Banks, Inc. (FSLB)
First United Bancorporation (FUSC)
First United Bancshares, Inc. (UNTD)
First United Capital Trust (FUNCP)
First United Corporation (FUNC)
First Victoria National Bank (FVNB)
First Virtual Corporation (FVCX)
First Years, Inc. (The) (KIDD)
Firstar Corporation (FSRPZ)
FirstBank Corp. (FBNW)
Firstbank of Illinois Co. (FBIC)
FirstCity Financial (FCFCP)
FirstFed Bancorp, Inc. (FFDB)
FirstFederal Financial (FFSWO)
Firstmark Corp. (FIRM)
Flagstar Bancorp, Inc. (FLGSP)
Flamemaster Corporation (The) (FAME)
FlashNet Communications, Inc. (FLAS)
Fletcher's Fine Foods Ltd. (FLCHF)
FlexiInternational Software (FLXI)
Flexsteel Industries, Inc. (FLXS)
Florida Banks, Inc. (FLBK)
Florida Gaming Corporation (BETS)
FloridaFirst Bancorp (FFBK)
Florsheim Group Inc. (FLSC)
Fluor Daniel GTI, Inc. (FDGT)
Flycast Communications Corp. (FCST)
FMS Financial Corporation (FMCO)
F.N.B. Corporation (FBAN)
F.N.B. Corporation (FBANP)
FNB Corp. (FNBN)
FNB Corporation (FNBP)
FNB Financial Services (FNBF)
Focal Communications Corp. (FCOM)
Foilmark, Inc. (FLMK)
Food Court Entertainment (FCENA)
Food Court Entertainment (FCENZ)
Food Technology Service, Inc. (VIFL)
Foothill Independent Bancorp (FOOT)
For Better Living, Inc. (FBTR)
Formula Systems (1985) Ltd. (FORTY)
Fort Thomas Financial (FTSB)
FP Bancorp Inc. (FPBN)
Franklin Bank, National (FSVB)
Franklin Electric Co., Inc. (FELE)
Freeserve PLC (FREE)
Frontier Natural Gas (FNGC)
Frontier Natural Gas (FNGCP)
Frontier Natural Gas (FNGCW)
FRP Properties, Inc. (FRPP)

COMPANY (SYMBOL)

Fulton Financial Corporation (FULT)
Fundtech, Ltd. (FNDTF)
Fusion Systems Corporation (FUSNR)

G

G. Willi-Food International (WILCF)
G. Willi-Food International (WILWF)
Gadzoox Networks, Inc. (ZOOX)
Gaston Federal Bancorp, Inc. (GBNK)
GB&T Bancshares, Inc. (GBTB)
General Binding Corporation (GBND)
Genesee & Wyoming Inc. (GNWR)
Genesee Corporation (GENBB)
Genesis Direct, Inc. (GEND)
Genesis Microchip, Inc. (GNSSF)
GenesisIntermedia.com, Inc. (GENI)
Genisys Reservation Systems (GENSW)
Genisys Reservation Systems (GENSZ)
Genta Incorporated (GNTA)
Genzyme Molecular Oncology (GZMO)
GeoResources, Inc. (GEOI)
George Mason Bankshares, Inc. (GMBS)
Gerald Stevens, Inc. (GIFT)
German American Bancorp. (GABC)
GFS Bancorp, Inc. (GFSB)
Giant Cement Holding, Inc. (GCHI)
Gibbs Construction, Inc. (GBSEW)
Giga Information Group, Inc. (GIGX)
Gilman & Ciocia, Inc. (GTAXW)
Gish Biomedical, Inc. (GISH)
GKN Holding Corp. (GKNS)
Glacier Bancorp, Inc. (GBCI)
Glassmaster Company (GLMA)
Global Crossing Ltd. (GBLX)
Global Imaging Systems, Inc. (GISX)
Global Intellicom, Inc. (GBIT)
Global Med Technologies, Inc. (GLOB)
Global Pharmaceutical (GLPC)
Global Sports, Inc. (GSPT)
Global TeleSystems Group, Inc. (GTSG)
GlobeSpan, Inc. (GSPN)
Gold Banc Corporation, Inc. (GLDB)
Gold Fields of South Africa (GLDFY)
Golden Eagle Group, Inc. (GEGPW)
Golden Isles Financial (GIFHU)
Golden State Vintners, Inc. (VINT)
Golf Training Systems, Inc. (GTSX)
Good Times Restaurants Inc. (GTIM)
GoodNoise Corporation (EMUS)
Goran Capital, Inc. (GNCNF)
GoTo.com, Inc. (GOTO)
Gradco Systems, Inc. (GRCO)
Grand Court Lifestyles, Inc. (GCLI)
Granite Broadcasting (GBTVP)
Granite Financial, Inc. (GFNI)

COMPANY (SYMBOL)

Granite State Bankshares, Inc. (GSBI)
Grease Monkey Holding (GMHC)
Great American Bancorp, Inc. (GTPS)
Great Bee Dee Bancorp, Inc. (PEDE)
Great Central Mines Ltd. (GTCMY)
Great Pee Dee Bancorp, Inc. (PEDE)
Greater Atlantic Financial Corp. (GAFC)
Greater Bay Bancorp (GBBK)
Greater Bay Bancorp (GBBKP)
Greater Community Bancorp (GFLSP)
Green Mountain Coffee, Inc. (GMCR)
Greene County Bancorp. Inc. (GCBC)
Greenstone Roberts (GRRI)
Greif Bros. Corporation (GBCOA)
Griffin Land & Nurseries, Inc. (GRIF)
Grist Mill Co. (GRST)
GSB Financial Corporation (GOSB)
GST Telecommunications (GSTX)
Guaranty Bancshares, Inc. (GNTY)
Guaranty Financial Corporation (GSLC)
Gulf West Banks, Inc. (GWBK)
Gyrodyne Company of America (GYRO)
GZA GeoEnvironmental (GZEA)

H

H. D. Vest, Inc. (HDVS)
Habersham Bancorp (HABC)
Hahn Automotive Warehouse (HAHN)
Hampshire Group, Limited (HAMP)
Hanover Gold Company, Inc. (HYGO)
Happy Kids, Inc. (HKID)
Harbor Federal Bancorp, Inc. (HRBF)
Hardin Bancorp, Inc. (HFSA)
Hardinge, Inc. (HDNG)
Harleysville National (HNBC)
Harmon Industries, Inc. (HRMN)
Harmony Brook, Inc. (HBRK)
Harrington Financial Group (HFGI)
Harrodsburg First Financial (HFFB)
Harvard Industries, Inc. (HAVAV)
Harvest Restaurant Group, Inc. (ROTIZ)
Hastings Entertainment, Inc. (HAST)
Hathaway Corporation (HATH)
Haverty Furniture Companies (HAVTA)
Hawaiian Natural Water (HNWC)
Hawaiian Natural Water (HNWCU)
Hawker Pacific Aerospace (HPAC)
Hawkins Chemical, Inc. (HWKN)
Hayes Corporation (HAYZ)
HCB Bancshares, Inc. (HCBB)
HeadHunter.NET, Inc. (HHNT)
Health Systems Design (HSDC)
Healtheon Corp. (HLTH)
HealthRite Inc. (HLRT)
Hechinger Company (HECHH)

COMPANY (SYMBOL)

Hector Communications (HCCO)
Hector Communications (HCCOG)
Heidrick & Struggles International (HSII)
Helisys, Inc. (HELI)
Help At Home, Inc. (HAHI)
Hemagen Diagnostics, Inc. (HMGN)
Hemlock Federal Financial (HMLK)
Henley Healthcare, Inc. (HENL)
Heritage Bancorp, Inc. (HBCI)
Heritage Financial Corporation (HFWA)
Herley Industries, Inc. (HRLYW)
Hertz Technology Group, Inc. (HERZ)
Herzfeld Caribbean Basin Fund (CUBA)
Heuristic Development Group (IFIT)
Heuristic Development Group (IFITU)
Heuristic Development Group (IFITW)
Heuristic Development Group (IFITZ)
HF Financial Corp. (HFFC)
Hibernia Foods Public Limited (HIBWF)
Hickok Incorporated (HICKA)
Hickory Tech Corporation (HTCO)
hi/fn, inc. (HIFN)
High Country Bancorp, Inc. (HCBC)
High Speed Access Corporation (HSAC)
Highland Bancorp, Inc. (HBNK)
Highway Holdings Limited (HIHWF)
Highwood Resources Ltd. (HIWDF)
Hines Horticulture, Inc. (HORT)
Hirel Holdings, Inc. (HIRL)
HLM Design, Inc. (HLMD)
HMT Technology Corporation (HMTTG)
Holiday RV Superstores, Inc. (RVEE)
Hollinger Inc. (HLGUF)
Holt's Cigar Holdings, Inc. (HOLT)
Home Bancorp (HBFW)
Home Building Bancorp, Inc. (HBBI)
Home Centers (DIY), Limited (HOMEF)
Home Loan Financial Corporation (HLFC)
HomeCorp, Inc. (HMCI)
homestore.com, Inc. (HOMS)
Hometown Auto Retailers, Inc. (HCAR)
Hoover's, Inc. (HOOV)
HopFed Bancorp, Inc. (HFBC)
Horizon Bancorp, Inc. (HZWV)
Horizon Medical Products, Inc. (HMPS)
Horizon Offshore, Inc. (HOFF)
Horizon Organic Holding Corp. (HCOW)
Hotel Discovery, Inc. (HOTDU)
Hotel Discovery, Inc. (HOTDW)
HotJobs.com, Ltd. (HOTJ)
Howell Corporation (HWLLP)
Hudson City Bancorp, Inc. (HCBK)
Hudson Hotels Corporation (HUDS)
Hudson River Bancorp, Inc. (HRBT)
Hungarian Broadcasting Corp. (HBCOP)

COMPANY (SYMBOL)

Hyde Athletic Industries, Inc. (HYDEA)
HyperMedia Communications (HYPR)

I

I V C Industries, Inc. (IVCO)
I.D. Systems, Inc. (IDSY)
ICHOR Corporation (ICHR)
ICO Global Communications, Limited (ICOGF)
ICON PLC (ICLRY)
IDG Books Worldwide, Inc. (IDGB)
IIC Industries Inc. (IICR)
IL Foranio (America) (ILFO)
Image Sensing Systems, Inc. (ISNS)
Image Systems Corporation (IMSG)
ImageX.com, Inc. (IMGX)
Imark Technologies, Inc. (MAXXW)
ImmuCell Corporation (ICCC)
ImmuLogic Pharmaceutical (IMUL)
Immunex Corporation (IMNX)
Imtec, Inc. (IMTC)
Independence Brewing Company (IBCO)
Independence Community Bank Corp. (ICBC)
Independence Federal Savings (IFSB)
Independent Bank Corporation (IBCP)
Independent Energy Holdings PLC (INDYY)
Indiana Community Bank, SB (INCB)
Indiana United Bancorp (IUBCP)
Indigo Aviation AB (IAABY)
Industrial Acoustics Company (IACI)
Industrial Bancorp, Inc. (INBI)
Industrial Holdings, Inc. (IHIIL)
Industrial Holdings, Inc. (IHIIZ)
Industrial Services of America (IDSA)
Indusri-Matematik (IMIC)
Inet Technologies, Inc. (INTI)
Infinite Machines Corp. (IMCIW)
InfoCure Corp. (INCX)
Informatica Corporation (INFA)
Information Management (IMAA)
Infosafe Systems, Inc. (ISFEU)
Infosafe Systems, Inc. (ISFEW)
InfoSpace.com, Inc. (INSP)
Infosys Technologies Limited (INFY)
Initio, Inc. (INTO)
Inkine Pharmaceutical Company (INKPW)
Inktomi Corporation (INKT)
Inland Casino Corporation (INLD)
Inmark Enterprises, Inc. (IMKE)
InnoPet Brands Corp. (INBC)
InnoPet Brands Corp. (INBCW)
InnoServ Technologies Inc. (ISER)
Innotrac Corporation (INOC)

COMPANY (SYMBOL)

INSCI Corporation (INSIW)
Insight Communications Company (ICCI)
Insilco Corporation (INSL)
Insituform East, Incorporated (INEI)
Instrumentarium Corporation (INMRY)
Insurance Management Solutions Group
  (INMG)
InsWeb Corporation (INSW)
Integral Systems, Inc. (ISYS)
Integrated Measurement (IMSC)
Integrated Systems Consulting (ISCG)
Intellicall, Inc. (ICL)
Intellicell Corp. (FONE)
Intelligent Life Corporation (ILIF)
Intensiva HealthCare (IHCC)
Interactive Magic, Inc. (IMGK)
Interactive Pictures Corporation (IPIX)
InterCept Group, Inc. (The) (ICPT)
Intercontinental Life (ILCO)
Intergroup Corporation (The) (INTG)
Interliant, Inc. (INIT)
International Aircraft (IAIS)
International Assets Holding (IAAC)
International Bancshares Corp. (IBOC)
International Integration, Inc. (ICUB)
International Microcomputer (IMSI)
International Nursing Services (NURS)
International Sports (ISWI)
International Sports (ISWIW)
Internet America, Inc. (GEEK)
Internet Capital Group (ICGE)
Internet Gold (IGLD)
internet.com LLC (INTM)
Interplay Entertainment Corporation
  (IPLY)
Interstate National Dealer (ISTN)
Intervisual Books, Inc. (IVBK)
InterWest Bancorp Inc. (IWBK)
Interwest Home Medical, Inc. (IWHM)
InterWorld Corporation (INTW)
InTime Systems International (TAMSA)
InTime Systems International (TAMSW)
Intraware, Inc. (ITRA)
Investors Real Estate Trust (IRETS)
Invitrogen Corporation (IVGN)
Ionic Fuel Technology, Inc. (IFTIW)
Ionic Fuel Technology, Inc. (IFTIZ)
IPL Energy Inc. (IPPIF)
Ipswich Savings Bank (IPSW)
IRATA, Inc. (IRATW)
Iroquois Bancorp, Inc. (IROQ)
Irwin Financial Corporation (IRWNP)
I.S.G. Technologies, Inc. (ISGTF)
Israel Land Development (ILDCY)

COMPANY (SYMBOL)

Isramco, Inc. (ISRLZ)
ISS Group, Inc. (ISSX)
iTurf, Inc. (TURF)
iVillage Inc. (IVIL)
IWL Communications (IWLC)
iXL Enterprises, Inc. (IIXL)
Ixnet, Inc. (EXNT)
IXOS Software AG (XOSY)

J

J2 Communications (JTWOW)
Jacksonville Bancorp, Inc. (JXVL)
Jacksonville Savings Bank (JXSB)
Jacobson Stores Inc. (JCBSG)
Jacor Communications, Inc. (JCORL)
Jacor Communications, Inc. (JCORM)
Jannock Limited (JANNF)
Japan Air Lines Company, Ltd. (JAPNY)
Jason Incorporated (JASN)
Javelin Systems, Inc. (JVLN)
JB Oxford Holdings, Inc. (JBOH)
Jean Philippe Fragrances, Inc. (JEAN)
JeffBanks, Inc. (JEFF)
JeffBanks, Inc. (JEFFP)
Jenkon International, Inc. (JNKN)
Jenna Lane, Inc. (JLNY)
JetForm Corporation (FORMF)
JFAX.COM, Inc. (JFAX)
JG Industries, Inc. (JGIN)
JLM Industries, Inc. (JLMI)
JMAR Industries, Inc. (JMARU)
JMAR Industries, Inc. (JMARW)
Joachim Bancorp, Inc. (JOAC)
John B. Sanfilippo & Son, Inc. (JBSS)
Johnson Worldwide Associates (JWAIA)
Jones Intercable, Inc. (JOIN)
JPS Textile Group, Inc. (JPST)
Juniper Networks, Inc. (JNPR)
Juno Online Services, Inc. (JWEB)

K

K2 Design, Inc. (KTWO)
K2 Design, Inc. (KTWOW)
Kaiser Ventures, Inc. (KRSC)
Kaman Corporation (KAMNG)
Karts International (KINTW)
Kaye Group, Inc. (KAYE)
Keith Companies, Inc. (The) (TKCI)
Kenan Transport Company (KTCO)
Kendle International Inc. (KNDL)
Kent Financial Services, Inc. (KENT)
Kentucky Electric Steel, Inc. (KESI)
Kevco, Inc. (KVCO)
Kewaunee Scientific (KEQU)

COMPANY (SYMBOL)

Key Florida Bancorp, Inc. (KEYB)
King Pharmaceuticals, Inc. (KING)
Kinnard Investments, Inc. (KINN)
KLLM Transport Services, Inc. (KLLM)
Knape & Vogt Manufacturing (KNAP)
Knight/Trimark Group, Inc. (NITE)
Koala Corporation (KARE)
Koss Corporation (KOSS)
KS Bancorp, Inc. (KSAV)
KSB Bancorp, Inc. (KSBK)
K-Tron International, Inc. (KTII)
KWG Resources, Inc. (KWGDF)
Kyzen Corporation (KYZNW)

L

L. B. Foster Company (FSTRA)
Lab Holdings, Inc. (LABH)
LaCrosse Footwear, Inc. (BOOT)
Ladish Company (LDSH)
Lady Luck Gaming Corporation (LUCK)
LaJolla Pharmaceutical Company (LJPC)
Lake Ariel Bancorp, Inc. (LABN)
Lakeland Financial Corporation (LKFN)
Lakeland Financial Corporation (LKFNP)
Lakeland Industries, Inc. (LAKE)
Lakes Gaming, Inc. (LACO)
Lam Research Corporation (LRCX)
Lamar Capital Corporation (LCCO)
Laminating Technologies, Inc. (LAMT)
Laminating Technologies, Inc. (LAMTU)
Lancaster Colony Corporation (LANC)
Lancit Media Entertainment Ltd. (LNCT)
Landmark Bancshares, Inc. (LARK)
Langer Biomechanics Group (GAIT)
Las Vegas Entertainment (LVENZ)
Laser Corporation (LSER)
Laser Power Corporation (LPWR)
Latin American Casinos, Inc. (LACI)
Latin American Casinos, Inc. (LACIW)
Latitude Communications, Inc. (LATD)
Lattice Semiconductor (LSCC)
Launch Media, Inc. (LAUN)
Laurel Capital Group, Inc. (LARL)
Lawrence Savings Bank (LSBX)
Leadville Corporation (LEAD)
Learning Tree International (LTRE)
LEC Technologies, Inc. (LECEP)
Leeds Federal Savings Bank (LFED)
Legacy Software, Inc. (LGCY)
Leisureways Marketing Ltd. (LMLAF)
Letchworth Independent (LEBC)
Level 3 Communications, Inc. (LVLT)
Lexford Inc. (CRSI)
Lexington B & L Financial (LXMO)

COMPANY (SYMBOL)

Lexington Global Asset (LGAM)
Lexington Healthcare Group (LEXI)
Lexington Healthcare Group (LEXIW)
LGS Group Inc. (LGSAF)
Liberate Technologies, Inc. (LBRT)
Liberty Bancorp, Inc. (LIBB)
Liberty Homes, Inc. (LIBHB)
Liberty Technologies, Inc. (LIBT)
Life Medical Sciences, Inc. (CHAIZ)
Lifetime Hoan Corporation (LCUT)
Lifeway Foods, Inc. (LWAY)
LightPath Technologies, Inc. (LPTHA)
LightPath Technologies, Inc. (LPTHW)
Lihir Gold, Limited (LIHRY)
Lincare Holdings, Inc. (LNCR)
Lincoln Bancorp (LNCB)
Lindal Cedar Homes, Inc. (LNDL)
Lindberg Corporation (LIND)
Lionbridge Technologies, Inc. (LIOX)
Liqui-Box Corporation (LIQB)
Liquid Audio, Inc. (LQID)
Litchfield Financial (LTCH)
Litronic Inc. (LTNX)
Littlefuse, Inc. (LFUSW)
Liuski International, Inc. (LSKI)
LJL Biosystems, Inc. (LJLB)
LM Ericsson Telephone Company (ERICY)
LMI Aerospace, Inc. (LMIA)
Local Financial Corporation (LFIN)
Log On America, Inc. (LOAX)
London Financial Corporation (LONF)
London International Group PLC
  (LONDY)
London Pacific Group, Limited (LPGLY)
LookSmart, Ltd. (LOOK)
Lowrance Electronics, Inc. (LEIX)
Lucor, Inc. (LUCR)
Lufkin Industries, Inc. (LUFK)
Lukens Medical Corporation (LUKN)
Lycos, Inc. (LCOS)
Lynx Therapeutics, Inc. (LYNX)

M

MACC Private Equities Inc. (MACC)
MacDermid, Incorporated (MACD)
Mackenzie Financial (MKFCF)
Mackie Designs, Inc. (MKIE)
Made2Manage Systems, Inc. (MTMS)
Madison Bancshares Group, Ltd. (MADB)
Magainin Pharmaceuticals Inc. (MAGN)
Mahaska Investment Company (OSKY)
Mahoning National Bancorp (MGNB)
Mail.com, Inc. (MAIL)
Maker Communications, Inc. (MAKR)

COMPANY (SYMBOL)

Makita Corp. (MKTAY)
Managed Care Solutions, Inc. (MCSX)
Manatron, Inc. (MANA)
Manhattan Associates, Inc. (MANH)
Mannatech, Inc. (MTEX)
Mansur Industries Inc. (MANS)
MapQuest.com, Inc. (MQST)
Marimba, Inc. (MRBA)
Marine Management Systems (MMSY)
Marine Management Systems (MMSYW)
Market Financial Corporation (MRKF)
MarketWatch.com, Inc. (MKTW)
Marquette Medical Systems, Inc. (MARQ)
Marsh Supermarkets, Inc. (MARSA)
MAS Technology Limited (MASSY)
Mason-Dixon Bancshares, Inc. (MSDXP)
MASSBANK Corp. (MASB)
Master Graphics, Inc. (MAGR)
Maverick Tube Corporation (MAVK)
Max & Erma's Restaurants, Inc. (MAXE)
Maxco, Inc. (MAXC)
Maxtor Corp. (MXTR)
Maxwell Shoe Company Inc. (MAXS)
Mayflower Co-operative Bank (MFLR)
Maynard Oil Company (MOIL)
Mazel Stores, Inc. (MAZL)
MBLA Financial Corporation (MBLF)
MBV Corp. (MFBC)
McClain Industries, Inc. (MCCL)
McGrath RentCorp (MGRC)
McLeod USA, Inc. (MCLDP)
McLeodUSA Incorporated (MCLD)
MCM Capital Group, Inc. (MCMC)
MDC Communications Corporation
  (MDCAF)
Meadow Valley Corporation (MVCO)
Meadowbrook Rehabilitation (MBRK)
Mechanical Technology, Inc. (MKTY)
MEDE AMERICA Corp. (MEDE)
Media Metrix, Inc. (MMXI)
Medical Control, Inc. (MDCL)
Medical Graphics Corporation (MGCC)
Mediconsult.com, Inc. (MCNS)
Medwave, Inc. (MDWV)
MEEMIC Holdings, Inc. (MEMH)
MegaBank Financial Corp. (MBFC)
Men's Wearhouse, Inc. (The) (SUITG)
Mercantile Bank Corporation (MBWM)
Merchants Bancshares, Inc. (MBVT)
Merchants New York Bancorp (MBNY)
Mercury Computer Systems (MRCY)
Meridian Insurance Group, Inc. (MIGI)
Meritrust Federal Savings Bank (MERI)
Merkert American Corporation (MERK)
Merrill Merchants Bancshares, Inc. (MERB)

COMPANY (SYMBOL)

Mes/Waste, Inc. (MWDS)
Methode Electronics, Inc. (METHB)
Metro Global Media, Inc. (MCMA)
Metro Information Services (MISI)
MetroBanCorp (METB)
MetroCorp Bancshares, Inc. (MCBI)
Metropolitan Financial Corp. (METF)
Metrotrans Corporation (MTRN)
MFRI, Inc. (MFRI)
MGC Communications, Inc. (MGCX)
Michigan Financial Corporation (MFCB)
Microcide Pharmaceuticals (MCDE)
Microenergy, Inc. (MICRP)
Microfield Graphics, Inc. (MICG)
Microframe, Inc. (MCFR)
Micro-Integration Corp. (MINT)
Micromuse, Inc. (MUSE)
Micron Electronics, Inc. (MUEI)
Micronetics Wireless, Inc. (NOIZ)
Microsoft Corporation (MSFT)
Microsoft Corporation (MSFTP)
Microstrategy, Inc. (MSTR)
Microtest, Inc. (MTST)
Mid Continent Bancshares, Inc. (MCBS)
Mid-Atlantic Community (MABG)
Midatlantic Corp. (PNCCG)
Mid-Coast Bancorp, Inc. (MCBN)
Middle Bay Oil Company, Inc. (MBOC)
Middlesex Water Company (MSEX)
Midland Company (The) (MLAN)
Midway Airlines Corporation (MDWY)
Midwest Bancshares, Inc. (MWBI)
Midwest Bank Holdings, Inc. (MBHI)
Midwest Grain Products, Inc. (MWGP)
MIH Ltd. (MIHL)
Mikron Instrument Company (MIKR)
Milbrook Press, Inc. (The) (MILB)
Miller Building Systems, Inc. (MBSI)
Miller Exploration Company (MEXP)
Milton Federal Financial (MFFC)
Mine Safety Appliances Company (MNES)
Mining Services International (MSIX)
MiningCo.com, Inc. (MINE)
Minuteman International Inc. (MMAN)
MIPS Technologies, Inc. (MIPS)
Mission Critical Software, Inc. (MCSW)
Mississippi Valley Bancshares (MVBIP)
Mississippi View Holding (MIVI)
Mitsui & Company, Ltd. (MITSY)
Mity-Life, Inc. (MITY)
MKS Instruments, Inc. (MKSI)
MLC Holdings, Inc. (MLCH)
MNB Bancshares Inc. (MNBB)
Mobile Mini, Inc. (MINIW)
Mobile Mini, Inc. (MINIZ)

COMPANY (SYMBOL)

Mobius Management Systems, Inc. (MOBI)
Modern Controls, Inc. (MOCO)
Modern Media Poppe Tyson, Inc. (MMPT)
Momentum Business Applications, Inc. (MMTM)
Monarch Avalon, Inc. (MAHI)
Monmouth Capital Corporation (MONM)
Moore Products Co. (MORP)
Moore-Handley, Inc. (MHCO)
Mortgage.com, Inc. (MDCM)
Motor Cargo Industries, Inc. (CRGO)
Motor Club of America (MOTR)
Motro Vac Technologies, Inc. (MVAC)
Movado Group Inc. (MOVA)
Moyco Technologies, Inc. (MOYC)
MP3.com, Inc. (MPPP)
Mpath Interactive, Inc. (MPTH)
MPW Industrial Services Group (MPWG)
MSB Financial, Inc. (MSBF)
Multex.com, Inc. (MLTX)
Multi-Color Corporation (LABL)
Multimedia Games, Inc. (MGAMW)
Multimedia Games, Inc. (MGAMZ)
Musicmaker.com, Inc. (HITS)
M-WAVE, Inc. (MWAV)
Mycogen Corporation (MYCO)
MyPoints.com, Inc. (MYPT)
Mystic Financial, Inc. (MYST)

N

N2H2, Inc. (NTWO)
NAM Corporation (NAMC)
NAM Corporation (NAMCU)
NAM Corporation (NAMCW)
Nanoen, Inc. (NGEN)
Napco Security Systems, Inc. (NSSC)
Nara Bank, National Association (NARA)
Nastech Pharmaceutical (NSTK)
National Bancorp of Alaska (NBAK)
National City Bancorporation (NCBM)
National City Bancshares, Inc. (NCBE)
National Datacomputer, Inc. (IDCP)
National Environmental Service (NESC)
National Home Centers, Inc. (NHCI)
National Home Health Care (NHHC)
National Income Realty Trust (NIRTS)
National Information Consortium (EGOV)
National Medical Health Card Systems (NMHC)
National Security Group, Inc. (NSEC)
Natrol, Inc. (NTOL)
NAVIDEC, Inc. (NVDC)
Navigant International, Inc. (FLYR)
NEI WebWorld, Inc. (NEIP)
Neo Therapeutics, Inc. (NEOTW)

COMPANY (SYMBOL)

NEON Systems, Inc. (NESY)
NeoPharm, Inc. (NPRMW)
NeoRx Corporation (NERX)
NeoRx Corporation (NERXP)
NeoRx Corporation (NERXW)
Neose Technologies, Inc. (NTEC)
Nera AS (NERAY)
Net Perceptions, Inc. (NETP)
Net2Phone, Inc. (NTOP)
Net.B@ank, Inc. (NTBK)
NetCom Systems, AB (publ) (NECSY)
NetGravity, Inc. (NETG)
Netia Holdings SA (NTIA)
NetIQ Corporation (NTIQ)
Netivation.com Inc. (NTVN)
NetObjects, Inc. (NETO)
Netro Corporation (NTRO)
NetScout Systems, Inc. (NTCT)
Netter Digital Entertainment (NETT)
Netter Digital Entertainment (NETTW)
Network Access Solutions Corp. (NASC)
Network Computing Devices (NCDI)
Network Connection, Inc. (The) (TNCX)
Network Imaging Corporation (IMGXP)
Network Imaging Corporation (IMGXW)
Network Plus Corp. (NPLS)
Network Six, Inc. (NWSS)
Neutral Posture Ergonomics (NTRL)
NevStar Gaming Corporation (NVSTW)
New Brunswick Scientific Co. (NBSC)
New England Community Bancorp (NECB)
New England Realty Associates (NEWRZ)
New Hampshire Thrift (NHTB)
New Horizon Kids Quest, Inc. (KIDQ)
New York Health Care, Inc. (NYHC)
NewCare Health Corporation (NWCA)
Newgen Results Corporation (NWGN)
Newmark Homes Corporation (NHCH)
NewMil Bancorp, Inc. (NMSB)
NewSouth Bancorp, Inc. (NSBC)
NextCard, Inc. (NXCD)
Nextel Communications, Inc. (NXTL)
Nextera Enterprises, Inc. (NXRA)
NextHealth, Inc. (NEXT)
nFront, Inc. (NFNT)
Niagara Bancorp, Inc. (NBCP)
Nicholas Financial, Inc. (NICKF)
Nicollet Process Engineering (NPET)
Nitches, Inc. (NICH)
NMBT CORP (NMBT)
Noble International, Ltd. (NOBLN)
Noland Company (NOLD)
Norstan, Inc. (NRRD)
Nortech Systems Incorporated (NSYS)
North American Palladium Ltd. (PDLCF)

COMPANY (SYMBOL)

North American Scientific, Inc. (NASI)
North Bancshares, Inc. (NBSI)
North County Bancorp (NCBH)
North Pittsburgh Systems, Inc. (NPSI)
Northeast Indiana Bancorp (NEIB)
NorthEast Optic Network, Inc. (NOPT)
Northern States Financial (NSFC)
NorthPoint Communications Group, Inc. (NPNT)
Northrim Bank (NRIM)
Northway Financial Inc. (NWFI)
Northwest Teleproductions (NWTL)
Norwood Financial Corp. (NWFL)
Norwood Promotional (NPPI)
Notify Corporation (NTFY)
Notify Corporation (NTFYU)
Notify Corporation (NTFYW)
Novadigm, Inc. (NVDM)
NovaMed Eyecare, Inc. (NOVA)
Novamerican Steel, Inc. (TONSF)
Novametrix Medical Systems (NMTXZ)
Novitron International, Inc. (NOVI)
NPC International, Inc. (NPCI)
NRG Generating (U.S.) Inc. (NRGG)
NS&L Bancorp, Inc. (NSLB)
NSD Bancorp, Inc. (NSDB)
NTL Incorporated (NTLI)
NTN Canada, Inc. (NTNC)
Nucentrix Broadband Networks (NCNX)
Nutmeg Federal Savings & Loan (NTMG)
Nutmeg Federal Savings & Loan (NTMGP)
Nutraceutical International Corp. (NUTR)
Nutrition For Life (NFLIW)
NuWave Technologies, Inc. (WAVE)
NuWave Technologies, Inc. (WAVEW)
NVIDIA Corp. (NVDA)
N-Viro International (NVIC)

O

Oak Hill Financial, Inc. (OAKF)
Oakhurst Company, Inc. (OAKC)
Obie Media Corporation (OBIE)
ObjectSoft Corporation (OSFT)
ObjectSoft Corporation (OSFTW)
Oce NV (OCENY)
Officeland Inc. (OFLUF)
Ohio Valley Banc Corp. (OVBC)
OHM Corporation (OHMCG)
OHSL Financial Corp. (OHSL)
Oilgear Company (The) (OLGR)
Old Kent Financial Corporation (OKEN)
Old Second Bancorp, Inc. (OSBC)
Olicom A/S (OLCWF)
Olympic Cascade Financial (NATS)
Olympic Steel, Inc. (ZEUS)

COMPANY (SYMBOL)

OMNI Energy Services Corp. (OMNI)
Omni Insurance Group, Inc. (OMGR)
On Stage Entertainment, Inc. (ONSTW)
OneLink Communication, Inc. (ONEL)
OneMain.com, Inc. (ONEM)
OneSource Information Services (ONES)
Online Resource & Communications (ORCC)
Online System Services, Inc. (WEBB)
onlinetradinginc.com (LINE)
On-Site Sourcing, Inc. (ONSSU)
On-Site Sourcing, Inc. (ONSSW)
ONYX Software Corporation (ONXS)
Open Plan Systems, Inc. (PLAN)
Ophthalmic Imaging Systems (OISI)
Optelecom, Inc. (OPTC)
Optibase Ltd. (OBAS)
Optika Imaging Systems, Inc. (OPTK)
Optimax Industries, Inc. (OPMXZ)
OptiSystems Solutions, Ltd. (OPTLF)
OptiSystems Solutions, Ltd. (OPTWF)
Oracle Corporation (ORCL)
Orange National Bancorp (OGNB)
Oregon Trail Financial Corp. (OTFC)
Orlando Predators (The) (PRED)
Orlando Predators (The) (PREDW)
OroAmerica, Inc. (OROA)
Ortec International, Inc. (ORTC)
Ortec International, Inc. (ORTCW)
Ortec International, Inc. (ORTCZ)
OrthAlliance, Inc. (ORAL)
Oshkosh Truck Corporation (OTRKB)
OSI Systems, Inc. (OSIS)
Otter Tail Power Company (OTTR)
Outlook Group Corp. (OUTL)
OYO Geospace Corporation (OYOG)
Ozark Capital Trust (OZRKP)

P

P & F Industries, Inc. (PFINA)
P. F. Chang's China Bistro, Inc. (PCFB)
PACE Health Management (PCES)
Pacific Capital Bancorp (PABN)
Pacific Coast Apparel Company (ACAJ)
Pacific Crest Capital, Inc. (PCCI)
Pacific Crest Capital, Inc. (PCCIP)
PacifiCare Health Systems (PHSYB)
Packaged Ice, Inc. (ICED)
Packeteer, Inc. (PKTR)
PalEx, Inc. (PALX)
Palm Harbor Homes, Inc. (PHHM)
Pamrapo Bancorp, Inc. (PBCI)
Pancho's Mexican Buffet, Inc. (PAMX)
Paradigm Geophysical, Ltd. (PGEOF)
Paradigm Medical Industries (PMED)

COMPANY (SYMBOL)

Paradise, Inc. (PARF)
Paradise Music & Entertainment (PDSE)
Paradise Music & Entertainment (PDSEW)
Paradyne Networks, Inc. (PDYN)
Paramark Enterprises, Inc. (TJCWC)
Paramark Enterprises, Inc. (TJCZC)
Paramount Financial (PARAW)
Paris Corporation (PBFI)
Pathfinder Bancorp, Inc. (PBHC)
Patient Infosystems, Inc. (PATI)
Patriot Bank Corp. (PBIX)
Paul Harris Stores, Inc. (PAUH)
Paul Mueller Company (MUEL)
Paulson Capital Corp. (PLCC)
PBOC Holdings, Inc. (PBOC)
PC Connection, Inc. (PCCC)
PC411, Inc. (PCFRU)
PC411, Inc. (PCFRW)
PCA International, Inc. (PCAI)
PCC Group, Inc. (PCCG)
pcOrder.com, Inc. (PCOR)
PDK Labs, Inc. (PDKLP)
Peak International Limited (PEAKF)
Pease Oil & Gas Company (WPOGW)
Peekskill Financial (PEEK)
Peerless Manufacturing Company (PMFG)
Pegasus Communications (PGTV)
Penn National Gaming, Inc. (PENN)
PennFed Financial Services (PFSBP)
PennFirst Bancorp, Inc. (PWBC)
PennFirst Bancorp, Inc. (PWBCP)
Pennichuck Corporation (PNNW)
Pennsylvania Manufacturers Corp.
  (PMFRA)
Pennwood Bancorp, Inc. (PWBK)
People's Bancshares, Inc. (PBKBP)
Peoples BancTrust Company (PBTC)
Peoples Bank (PEBK)
Peoples Financial Corporation (PFFC)
Peoples First Corporation (PFKY)
Peoples Home Savings Bank (PHSB)
Permanent Bancorp, Inc. (PERM)
Perpetual Midwest Financial (PMFI)
Perry County Financial (PCBC)
PerSeptive Biosystems, Inc. (PBIO)
PerSeptive Biosystems, Inc. (PBIOW)
Persistence Software, Inc. (PRSW)
Pete's Brewing Company (WIKD)
Petro Union, Inc. d/b/a (HVNV)
PetroCorp Incorporated (PETR)
Petroglyph Energy, Inc. (PGEI)
Petroleum Helicopters, Inc. (PHEL)
Petroleum Helicopters, Inc. (PHELK)
Petromet Resources Limited (PNTGF)
Petrominerals Corporation (PTRO)

COMPANY (SYMBOL)

Phar-Mor, Inc. (PMORW)
PHC, Inc. (PIHCW)
Phoenix International Ltd. (PHXX)
Phoenix International Sciences, Inc. (PHXI)
Phone.com, Inc. (PHCM)
Photo Control Corporation (PHOC)
Photoelectron Corporation (PECX)
Photomatrix, Inc. (PHRX)
PhyCor, Inc. (PHYCH)
Physicians Health Services (PHSV)
Physicians' Specialty Corp. (ENTS)
PICO Holdings Inc. (PICO)
PictureTel Corporation (PCTL)
Piemonte Foods, Inc. (PIFI)
Piercing Pagoda, Inc. (PGDA)
Pilot Network Services, Inc. (PILT)
Pinnacle Financial Services (PNFI)
Pinnacle Holdings Inc. (BIGT)
Pioneer Commercial Funding (PCFC)
Piranha Interactive Publishing (PRAN)
Pittsburgh Home Capital Trust I (PHFCP)
Pittsburgh Home Financial (PHFC)
Pivotal Corporation (PVTL)
Plasti-Line, Inc. (SIGN)
PLX Technology, Inc. (PLXT)
Polymer Research Corp. of America (PROA)
PNB Financial Group (PNBF)
Pocahontas Federal Savings (PFSL)
Point of Sale Limited (POSIF)
Pointe Financial Corporation (PNTE)
PolyMedica Corporation (PLMD)
Pope Resources (POPEZ)
Popular, Inc. (BPOPP)
Portal Software, Inc. (PRSF)
Potters Financial Corporation (PTRS)
Premier Concepts, Inc. (FAUX)
Premier Financial Bancorp (PFBI)
Prestige Bancorp, Inc. (PRBC)
Priceline.com, Inc. (PCLN)
Pride Automotive Group, Inc. (LEAS)
Prima Energy Corporation (PENG)
PrimaCom AG (PCAG)
Prime Bancshares, Inc. (PBTX)
Prime Capital Corporation (PMCP)
PrimeEnergy Corporation (PNRG)
Primus Knowledge Solutions (PKSI)
Princeton National Bancorp (PNBC)
Printware, Inc. (PRTW)
Priority Healthcare (PHCC)
Private Business, Inc. (PBIZ)
Private Media Group, Inc. (PRVT)
PrivateBancorp, Inc. (PVTB)
Prodigy Communications Corp. (PRGY)
Producers Entertainment Group (TPEGP)
Producers Entertainment Group (TPEGW)

COMPANY (SYMBOL)

Productivity Technologies (PRAC)
Productivity Technologies (PRACW)
Professional Detailing, Inc. (PDII)
Professional Transportation (TRUC)
Professional Transportation (TRUCW)
Profile Technologies, Inc. (PRTK)
Progenitor, Inc. (PGENW)
Progressive Bank, Inc. (PSBK)
Projectavision, Inc. (PJTVP)
PROLOGIC Management Systems (PRLO)
PROLOGIC Management Systems
  (PRLOW)
ProMedCo Management Company (PMCO)
Prophet 21, Inc. (PXXI)
Prosperity Bancshares, Inc. (PRSP)
Protein Polymer Technologies (PPTIW)
Provant, Inc. (POVT)
Provident American Corporation (PAMC)
Provident Bancorp, Incorporated (PBCP)
Province Healthcare Company (PRHC)
Proxicom, Inc. (PXCM)
PS Financial, Inc. (PSFI)
Pulaski Financial Corp. (PULB)
Pulse Bancorp, Inc. (PULS)
Pure World, Inc. (PURW)

Q

QIAGEN N.V. (QGENF)
Quadrax Corporation (QDRXZ)
Quepasa.com, Inc. (PASA)
Quest Medical, Inc. (QMED)
Quest Software, Inc. (USFT)
Questa Oil & Gas Co. (QUES)
QuesTech, Inc. (QTEC)
Quidel Corporation (QDELW)
Quiksilver, Inc. (QUIK)
Quizno's Corporation (QUIZ)
Quokka Sports, Inc. (QKKA)
Quotesmith.com, Inc. (QUOT)
Qwest Communications International, Inc.
  (QWST)

R

R & R, Inc. (RBIN)
Radio One, Inc. (ROIA)
Rag Shops, Inc. (RAGS)
RailWorks Corp. (RWKS)
Rainbow Rentals, Inc. (RBOW)
Ramp Networks, Inc. (RAMP)
Rand Capital Corporation (RAND)
Randgold & Exploration (RANGY)
Rankin Automotive Group, Inc. (RAVE)
Raven Industries, Inc. (RAVN)
Ravenswood Winery, Inc. (RVWD)

COMPANY (SYMBOL)

RAVISENT Technologies Inc. (RVST)
Rawson-Koenig, Inc. (RAKO)
Razorfish, Inc. (RAZF)
RCM Technologies, Inc. (RCMTZ)
Reading Entertainment, Inc. (RDGE)
Real Goods Trading Corporation (RGTC)
Realco, Inc. (RLCO)
Realco, Inc. (RLCOW)
Reality Interactive, Inc. (RINT)
Reality Interactive, Inc. (RINTW)
Realty Information Group, Inc. (RIGX)
Reckson Services Industries, Inc. (RSII)
Reconditioned Systems, Inc. (RESY)
Recovery Network, Inc. (The) (RNETU)
Red Hat, Inc. (RHAT)
Red Hot Concepts, Inc. (RHCDC)
Redback Networks, Inc. (RBAK)
Redwood Empire Bancorp (REBC)
Reeds Jewelers, Inc. (REED)
Regency Bancorp (REFN)
Regeneron Pharmaceuticals (REGN)
Regent Assist Living, Inc. (RGNT)
Regent Bancshares Corp. (RBNK)
Reliv' International, Inc. (RELV)
Remington Oil and Gas (ROILAA)
Renaissance Capital Growth & Income
  Fund III, Inc. (RENN)
Renaissance Entertainment (FAIRW)
Renaissance Entertainment (FAIRZ)
Rent-A-Wreck of America, Inc. (RAWA)
Reptron Electronics, Inc. (REPT)
Republic Bancorp Inc., Class A (RBCAA)
Republic Bancshares, Inc. (REPB)
Republic Bancshares, Inc. (REPBP)
Republic Security Financial (RSFCO)
Research in Motion Ltd. (RIMM)
Resource Bank (RBKV)
Restoration Hardware, Inc. (RSTO)
Resurgence Properties, Inc. (RPIA)
Retrospettiva, Inc. (RTRO)
Reunion Industries Inc. (RUNI)
Reuters Holdings PLC ADR (RTRSY)
Revenue Properties Company (RPCLF)
Rexall Sundown, Inc. (REXD)
Rexall Sundown, Inc. (RXSD)
Rexhall Industries, Inc. (REXL)
RF Industries, Inc. (RFIL)
Rhythms NetConnections, Inc. (RTHM)
Richmond County Financial Corp. (RCBK)
Ridgeview, Inc. (RIDG)
Ridgewood Financial, Incorporated (RSBI)
Rimage Corporation (RIMG)
Ringer Corporation (RING)
Risk Capital Holdings, Inc. (RCHI)

COMPANY (SYMBOL)

Riverview Bancorp Inc. (RVSB)
Riviana Foods Inc. (RVFD)
Roanoke Gas Company (RGCO)
Roberds, Inc. (RBDS)
RockShox, Inc. (RSHX)
Rocky Mountain Chocolate (RMCF)
Rocky Mountain Internet, Inc. (RMIIU)
Romac International, Inc. (ROMC)
Ronson Corporation (RONC)
Room Plus, Inc. (PLUS)
Room Plus, Inc. (PLUSW)
Rose's Holdings Inc. (RSTOW)
Rottlund Company, Inc. (The) (RHOM)
RoweCom Inc. (ROWE)
Roy F. Weston, Inc. (WSTNA)
Royal Gold, Inc. (RGLD)
Royal Olympic Cruise Lines, Inc. (ROCLF)
Royal Precision, Inc. (RIFL)
RPM, Inc. (RPOWG)
RSI Systems, Inc. (RSIS)
Rubio's Restaurants, Inc. (RUBO)
Russel Metals, Inc. (RUSAF)
Ryan, Beck & Co., Inc. (RBCO)

S

S & K Famous Brands, Inc. (SKFB)
S I Technologies Inc. (SISI)
S & T Bancorp, Inc. (STBA)
S2 Golf Inc. (GOLF)
SAES Getters S.P.A. (SAESY)
Sage Laboratories, Inc. (SLAB)
Sagebrush, Inc. (SAGE)
Sagent Technology, Inc. (SGNT)
Saint Andrews Golf Corporation (SAGC)
Salem Communications Corp. (SALM)
SalesLogix Corporation (SLGX)
Saliva Diagnostic Systems (SALVW)
Salon.com Inc. (SALN)
Sands Regent (The) (SNDS)
Sandy Spring Bancorp, Inc. (SASR)
Sanmina Corporation (SANM)
Santa Barbara Bancorp (SABB)
Santa Fe Financial Corporation (SFEF)
Santos, Ltd. (STOSY)
SanVec Company (1990), Ltd. (SVECF)
Sanyo Electric Co., Ltd. (SANYY)
Sawako Corporation (SWKOY)
SBA Communications Corp. (SBAC)
SCC Communications Corp. (SCCX)
Scherer Healthcare, Inc. (SCHR)
School Specialty, Inc. (SCHS)
Schuler Homes, Inc. (SHLRG)
Schultz Sav-O Stores, Inc. (SAVO)
Scient Corporation (SCNT)

COMPANY (SYMBOL)

Scientific Learning Corp. (SCIL)
Scientific Technologies (STIZ)
Scottish Annuity & Life Holdings, Ltd. (SCTLF)
Seacoast Banking Corporation (SBCFA)
Seacoast Financial Services Corp. (SCFS)
Search Financial Services Inc. (SFSI)
Search Financial Services, Inc. (SFSIP)
Seaway Food Town, Inc. (SEWY)
Second Bancorp, Incorporated (SECD)
Second National Financial Corp. (SEFC)
Security First Corp. (SFSL)
Security National Financial (SNFCA)
Seibels Bruce Group, Inc. (SBIG)
Select Comfort Corporation (AIRB)
SEMCO Energy, Inc. (SMGS)
Seminis, Inc. (SMNS)
Senior Tour Players (SRTR)
Senior Tour Players (SRTRW)
Sento Technical Innovations (SNTO)
SERENA Software, Inc. (SRNA)
Serengeti Eyewear, Inc. (SOLR)
Serengeti Eyewear Inc. (SOLRW)
Sevenson Environmental (SEVN)
SFS Bancorp, Inc. (SFED)
SFX Broadcasting, Inc. (SFXBW)
SGV Bancorp, Inc. (SGVB)
Sheridan Energy, Inc. (SHDN)
Shire Pharmaceuticals Group (SHPY)
Shoe Pavilion, Inc. (SHOE)
Sho-Me Financial Corp. (SMFC)
Shoreline Financial (SLFC)
Showcase Corporation (SHWC)
SI Handling Systems, Inc. (SIHS)
Siebel Systems, Inc. (SEBL)
Siebert Financial Corp. (SIEB)
SigmaTron International, Inc. (SGMA)
Signature Inns, Inc. (SNGSP)
Silknet Software, Inc. (SILK)
SilverStream Software, Inc. (SSSW)
Simmons First National (SFNCA)
Simmons First National (SFNCP)
Simulation Sciences, Inc. (SMCI)
Simulations Plus, Inc. (SIMU)
Sinclair Broadcast Group, Inc. (SBGIP)
Six Rivers National Bank (SIXR)
SJNB Financial Corp. (SJNB)
Sky Network Television Limited (NZSKY)
SkyePharma PLC (SKYYV)
Skylands Community Bank (SKCB)
Skyline Multimedia (SKYL)
Skyline Multimedia (SKYLU)
Skyline Multimedia (SKYLW)
Smartserv Online, Inc. (SSOLW)

COMPANY (SYMBOL)

SMED International, Inc. (SMEDF)
Smithfield Companies, Inc. (HAMS)
Smith-Gardner & Associates, Inc. (SGAI)
Smith-Midland Corporation (SMIDW)
SNB Bancshares, Inc. (SNBJ)
Sobieski Bancorp, Inc. (SOBI)
Societe Europeenne de Communication S.A.
  (SECAY)
Societe Europeenne de Communication S.A.
  (SECBY)
SoftNet Systems, Inc. (SOFTN)
Software.com, Inc. (SWCM)
software.net Corporation (SWNT)
SOFTWORKS, Inc. (SWRX)
Sound Advice, Inc. (SUND)
Sound Federal Bancorp (SFFS)
South Alabama Bancorporation (SABC)
South Carolina Community (SCCB)
South Jersey Financial Corporation (SJFC)
South Street Financial (SSFC)
Southern Community Bancshares (SCBS)
Southern Missouri Bancorp (SMBC)
Southern Pacific Petroleum N.L. (SPPTY)
Southern Security Life (SSLI)
Southside Bancshares Corp. (SBCO)
Southside Bancshares, Inc. (SBSIP)
Southwest Bancorp, Inc. (OKSBO)
Southwest Bancorp, Inc. (OKSBP)
Southwest Bancshares, Inc. (SWBI)
Southwest Water Company (SWWC)
Span-America Medical Systems (SPAN)
Spanlink Communications, Inc. (SPLK)
Sparta Foods, Inc. (SPFO)
Sparta Pharmaceuticals, Inc. (SPTAL)
Sparta Pharmaceuticals, Inc. (SPTAU)
Sparta Pharmaceuticals, Inc. (SPTAW)
Specialized Health Products (SHPI)
Specialty Catalog Corp. (CTLG)
Spec's Music, Inc. (SPEK)
Spectra-Physics Lasers, Inc. (SPLI)
SpectraScience, Inc. (SPSI)
Spectrx, Inc. (SPRX)
Splitrock Services, Inc. (SPLT)
Sport Chalet, Inc. (SPCH)
Sportman's Guide, Inc. (SGDE)
SQL Financials International, Inc. (SQLF)
St. Helena Gold Mines Limited (SGOLY)
Stacey's Buffet, Inc. (SBUFW)
Stake Technology Ltd. (STKLF)
Stamps.com Inc. (STMP)
Stanley Furniture Company (STLY)
Star City Holdings Limited (SCITY)
Star Multi Care Services, Inc. (SMCS)
Star Resources Corporation (SRRCF)
Starcraft Corporation (STCR)

COMPANY (SYMBOL)

StarMedia Network, Inc. (STRM)
Starmet Corporation (STMT)
State Auto Financial (STFC)
State Financial Services (SFSW)
State of The Art, Inc. (SOTA)
StateFed Financial Corporation (SFFC)
Statis Terminals Group NV (STNV)
Stearns & Lehman, Inc. (SLHN)
Steel Dynamics, Inc. (STLD)
Sterling Bancshares, Inc. (SBIBP)
Sterling Financial Corporation (SLFI)
Sterling Financial Corporation (STSAO)
Sterling West Bancorp (SWBC)
Stet Hellas Telecomm SA (STHLY)
Steven Myers & Associates, Inc. (WINS)
Stirling Cooke Brown Holdings (SCBHF)
Strategic Distribution, Inc. (STRD)
Streamline.com, Inc. (SLNE)
Student Advantage, Inc. (STAD)
STV Group, Inc. (STVI)
Success Bancshares, Inc. (SXNB)
Suffolk Bancorp (SUBK)
Sumitomo Bank of California (SUMI)
Sumitomo Bank of California (SUMIZ)
Summit Bancshares, Inc. (SBIT)
Summit Bank Corporation (SBGA)
Summit Financial Corporation (SUMM)
Sun Bancorp, Inc. (SNBC)
Sun Community Bancorp, Ltd. (SCBL)
Sun Hydraulics Corporation (SNHY)
SunPharm Corporation (SUNPU)
Sunshine Mining and Refining (SILVZ)
Super Vision International (SUPVA)
Super Vision International (SUPVZ)
Superior National Insurance (SNTL)
SurModics, Inc. (SRDX)
Surrey, Inc. (SOAPU)
Swedish Match, AB (SWMAY)
Swiss Army Brands Inc. (SABI)
Symbollon Corporation (SYMBA)
Symbollon Corporation (SYMBW)
Symons International Group (SIGC)
Symphonix Devices, Inc. (SMPX)
Synalloy Corporation (SYNC)
Synaptic Pharmaceutical (SNAP)
Synbiotics Corporation (SBIO)
SYNSORB Biotech, Inc. (SYBBF)
Synthetic Industries, Inc. (SIND)
Syscomm International (SYCM)
System Software Associates (SSAXG)
Systems & Computer Technology (SCTCG)

T

Take-Two Interactive Software (TTWOW)
Talk City, Inc. (TCTY)

COMPANY (SYMBOL)

Tandy Brands Accessories, Inc. (TBAC)
Tappan Zee Financial, Inc. (TPNZ)
Taylor Devices, Inc. (TAYD)
TBA Entertainment Corporation (TBAEW)
TBC Corporation (TBCC)
TC Pipelines, LP (TCLPZ)
TEAM America Corporation (TMAM)
Team Financial, Inc. (TFIN)
TearDrop Golf Company (TDRPW)
Tech Data Corporation (TECD)
Technisouce, Inc. (TSRC)
TEKELEC (TKLC)
Tekgraf, Inc. (TKGFW)
TeleBanc Financial Corp. (TBFC)
Tele-Communications, Inc. (TCOMP)
Telemundo Group, Inc. (TLMDW)
TelePad Corporation (TPADU)
TelePad Corporation (TPADW)
Telesystem International Wireless of Canada
 (TIWIF)
Teletouch Communications, Inc. (TELL)
Teletouch Communications, Inc. (TELLW)
Telident, Inc. (TLDT)
Tellabs, Inc. (TLAB)
Tellurian, Inc. (TLRN)
Telscape International, Inc. (TSCPW)
Telular Corporation (WRLS)
Temtex Industries, Inc. (TMTX)
TenFold Corporation (TENF)
Terayon Communication Systems, Inc.
 (TERN)
Tesco Corporation (TESOF)
Tescorp, Inc. (TESCP)
Tetra Tech, Inc. (WATR)
Texoil, Inc. (TXLI)
Texoil, Inc. (TXLIW)
Texoil, Inc. (TXLIZ)
TGC Industries, Inc. (TGCI)
TGC Industries, Inc. (TGCIP)
theglobe.com, Inc. (TGLO)
Thermo-Mizer Environmental (THMZW)
TheStreet.com, Inc. (TSCM)
Thinking Tools, Inc. (TSIM)
Thistle Group Holdings, Co. (THTL)
Thomaston Mills, Inc. (TMSTA)
TIB Financial Corporation (TIBB)
TIBCO Software, Inc. (TIBX)
Ticketmaster Online-CitySearch, Inc.
 (TMCS)
Timber Lodge Steakhouse, Inc. (TBRL)
Timberland Bancorp, Inc. (TSBK)
Time Warner Telecom, Inc. (TWTC)
Titan Pharmaceuticals, Inc. (TTNP)
TLII Liquidating Corporation (TLII)
Top Image Systems, Ltd. (TISWF)

COMPANY (SYMBOL)

topjobs.net PLC (TJOB)
TOPRO Incorporated (TPROW)
Total Entertainment Restaurant (TENT)
Total-Tel USA Communications (TELU)
Tower Tech, Inc. (TTMT)
Towne Services, Inc. (TWNE)
Tracor, Inc. (TTRRW)
Tractor Supply Company (TSCO)
Trailer Bridge, Inc. (TRBR)
Tramford International, Ltd. (TRFDF)
Transaction Systems Architects (TSAI)
TransAmerican Waste Industries (WSTE)
TransCor Waste Services, Inc. (TRCW)
Transgene SA (TRGNY)
Trans-Global Resources N.L. (TGBRY)
Transglobe Energy Corporation (TGLEF)
Trans-Industries, Inc. (TRNI)
Transit Group Inc. (TRGPW)
Transmation, Inc. (TRNS)
Transmedia Asia Pacific, Inc. (MBTA)
Trend Micro, Inc. (TMICV)
Triangle Pacific Corp. (TRIP)
Tri-County Bancorp, Inc. (TRIC)
Trimark Holdings, Inc. (TMRK)
Trimedyne, Inc. (TMED)
Trinity Biotech PLC (TRIBY)
Trinity Biotech PLC (TRIZF)
Trio-Tech International (TRTC)
Triple S Plastics, Inc. (TSSS)
Troy Financial Corp. (TRYF)
Troy Group, Inc. (TROY)
TSI International Software Ltd. (TSFW)
Tuesday Morning Corporation (TUES)
Tufco Technologies, Inc. (TFCO)
Tumbleweed, Inc. (TWED)
Tumbleweed Software Corporation
 (TMWD)
Tut Systems, Inc. (TUTS)
T.V.G. Technologies Ltd. (TVGLF)
T.V.G. Technologies Ltd. (TVGWF)
T.V.G. Technologies Ltd. (TVGZF)
Tweeter Home Entertainment Group, Inc.
 (TWTR)

U

UBICS, Inc. (UBIX)
uBid, Inc. (UBID)
UFP Technologies, Inc. (UFPT)
Ultimate Software Group, Inc. (The) (ULTI)
Ultradata Systems (ULTR)
Uncle B's Bakery, Inc. (UNCB)
UNIDYNE Corporation (UDYN)
UNIFAB International, Inc. (UFAB)
UniHolding Corp. (UHLD)
Union Bankshares Corporation (UBSH)

COMPANY (SYMBOL)

Union Bankshares Capital Trust I
(UBSCP)
Union Community Bancorp (UCBC)
Union Community Bank (UCBC)
UnionBancorp, Inc. (UBCD)
Uniphase Corporation (UNPH)
Unique Casual Restaurants, Inc. (UNIQ)
Uniservice Corp. (UNSRW)
Uniservice Corp. (USNRA)
United Bancorp, Inc. (UBCP)
United Community Financial (UCFC)
United Financial Corp. (UBMT)
United Investors Realty Trust (UIRT)
United News & Media, p.l.c. (UNEWY)
United PanAm Financial Corporation
(UPFC)
United Pan-Europe Communications NV
(UPCOY)
United Road Services, Inc. (URSI)
United Security Bancorporation (USBN)
United Television, Inc. (UTVI)
United Therapeutics Corp. (UTHR)
Unity Bancorp, Inc. (UNTY)
Universal American Financial (UHCO)
Universal American Financial (UHCOW)
Universal Automotive (UVSL)
Universal Display Corporation (PANL)
Universal Hospital Services (UHOS)
Universal Mfg. Co. (UFMG)
Universal Stainless & Alloy (USAP)
Ursus Telecom Corporation (UTCC)
US LEC Corp. (CLEC)
US SEARCH.com Inc. (SRCH)
U.S. Bancorp (FBSWW)
U.S. Concrete, Inc. (RMIX)
U.S. Energy Corp. (USEG)
U.S. Energy Systems, Inc. (USEY)
U.S. Home & Garden, Inc. (USHGW)
U.S. Interactive, Inc. (USIT)
U.S. Physical Therapy, Inc. (USPH)
U.S. Plastic Lumber Co. (USPL)
U.S. Transportation Systems (USTSW)
U.S. Vision, Inc. (USVI)
U.S. Xpress Enterprises, Inc. (XPRSA)
U.S.-China Industrial (CHDXW)
USA Networks, Inc. (USAI)
USA Truck, Inc. (USAK)
USANA, Inc. (USNA)
USBANCORP, Inc. (UBAN)
USDATA Corporation (USDC)
USFreightways Corporation (USFC)
Usinternetworking, Inc. (USIX)
USN Communications, Inc. (USNC)
USP Real Estate Investment (USPTS)

COMPANY (SYMBOL)

V

V.I. Technologies, Inc. (VITX)
Vail Banks, Inc. (VAIL)
Valle de Oro Bank NA (VADO)
Vallen Corporation (VALN)
Valley Independent Bank (VAIB)
Valley Media, Inc. (VMIX)
Value America, Inc. (VUSA)
Value Line, Inc. (VALU)
Varian Inc. (VARIV)
VaxGen, Inc. (VXGN)
Vectra Banking Corporation (VTRAO)
Velcro Industries N.V. (VELCF)
Venturian Corp. (VENT)
Verisign, Inc. (VRSN)
VERITAS Software Corporation (VRTS)
Versatel Telecom International (VRSA)
Versatility Inc. (VERS)
VerticaNet, Inc. (VERT)
VIALOG Corp. (VLOG)
Viant Corporation (VIAN)
ViaSat, Inc. (VSAT)
Video Display Corporation (VIDE)
Video Services Corporation (VSCX)
Videonics, Inc. (VDNX)
View Tech, Inc. (VUTKW)
Vignette Corporation (VIGN)
Vinings Investment Properties (VIPIS)
Vion Pharmaceuticals, Inc. (VIONU)
Vion Pharmaceuticals, Inc. (VIONW)
Virginia Capital Bancshares, Inc. (VCAP)
Virginia Commerce Bank (VCBK)
Virginia Gas Company (VGCO)
Virginia Gas Company (VGCOW)
Visual Data Corporation (VDAT)
Visual Networks, Inc. (VNWK)
VISX, Incorporated (VISX)
Vitesse Semiconductor Corporation (VTSS)
Vitran Corporation, Inc. (VTNAF)
Voice It Worldwide, Inc. (MEMO)
VoiceStream Wireless Corporation (VSTR)
Volvo (A B) (VOLVY)
V-ONE Corporation (VONE)
VOXEL (VOXLU)
Voyager.net, Inc. (VOYN)
VRB Bancorp (VRBA)
Vyrex Corporation (VYRXW)
Vysis, Inc. (VYSI)

W

Wall Street Deli, Inc. (WSDI)
Walnut Financial Services (WNUT)
Walsh International, Inc. (WSHI)
Walshire Assurance Company (WALS)

COMPANY (SYMBOL)

Wandel & Goltermann (WGTI)
Warner Chilcott Public Limited (WCRXY)
Warrantech Corporation (WTEC)
Warren Bancorp, Inc. (WRNB)
Warwick Community Bancorp, Inc. (WSBI)
Warwick Valley Telephone Company
  (WWVY)
Washington Banking Company (WBCO)
Washington Federal, Inc. (WFSL)
Washington Mutual, Inc. (WAMU)
Washington Mutual, Inc. (WAMUM)
Washington Scientific (WSCI)
Waste Connections, Inc. (WCNX)
Waste Industries, Inc. (WWIN)
Waste Systems International (WSII)
WasteMasters, Inc. (WAST)
Waterford Wedgewood PLC (WATFZ)
Water-Jel Technologies Inc. (XCED)
Waters Instruments, Inc. (WTRS)
Watson General Corporation (WGEN)
Wausau-Mosinee Paper (WSAU)
Wave Systems Corp. (WAVX)
Wave Technologies (WAVT)
Wavecom SA (WVCM)
WavePhore, Inc. (WAVO)
Waverly, Inc. (WAVR)
Wayne Bancorp, Inc. (WNNB)
Wayne Bancorp, Inc. (WYNE)
Wayne Savings Bancshares Inc. (WAYN)
WD-40 Company (WDFC)
Webster City Federal Savings (WCFB)
Webster Financial Corporation (WBST)
WebTrends Corporation (WEBT)
Wegener Corporation (WGNR)
WellCare Management Group (The) (WELL)
Wellington Properties Trust (WLPT)
Werner Enterprises, Inc. (WERN)
WesBanco, Inc. (WSBC)
Wescast Industries, Inc. (WCSTF)
Wesley Jessen VisionCare, Inc. (WJCO)
West Coast Bancorp (WCBO)
West Coast Entertainment Corp. (WCEC)
West Essex Bancorp, Inc. (WEBK)
West Marine, Inc. (WMAR)
West TeleServices Corporation (WTSC)
WestAmerica Corporation (WACC)
WestBank Corporation (WBKC)
Westell Technologies, Inc. (WSTL)
Westerbeke Corporation (WTBK)
WesterFed Financial (WSTR)
Western Bancorp (WEBC)
Western Bancorp (WEFC)
Western Beef, Inc. (BEEF)
Western Country Clubs, Inc. (WCCI)

COMPANY (SYMBOL)

Western Deep Levels Ltd. (WDEPY)
Western Ohio Financial (WOFC)
Western Power & Equipment (WPEC)
Western Sierra Bancorp (WSBA)
Western Staff Services, Inc. (WSTF)
Western Water Company (WWTR)
Western Wireless Corporation (WWCA)
Westernbank Puerto Rico (WBPR)
Westmark Group Holdings, Inc. (WGHI)
WestPoint Stevens Inc. (WPSN)
Westwood Homestead Financial (WEHO)
Westwood One, Inc. (WONE)
Wet Seal, Inc. (The) (WTSLA)
Weyco Group, Inc. (WEYS)
WFS Financial, Inc. (WFSI)
Wheels Sports Group, Inc. (WHEL)
Wheels Sports Group, Inc. (WHELW)
WHG Bancshares Corporation (WHGB)
White Cap Industries, Inc. (WHCP)
White Pine Software, Inc. (WPNE)
White River Corporation (WHRC)
Whitney Holding Corporation (WTNY)
Whittman-Hart, Inc. (WHIT)
Whole Foods Market, Inc. (WFMI)
Wickes Inc. (WIKS)
WideCom Group, Inc. (The) (WIDEF)
WideCom Group, Inc. (The) (WIDWF)
Williamette Valley Vineyards (WVVI)
Williams Controls, Inc. (WMCO)
Williams Industries, Inc. (WMSI)
Williams-Sonoma, Inc. (WSGC)
Willis Lease Finance (WLFC)
Willow Grove Bancorp, Inc. (WGBC)
Wilmar Industries, Inc. (WLMR)
Wilshire Real Estate Investment Trust, Inc.
  (WREI)
Wilshire State Bank (WSBK)
Wilsons The Leather Experts (WLSN)
Wilsons The Leather Experts (WLSNW)
Wind River Systems, Inc. (WIND)
Winfield Capital Corp. (WCAP)
Wink Communications, Inc. (WINK)
Winland Electronics, Inc. (WLET)
WinStar Communications, Inc. (WCII)
Wintrust Capital Trust I (WTFCP)
Wintrust Financial Corporation (WTFC)
Wireless One, Inc. (WIRL)
Wit Capital Group, Inc. (WITC)
Wiztec Solutions, Limited (WIZTF)
WLR Foods, Inc. (WLRF)
WMF Group, Ltd. (The) (WMFG)
Wolohan Lumber Company (WLHN)
Women First Healthcare (WFHC)
Wonderware Corporation (WNDR)

COMPANY (SYMBOL)

Woodhead Industries, Inc. (WDHD)
Woodroast Systems, Inc. (WRSI)
Woodward Governor Company (WGOV)
Workgroup Technology (WKGP)
World Acceptance Corporation (WRLD)
World Access, Inc. (WAXS)
World Airways, Inc. (WLDA)
World Heart Corporation (WHRTF)
World of Science, Inc. (WOSI)
WorldCom, Inc. (WCOM)
WorldCom, Inc. (WCOMP)
WorldGate Communications, Inc. (WGAT)
Worldtalk Communications (WTLK)
Worthington Foods, Inc. (WFDS)
Worthington Industries, Inc. (WTHG)
WPI Group, Inc. (WPIC)
WPP Group PLC (WPPGY)
WSFS Financial Corporation (WSFS)
WSMP, Inc. (WSMP)
WTD Industries, Inc. (WTDI)
Wyant Corporation (WYNT)
Wyman-Gordon Company (WYMN)

X

XATA Corporation (XATA)
Xeikon, N.V. (XEIKY)
Xenometrix, Inc. (XENOW)
Xenova Group PLC (XNVAY)
Xeta Corporation (XETA)
XETel Corporation (XTEL)
XIOX (XICO)
Xircom, Inc. (XIRC)
XLConnect Solutions, Inc. (XLCT)
XOMA Corporation (XOMA)
Xomed Surgical Products, Inc. (XOMD)
Xoom.com, Inc. (XMCM)
XOX Corporation (XOXC)
XOX Corporation (XOXCW)

COMPANY (SYMBOL)

Xpedite Systems, Inc. (XPED)
X-Rite, Incorporated (XRIT)
XXsys Technologies, Inc. (XSYS)
Xybernaut Corporation (XYBR)

Y

Yahoo! Inc. (YHOO)
Yellow Corporation (YELL)
YES! Entertainment Corporation (YESS)
YieldUP International (YILD)
YieldUp International (YILDZ)
York Financial Group (YFED)
York Group, Inc. (The) (YRKG)
York Research Corporation (YORK)
Youbet.com, Inc. (UBET)
Young Broadcasting, Inc. (YBTVA)
Yurie Systems, Inc. (YURI)

Z

Zany Brainy, Inc. (ZANY)
Zebra Technologies Corporation (ZBRA)
Zegarelli Group International, (ZEGG)
ZEVEX International, Inc. (ZVXI)
Zi Corporation (ZICAF)
Zila, Inc. (ZILA)
Zindart Limited (ZNDTY)
Zions Bancorporation (ZION)
ZipLink, Inc. (ZIPL)
Zitel Corporation (ZITL)
Zoll Medical Corporation (ZOLL)
Zomax Optical Media, Inc. (ZOMX)
Zonagen, Inc. (ZONA)
Zoom Telephonics, Inc. (ZOOM)
Zoran Corporation (ZRAN)
Z-Seven Fund, Inc. (ZSEV)
Zygo Corporation (ZIGO)
ZYMETX, Inc. (ZMTX)

Contract Specifications

UNITED STATES

Chicago Board of Trade

Commodity	Symbol	Contract Months	Trading Hours	Contract Size	Minimum Fluctuation	Daily Limit
Corn	C	H,K,N,U,Z	9:30–1:15	5,000 bu.	¼c/bu.=$12.50	12c/bu.=$600
Wheat	W	H,K,N,U,Z	9:30–1:15	5,000 bu.	¼c/bu.=$12.50	20c/bu.=$1,000
Oats	0	H,K,N,U,Z	9:30–1:15	5,000 bu.	¼c/bu.=$12.50	10c/bu.=$500
Rough Rice	RR	F,H,K,N,U,X	9:15–1:30	2,000 cwt. (200,000 lbs.)	½c/cst.=$10	30c/cwt.=$600
Soybeans	S	F,H,K,N,Q,U,X	9:30–1:15	5,000 bu.	¼c/bu.=$12.50	30c/bu.=$1,500, expands to 45c
Soybean Meal	SM	F,H,K,N,Q,U,V,Z	9:30–1:15	100 tons	10c/ton=$10	$10/ton=$1,000
Soybean Oil	BO	F,H,K,N,Q,U,V,Z	9:30–1:15	60,000 lb.	1/100c/lb.=$6	1c/lb=$600
U.S. Treasury Bonds	US	H,M,U,Z	7:20–2:00	$100,000	1/32 pt.=$31.25	3 pt.=$3,000, expands to 4.5
10-Year U.S. T-Notes	TY	H,M,U,Z	7:20–2:00	$100,000	1/32 pt.=$31.25	3 pt.=$3,000, expands to 4.5
5-Year U.S. T-Notes	FV	H,M,U,Z	7:20–2:00	$100,000	1/32 pt.=$15.625	3 pt.=$3,000, expands to 4.5
2-Year U.S. T-Notes	TU	H,M,U,Z	7:20–2:00	$200,000	¼ of 1/32 pt.= $15.625	1 pt.=$2,000, expands to1.5pts.
3-Day Fed Funds	FF	All months	7:20–2:00	$5,000,000	0.01%=$51.67	150 basis pt.
Municipal Bond Index	MB	H,M,U,Z	7:20–2:00	$1,000 × bond	1/32 pt.=$31.25	3 pt.=$3,000, expands to 4.5
Flexible U.S. T-Bonds	CG,PG	Flexible	7:20–2:00	$100,000 face value	1/65 pt.=$15.625	3 pt.=$3,000, expands to 4.5
Flexible 10-Year U.S. T-Notes	TC,TP	Flexible	7:20–2:00	$100,000 face value	1/64 pt.=$15.625	3 pt.=$3,000, expands to 4.5
Flexible 5-Year T-Notes	FL,FP	Flexible	7:20–2:00	$100,000 face value	1/64 pt.=$15,625	3 pt.=$3,000, expands to 4.5
Flexible 2-Year T-Notes	TUC,TUP	Flexible	7:20–2:00	$200,000 face value	½ of 1/64 pt.= $15.625	1 pt.=$2,000, expands to 1.5
Dow Jones Industrial Average Index	DJ	H,M,U,Z	8:30–3:15	$10 × index	1 pt.=$10	350, 550, 700 pts. below set price previous reg session
Gold	KI	Current mo., next 2mos. plus G,J,M,Q,V,Z	7:20–1:40	1 kg.=32.15 troy oz.	10c/troy oz.=$3.22	$50/troy oz.= $1,607.50, expands to $75
Gold	GH	Current mo., next 2 mos., plus G,J,M,Q,V,Z	7:20–1:40, 5:20–8:05	100 fine troy oz.	10c/troy oz.=$10	$50/troy oz.= $5,000, expands to $75
Silver	SV	Current mo., next 2 mos. plus G,J,M,Q,V,Z	7:25–1:25, 5:20–8:05	5,000 troy oz.	1/100c troy oz.=$5	$1/troy oz.= $5,000, expands to $1.50

Chicago Board of Trade *(Continued)*

Commodity	Symbol	Contract Months	Trading Hours	Contract Size	Minimum Fluctuation	Daily Limit
Silver	AG	Current mo., next 2mos. plus G,J,M,Q,V,Z	7:25–1:25	1,000 troy oz.	$\frac{1}{100}$c/troy oz.=$1	$1/troy oz.= $1,000, expands to $1.50
National Catastrophe Insurance	UN	H,M,U,Z	8:30–12:30	$25,000 × ratio of losses/ premiums	$\frac{1}{10}$ pt.=$25	10 pt.=$2,500, var. limits: 15 pt.=$3,750
Eastern Catastrophe Insurance	UE	H,M,U,Z	8:30–12:30	$25,000 × ratio of losses/ premiums	$\frac{1}{10}$ pt.=$25	10 pt.=$2,500, var. limits: 15 pt.=$3,750
Midwestern Catastrophe Insurance	UM	H,M,U,Z	8:30–12:30	$25,000 × ratio of losses/ premiums	$\frac{1}{10}$ pt.=$25	10 pt.=$2,500, var. limits: 15 pt.=$3,750
Western Quarterly Catastrophe Insurance	UW	H,M,U,Z	8:30–12:30	$25,000 × ratio of losses/ premiums	$\frac{1}{10}$ pt.=$25	10 pt.=$2,500, var. limits: 15 pt.=$3,750
Western Annual Catastrophe Insurance	WA	All months	8:30–12:30	$25,000 × ratio of losses/ premiums	$\frac{1}{10}$ pt.=$25	10 pt.=$2,500, var. limits: 15 pt.=$3,750
Iowa Corn Yield Insurance	CA	F,U	10:30–12:45	Iowa corn yield estimate × $100	$\frac{1}{10}$ bu.=$10	15 bu.=$1,500
Chicago Mercantile Exchange						
Feeder Cattle	FC	F,H,J,K,Q,U,V,X	9:05–1:00	50,000 lb.	2.5c/cwt.=$12.50	1.5c/lb.=$750
Live Cattle	LC	G,H,J,M,Q,V,Z	9:05–1:00	40,000 lb.	2.5c/cwt.=$10	1.5c/lb.=$600
Lean Hogs	LN	G,J,M,N,Q,V,Z	9:10–1:00	40,000 lb.	2.5c/cwt.=$10	2c/lb.=$800
Boneless Beef	BB	G,J,M,Q,V,Z	8:50–1:00	20,000 lb.	$0.001/lb.=$20	$600
Pork Bellies	PB	G,H,K,N,Q	9:10–1:00	40,000 lb.	2.5c/cwt.=$10	3c/lb.=$1,200
BFP Milk	DA	All months	8:00–1:10	200,000 lb.	1c/100 lb.=$20	1.5c/lb.=$3,000
Butter	DB	G,J,M,N,U,X	8:00–1:10	40,000 lb.	2.5c/100 lb.-$10	2.5c/lb.=$1,000
Cheddar Cheese	DC	F,H,K,N,U,X	8:00–1:00	40,000 lb.	2.5c/100 lb.=$10	2.5c/lb.=$1,000
Lumber	LU(b)	F,H,K,N,U,X	9:00–1:05	80,000 bd. ft.	10c/ 1,000 bd. ft.=$8	$10/ 1,000 bd. ft.
Oriented Strand Board	OSB	F,H,K,N,U,X	9:00–1:05	100,000 sq. ft.	10c/ 1,000 sq. ft.=$10	$10/ 1,000 sq. ft.
International Monetary Market Division of the CME (IMM)						
Deutsche Mark	DM	F,H,J,M,N,U,V,Z	7:20–2:00	DM125,000	$0.0001/ DM=$12.50	$0.0400 EPLI
Canadian Dollar	CD	F,H,J,M,N,U,V,Z	7:20–2:00	C$100,000	$0.0001/C$=$10	$0.0400 EPLI
Swiss Franc	SF	F,H,J,M,N,U,V,Z	7:20–2:00	SF125,000	$0.0001/ SF=$12.50	$0.0400 EPLI

International Monetary Market Division of the CME (IMM) *(Continued)*

Commodity	Symbol	Contract Months	Trading Hours	Contract Size	Minimum Fluctuation	Daily Limit
British Pound	BP	F,H,J,M,N,U,V,Z	7:20–2:00	£62,500	$0.0002/ £=$12.50	$0.0800 ELPI
Japanese Yen	JY	F,H,J,M,N,U,V,Z	7:20–2:00	¥12,500,000	$0.000001/ ¥=$12.50	$0.000400 EPLI
Australian Dollar	AD	F,H,J,M,N,U,V,Z	7:20–2:00	A$100,000	$0.0001/A$=$10	$0.0400 ELPI
French Franc	FR	F,H,J,M,N,U,V,Z	7:20–2:00	FF500,000	$0.00002/ FF=$10	$0.01000 ELPI
Euroyen	EY	H,M,U,Z & serial mos.	7:20–2:00	¥100,000,000	$0.01/¥=¥2,500	NA
Deutsche Mark/ Japanese Yen Cross Rate	DJ	H,M,U,Z	7:20–2:00	DM250,000	0.005- 1,250	None
British Pound/ Deutsche Mark Cross Rate	IP	H,M,U,Z	7:20–2:00	£125,000	0.0001= DM$12.50	
London Interbank Offered Rate (LIBOR)	EM	All months	7:20–2:00	$3,000,000	1 pt.=$25	—
13-Week T-Bills	TB	H,M,U,Z & 2 serial mos.	7:20–2:00	$1,000,000	½ pt.=$12.50	None
1-Year T-Bills	YR	H,M,U,Z	7:20–2:00	$500,000	½ pt.=$25	None
Eurodollar Time Deposit	ED	H,M,U,Z & serial mos.	7:20–2:00	$1,000,000	1 pt.=$25	None
British Pound Rolling Spot	RP	H,M,U,Z	7:00–2:00	£250,000	1 pt.=$25	—
Japanese Yen Currency Forward	FE	12 mos. plus 4 in the Mar cycle	7:00–2:00	$250,000	¼ pt.=¥625	NA
Japanese Yen Rolling Spot	RY	H,M,U,Z	7:00–2:00	$250,000	1 pt.=¥2,500	NA
Deutsche Mark	RD	H,M,U,Z	7:00–2:00	$250,000	1 pt.=DM25	—
Deutsche Mark Currency Forward	FM	12 mos. plus 4 in the Mar cycle	7:00–2:00	$250,000	¼ pt.=DM6.25	NA
3-Month Euromark	EK	H,M,U,Z	7:20–2:00	DM1,000,000	1 pt.=DM25	None
91-Day Mexican T-Bill (Cetes)	TS	H,M,U,Z	7:20–2:00	MP2,000,000	1 pt.=MP50	None
28-Day Mexican TIIE	TE	All months	7:20–2:00	MP6,000,000	1 pt.=MP50	None
Fed Funds Rate	FT	All months	7:20–2:00	$3,000,000	½ pt.=$12.50	None
Index and Option Market Division of the CME (IOM)						
Nikkei 225 Stock Average	NK	H,M,U,Z	8:00–3:15	$5 × index	5 pt.=$25	Varies
S&P 500 Stock Index	SP	H,M,U,Z	8:30–3:15	$500 × index	5 pt.-$25	Varies
E-Mini S&P 500 Stock Index	ES	H,M,U,Z	8:30–3:15	$50 × index	25 pt.=$12.50	Varies
S&P MidCap 400 Index	MD	H,M,U,Z	8:30–3:15	$500 × index	5 pt.=$25	Varies

Index and Option Market Division of the CME (IOM) *(Continued)*

Commodity	Symbol	Contract Months	Trading Hours	Contract Size	Minimum Fluctuation	Daily Limit
S&P 500/BARRA Growth Index	SG	H,M,U,Z	8:30–3:15	$500 × index	5 pt.=$25	Varies
S&P 500/BARRA Value Index	SU	H,M,U,Z	8:30–3:15	$500 × index	5 pt.=$25	Varies
NASDAQ 100 Index	ND	H,M,U,Z	8:30–3:15	$100 × index	5 pt.=$5	Varies
Coffee, Sugar & Cocoa Exchange, Inc. (CSCE)						
Brazil Differential		H,K,N,U,Z	9:05–1:35	37,500/lb.	^{5}/$_{100}$c/lb.=$18.75	None
Coffee	KB					
Cocoa	CC	H,K,N,U,Z	9:00–2:00	10 metric tons	$1/ton=$10	$88/ton= $88
Coffee "C"	KC	H,K,N,U,Z	9:15–1:35	37,500 lb.	^{5}/$_{100}$c/lb.=$18.75	6c/lb.
Sugar No. 11 (world)	SB	H,K,N,V	9:30–1:20	112,000 lb.	^{1}/$_{100}$c/lb.=$11.20	½c/lb.
Sugar No. 14	SE	F,H,K,N,U,X	9:10–1:15	112,000 lb.	^{1}/$_{100}$c/lb.=$11.20	½c/lb.= $560
Sugar (white)	WS	H,K,N,V,Z	9:15–1:20	50 metric tons	20c/ton=$10	$10/ton
Cheddar Cheese	EZ	#	9:00–2:00	10,500 lbs.	^{10}/$_{100}$c/lb.=$10.50	6c/lb.
Nonfat Dry Milk	MU	#	9:00–2:00	11,000 lbs.	^{10}/$_{100}$c/lb.=$11	6c/lb.
Milk	MI	#	9:00–2:00	50,000 lbs.	1c/lb.=$5	50c/lb.
Basic Formula Price (BFP) Milk	MJ	Each mo. in 13-mo. cycle	9:00–2:00	100,000 lbs.	1c/lb.=$10	50c/lb.
Butter	BW	#	9:00–2:00	10,000	^{10}/$_{100}$c/lb.=$10	6c/lb.
Kansas City Board of Trade (KCBT)						
Wheat	KW	H,K,N,U,Z	9:30–1:15	5,000 bu.	¼c/bu.=$12.50	25c/bu.=$1,250
Value Line	KV	H,M,U,Z	8:30–3:15	500 × index	0.05=$25	Check with exchange
Mini Value Line	MV	H,M,U,Z	8:30–3:15	100 × index	0.05=$5	Check with exchange
Western Natural Gas	KG	18 serial mos.	8:30–2:30	10 MMBtu	^{1}/$_{10}$c/bu.=$5	15c
New York Cotton Exchange (NYCE)						
Cotton	CT,CO	H,K,N,V,Z	10:30–2:40	50,000 lb. (100 bales)	^{1}/$_{100}$c/lb.=$5	3c/lb.=$1,500
Potato	PT	F,H,K,N,U,X	9:45–2:00	85,000 lb.	1c/cwt.=$.01	$2/cwt.=200 pts.
Citrus Associates of the New York Cotton Exchange, Inc.						
Frozen Concentrated	JO,OJ	F,H,K,N,U,X	10:15–2:15	15,000 lb.	^{5}/$_{100}$c/lb.=$7.50	5c/lb.=$750
Finex						
U.S. Dollar Index (USDX)	DX,DO	H,M,U,Z	*	$1,000 × index	0.01 (1 basis pt.) = $10	***
2-Year Treasury Auction Notes	TW	All months	8:20–3:00	$100 × basis pt. of yield	0.005 pt.=$50	None
5-Year Treasury Auction Notes	FY	All months	8:20–3:00	$100 × basis pt. of yield	0.005 pt.=$50	None

Finex *(Continued)*

Commodity	Symbol	Contract Months	Trading Hours	Contract Size	Minimum Fluctuation	Daily Limit
Sterling/D-Mark Cross-Rate	MP	H,M,U,Z	**	£125,000	DM0.001 pt.= DM12.50	None
Sterling/Yen Cross-Rate	SY	H,M,U,Z	**	£125,000	¥0.01 pt.=¥1,250	None
Sterling/ Swiss Franc Cross-Rate	SS	H,M,U,Z	**	125,000	SF0.0001 pt.= SF12.50	None
D-Mark/Yen Cross-Rate	MY	H,M,U,Z	**	DM125,000	0.01 pt.= 1,250	None
D-Mark/Krona Cross-Rate	MK	H,M,U,Z	**	DM125,000	KR0.0005 pt.= KR62.50	None
D-Mark/French Franc Cross-Rate	MF	H,M,U,Z	**	DM500,000	FF0.0001 pt.=FF50	None
D-Mark/Lira Cross-Rate	ML	H,M,U,Z	**	DM250,000	ItL0.05 pt.= ItL12,500	None
D-Mark/Swiss Franc Cross-Rate	MH	H,M,U,Z	8:20–3:00	DM125,000	FR0.0001 pt.= FR12.5	None
D-Mark/Spanish Peseta Cross-Rate	MT	H,M,U,Z	**	DM250,000	Pst0.01 pt.= Pst.2,500	None
U.S. Dollar/Pound	YP	H,M,U,Z	*	£62,500	$0.0001 pt.= $6.25	None
U.S. Dollar/D-Mark	YM	H,M,U,Z	*	DM125,000	$0.0001 pt.= $12.50	None
U.S. Dollar/Yen	YY	H,M,U,Z	*	¥12,500,000	$0.000001 pt. = $12.50	None
U.S. Dollar/Swiss Franc	YF	H,M,U,Z	*	SF125,000	$0.0001 pt. = $12.50	None
U.S. Dollar/ Canadian Dollar	YD	H,M,U,Z	*	$200,000	C$0.0001 pt. = C$20	None
U.S. Dollar/South African Rand	ZR	H,M,U,Z	*	$100,000	R0.0005 pt.=R$50	None
Sterling/U.S. Dollar	YP	H,M,U,Z	*	£125,000	$0.0001 pt.= $12.50	None
Australian Dollar/ U.S. Dollar	AU	H,M,U,Z	*	A$200,000	$0.0001 pt.=$20	None
New Zealand Dollar/U.S. Dollar	ZX	H,M,U,Z	*	$100,000	$0.0001 pt.=$20	None
New York Futures Exchange (NYFE)						
NYSE Composite Index	YX	H,M,U,Z	9:30–4:15	$500 × index	0.05 pt.–$25	18 pt.
NYSE Large Composite Index	YL	H,M,U,Z	9:30–4:15	$1,000 × index	0.05 pt.=$50	26 pt.
CRB Futures Price Index	CR	H,K,N,U,Z	9:40–2:45 (3:15 on LTD)	$500 × index	0.05 pt.=$25	None
PSE Tech 100 Index	TK	H,M,U,Z	9:30–4:15	$500 × index	0.05 pt.=$25	None

New York Mercantile Exchange

Commodity	Symbol	Contract Months	Trading Hours	Contract Size	Minimum Fluctuation	Daily Limit
Nymex Division						
Palladium	PA	H,M,U,Z	8:10–2:20	100 troy oz.	5c/oz.=$5	$6/oz.=$600
Platinum	PL,PO	F,J,N,V	8:20–2:30	50 troy oz.	10c/oz.=$5	$25/oz.=$1,200
Heating Oil	HO,OH	Next 18 mths.	9:50–3:10	42,000 gal.	0.01c/gal.=$4.20	40c/gal.=$16,800
New York Harbor Unleaded Gasoline	HU,GO	Next 18 mths.	9:50–3:10	42,000 gal.	0.01c/gal.=$4.20	40c/gal.=$16,800
Gulf Coast Unleaded Gasoline	GU	Next 18 mths.	9:40–3:10	42,000 gal.	0.01c/gal.=$4.20	40c/gal=$1,680
Crude Oil	C1,LO	Next 30 mos. plus 36,48,60, 72,& 84	9:45–3:10	1,000 barrels (42,000 gal.)	1c/barrel=$10	$15/barrel=$15,000
Sour Crude Oil	SC	Next 18 mths.	9:35–3:20	1,000 barrels	1c/barrel=$10	$15/barrel=$15,000
Henry Hub Natural Gas	NG,ON	Next 30 mos. plus	10:00–3:10	10,000 MMBtu	0.1c/MMBtu =$10	$1.50/ MMBtu= $15,000
Propane Gas	PN	Next 15 months	9:55–3:00	42,000 gal.	0.01c/gal.=$4.20	40c/gal.=$16,800
Permian Basin Natural Gas	NG,ON	Next 18 mths.	10:10–3:10	10,000 MMBtu	0.001c/ MMBtu–$10	$1.50/ MMBtu= $15,000
Alberta Natural Gas	NG,ON	Next 18 mths.	10:00–3:10	10,000 MMBtu	0.001c/ MMBtu=$10	$1.50/ MMBtu= $15,000
Calif./Oregon Border Electricity	MW,WO	Next 18 mths.	9:55–3:30	736 Mwh= $7.36	0.01c/Mwh	$15/Mwh= $11,040
Palo Verde Electricity	KV,VO	Next 18 mths.	9:55–3:25	736 Mwh= $7.36	0.01c/Mwh	$15/Mwh= $11,040
Heating Oil/Crude Spread	CH	Next 6 mos. plus 2 quarterly mos. on H,M,U,Z cycle	9:50–3:10	1,000 barrels each	$0.01/bbl=$10	None
Gasoline/Crude Spread	CF	Next 6 mos. plus 2 quarterly mos. on H,M,U,Z cycle	9:50–3:10	1,000 barrels each	$0.01/bbl=$10	None
Comex Division						
Copper	HG,HX	Current plus 23 mo.	8:10–2:00	25,000 lb.	$\frac{5}{100}$c/lb. =$12.50	20c/lb.=$5,000
Silver	SI,SO	Current plus 2 mo. plus F,H, K,N,U,Z	8:25–2:25	5,000 troy oz.	0.5c/oz.=$25	$1.50/oz.= $7,500
Gold	GC,OG	Current plus next 2 mo. plus G,J,Q,V	8:20–2:30	100 troy oz.	10c/oz.=$10	$75/oz.=$7,500
Eurotop 100 Stock Index	ER,EQ	H,K,N,Z	5:30–11:30	$100 × index	0.1 pt.=$10	None

CANADA

The Winnipeg Commodity Exchange (WCE)

Commodity	Symbol	Contract Months	Trading Hours	Contract Size	Minimum Fluctuation	Daily Limit
Western Domestic Feed Barley	AB	H,K,N,V,Z	9:30–1:15	20 metric tons	C10c/ton=$2	C$5/ton = C$100
Canola	RS	F,H,K,N,Q,U,X	9:30–1:15	$20/_{100}$ metric tons	C10c/ton= C$2/C$10	C$10/ton =C$200/ $1,000
Flaxseed	WF	F,H,N,U,X	9:30–1:15	$20/_{100}$ metric tons	C10c/ton= C$2/C$10	C$10/ton =C$200/ $1,000
Oats	WO	H,K,N,V,Z	9:30–1:15	$20/_{100}$ metric tons	10c/ton=$2/$10	$5/ton= $100/ $500
Domestic Feed	WW	H,K,N,V,Z	9:30–1:15	$20/_{100}$ metric tons	C10c/ton= C$2/C$10	C$5/ ton= C$100/ C$500
Feed Peas	WP	G,K,N,V,Z	9:30–1:15	$20/_{100}$ metric tons	10c/ton=$2/$10	$5/ton= $100/ $500

FRANCE

Marche a Terme International de France (MATIF)

Long-Term National Bond	NNN	H,M,U,Z	8:30–4:30	FF500,000	0.02%=FF100	
5-Year Bond	YR5	H,M,U,Z	8:30–4:30	FF500,000	0.01%=FF50	
3-Month PIBOR	PIB	2 mo.+20 qtrly. expirations of H,M,U,Z	8:30–4:30	FF5,000,000	0.01%=FF125	
ECU Bond	ECU	H,M,U,Z	8:30–4:30	100,000 XEU	0.02%=20 XEU	
CAC 40 Stock Index	CAC	3 mos. plus 3 qtrly plus 2 six-mo. (H,U)	10:00–5:00	FF200 × futures index	0.5 pt.=FF100	
45 Icumsa White Sugar	SUD,OSU	H,K,Q,V,Z	11:00–1:00, 3:00–7:30	50 metric tons	10c/ton= $5/contract	
100 Icumsa White Sugar	SUB	H,K,Q,V,Z	10:45–1:00, 3:00–7:30	50 metric tons	10c/ton = $5/ contract	
European Milling Wheat	BLE	U,X,G,K	10:30–12:30: 3:15–6:15	50 metric tons	FRF1/ton= FRF50/contract	
European Rapeseed	COM	G,K,Q,X	11:00–1:00, 3:30–6:30	50 metric tons	DM1/ton =DM50/ contract	

Marche des Options Negociables de Paris (MONEP)

Short-Term CAC 40 Stock Index	PX1	2 nearest & 1 qtrly.H,M,U,Z	10:00–5:00	FF200 × index	FF0.01/pt.=FF2	
Long-Term CAC 40 Stock Index	PXL	H,U up to 2 yrs.	10:00–5:00	FF50 × index	FF0.01/pt.=FF0.50	

Marche des Options Negociables de Paris (MONEP) *(Continued)*

Commodity	Symbol	Contract Months	Trading Hours	Contract Size	Minimum Fluctuation	Daily Limit
CAC 40*		3 nearest & 3 qtrly.& 2 semi-mthly.(H,U)	10:00–5:00	FF200 × index	FF0.5/pt.=FF100	
Short-Term Equities (50 stocks)	H,M,U,Z		10:10–5:00	20-500 shares (mostly 100)	FF0.01 to FF0.50@	
Long-Term Equities (35 stocks)	H,U (up to 2 yrs)		10:10–5:00	20-500 shares (mostly 100)	FF0.01 to FF0.50@	

GERMANY

DTB (Deutsche Terminborse)

Commodity	Symbol	Contract Months	Trading Hours	Contract Size	Minimum Fluctuation	Daily Limit
Long-Term Govt.Bond (Bund: 8½– 10 yrs)		3 next qtr., end mos. of H,M,U,Z	8:00–7:00	DM250,000 (6% coupon)	0.01 pt.=DM25	
Medium-Term Govt.Bond (Bobl: 3½-5 yrs)		3 next qtr. end mos. of H,M,U,Z	8:00–7:00	DM250,000 (6% coupon)	0.01 pt.=DM25	
DAX		Next 3 mos. of H,M,U,Z	8:30–5:00	DM100 × index	0.5 pt.=DM50	
DAX		Next 3 mos. & qtrly. mos. of H,M,U,Z and next 2 mos. of M,Z	8:30–5:00	DM10 × index	0.1 pt.=DM1	
Midcap DAX (MDAX)		Next 3 mos. of H,M,U,Z	8:30–5:00	DM10 × index	0.5 pt.=DM5	
Schatz		3 next qtr. end mos. of H,M,U,Z	8:00–7:00	DM100 × index	0.1%=DM25	
Equities		Next 3 mos. and next 2 mos. of H,M,U,Z	9:00–5:00	Varies	DM0.1=DM5	
1-, 3-Month Euromark		1-mo.: next 6 mos. 3-mo.: next 3 mos.,and next 11 qtrly. mos of H,M,U,Z	1-mo.: 8:45–7:00 3-mo.: 8:30–7:00	DM1,000,000	0.1%=DM25	

HONG KONG

Hong Kong Futures Exchange

Commodity	Symbol	Contract Months	Trading Hours	Contract Size	Minimum Fluctuation	Daily Limit
Gold		G,J,M,Q,V,Z, spot and next 2 mths.	9:00–12:00, 2:30–5:30	100 troy oz.	10c/oz.=$10	
Hang Seng Stock Index		Spot, next 2 qtrly.mos.	10–12:30, 2:30–4:00	HK$50 × index	1 index pt.=HK$50	
Hang Seng Stock Index		Next 2 of M,Z	10:00–12:30, 2:30–4:00	HK$50 × index	1 index pt.=HK$50	

Hong Kong Futures Exchange *(Continued)*

Commodity	Symbol	Contract Months	Trading Hours	Contract Size	Minimum Fluctuation	Daily Limit
3-Month Hong Kong Interbank Offer (HIBOR)		8 calendar qtrly.	9:00–11:00, 2:00–4:30	HK$1 million	1 pt.=HK$25	
Hang Seng China-Affiliated Corporations Index		Spot, next and next 2 qtrly. mos	10:00–12:30, 2:30–4:00	HK$50 × index	1 pt.=HK$50	
Equities		Spot, next and next 1 qtrly. mos.	10:00–12:30, 2:30–3:55	Varies	Varies	
Rolling Deutsche Mark		Does not expire	@	$50,000	DM5	
Rolling Japanese Yen		Does not expire	@	$50,000	¥500	
Rolling British Pound		Does not expire	@	£50,000	$5	

The Stock Exchange of Hong Kong (SEHK)

Commodity	Symbol	Contract Months	Trading Hours	Contract Size	Minimum Fluctuation	Daily Limit
Equities (15 stocks)		Next 3 mos. & next 2 mos. of H,M,U,Z	10:00–12:30, 2:30–3:55	Varies	HK$0.01; HK$0.05 if premium is >HK$5	

JAPAN

Chubu Commodity Exchange (C-COM)

Commodity	Symbol	Contract Months	Trading Hours	Contract Size	Minimum Fluctuation	Daily Limit
Cotton Yarn		Next 6 months	9:20–10:30, 1:20–2:30	4,000 lbs.	10 Sen./lb.	
Woolen Yarn		Next 6 months	9:20–10:30, 1:20–2:30	500 kg.	¥1/kg.	
Staple Fiber Yarn		Next 6 months	9:20–10:30, 1:20–2:30	5,000 lbs.	10 Sen./lb.	
Red Beans (Azuki)		Next 6 months	9:00–11:00, 1:00–3:00	80 bags (2,400 kg.)	¥10/bag	
Soybeans (Imported)		Next 6 odd months	9:00–11:00, 1:00–3:00	30,000 kg.	¥10/1,000 kg.	
Refined White Soft Sugar		Next 6 months	9:00–10:00, 1:00–3:00	9,000 kg.	¥0.1/kg.	
Sweet Potato Starch		Next 3 months	9:00–11:00, 1:00–3:00	100 bags (2,500 kg.)	¥1/25 kg. bag	
Dried Cocoon		Next 6 months	9:40–11:30, 1:40–3:30	300 kg.	¥1/kg.	

Kansai Commodities Exchange (KANEX)

Commodity	Symbol	Contract Months	Trading Hours	Contract Size	Minimum Fluctuation	Daily Limit
Azuki Beans		Next 6 months	9:00, 10:00, 11:00, 12:00, 3:00	2,400 kg.	¥10/30 kg.	
Imported Soybeans	G,J,M,Q,V,Z		10:00, 11:00, 1:00, 2:00, 3:00	30,000 kg.	¥10/ton	
Raw Sugar	F,H,K,N,U,X		9:20, 10:20, 12:50, 1:50, 2:50	50,000 kg.	¥10/ton	

Osaka Mercantile Exchange (OME)

Commodity	Symbol	Contract Months	Trading Hours	Contract Size	Minimum Fluctuation	Daily Limit
Refined Sugar		Next 6 months	9:10, 10:20, 12:50, 1:50, 2:50	90,000 kg.	¥0.10/kg.	
Raw Silk		Next 6 months	9:15, 11:20, 1:15, 2:50	300 kg.	¥1/kg.	
Natural Rubber		Next 5 months	9:30, 10:30, 1:30, 2:30, 3:30, 5:00	5,000 kg.	¥0.1/kg.=¥500	
Rubber Index		Next 5 months	9:15, 10:15, 1:15, 2:15, 3:15	20,000 × index	0.01=¥200	
Cotton Yarn		Next 6 months	9:40, 10:40	20s, 30s: 2,000 lb. 40s: 4,000 lb.	¥0.1/lb.=¥200	
Staple Fiber Yarn		Next 6 months	9:40, 1:40	5,000 lb.	¥0.1/lb=¥500	
Woolen Yarn		Next 6 months	9:20, 11:20, 2:20, 3:20	500 kg.	¥1/kg.=¥500	
Aluminum		6 mos. of F,H,K, N,U,X	10:00, 11:00, 2:00, 3:00, 5:15	5,000 kg.	¥0.1/kg.=¥500	

Tokyo Grain Exchange (TGE)

Commodity	Symbol	Contract Months	Trading Hours	Contract Size	Minimum Fluctuation	Daily Limit
U.S. Soybeans	G,J,M,Q,V,Z		10:00, 11:00, 1:00, 2:00	30,000 kg.	¥10/1,000 kg.	
Azuki (Red Beans)		Next 6 months	9:00, 10:00, 11:00, 1:00, 2:00, 3:00	80 bags (2,400 kg.)	¥10/1 bag (30 kg.)	
Corn	F,H,K,N,U,X		9:00, 11:00, 1:00, 3:00	100,000 kg.	¥10/1,000 kg.	
Refined Sugar		Next 6 months	9:05, 10:15, 12:55, 1:55, 2:55	9,000 kg.	¥0.10/kg.	
Raw Sugar	F,H,K,N,U,X		9:00, 10:00, 1:00, 2:00, 3:00	50,000 kg.	¥10/1,000 kg.	

Tokyo International Financial Futures Exchange (TIFFE)

Commodity	Symbol	Contract Months	Trading Hours	Contract Size	Minimum Fluctuation	Daily Limit
3-Month Euroyen	EY,EYO	M,U,Z H,M,U,Z	09:00–11:30, 12:30–3:30, 4:00–6:00	¥100,000,000	0.01 pt.=¥2,500	
3-Month Eurodollar	ED	H,M,U,Z	9:00–11:30, 12:30–3:30	$1,000,000	0.01 pt.=$25	
U.S. Dollar/ Japanese Yen	UD	H,M,U,Z	9:00–11:30, 12:30–3:30	$50,000	0.05 pt.=¥2,500	
1-Year Euroyen	EY1Y	H,M,U,Z	9:00–11:30, 12:30–3:30, 4:00–6:00	¥100,000,000	0.01 pt.=¥10,000	

Tokyo Commodity Exchange (TOCOM)

Commodity	Symbol	Contract Months	Trading Hours	Contract Size	Minimum Fluctuation	Daily Limit
Gold		Current or next odd mo. & even mos. within a year	9:00–11:00, 1:00–3:30	1 kg.	¥1/gram	
Silver	"		9:00–11:00, 1:00–3:30	60 kg.	¥0.1/10 grams	
Platinum	"		9:00–11:00, 1:00–3:30	500 grams	¥1/gram	
Palladium	"		9:00–11:00, 1:00–3:30	1.5 kg.	¥1/gram	
Rubber		Next 6 months	9:45, 10:45, 1:45, 2:45, 3:30	5,000 kg.	¥0.10/kg.	
Cotton Yarn		Next 6 months	8:50, 10:15, 12:50, 3:10	1,814.36 kg.	¥0.10/lb.	
Wool Yarn		Next 6 months	"	500 kg.	¥1/kg.	
Aluminum		Current or next odd mo. & even mos. within a year	9:00–11:00, 1:00–3:30	10 tons	¥0.1/kg.	

SINGAPORE

Singapore Commodity Exchange Ltd.

Commodity	Symbol	Contract Months	Trading Hours	Contract Size	Minimum Fluctuation	Daily Limit
Rubber RSS1		Single months Quarters out 15 months	10:00–11:40, 3:30–4:40, 5:08–5:30	5 metric tons 15 metric tons	S0.25c/kg.=S$12.50 S0.25c/kg.=S$37.50	
Rubber RSS3	(Same contract specs as above, but prices in U.S. Dollars)					
Rubber TSR 20 (FOB)		Single months Quarters out 15 months	10:00–11:40, 12:08–1:00, 3:30–4:40, 5:08–5:30	20 metric tons 60 metric tons	$0.25/kg.=$50 $0.25/kg.=$150	
Robusta Coffee		7 con-secutive odd months	#	10 metric tons	$1/kg.=$10	
RCS Index		9 con-secutive odd months	10:00–1:00, 3:30–5:30	1 lot of 5,000 × RCS Index	$0.01/kg.=$5	

Singapore International Monetary Exchange Ltd. (SIMEX)

Commodity	Symbol	Contract Months	Trading Hours	Contract Size	Minimum Fluctuation	Daily Limit
Japanese Government Bonds	JB	5 qtrly mos. on H,M,U,Z cycle	7:45am– 7:10pm	¥50,000,000 (10-yr. 6% coupon)	¥0.01=¥5,000	
Euroyen	EY	H,M,U,Z (2-yr. cycle)	7:58am– 8:05pm	¥100,000,000	Front 1 qtrly. mos. 0.005=¥1,250	
Eurodollar	ED	2 serial mos. & H,M,U,Z	7:58am– 7:00pm	$1,000,000	Front yr. mos.: 0.005 pt.=$12.50	

Singapore International Monetary Exchange Ltd. (SIMEX) *(Continued)*

Commodity	Symbol	Contract Months	Trading Hours	Contract Size	Minimum Fluctuation	Daily Limit
Euromark	EM	H,M,U,Z (2-yr. cycle)	10:00am–7:10pm, 7:35pm–1:00am	DM1,000,000	0.01 pt.=DM25	
Nikkei 225 Stock Index	NK	H,M,U,Z for 5 quarters	7:55am–10:15am, 11:15am–2:15pm	¥500 × average	5 pt.=¥2,500	
Nikkei 300 Stock Index	N3	H,M,U,Z for 5 quarters	8:00am–10:15am, 11:15am–2:15pm	¥10,000 × futures price	0.1 pt.=¥1,000	
SIMEX MSCI Taiwan Index	T,W	*	M–F, 8:45am–12:15pm; Sat. 8:45am–11:15am	$100 × index	0.1 pt.=$10	
Deferred Spot US Dollar/Yen	DY	H,M,U,Z	8:00am–7:00pm, 7:35pm–1:00am	$100,000	¥0.01/$=¥1,000	
Deferred Spot U.S. Dollar/Mark	UM	H,M,U,Z	8:05am–7:05pm 7:35pm–1:00am	$100,000	DM0.0001/$=DM10	
Gold	GD	G,J,M,Q,V,Z listed on 1-yr. cycle	9:00am–5:15pm, 7:35pm–1:00am	100 troy oz.	US5c/oz.=$5	
Fuel Oil	SF	9 consecutive months	9:30am–12:30pm 2:00pm–7:00pm	100 metric tons	US10c/ton=$10	
Brent Crude Oil	BC	12 consecutive months	9:25am–12:30pm 2:00pm–5:58pm; 6:02pm–4:15am	1,000 barrels	$0.01/barrel=$10	

UNITED KINGDOM

International Petroleum Exchange of London Ltd. (PE)

Commodity	Symbol	Contract Months	Trading Hours	Contract Size	Minimum Fluctuation	Daily Limit
Brent Crude Oil	FB,OB CB,PB	Next 12 months	10:01–8:15	1,000 barrels	1c/barrel=US$10	
Gas Oil	FB,OP, CP,PP	Up to 18 mths.	9:15–5:27	100 metric tons	25c/ton=$25	
Natural Gas	MN	Next 12 months	10:01–4:59	1,000 therms	0.1 pence sterling/ therm	

London International Financial Futures and Options Exchange (LIFFE)

Commodity	Symbol	Contract Months	Trading Hours	Contract Size	Minimum Fluctuation	Daily Limit
Long Gilt		H,M,U,Z	8:00–4:15, APT: 4:30–6:00	£50,000 (nominal value, 9% coupon)	£¹⁄₃₂=£15.625	

London International Financial Futures and Options Exchange (LIFFE) *(Continued)*

Commodity	Symbol	Contract Months	Trading Hours	Contract Size	Minimum Fluctuation	Daily Limit
1-Month Euromark Interest Rate		All months	7:30–4:10, APT: 4:25–5:59	DM3,000,000	1 pt. (0.01%) =DM25	
3-Month Euromark Interest Rate	H,M,U,Z		7:30–4:10, APT: 4:25–5:59	DM1,000,000	1 pt. (0.01%) =DM25	
3-Month Euroyen Interest Rate	H,M,U,Z		9:00–4:00	¥100,000,000	0.01 pt.=¥2,500	
3-Month Euroswiss Interest Rate	H,M,U,Z		8:10–4:05, APT: 4:24–5:55	SF1,000,000	0.01 pt.=SF25	
3-Month Sterling Interest Rate	H,M,U,Z		8:05–4:05, APT: 4:22–5:57	£500,000	1 pt. (0.01%) =£12.50	
3-Month Eurolira Interest Rate	H,M,U,Z		7:55–4:10, APT: 4:23–5:58	itL 1,000,000,000	itL0.01=itL25,000	
3-Month ECU Interest Rate	H,M,U,Z		8:05–4:05	ECU1,000,000	0.01 pt.=ECU25	
German Government Bonds (Bund)	H,M,U,Z		7:00–4:15, APT: 4:20–5:55	DM250,000 (nominal value, 6% coupon)	DM0.01=DM25	
German Government Bonds (Bobl)	H,M,U,Z		7:30–4:15 APT: 4:20–5:55	DM1,000,000 (nominal value, 6% coupon)	0.01 pt.=DM25	
Japanese Government Bonds	H,M,U,Z		APT: 7:00–4:00	¥100,000,000 (6% coupon)	¥0.01=¥10,000	
Italian Government Bonds	H,M,U,Z		8:00–4:10, APT: 4:21–5:58	itL200,000,000 (nominal value, 12% coupon)	itL0.01=itL20,000	
U.S. T-Bond	H,M,U,Z		7:30–1:00	$100,000 (nominal value, 8% coupon)	$\frac{1}{32}$ pt.=$31.25	
FT-SE 100 Index	H,M,U,Z		8:35–4:10, APT: 4:32–5:30	£25 × index	0.5 pt.=£12.50	
FT-SE 100 Index (American Style)		Next 4 mths. plus M,Z	8:35–4:10	£10 × index	0.5 pt.-£5	
FT-SE 100 Index (European Style)		Next 3 mths. plus H,M,U,Z	8:35–4:10	£10 × index	0.5 pt.=£5	
FT-SE 100 Index FLEX (European Style)		#	9:00–3:45	£10 × index	0.5 pt.=£5	
FT-SE Mid 250 Index	H,M,U,Z		8:30–4:05	£10 × index	0.5 pt.=£5	
Equities		Three cycles	8:35–4:10	1,000 shares	0.5 pence/share=£5	

London International Financial Futures and Options Exchange (LIFFE) *(Continued)*

Commodity	Symbol	Contract Months	Trading Hours	Contract Size	Minimum Fluctuation	Daily Limit
LIFFE Commodity Products						
Cocoa No. 7	H,K,N,U,Z	9:30–12:28, 2:00–4:45	10 metric tons	£1/ton	
Coffee (Robusta)	F,H,K,N,UX	9:45–12:32, 2:30–5:00	5 metric tons	$1/ton	
Sugar No. 5 (White)	H,K,Q,V,Z	9:45–6:30	50 metric tons	10c/ton	
Baltic Freight Index (BIFFEX)		Spot month & 2 mos. plus F,J,N,V	10:15–12:30, 2:30–4:30	$10 × index	1 pt.=$10	
ECC Wheat	U,X,F,H,K,N	10:30–12:30, 2:30–4:00	100 metric tons	5 pence/ton=£5	
ECC Barley	U,X,F,H,K,N	10:30–12:30, 2:30–4:00	100 metric tons	5 pence/ton=£5	
Potatoes	X,H,J,K,M	11:00–12:30, 2:30–4:00	20 metric tons	10 pence/ton=£2	
London Metal Exchange (LME)						
Aluminum	**		11:55, 12:55, 3:35, 4:15	25 metric tons	50c/ton=$12.50	
Aluminum Alloy	**		11:45, 1:05, 3:50, 4:30	20 metric tons	50c/ton=$10	
Copper	**		Noon, 12:30, 3:30, 4:10	25 metric tons	50c/ton=$12.50	
Lead	**		12:05, 12:45, 3:20, 4:00	25 metric tons	50c/ton=$12.50	
Nickel	**		12:15, 1:00, 3:45, 4:25	6 metric tons	$1/ton=$6	
Tin	**		11:50, 12:40, 3:40, 4:20	5 metric tons	$1/ton=$5	
Zinc	**		12:10, 12:50, 3:25, 4:05	25 metric tons	50c/ton=$12.50	

The Language

A Glossary of the Securities Markets

Accounts Payable: Money a company owes for services and supplies.

Accrued Interest: The interest due on a bond since the last interest payment was made. The buyer of the bond pays the market price plus accrued interest.

Acquisition: Acquiring control of one corporation by another. In "unfriendly" takeover attempts, the potential buying company may offer a price well above current market values, new securities, and other inducements to stockholders. The management of the subject company might ask for a better price or try to join up with a third company. (*See also* Merger, Proxy.)

ADR: American Depositary Receipt. A security issued by a U.S. bank in place of foreign shares held in trust by that bank. ADRs facilitate the trading of foreign shares in U.S. markets.

Advanced Computerized Execution System (ACES): Customized facility offered by the NASD that permits broker/dealers to automate their internal execution and record-keeping functions.

Affirmative Obligations: Requirements imposed on Nasdaq market makers by the NASD. These include quoting firm prices, making two-sided markets (quoting both a bid and an ask price) on a continuous basis, participating in the automated execution system (Small Order Execution System) for processing small order agency executions, and reporting price and volume data for each transaction in a Nasdaq security within 90 seconds of execution. (*See also* Market Maker.)

Aftermarket: Trading activity in a security immediately following its initial offering to the public.

Agency Order: An order that a broker/dealer executes for the account of a customer with another professional or retail investor and for which a commission is typically charged.

American Stock Exchange: The second largest stock exchange in New York, located in the financial district of New York City.

AMEX: American Stock Exchange.

Amortization: Accounting for expenses or charges as applicable rather than as paid. Includes such practices as depreciation, depletion, write-off of intangibles, prepaid expenses, and deferred charges.

Annual Report: The formal financial statement issued yearly by a publicly owned corporation. The report shows assets, liabilities, revenues, expenses, and earnings. The report also shows the company's financial condition at the close of the business year and other basic information of interest to shareholders.

Arbitrage: Arbitrage involves the simultaneous purchase of a security in one market and the sale of it or a derivative product in another market to profit from price differentials between the two markets. If, for example, ABC stock can be bought in New York for $10 a share and sold in London at $10.50, an arbitrageur may simultaneously purchase ABC stock in New York and sell the same amount in London, making a profit of 50 cents a share, less expenses. Arbitrage may also involve the purchase of rights to subscribe to a security, or the purchase of convertible security, and the sale at or about the same time of the security obtainable through exercise of the rights or of the security obtainable through conversion. (*See also* Convertible, Rights, Derivative.)

Arbitral Immunity: Arbitrators are protected from suits arising out of their quasijudicial conduct in arbitration proceedings. (*See also* Arbitrator.)

Arbitration: A method where conflict between two or more parties is resolved by impartial persons—arbitrators—who are knowledgeable in the areas in controversy. A low-cost alternative to settling disputes over securities transactions in the court system. The NYSE administers this service. (*See also* Mediation.)

Arbitration Counsel: Also called *arbitration administrator,* the person at the sponsoring organization who handles administrative matters in arbitration proceedings. (*See also* Arbitration.)

Arbitrator: A private, disinterested person chosen to decide disputes between parties. (*See also* Arbitration.)

Arbitrators Code of Ethics: A guide for the conduct and ethical responsibility of arbitrators in commercial disputes.

Ask: The price at which a holder of a security is willing to sell (as opposed to the bid price, which is what someone is willing to pay).

Asset: Anything a person, company, or group owns or is owed, including money, investments, and property.

Assignment: Notice to an option writer that an option holder has exercised the option and that the writer will now be required to deliver (receive) under the terms of the contract.

Associated Person: A person engaged in the investment banking or securities business who is directly or indirectly controlled by an NASD member, whether or not this person is registered or exempt from registration with NASD. Every sole proprietor, partner, officer, director, or branch manager of any NASD member.

Association of Publicly Traded Companies (APTC, formerly NAOTC):   This organization, which is not connected with the NASD, provides publicly traded companies with a forum for addressing regulatory and legislative issues that affect them.

Auction Market: The system of trading securities through brokers or agents on an exchange, such as the New York Stock Exchange. Buyers compete with other buyers and sellers compete with other sellers for the most advantageous price.

Auditor's Report: Often called the *accountant's opinion,* it is the statement of the accounting firm's work and its opinion of a corporation's financial statements, especially if they conform to the normal and generally accepted practices of accountancy.

Automated Confirmation Transaction Service^{SM} (ACT^{SM}):   NASD service that allows parties to a telephone negotiation to speed the steps involved in completing a transaction.

Averages: Various ways of measuring the trend of securities prices, one of the most popular of which is the Dow Jones average of 30 industrial stocks listed on the New York Stock Exchange. The prices of the 30 stocks are totaled and then divided by a divisor that is intended to compensate for past stock splits and stock dividends and that is changed from time to time. As a result, point changes in the average have only the vaguest relationship to dollar price changes in stocks included in the average. (*See also* NYSE Composite Index.)

Averaging: *See* Dollar Cost Averaging.

Balance Sheet: A condensed financial statement showing the nature and amount of a company's assets, liabilities, and capital on a given date. In dollar amounts, the balance sheet shows what the company owned, what it owed, and the ownership interest in the company of its stockholders. (*See also* Assets, Earnings Report.)

Basis Point: One gradation on a 100-point scale representing 1 percent; used especially in expressing variations in the yields of bonds. Fixed-income yields vary often and slightly, within 1 percent. The basis point scale easily expresses these changes in hundredths of 1 percent. For example, the difference between 12.83 percent and 12.88 percent is 5 basis points.

Bear: Someone who believes the market will decline. (*See also* Bull.)

Bear Market: A condition of the stock market when prices of stocks are generally declining.

Bearer Bond: A bond that does not have the owner's name registered on the books of the issuer. Interest and principal, when due, are payable to the owner. (*See also* Coupon Bond, Registered Bond.)

Beta: A statistical measure of a stock's volatility compared with the overall market. A beta of less than 1 indicates lower risk than the market; a beta of more than 1 indicates higher risk than the market. (*See also* Volatility.)

Bid: The price at which someone is willing to buy a security.

Bid and Asked: Often referred to as a quotation, or quote. The bid is the highest price anyone wants to pay for a security at a given time; the asked is the lowest price anyone will take at the same time. (*See also* Quote.)

Bid/Ask Spread: The difference between the price at which a market maker is willing to buy a security (bid), and the price at which the firm is willing to sell it (ask). The spread narrows or widens according to the supply and demand for the security being traded. (*See also* Inside Quote, Spread.)

Block: A large holding or transaction of stock, popularly considered to be 10,000 shares or more.

Blue-Chip Stock: Stock in a company with a national reputation for quality, reliability, and the ability to operate profitably in good and bad times.

Blue-Sky Laws: State laws that require issuers of securities to register their offerings with the state before they can be sold to its residents.

Bond: Basically, an I.O.U. or promissory note of a corporation or municipality, usually issued in multiples of $1000 or $5000. A bond is an evidence of debt, on which the issuing company usually promises to pay the bondholder a specified amount of interest for a specified length of time and to repay the loan on the expiration date. A bondholder is a creditor of the corporation, not a part owner as is the shareholder. While the interest paid on corporate bonds is fully taxable, the interest on municipal bonds is usually exempt from federal income tax and state and local taxes within the state of issue.

Book Value: An accounting term, the book value of a stock is determined from a company's records by adding all assets, then deducting all debts and other liabilities, plus the liquidation price of any preferred issues. The sum arrived at is divided by the number of common shares outstanding, and the result is book value per common share. Book value of the assets of a company or a security may have little relationship to market value.

Booths: The workspaces (about 1,400), each equipped with a computer system, around the perimeter of the NYSE trading floor. They are where member firms and independent brokers receive orders.

Borrowing: A way of acquiring necessary capital. One form of borrowing is when individuals or companies ask a bank to loan them a certain amount of money, over a certain period of time, and agree to pay a certain amount of interest.

Broker: An agent who handles the public's orders to buy and sell securities, commodities, or other property. For this service a commission is charged.

Broker Booth Support System (BBSS):   A state-of-the-art order management system designed exclusively for NYSE members. BBSS enables member firms to quickly and efficiently process and manage their orders and selectively route orders via SuperDot directly to either the trading post or the booths on the NYSE trading floor.

Broker/Dealer: NASD member firms that act as securities dealers or brokers or perform both functions.

Brokers' Loan: Money borrowed by brokers from banks or other brokers for a variety of uses. It may be used by specialists to help finance investments of stock they deal in; by brokerage firms to finance the underwriting of new issues of corporate and municipal securities; to help finance a firm's own investments; and to help finance the purchase of securities for customers who prefer to use the broker's credit when they buy securities. (*See also* Margin.)

Bull: One who believes the market will rise. (*See also* Bear.)

Bull Market: A condition of the stock market when prices of stocks are generally rising.

Buttonwood Agreement: A 1792 trade agreement banding the original 24 brokers in New York together into an investment community. The agreement was named for a Buttonwood tree that served as their informal meeting place on Wall Street.

Buy Side: An institution who buys services from a broker/dealer, i.e., pays a commission on the execution of an order.

Call: *Bonds:* The right to redeem outstanding bonds before their scheduled maturity. *Options:* The right to buy a specific number of shares at a specified price by a fixed date. (*See also* Put, Option.)

Callable: A bond issue all or parts of which may be redeemed by the issuing corporation under specified conditions before maturity. The term also applies to preferred shares that may be redeemed by the issuing corporation.

Capital Gain: Profit made on securities, either through dividends or by selling the securities for a higher price than they originally cost.

Capital Stock: All shares representing ownership of a business, including preferred and common. (*See also* Common Stock, Preferred Stock.)

Capitalization: The total amount of various securities issued by a corporation. Capitalization may include bonds, debentures, preferred and common stock, and surplus.

Cash Flow: Reported net income of a corporation, plus amounts charged for depreciation, depletion, amortization, extraordinary charges to reserves, which are bookkeeping deductions and not paid out in actual dollars and cents. (*See also* Amortization, Depreciation.)

Certificate: The actual piece of paper that is evidence of ownership of stock in a corporation. Watermarked paper is finely engraved with delicate etchings to discourage forgery.

Certificate of Deposit (CD):   An agreement with a bank that you will leave your money on deposit for a specified period of time in return for a specific amount of interest.

CFTC: The Commodity Futures Trading Commission, created by Congress in 1974 to regulate exchange trading in futures.

Change: The dollar difference between the preceding day's closing price and the most recent price of a stock.

Chinese Wall: A term used to describe procedures enforced within a securities firm that separate the firm's departments to restrict access to nonpublic, material information. The procedures help NASD members avoid the illegal use of "inside" information.

Churning: *See* Excess Trading.

Circuit Breaker: A procedure that temporarily halts trading on all U.S. stock markets for one hour when the Dow Jones Industrial Average falls 250 points or more within a trading day. The pause is designed to allow time for the markets to absorb the news that precipitated the decline. Should the average fall another 150 points within the same day, trading would again be halted, this time for two hours.

Clearance: The conclusion of an exchange of securities. (*See also* Settlement.)

Closed-End Investment Company: *See* Investment Company.

Collateral: Securities or other property pledged by a borrower to secure repayment of a loan.

Commercial Paper: Debt instruments issued by companies to meet short-term financing needs.

Commission: The broker's basic fee for purchasing or selling securities or property as an agent.

Commission Broker: An agent who executes the public's order for the purchase or sale of securities or commodities.

Committee on Uniform Security Identification Procedures (CUSIP) number: A unique nine-character alphanumeric code appearing on the face of each stock certificate that is assigned to a security by Standard & Poor's Corporation. The number is used to expedite clearance and settlement. (*See also* Clearance, Settlement, Standard & Poor's.)

Commodities: *See* Futures.

Common Stock: One of two types of stock an investor may purchase in a company. Most stock is common stock. Investors who purchase it have voting rights at the company's annual stockholders' meeting. Common stockholders are not guaranteed dividends, but they may receive higher dividends during the company's prosperous periods. If a company fails or liquidates, common stockholders are paid after bondholders and preferred stockholders. (*See also* Preferred Stock.)

Competitive Trader: A member of an exchange who trades in stocks on the floor for an account in which the member firm has an interest. Also known as *registered trader.*

Compliance Departments: Departments set up in all organized stock markets to oversee market activity and make sure that trading complies with Securities and Exchange Commission and other exchange regulations.

Computer Assisted Execution System (CAES): Nasdaq service that automates order routing and execution for securities listed on domestic exchanges in the Intermarket Trading System (ITS). When linked to ITS, market makers can execute trades in exchange-listed securities through CAES with specialists on an exchange floor. (*See also* Intermarket Trading System, Market Maker, Specialist.)

Confirmation: Formal memorandum from a broker to a client giving details of a securities transaction. When a broker acts as a dealer, the confirmation must disclose that fact to a customer.

Conglomerate: A corporation that has diversified its operations, usually by acquiring enterprises in widely varied industries.

Consolidated Balance Sheet: A balance sheet showing the financial condition of a corporation and its subsidiaries. (*See also* Balance Sheet.)

Consolidated Quotation System (CQS): An electronic service that provides quotations on issues listed on the New York and American stock exchanges, regional stock exchanges, and issues traded by NASD member firms in the third market. Nasdaq processes this data and provides it to its subscribers as the Composite Quotation Service. The initials may be used either for the exchange system or the Nasdaq service. (*See also* Third Market.)

Consolidated Tape: The ticker tape reporting transactions in NYSE-listed securities that take place on the NYSE or any of the participating regional stock exchanges and other markets. Similarly, transactions in Amex-listed securities and certain other securities listed on regional stock exchanges are reported on a separate tape.

Convertible: A bond, debenture, or preferred share that may be exchanged by the owner for common stock or another security, usually of the same company, in accordance with the terms of the issue.

Corporate Bond: A bond issued by a corporation.

Correspondent: A securities firm, bank, or other financial organization that regularly performs services for another in a place or market to which the other does not have direct access. Securities firms may have correspondents in foreign countries or on exchanges of which they are not members. Correspondents are frequently linked by private wires. Member organizations of the NYSE with offices in New York City may also act as correspondents for out-of-town member organizations that do not maintain New York offices.

Coupon Bond: Bond with interest coupons attached. The coupons are clipped as they come due and presented by the holder for payment of interest. (*See also* Bearer Bond, Registered Bond.)

Covered Option: An option position that is offset by an equal and opposite position in the underlying security.

Cumulative Preferred: A stock having a provision that if one or more dividends are omitted, the omitted dividends must be paid before dividends may be paid on the company's common stock.

Cumulative Voting: A method of voting for corporate directors that enables the shareholders to multiply the number of their shares by the number of directorships being voted on and to cast the total for one director or a selected group of directors. A holder of 10 shares normally casts 10 votes for each of, say, 12 nominees to the board of directors. One thus has 120 votes. Under the cumulative voting principle, one may do that or may cast 120 (10 × 2) votes for only one nominee, 60 each for two, 40 each for three, or any other distribution one chooses. Cumulative voting is required under the corporate laws of some states and is permitted in most others.

Current Assets: Those assets of a company that are reasonably expected to be realized in cash, or sold, or consumed during one year. These include cash, U.S. government bonds, receivables and money due usually within one year, and inventories.

Current Return: *See* Yield.

Day Order: An order to buy or sell which, if not executed, expires at the end of the trading day on which it was entered.

Day's High: The highest price of a security during the current day's trading.

Day's Low: The lowest price of a security during the current day's trading.

Dealer: An individual or firm in the securities business who buys and sells stocks and bonds as a principal rather than as an agent. The dealer's profit or loss is the difference between the price paid and the price received for the same security. The dealer's confirmation must disclose to the customer that the principal has been acted upon. The same individual or firm may function, at different times, either as broker or dealer. (*See also* NASD, Specialist.)

Dealer Market: Nasdaq is a competing dealer market, which differs from an auction market in that many dealers, called *market makers,* use their own capital, research, retail, and/or systems resources to represent a stock. Many market makers can represent the same stock; thus, they compete with each other to buy and sell that stock. Auction markets have only one person, a specialist, who in a centralized location or "floor," matches incoming orders to buy and sell each stock. Specialists are not allowed to provide research or retail sales support, and are limited to only one firm's available capital. The average Nasdaq stock has 11 market-making firms that risk and invest their capital.

Debenture: A promissory note backed by the general credit of a company and usually not secured by any specific collateral, such as a mortgage or property.

Debit Balance: In a customer's margin account, that portion of the purchase price of stock, bonds, or commodities that is covered by credit extended by the broker to the margin customer. (*See also* Margin.)

Delayed Opening: The postponement of trading of an issue on a stock exchange beyond the normal opening of a day's trading because of market conditions that have been judged by exchange officials to warrant such a delay. Reasons for the delay may be an influx of either buy or sell orders, an imbalance of buyers and sellers, or pending corporate news that requires time for dissemination.

Depletion Accounting: Natural resources, such as metals, oil, gas, and timber, which conceivably can be reduced to zero over the years, present a special problem in capital management. Depletion is an accounting practice consisting of charges against earnings based upon the amount of the asset taken out of the total reserves in the period for which accounting is made. A bookkeeping entry, it does not represent any cash outlay, nor are funds earmarked for that purpose.

Depository Trust Company (DTC):   A central securities certificate depository through which members effect security deliveries between each other via computerized bookkeeping entries, thereby reducing the physical movement of stock certificates.

Depreciation: Normally, charges against earnings to write off the cost, less salvage value, of an asset over its estimated useful life. It is a bookkeeping entry and does not represent any cash outlay, nor are funds earmarked for the purpose.

Depth of Market: The number of shares of a security that can be bought or sold at the bid and ask prices near the market without causing a dramatic change in price. (*See also* Liquidity Ratio.)

Derivative: A generic term often applied to a wide variety of financial instruments that derive their cash flows, and therefore their value, by reference to an underlying asset, reference rate, or index.

Director: Person elected by shareholders, usually during an annual meeting, to serve on the board of directors of a corporation. The directors appoint the president, vice president, and all other operating officers. Directors decide, among other matters, if and when dividends will be paid.

Discount: The amount by which a preferred stock or bond may sell below its par value. Also used as a verb to mean "takes into account," such as in: The price of the stock has *discounted* the expected dividend cut. (*See also* Proxy.)

Discretionary Account: An account in which the customer gives the broker or someone else discretion to buy and sell securities or commodities, including selection, timing, amount, and price to be paid or received.

Diversification: Spreading investments among different types of securities and various companies in different fields.

Dividend: The payment designated by the board of directors to be distributed pro rata among the shares outstanding. For preferred shares, the dividend is usually a fixed amount. For common shares, the dividend varies with the fortunes of the company and the amount of cash on hand, and may be omitted if business is poor or if the directors determine to withhold earnings to invest in plant and equipment. Sometimes a company will pay a dividend out of past earnings even if it is not currently operating at a profit.

Dividend Reinvestment Plan (DRIP): A program offered by companies that allow investors to buy their stock directly from the company, i.e., without using a brokerage firm. DRIPs allow investors to use their dividends to purchase additional shares of stock in the company.

Dividends Paid per Share: The cash payment per share made by the company to its shareholders.

Dollar Cost Averaging: A system of buying securities at regular intervals in a fixed dollar amount. Under this system, investors buy by the dollars' worth rather than by the number of shares. If each investment is of the same number of dollars, payments buy more shares when the price is low and fewer when it rises. Thus, temporary downswings in price benefit investors if they continue periodic purchases in both good times and bad and the price at which the shares are sold is more than their average cost. (*See also* Formula Investing.)

Dow Theory: A theory of market analysis based upon the performance of the Dow Jones Industrial and Transportation Stock price averages. The theory says that the market is in a basic upward trend if one of these averages advances above a previous important high, accompanied or followed by a similar advance in the other. When the averages both dip below previous important lows, this is regarded as confirmation of a downward trend. The Dow Jones is one type of market index. (*See also* NYSE Composite Index.)

Downtick: A transaction executed at a price lower than the preceding transaction in that security, or a new quote registered at a lower price than the preceding quote in that security. (*See also* Uptick.)

Earnings Per Share (EPS): Net income divided by common shares outstanding.

Earnings Report: A statement—also called an *income statement*—issued by a company showing its earnings or losses over a given period. The earnings report lists the income earned, expenses, and the net result. (*See also* Balance Sheet.)

Economic Indicator: A key statistic in the overall economy that experts use as a yardstick to predict the performance of the stock market.

EDGAR: Electronic Data Gathering, Analysis, and Retrieval, EDGAR is an electronic system developed by the Securities and Exchange Commission. EDGAR permits companies to file electronically with the SEC all documents required for securities offerings and ongoing disclosure obligations. EDGAR became fully operational in mid-1995. (*See also* Securities and Exchange Commission.)

Electronic Communication Network (ECN): Any electronic system that widely disseminates to third parties orders entered by an exchange market maker or OTC market maker and permits such orders to be executed against in whole or part. (*See also* Market Maker.)

Equipment Trust Certificate: A type of security to pay for new equipment, generally issued by a railroad. Title to the equipment, such as a locomotive, is held by a trustee until the notes are paid off. An equipment trust certificate is usually secured by a first claim on the equipment.

Equity: The ownership interest of stockholders in a company. Also, the excess of the market value of securities over monies owed to a broker/dealer in a margin account. (*See also* Margin.)

Exchange: The organization that provides for the trading of a listed security.

Excess Trading: A broker excessively trades an account for the purpose of increasing his or her commissions rather than to further the customer's investment goals.

Excess Spread Policy: The NASD requirement that prohibits market makers from entering quotations on the Nasdaq Stock Market that exceed prescribed limits for maximum allowable spreads. (*See also* Market Maker, Spread.)

Ex-Dividend: A synonym for "without dividend." The buyer of a stock selling ex-dividend does not receive the recently declared dividend. Every dividend is payable on a fixed date to all shareholders recorded on the books of the company as of a previous date of record. For example, a dividend may be declared as payable to holders of record on the books of the company on a given Friday. Since three business days are allowed for delivery of stock in a "regular way" transaction on the New York Stock Exchange, the exchange would declare the stock ex-dividend as of the opening of the market on the preceding Wednesday. That means anyone who bought it on or after that Wednesday would not be entitled to that dividend. When stocks go ex-dividend, the stock tables include the symbol x after the name. (*See also* Net Change, Transfer.)

Exercise: Action taken by an option holder that requires the writer to perform the terms of the contract.

Exercise Prices: The prices at which an option may be exercised. Also called *strike prices.*

Ex-Rights: Without the rights. Corporations raising additional money may do so by offering their stockholders the right to subscribe to new or additional stock, usually at a discount from the prevailing market price. The buyer of a stock selling ex-rights is not entitled to the rights. (*See also* Ex-Dividend, Rights.)

Extra: The short form of *extra dividend.* A dividend in the form of stock or cash in addition to the regular or usual dividend the company has been paying.

52-Week High: The highest price for a security or fund during the past year.

52-Week Low: The lowest price for a security or fund during the past year.

Face Value: The value of a bond that appears on the face of the bond, unless the value is otherwise specified by the issuing company. Face value is ordinarily the amount the issuing company promises to pay at maturity. Face value is not an indication of market value. Also sometimes referred to as *par value.* (*See also* Par.)

Failure to Execute: The failure of a broker to execute an order of his or her customer.

Fair Market Price: A reasonable price for securities based on supply and demand.

Federal Reserve System: A federal government institution created by Congress to administer the nation's credit and monetary policies. Among other things, the Board of Governors of the Federal Reserve System sets the initial amount of credit that broker/dealers (as well as other lenders) may extend to customers to purchase securities.

Financial Futures: Futures contracts based on financial instruments, such as U.S. Treasury bonds, CDs, and other interest-sensitive issues, currencies, and stock market indicators. (*See also* Futures, Stock Index Futures.)

Firm Quotation: The NASD requirement that a market maker execute an order form with another broker/dealer at its displayed Nasdaq price for the normal unit of trading, or for its displayed size, whichever is greater. (*See also* Market Maker.)

Fiscal Year: A corporation's accounting year. Due to the nature of their particular business, some companies do not use the calendar year for their bookkeeping. A typical example is the department store that finds December 31 too early a date to close its books after the Christmas rush. For that reason, many stores wind up their accounting year January 31. Their fiscal year, therefore, runs from February 1 of one year through January 31 of the next. The fiscal year of other companies may run from July 1 through the following June 30. Most companies, though, operate on a calendar year basis.

Fixed Charges: A company's fixed expenses, such as bond interest, which it has agreed to pay whether or not earned, and which are deducted from income before earnings in equity capital are computed.

Flat Income Bond: This term means that the price at which a bond is traded includes consideration for all unpaid accruals of interest. Bonds that are in default of interest or principal are traded flat. Income bonds that pay interest only to the extent earned are usually dealt in *and interest,* which means that the buyer pays to the seller the market price plus interest accrued since the last payment date.

Floor: The trading area where stocks are bought and sold.

Floor Brokers: The largest single membership group of the NYSE. There are two main types: *Commission brokers,* employed by brokerage houses, buy and sell securities on the NYSE floor for the general public. *Independent floor brokers* work for themselves. They execute orders for brokerages without full-time commission brokers or for overly busy brokers.

Formula Investing: An investment technique. One formula, for example, calls for the shifting of funds from common shares to preferred shares or bonds as a selected market indicator rises above a certain predetermined point, and the return of funds to common share investments as the market average declines. (*See also* Dollar Cost Averaging.)

Fourth Market: The direct trading of large blocks of securities between institutional investors through a computer network called INSTINET, which allows subscribers to display tentative bid and ask quotes. (*See also* Third Market.)

Free and Open Market: A market in which supply and demand are freely expressed in terms of price. Contrasts with a controlled market in which supply, demand, and price may all be regulated.

Fundamental Research: Analysis of industries and companies based on such factors as sales, assets, earnings, products or services, markets, and management. As applied to the economy, fundamental research includes consideration of gross national product, interest rates, unemployment, inventories, savings, etc. (*See also* Technical Research.)

Fundamentals: All the factors about a specific business that an investor might use in deciding whether to invest.

Futures: A contract specifying a future date of delivery or receipt of a certain amount of a specific tangible or intangible product. The commodities traded in futures markets include stock index futures; agricultural products like wheat, soybeans, and pork bellies; metals; and financial instruments. Futures are used by businesses as a hedge against unfavorable price changes and by speculators who hope to profit from such changes.

General Mortgage Bond: A bond that is secured by a blanket mortgage on the company's property but which may be outranked by one or more other mortgages.

Gilt-Edged: High-grade bond issued by a company that has demonstrated its ability to earn a comfortable profit over a period of years and pay its bondholders their interest without interruption.

Give-Up: A term with many different meanings. For one, a member of an exchange on the floor may act for a second member by executing an order for him with a third member. The first member tells the third member that he is acting on behalf of the second member and "gives up" the second member's name rather than his own.

Gold Fix: The setting of the price of gold by dealers (especially in a twice-daily London meeting at the central bank). The fix is the fundamental worldwide price for setting the price of gold bullion and gold-related contracts and products.

Good Delivery: Certain basic qualifications must be met before a security sold on the exchange may be delivered. The security must be in proper form to comply with the contract of sale and to transfer title to the purchaser.

Good 'til Canceled (GTC) Order: An order to buy or sell at a specific price until the investor cancels the order.

Going Public: When a company sells shares of itself to the public to raise capital.

Government Bond: A bond issued by the federal government.

Government Securities Broker: Any person or company regularly engaged in the business of effecting transactions in government securities for the account of others. The definition does not include corporations that issue securities exempted by the secretary of the treasury, corporations that are empowered by law to issue exempt securities, banks, or other insured financial institutions.

Growth Stock: Stock of a company with a record of earnings growth at a relatively high rate.

Hedging: The purchase or sale of a derivative security (such as options or futures) in order to reduce or neutralize all or some portion of the risk of holding another security.

Held: A situation where a security is temporarily not available for trading. Market makers are not allowed to display quotes of held securities.

Holding Company: A corporation that owns the securities of another, in most cases with voting control.

House: A person or company doing business as a broker or dealer in securities, investment banking, or related services.

House Spread: Among market maker firms, the house spread is the difference between the highest price bid for a security and the highest price asked, or the difference between best bid and best ask. (*See also* Best Ask, Best Bid, Inside Market, Inside Quote.)

Hypothecation: The pledging of securities as collateral, for example, to secure the debit balance in a margin account.

Income Bond: Generally, income bonds promise to repay principal but to pay interest only when it is earned. In some cases, unpaid interest on an income bond may accumulate as a claim against the corporation when the bond becomes due. An income bond may also be issued in lieu of preferred stock.

Income Statement: A report on a company's financial status over a period of time. It totals profits, subtracts expenses, and pinpoints how much money the company can reinvest.

Indenture: A written agreement under which bonds and debentures are issued, setting forth maturity date, interest rate, and other terms.

Independent Broker: Member on the floor of an exchange who executes orders for other brokers having more business at that time than they can handle themselves, or for firms who do not have their exchange member on the floor. Formerly known on the NYSE as two-dollar brokers, from the time when these independent brokers received $2 per hundred shares of such orders executed. Their fees are paid by the commission brokers. (*See also* Commission Broker.)

Index: A statistical yardstick expressed in terms of percentages of a base year or years. For instance, the NYSE Composite Index of all NYSE common stocks is based on year-end 1965 as 50. An index is not an average. (*See also* Averages, NYSE Composite Index.)

Individual Investor: A person who buys or sells securities for his or her own account. The individual investor is also called a *retail investor* or *retail shareholder*.

Inflation: Increase in the prices for goods and services.

Inflation Rate: An important economic indicator. The rate at which prices are rising.

Initial Public Offering (IPO): A company's first sale of stock to the public. Companies making an IPO are seeking outside equity capital and a public market for their stock. (*See also* Syndicate, Underwriter.)

Inside Market: The highest bid and the lowest ask (offer) prices among all market makers competing in a Nasdaq security; the best bid and ask prices for a security. (*See also* Best Bid, Best Ask.)

Inside Spread (Inside Quote): The difference between the best bid and best ask among all securities is the highest bid and the lowest offer being quoted among all of the market makers competing in a security. Since the spread is the aggregate of individual market maker spreads, it is narrower than an individual dealer spread or quote. (*See also* Market Maker, Market Maker Spread.)

Institutional Investor: A bank, mutual fund, pension fund, or other corporate entity that trades securities in large volumes. (*See also* Buy-Side, Fourth Market, Qualified Institutional Investor.)

Interest: Payments borrowers pay lenders for the use of their money. A corporation pays interest on its bonds to its bondholders.

Interest Rate: Another important economic indicator. The price, calculated as a percentage of the money loaned, that banks are charging borrowers for the use of the banks' money.

Intermarket Trading System (ITS): An electronic network of U.S. exchanges and NASD broker/dealers. The ITS displays quotes of stocks traded on multiple exchanges. This allows specialists and traders to get the best possible price of a stock for their customers.

Interrogation Device: A computer terminal that provides market information—last sale price, quotes, volume, etc.—on a screen or paper tape.

Intrinsic Value: The dollar amount of the difference between the exercise price of an option and the current cash value of the underlying security. Intrinsic value and time value are the two components of an option premium, or price.

Inventory: All the raw materials and finished products a company has in its possession.

Investment: The use of money for the purpose of making more money, to gain income or increase capital, or both.

Investment Banker: Also known as an *underwriter,* the "middleman" between a corporation issuing new securities and the public. The usual practice is for one or more investment bankers to buy outright from a corporation a new issue of stocks or bonds. The group forms a syndicate to sell the securities to individuals and institutions. Investment bankers also distribute very large blocks of stock or bonds—perhaps held by an estate.

Investment Company: A company or trust that uses its capital to invest in other companies. There are two principal types: the closed-end and the open-end, also known as a mutual fund. Shares of closed-end investment companies, most of which are listed on the NYSE, are readily transferable in the open market and are bought and sold like stock. Capitalization of these companies remains the same unless action is taken to change, which is rare. Open-end funds sell their own new shares to investors, stand ready to buy back their old shares, and are not listed. Open-end funds are so called because their capitalization is not fixed; they issue more shares as people want them.

Investment Counsel: One whose principal business consists of acting as investment adviser and rendering investment supervisory services.

Investment Portfolio: A variety of securities owned by an individual or an institution.

Investor: A person who buys or sells securities for his or her own account or the accounts of others. (*See also* Individual Investor, Institutional Investor.)

IRA: Individual Retirement Account. A pension plan with tax advantages. An IRA permits investment through intermediaries like mutual funds, insurance companies, and banks, or directly in stocks and bonds through stockbrokers. (*See also* Keogh Plan.)

Issue: Any of a company's securities, or the act of distributing such securities.

Issuer: A corporation that has distributed to the public securities registered with the Securities and Exchange Commission.

Keogh Plan: Tax advantaged personal retirement program that can be established by a self-employed individual. (*See also* IRA.)

Last: The current trading price of one unit of a particular security.

Last-Sale Service: A service that allows real-time access to last-sale information reported by market makers. (*See also* Last-Sale Reporting.)

Last-Sale Reporting: The electronic notification by a market maker to the Nasdaq Stock Market of the price and the number of shares involved in a transaction in a Nasdaq security. The notification must be made within 90 seconds of the execution of an order.

Legal List: A list of investments selected by various states in which certain institutions and fiduciaries, such as insurance companies and banks, may invest. Legal lists are often restricted to high quality securities meeting certain specifications. (*See also* Prudent Man Rule.)

Level 1 Service: A vendor-distributed service consisting of real-time inside bid/ask quotations for securities quoted in the Nasdaq system and comparable information for securities quoted in the OTC Bulletin Board Service. (*See also* OTC Bulletin Board Service.)

Level 2 Service: A component of Nasdaq Workstation II service consisting of real-time access to the quotations of individual market makers registered in every Nasdaq-listed security as well as market makers' quotations in OTC Bulletin Board securities.

Level 3 Service: Consists of Level 2 Service plus the ability to enter quotations, direct/execute orders, and send information. This service is restricted to NASD member firms that function as registered market makers in either Nasdaq, exchange-listed, or OTC Bulletin Board securities.

Leverage: The effect on a company when the company has bonds, preferred stock, or both outstanding. Example: If the earnings of a company with 1,000,000 common shares increases from $1,000,000 to $1,500,000, earnings per share would go from $1 to $1.50, or an increase of 50 percent. But if earnings of a company that had to pay $500,000 in bond interest increased that much—earnings per common share would jump from 50 cents to $1 a share, or 100 percent.

Liabilities: All the claims against a corporation. Liabilities include accounts, wages, and salaries payable; dividends declared payable; accrued taxes payable; fixed or long-term liabilities, such as mortgage bonds, debentures, and bank loans. (*See also* Assets, Balance Sheet.)

Limit Order: An order to buy or sell when and if a security reaches a specific price.

Liquidation: When a company fails, the process of converting all of its assets back into cash and distributing it to those with a claim on it.

Liquidity: (1) How easily one's assets can be converted back into cash. For example, money in an account that can't be withdrawn for 10 years is not very liquid. (2) The ability of the market in a particular security to absorb a reasonable amount of buying or selling at reasonable price changes. Liquidity is one of the most important characteristics of a good market.

Liquidity Ratio: A measure of the trading volume of a security associated with a 1 percent change in its price. The higher the ratio, the more shares that can be traded with little change in price.

Listed Stock: The stock of a company that is traded on a securities exchange. The various stock exchanges have different standards for listing. Some of the guidelines used by the New York Stock Exchange for an original listing are national interest in the company and a minimum of 1.1 million shares publicly held among no fewer than 2000 round-lot stockholders. The publicly held common shares should have a minimum aggregate market value of $40 million. The company should have net income in the latest year of over $2.5 million before federal income tax, and $2 million in each of the preceding two years.

Load: The portion of the offering price of shares of open-end investment companies in excess of the value of the underlying assets. Covers sales commissions and all other costs of distribution. The load is usually incurred only on purchase, there being, in most cases, no charge when the shares are sold (redeemed). (*See also* Investment Company.)

Locked In: Investors are said to be locked in when they have profit on a security they own but do not sell because their profit would immediately become subject to the capital gains tax.

Locked Quotations: Also called *crossed quotations,* this is a temporary and unusual condition where the ask (offer) price of one market maker for a security is the same or lower than the bid (buy) price of another market maker. Locked or crossed quotations may occur in fast-moving markets. (*See also* Ask Price, Bid Price, Market Maker.)

Long: Signifies ownership of securities. "I am long 100 U.S. Steel" means the speaker owns 100 shares. (*See also* Short Position, Short Sale.)

Maloney Act: Also called the Maloney Amendment, this provides for the regulation of over-the-counter securities markets through national associations registered with the Securities and Exchange Commission. The act was passed in 1938 to add Section 15A to the Securities Exchange Act of 1934. The National Association of Securities Dealers, Inc., is the only association ever to register under the act.

Manipulation: An illegal operation. Buying or selling a security for the purpose of creating the false or misleading appearance of active trading or for the purpose of raising or depressing the price to induce purchase or sale by others.

Margin: The amount paid by the customer when using a broker's credit to buy or sell a security. Under Federal Reserve regulations, the initial margin required since 1934 has ranged from 40 percent of the purchase price up to 100 percent. Since 1974, the current rate of 50 percent has been in effect. (*See also* Brokers' Loans, Equity.)

Margin Call: A demand upon a customer to put up money or securities with the broker. The call is made when a purchase is made; also if a customer's equity in a margin account declines below a minimum standard set by the exchange or by the firm.

Markdown and Markup: A markdown is a charge subtracted from the selling price of a security that a customer is selling to a broker/dealer for the broker/dealer's own account. The broker/dealer adds a markup to the price when it sells a security to a customer from its own account. The markdown or markup is the equivalent of a commission on the sale.

Market Capitalization: The value of a company's outstanding shares, as measured by shares times current price.

Market Maker: A firm that maintains a firm bid and offer price in a given security by standing ready to buy or sell at publicly quoted prices. The Nasdaq Stock Market is a decentralized network of competitive market makers. Market makers process orders for their own customers and for other NASD broker/dealers. All NASD securities are traded through market maker firms. Market makers also will buy securities from issuers for resale to customers or other broker/dealers. About 10 percent of NASD firms are market makers. A broker/dealer may become a market maker if the firm meets capitalization standards set down by NASD. (*See also* Specialist.)

Market Maker Spread: The difference between the price at which a market maker is willing to buy a security and the price at which the firm is willing to sell it. (*See also* Inside Market.)

Market Order: An order to buy or sell at the best price currently available on the trading floor.

Market Price: The last reported price at which the stock or bond sold, or the current quote. (*See also* Quote.)

Maturity Date: The date that a bond comes due and must be paid off.

Member Corporation (NYSE): A securities brokerage firm, organized as a corporation, with at least one member of the New York Stock Exchange who is an officer or employee of the corporation.

Member Firm: A securities brokerage firm, organized as a corporation, partnership, or sole proprietorship, with at least one member of the NYSE who is an officer or employee of the corporation. A broker/dealer that is a member of the National Association of Securities Dealers, Inc.

Merger: Combination of two or more corporations.

Money Market Account: An account in which your money is reinvested in short-term securities by the bank or investment firm managing the account.

Money Market Fund: A mutual fund whose investments are in high-yield money market instruments, such as federal securities, CDs, and commercial paper. Its intent is to make such instruments, normally purchased in large denominations by institutions, available indirectly to individuals. (*See also* Certificate of Deposit, Commercial Paper.)

Mortgage Bond: A bond secured by a mortgage on a property. The value of the property may or may not equal the value of the bond issued against it. (*See also* Bond, Debenture.)

Most Active: Most active stocks.

Municipal Bonds: Bonds issued by states, cities, counties, and towns to fund public capital projects like roads, schools, sanitation facilities, and bridges, as well as operating budgets. These bonds are exempt from federal taxation and from state and local taxes for the investors who reside in the state where the bond is issued.

Mutual Fund: *See* Investment Company.

Naked Option: An option position that is not offset by an equal and opposite position in the underlying security.

Nasdaq: An automated information network that provides brokers and dealers with price quotations on securities traded over-the-counter. (*See also* Over-the-Counter.)

Nasdaq Composite^{SM} Index: A statistical measure that indicates changes in the Nasdaq Stock Market. The Nasdaq Composite Index measures all Nasdaq domestic and foreign common stocks. As it is market-value weighted, each company's security affects the index in proportion to its market value.

Nasdaq International Service: The extension of the Nasdaq Stock Market to the United Kingdom. The service supports a European trading session from 3:30 a.m. to 9 a.m. eastern time (U.S.). This enables participants to monitor trade during London market hours. NASD members are eligible to participate in this session through their U.S. facilities or approved United Kingdom affiliates.

Nasdaq National Market®: More than 3900 companies that are the larger and generally more actively traded Nasdaq securities. (*See also* Nasdaq SmallCap Market.)

Nasdaq Quotation Dissemination ServiceSM **(NQDS):** The NQDS carries real-time quotation information for market makers and electronic communication networks (ECNs) in each Nasdaq National Market® and Nasdaq SmallCap Market SM issue. Using the NQDS data feed, market data vendors are able to create a level 2 display similar to the Nasdaq Workstation II™ to show the depth of market makers at each price level of a Nasdaq-listed security. (*See also* Electronic Communication Network (ECN), Market Maker, Nasdaq Workstation II™.)

Nasdaq SmallCap MarketSM**:** Securities of smaller, less-capitalized companies that do not qualify for inclusion in the Nasdaq National Market. There are more than 1300 companies on the SmallCap Market.

Nasdaq Stock MarketSM**:** The Nasdaq Stock Market is a major national and international stock market that uses computers and telecommunications for the trading and surveillance of thousands of securities. The Nasdaq Stock Market is built on a unique system of competing market maker firms that list specific prices for the sale or purchase of securities. It also is unique in its use of a flexible computer-screen trading system that enables people to trade by computer from wherever they are located.

Nasdaq Trade Dissemination ServiceSM **(NTDS):** The NTDS carries real-time trade price and volume data to market data vendors and other data feed recipients. NTDS carries the price and size for all trade reports that are submitted to the Automated Confirmation Transaction Service SM (ACTSM). For pricing purposes, the Nasdaq last sale information is bundled with Nasdaq 1 Service. (*See also* Automated Confirmation Transaction ServiceSM.)

National Association of Securities Dealers, Inc. (NASD®): The largest self-regulatory organization for the securities industry in the United States. NASD is responsible for the operation and regulation of Nasdaq and the over-the-counter securities markets. It is the parent company of NASD Regulation, Inc., and the Nasdaq Stock Market, Inc. (*See also* Nasdaq, The Nasdaq Stock Market, NASD Regulation, Inc.)

Negotiable: Refers to a security, title to which is transferable by delivery.

Net Asset Value: Usually used in connection with investment companies to mean net asset value per share. An investment company computes its assets daily, or even twice daily, by totaling the market value of all securities owned. All liabilities are deducted, and the balance is divided by the number of shares outstanding. The resulting figure is the net asset value per share. (*See also* Assets, Investment Company.)

Net Change: The change in the price of a security from the closing price of one day to the closing price on the next day on which the stock is traded. The net change is ordinarily the last figure in the newspaper stock price list. The mark +1⅛ means up $1.125 a share from the last sale on the previous day the stock traded.

New Issue: A stock or bond sold by a corporation for the first time. Proceeds may be used to retire outstanding securities of the company, for new plant or equipment, for additional working capital, or to acquire a public ownership interest in the company for private owners.

New York Stock Exchange (NYSE): The largest organized securities market in the United States, founded in 1792. The exchange itself does not buy, sell, own, or set the price of securities traded there. The prices are determined by public supply and demand. The exchange is a not-for-profit corporation of 1366 individual members, governed by a board of directors consisting of 12 public representatives, 12 member firm representatives, and a full-time chairman, executive vice chairman, and president.

Noncumulative: A type of preferred stock on which unpaid dividends do not accrue. Omitted dividends are, as a rule, gone forever. (*See also* Cumulative Preferred.)

North American Securities Administrators Association, Inc. (NASAA): An association of securities commissioners from each of the 50 states, the District of Columbia, Puerto Rico, and several of the Canadian provinces.

NYSE Composite Index: The composite index covering price movements of all common stocks listed on the New York Stock Exchange. It is based on the close of the market December 31, 1967 as 50.00 and is weighed according to the number of shares listed for each issue. The index is computed continuously and printed on the ticker tape. Point changes in the index are converted to dollars and cents so as to provide a meaningful measure of changes in the average price of listed stocks. The composite index is supplemented by separate indexes for four industry groups: industrial, transportation, utility, and finance. (*See also* Averages.)

Odd Lots: Stock transactions that involve less than 100 shares.

Off-Board: This term refers either to transactions over the counter in unlisted securities or to a transaction of listed shares that is not executed on a national securities exchange.

Offer: The price at which a person is ready to sell. Opposed to bid, the price at which one is ready to buy. (*See also* Bid and Asked.)

Open: The price paid in a security's first transaction of the current trading day.

Open-End Investment Company: *See* Investment Company.

Open Interest: In options and futures trading, the number of outstanding options contracts at a given point in time which have not been exercised and have not yet reached expiration.

Open Order: *See* Good 'til Canceled Order.

Option: A right to buy or sell a fixed amount of a given stock at a specified price within a limited period of time. If the right is not exercised, the option expires and the buyer forfeits the money.

Order Flow: Aggregated small orders to purchase or sell securities that brokers send to dealers, often in return for cash payments.

Order Matching: The market maker practice of pairing buy and sell orders for like amounts of securities at identical prices. (*See also* Market Maker, Small Order Execution System.)

Orders: Specific instructions for handling transactions.

The OTC Bulletin Board® (OTCBB): The OTC Bulletin Board is a regulated electronic quotation service that displays real-time quotes, last-sale prices, and volume information for unlisted, non-Nasdaq, over-the-counter securities. OTCBB securities are traded by a community of market makers that enter quotes and trade reports through a highly sophisticated, closed computer network, which is accessed through Nasdaq Workstation II™, a computerized trading tool that provides access to all Nasdaq markets for market makers, brokers, and institutions.

Overbought: An opinion as to price levels. It can refer either to a security that has had a sharp rise or to the market as a whole after a period of vigorous buying, which, it may be argued, has left prices "too high."

Oversold: The reverse of overbought. A single security or a market which, it is believed, has declined to an unreasonable level.

Over-the-Counter (OTC): A market for securities made up of dealers who may or may not be members of a securities exchange. The OTC market is conducted over the telephone and deals mainly with stocks of companies without sufficient shares, stockholders, or earnings to warrant listing on an exchange. OTC firms may act either as principals or dealers (buying or selling stock from their own inventories and charging a markup) or as brokers or agents and charging a commission.

Paper Profit (Loss): An unrealized profit or loss on a security still held. Paper profits and losses become realized only when the security is sold. (*See also* Profit-Taking.)

Par: Equal to the nominal or face value of a security.

Participating Preferred: A preferred stock that is entitled to its stated dividend and also to dividends on a specific basis upon payment of dividends on the common stock.

Partnership: A business relationship in which two or more people agree to share the risks and profits of running a business.

Passed Dividend: Omission of a regular or scheduled dividend.

Passive Market-Making: A process that allows a market-maker firm to be both underwriter and buyer of a company's securities in a secondary public offering, which is a registered offering of a large block of a security that has been previously issued to the public. An underwriting market maker may bid for the security during the issue's cooling-off period when a company's prospectus has been filed with the Security and Exchange Commission and before offering is made to the public if its bid is no higher than a competing, nonunderwriting market maker's. (*See also* Market Maker, Underwriter.)

P/E Ratio: Also known as the *P/E multiple,* this is the latest closing price divided by the latest 12 months' earnings per share.

Penny Stocks: Low-priced issues, often highly speculative, selling at less than $1 a share; frequently used as a term of disparagement, although some penny stocks have developed into investment-caliber issues.

Percent Change: The percentage difference between the preceding day's closing price and the current price.

Point: In the case of shares of stock, a point means $1. If ABC shares rise 3 points, each share has risen $3. In the case of bonds, a point means $10, since a bond is quoted as a percentage of $1000. A bond that rises 3 points gains 3 percent of $1000, or $30 in value. An advance from 87 to 90 would mean an advance in dollar value from $870 to $900. In the case of market averages, the word *point* means merely that and no more. If, for example, the NYSE Composite Index rises from 90.25 to 91.25, it has risen a point. A point in this index, however, is not equivalent to $1. (*See also* Indexes.)

Portfolio: A holding of securities by an individual or institution.

Preferred Stock: A class of stock with a claim on the company's earnings before payment may be made on common stock and usually entitled to priority over common stockholders if the company fails or liquidates. Preferred stock also is entitled to dividends at a specified rate when declared by the company's board of directors and before payment of a dividend on the common stock. Preferred stock normally does not include voting rights.

Premium: The amount by which a bond or preferred stock may sell above its par value. For options, it is the price that the buyer pays the writer for an option contract (*option premium* is synonymous with *the price of an option*). It may refer, also, to redemption price of a bond or preferred stock if it is higher than face value. (*See also* Discount.)

Previous Close: The price of a security at the end of the previous day's trading session.

Previous Day's Close: The previous trading day's last reported trade.

Price-Earnings Ratio: A popular way to compare stocks selling at various price levels. The PE ratio is the price of a share of stock divided by earnings per share for a 12-month period. For example, a stock selling for $50 a share that earned $5 a share is said to be selling at a price-earnings ratio of 10.

Primary Distribution: Also called *primary offering* or *public offering.* The original sale of a company's securities. (*See also* Investment Banker.)

Primary Market: The process by which a corporation's stock is issued for the first time. It is then sold to the public on the secondary market.

Prime Rate: The lowest interest rate charged by commercial banks to their most creditworthy and largest corporate customers. Other interest rates, such as personal, automobile, commercial, and financing loans are often pegged to the prime.

Profit-Taking: Selling stock which has appreciated in value since purchase in order to realize the profit. The term is often used to explain a downturn in the market following a period of rising prices. (*See also* Paper Profit.)

Prospectus: A document that provides details about a new offering of securities for sale to the public. It gives a detailed financial background of the issuing company, how the proceeds of the securities will be used, and other pertinent information investors will need to make an informed decision.

Proxy: Written authorization given by a shareholder to someone else to represent him and vote his share at a shareholders' meeting.

Proxy Statement: Information given to stockholders in conjunction with the solicitation of proxies.

Prudent Man Rule: An investment standard. In some states, the law requires that a fiduciary, such as a trustee, only invest the fund's money in a list of securities designated by the state, the so-called legal list. In other states, the trustee may invest in a security if it is one that would be bought by a prudent man of discretion and intelligence who is seeking a reasonable income and preservation of capital.

Public Float: The portion of a company's outstanding shares that is in the hands of public investors; shares not held by company officers, directors, or investors who hold a controlling interest in the company.

Public Offering: *See* Primary Distribution.

Put: *See* Option.

Qualified Institutional Investor: An institutional investor permitted under Securities and Exchange Commission rules to trade privately placed securities with other qualified institutional investors without registering the securities with the SEC. A qualified institutional investor must have at least $100 million under management.

Quotation Size: The maximum number of shares per order of a particular security that a market maker is willing to buy or sell at his or her current price.

Quote: The highest bid to buy and the lowest offer to sell any stock at a given time.

Quote Dissemination System (QDS): Provides Nasdaq market maker quotations to outside services and vendors.

Rally: A brisk rise following a decline in the general price level of the market or in the price of an individual stock.

Rate of Return: In stocks and bonds, the amount of money returned to investors on their investments. Also known as *yield.*

Recession: A period of no or negative economic growth and high unemployment.

Record Date: The date on which you must be registered as a shareholder of a company in order to receive a declared dividend or, among other things, to vote on company affairs. (*See also* Ex-Dividend, Transfer.)

Redemption Price: The price at which a bond may be redeemed before maturity, at the option of the issuing company. Redemption value also applies to the price the company must pay to call in certain types of preferred stock. (*See also* Callable.)

Red Herring: *See* Prospectus.

Refinancing: Same as *refunding.* New securities are sold by a company and the money is used to retire existing securities. The object may be to save interest costs, extend the maturity of the loan, or both.

Registered Bond: A bond that is registered on the books of the issuing company in the name of the owner. It can be transferred only when endorsed by the registered owner. (*See also* Bearer Bond, Coupon Bond.)

Registered Competitive Market Makers: Members of the New York Stock Exchange who trade on the floor for their own or their firm's account and who have an obligation, when called upon by an exchange official, to narrow a quote or improve the depth of an existing quote by their own bid or offer.

Registered Representative: The person, normally employed by a brokerage firm or broker/dealer, who acts as an account executive for customers to buy and sell securities. The term *registered* means the individual has passed qualifying securities examinations and is registered with the SEC.

Registrar: Usually a trust company or bank charged with the responsibility of keeping a record of the owners of a corporation's securities and preventing the issuance of more than the authorized amount. (*See also* Transfer.)

Registration: Before a public offering of new securities may be made by a company, the securities must be registered under the Securities Act of 1933. A registration statement is filed with the SEC by the issuer. It must disclose pertinent information related to the company's operations, securities, management, and the purpose of the public offering. Before a security may be admitted to dealings on a national security exchange, it must be registered under the Securities Exchange Act of 1934. The application for registration must be filed with the exchange and the SEC by the company issuing the securities.

Regular Way Delivery: Unless otherwise specified, securities sold on the New York Stock Exchange are to be delivered to the buying broker by the selling broker and payment made to the selling broker by the buying broker on the third business day after the transaction. Regular delivery for bonds is the following business day. (*See also* Transfer.)

Regulation T: The federal regulation governing the amount of credit that may be advanced by brokers and dealers to customers for the purchase of securities. (*See also* Margin.)

Regulation U: The federal regulation governing the amount of credit that may be advanced by a bank to its customers for the purchase of listed stock. (*See also* Margin.)

Regulatory Pyramid: A network of safeguards that surrounds the securities industry—from individual brokerages all the way up to the U.S. Congress.

Reinvest: Funneling of profits back into a company to enhance its operations. An individual stockowner can also reinvest by designating that dividends paid on stock be used to purchase additional shares of that stock.

REIT: Real Estate Investment Trust; an organization similar to an investment company in some respects, but concentrating its holdings in real estate investments. The yield is generally liberal, since REITs are required to distribute as much as 90 percent of their income. (*See also* Investment Company.)

Retained Earnings: Profits a company keeps for its operations, after paying taxes and dividends.

Rights: When a company wants to raise more funds by issuing additional securities, it may give its stockholders the opportunity, ahead of others, to buy the new securities in proportion to the number of shares each already owns. The piece of paper evidencing this privilege is called a *right*. Because the additional stock is usually offered to stockholders below the current market price, rights ordinarily have a market value of their own and are actively traded. In most cases, rights must be exercised within a relatively short period. Failure to exercise or sell rights may result in monetary loss to the holder. (*See also* Warrant.)

Right to Vote: The right of common stockholders to vote on matters of corporate policy at an annual stockholders' meeting. The impact of a stockholder's vote is proportionate to the amount of stock owned.

Round Lot Order: An order to buy or sell in multiples of 100 shares.

Scale Order: An order to buy (or sell) a security that specifies the total amount to be bought (or sold) at specified price variations.

Scripophily: A term coined in the mid-1970s to describe the hobby of collecting antique bonds, stocks, and other financial instruments. Value is affected, among other things, by beauty of the certificate and the issuer's role in world finance and economic development.

Seat: The traditional term for the right to trade on the trading floor of the NYSE. The owners of seats are considered members of the NYSE.

Secondary Distribution: Also known as *secondary offering*. The redistribution of a block of stock some time after it has been sold by the issuing company. The sale is handled off the NYSE by a securities firm or group of firms, and the shares are usually offered at a fixed price related to the current market price of the stock. Usually, the block is a large one, such as might be involved in the settlement of an estate. The security may be listed or unlisted. (*See also* Investment Banker, Primary Distribution.)

Secondary Market: When stocks or bonds are traded or resold, they are said to be sold on the secondary market. Most securities transactions take place on the secondary market.

Securities Analyst: An individual who does investment research and makes recommendations to buy, sell, or hold. Most analysts specialize in a single industry or business sector.

Securities and Exchange Commission (SEC):   A watchdog agency created by the U.S. Congress to monitor the securities industry and enforce punishments of those who violate the industry's regulations. The SEC administers the Securities Act of 1933, the Securities Exchange Act of 1934, the Securities Act Amendment of 1975, the Trust Indenture Act, the Investment Company Act, the Investment Advisers Act, and the Public Utility Holding Company Act.

Securities Industry Association (SIA):   The principal trade association and lobbying arm of the securities industry.

Securities Investors Protection Corporation (SIPC):   A safeguard for investors' capital created by Congress. The SIPC ensures that cash and securities on deposit with a brokerage are insured up to $500,000 per customer, in the event that the brokerage goes out of business.

Self-Regulation: The way in which the securities industry monitors itself to create a fair and orderly trading environment.

Sell Side: A broker/dealer who sells expertise in research, order execution, or any other service to an individual or institution.

Seller's Option: A special transaction on the NYSE that gives the seller the right to deliver the stock or bond at any time within a specified period, ranging from no less than 2 business days to no more than 60 days.

Serial Bond: An issue that matures in part at periodic stated intervals.

Settlement: Conclusion of a securities transaction when a customer pays a broker/dealer for securities purchased or delivers securities sold and receives from the broker the proceeds of a sale.

Shares Outstanding: The total number of a company's publicly traded shares.

Short Covering: Buying stock to return stock previously borrowed to make delivery on a short sale.

Short Dollars: Payment for brokerage services, such as research, through commissions or directed underwriting rather than fees.

Short Interest: The total number of shares of a security that have been sold short by customers and securities firms that have not been repurchased to settle short positions in the market. (*See also* Short Sale.)

Short Position: Stock options or futures contracts sold short and not covered as of a particular date. On the NYSE, a tabulation is issued once a month listing all issues on the exchange in which there is a short position of 5000 or more shares and issues in which the short position has changed by 2000 or more shares in the preceding month. *Short position* also means the total amount of stock an individual has sold short and has not covered, as of a particular date.

Short Sale: A transaction by a person who believes a security will decline and who sells it, even though he or she does not own the security. Say, for instance, you instruct your broker to sell 100 shares of XYZ. Your broker borrows the stock so delivery of the 100 shares can be made to the buyer. The money value of the shares borrowed is deposited by your broker with the lender. Sooner or later, you must cover your short sale by buying the same amount of stock you borrowed for return to the lender. If you are able to buy XYZ at a lower price than you sold it for, your profit is the difference between the two prices, not counting commission and taxes. But if you have to pay more for the stock than the price you received, that is the amount of your loss. Stock exchange and federal regulations govern and limit the conditions under which a short sale may be made on a national securities exchange. Sometimes, people will sell short a stock they already own in order to protect a paper profit. This is known as *selling short against the box.*

Short Sale Rule: A Nasdaq rule that prohibits NASD members from selling a Nasdaq National Market stock at or below the highest quoted bid of all competing market makers when that price is lower than the previous highest quoted bid in that stock. (*See also* Inside Spread, Short Sale.)

SIAC: The Securities Industry Automation Corporation, an independent organization established by the New York and American Stock exchanges as a jointly owned subsidiary to provide automation, data processing, clearing, and communication services.

Sinking Fund: Money regularly set aside by a company to redeem its bonds, debentures, or preferred stock from time to time, as specified in the indenture or charter.

SIPC: The Securities Investor Protection Corporation, which provides funds to protect customers' cash and securities that may be on deposit with an SIPC member firm in the event the firm fails and is liquidated under the provisions of the SIPC Act. SIPC is not a government agency. It is, however, a nonprofit membership corporation created by an act of Congress.

Sole Proprietorship: Any business that is owned and operated by a single individual.

Specialist: A member of the NYSE who has two primary functions. The first is to maintain an orderly market in the securities assigned to the specialist. To do this, the specialist must, to a reasonable degree, buy or sell for his own account when there is a temporary disparity between supply and demand. Second, the specialist acts as a broker's broker. When commission brokers on the exchange floor receive a limit order, say, to buy at $50 a stock then selling at $60, they cannot wait at the post where the stock is traded to see if the price reaches the specified level. They leave the order with the specialist, who will try to execute it in the market if and when the stock declines to the specified price. At all times, specialists must put their customers' interests above their own.

Speculation: The employment of funds by a speculator. Safety of principal is a secondary factor. (*See also* Investment.)

Spin Off: To separate a subsidiary or division of a corporation from its parent by issuing shares in a new corporate entity. Shareowners in the parent receive shares in the new company in proportion to their original holding, and the total value remains approximately the same.

Split: The division of the outstanding shares of a corporation into either a larger or smaller number of shares, without any immediate impact in individual shareholder equity. For example, a 3-for-1 forward split by a company with 1 million shares outstanding results in 3 million shares outstanding. Each holder of 100 shares before the split would have 300 shares, each worth less, although the proportionate equity in the company would stay the same. A reverse split would reduce the number of shares outstanding and each share would be worth more.

Spread: The difference between the bid price at which a market maker will buy a security and the ask price at which a market maker will sell a security. (*See also* Inside Spread.)

Standard & Poor's Corporation: A company well known for its rating of stocks and bonds according to investment risk (the Standard & Poor's Rating), and for compiling the Standard & Poor's Index—commonly called the Standard & Poor's 500—which tracks 400 industrial stocks, 20 transportation stocks, 40 financial stocks, and 40 public utilities as a measurement of broad changes in the market.

Stock: *See* Capital Stock, Common Stock, Preferred Stock.

Stock Exchange: An organized marketplace for securities, characterized by the centralization of supply and demand, for the transaction of orders by member brokers for institutional and individual investors. (*See also* New York Stock Exchange.)

Stock Dividend: A dividend paid in securities rather than cash. The dividend may be in additional shares of the issuing company or in shares of another company (usually a subsidiary) held by the company.

Stockholder of Record: A stockholder whose name is registered on the books of the issuing corporation. (*See also* Registrar.)

Stockholders' Equity: The value of all the stock owned by the shareholders of a particular company. Also known as *net worth.*

Stock Index: A way of using a select group of stocks for long-term evaluation. The performance of a group of stocks that experts regard as important is averaged, and over time, that average serves as an indicator of the market's general movement.

Stock Index Futures: Futures contracts based on market indexes.

Stock Ticker Symbols: Every corporation whose transactions are reported on the NYSE or AMEX ticker or on Nasdaq is given a unique identification symbol of up to four letters. These symbols abbreviate the complete corporate name and facilitate trading and ticker reporting. Some of the most famous symbols are T (American Telephone & Telegraph), XON (Exxon), GM (General Motors), IBM (International Business Machines), S (Sears Roebuck), and XRX (Xerox).

StockWatch: The NYSE's state-of-the-art computer surveillance unit. StockWatch monitors the stock market for suspicious signals and detects illegal transactions.

Stop-Limit Order: A stop order that becomes a limit order after the specified stop price has been reached. (*See also* Limit Order, Stop Order.)

Stop Order: An order to buy at a price above or sell at a price below the current market. Stop *buy* orders are generally used to limit or protect unrealized profits on a short sale. Stop *sell* orders are generally used to protect unrealized profits or limit loss on a holding.

A stop order becomes a market order when the stock sells at or beyond the specified price and, thus, may not necessarily be executed at that price.

Street Name: Securities held in the name of a broker instead of a customer's name are said to be carried in "street name." This occurs when the securities have been bought on margin or when the customer wishes the security to be held by the broker.

SuperDot: The electronic order-routing system through which NYSE member firms transmit market and limit orders directly to the trading post where the security is traded or to the member firm's booth. After the order has been completed in the auction market, a report of execution is returned directly to the member firm office over the same electronic circuit that brought the order to the trading floor.

Swapping: Selling one security and buying a similar one almost at the same time to take a loss, usually for tax purposes.

Syndicate: A group of investment bankers who, together, underwrite and distribute a new issue of securities or a large block of an outstanding issue.

Syndicate Manager: Also called the *managing underwriter* or simply *manager,* the syndicate manager works with a company to prepare a new stock issue and register it with the Securities and Exchange Commission. The manager often also organizes the syndicate to spread the risk of a new issue.

Technical Research: Analysis of the market and stocks based on supply and demand. The technician studies price movements, volume, trends, and patterns, which are revealed by charting these factors, and attempts to assess the possible effects of current market action or future supply and demand for securities and individual issues. (*See also* Fundamental Research.)

Tender Offer: A public offer to buy shares from existing stockholders of one public corporation by another company or other organization under specified terms good for a certain time period. Stockholders are asked to "tender" (surrender) their holdings for a stated value, usually at a premium above current market price, subject to the tendering of a minimum and maximum number of shares.

Third Market: Trading of stock-exchange-listed securities in the over-the-counter market by nonexchange-member brokers.

Ticker: A telegraphic system that continuously provides the last sale prices and volume of securities transactions on exchanges. Information is either printed or displayed on a moving tape after each trade.

Time Value: The part of an option premium that is in excess of the intrinsic value.

Trader: An individual who buys and sells for her or his own account for short-term profit. Also, an employee of a broker/dealer who specializes in handling purchases and sales of securities for the firm and/or its clients. (*See also* Investor.)

Trading Posts: The 17 horseshoe-shaped counters attended by clerks and specialists on the trading floor of the NYSE. They are like stores where individual stocks are bought and sold. Each trading post is responsible for over 100 stocks. The actual buying and selling takes place around each post.

Transfer: This term may refer to two different operations. For one, it is the delivery of a stock certificate from the seller's broker to the buyer's broker and legal change of ownership, which normally is accomplished within a few days. For another, it is to record the change of ownership on the books of the corporation by the transfer agent. When the purchaser's name is recorded, dividends, notices of meetings, proxies, financial reports, and all pertinent literature sent by the issuer to its securities holders are mailed directly to the new owner. (*See also* Registrar, Street Name.)

Transfer Agent: A transfer agent keeps a record of the name of each registered shareowner, his or her address, the number of shares owned, and sees that certificates presented for transfer are properly cancelled and new certificates issued in the name of the new owner. (*See also* Registrar.)

Treasuries: Debt obligations of the U.S. government. Treasuries are among the safest investments, since they are secured by the full faith and credit of the government. The interest on Treasuries is exempt from state and local taxes but is subject to federal income tax.

There are three types of treasuries: Treasury bills, with maturities of one year or less; Treasury notes, with maturities ranging from 1 to 10 years; and Treasury bonds, long-term instruments with maturities of 10 years or more.

Treasury Stock: Stock issued by a company but later reacquired. It may be held in the company's treasury indefinitely, reissued to the public, or retired. Treasury stock receives no dividend and has no vote while held by the company.

Triple Witching Hour: The last trading hour on the third Friday of March, June, September, and December, when options and futures on stock indexes expire concurrently. (*See also* Options and Futures.)

Turnover Rate: The volume of shares traded in a year as a percentage of total shares listed on an exchange, outstanding for an individual issue, or held in an institutional portfolio.

Underlying: The security that one has the right to buy or sell according to the terms of an option contract.

Underwriter: *See* Investment Banker.

Unlisted Stock: A security not listed on a stock exchange. (*See also* Over-the-Counter.)

Uptick: A term used to designate a transaction made at a price higher than the preceding transaction. Also called a *plus tick.* A "zero plus" tick is a term used for a transaction at the same price as the preceding trade but higher than the preceding different price. Conversely, a downtick, or *minus tick,* is a term used to designate a transaction made at a price lower than the preceding trade. A plus sign or minus sign is displayed throughout the day next to the last price of each stock at the trading post on the floor of the New York Stock Exchange.

Variable Annuity: A life insurance policy in which the annuity premium (a set amount of dollars) is immediately turned into units of a portfolio of stocks. Upon retirement, the policyholder is paid according to accumulated units, the dollar value of which varies according to the performance of the stock portfolio. Its objective is to enhance, through stock investment, the purchasing value of the annuity, which otherwise is subject to erosion through inflation.

Volatility: The degree of price fluctuation for a given asset, rate, or index, usually expressed as a variance or standard deviation. (*See also* Beta.)

Volume: The number of shares or contracts traded in a security or an entire market during a given period. Volume is usually considered on a daily basis, and a daily average is computed for longer periods.

Voting Right: The common stockholders' right to vote their stock in the affairs of a company. Preferred stock usually has the right to vote when preferred dividends are in default for a specified period. The right to vote may be delegated by the stockholder to another person. (*See also* Cumulative Voting, Proxy.)

Warrant: A certificate giving the holder the right to purchase securities at a stipulated price within a specified time limit or perpetually. Sometimes a warrant is offered with securities as an inducement to buy. (*See also* Rights.)

When Issued: A short form of "when, as, and if issued," the term indicates a conditional transaction in a security authorized for issuance but not as yet actually issued. All *when issued* transactions are on an *if* basis, to be settled if and when the actual security is issued and the exchange or National Association of Securities Dealers rules the transactions are to be settled.

Wire House: A firm whose branch offices are linked by a communications system that permits the rapid dissemination of prices, information, and research related to financial markets and individual securities.

Working Capital: The assets a company has that can be poured into the company's operations.

Working Control: Theoretically, ownership of 51 percent of a company's voting stock is necessary to exercise control. In practice—and this is particularly true in the case of a large corporation—effective control sometimes can be exerted through ownership, individually or by a group acting in concert, of less than 50 percent.

Wrap Fee: Charge for an investment program that bundles or "wraps" a number of services (brokerage, advisory, research, consulting, management, etc.) together and covers them with a single fee based on the value of assets under management.

Writer: A person who assumes the obligation to sell (call) or buy (put) the underlying security at an option's exercise.

Yield: In stocks and bonds, the amount of money returned to investors on their investments. Also known as *rate of return.*

Yield to Maturity: The yield of a bond to maturity takes into account the price discount from or premium over the face amount. It is greater than the current yield when the bond is selling at a discount and less than the current yield when the bond is selling at a premium.

Zero Coupon Bond: A bond which pays no interest, but which is priced, at issue, at a discount from its redemption price.

A Glossary of the Futures Markets

Abandon: The act of an option holder in electing not to exercise or offset an option.

Accommodation Trading: Noncompetitive trading entered into by a trader, usually to assist another with illegal trades.

Action Type: A uniform category of rule violation, such as floor record-keeping violations, sales practice violations, and trade practice violations.

Actuals: The physical or cash commodity, as distinguished from a commodity futures contract. (*See also* Cash Commodity, Spot Commodity.)

Adjudication: The determination of a controversy and pronouncement of a judgment based on evidence presented. Implies a final judgment of a court or other body deciding the matter, as opposed to a proceeding in which the merits of the cause of action were not reached.

Adjudication Committee: A committee empowered by a self-regulatory organization to determine an issue of fact and reach a decision on the basis of evidence presented.

Administrative Hearing: A proceeding wherein evidence is taken for the purpose of determining an issue of fact and reaching a decision on the basis of that evidence. An administrative hearing may take place outside the judicial process, before officials who have been expressly granted judicial authority to conduct such hearings.

Administrative Law: Law created by administrative agencies by way of rules, regulations, orders, and decisions.

Administrative Law Judge (ALJ): The presiding officer of an administrative hearing. An ALJ does not sit as a law judge, and his power is essentially that of recommendation. In the federal system, the ALJ is empowered to administer oaths and affirmations, issue subpoenas, rule on evidence presented, take depositions, regulate the course hearings, and make or recommend decisions.

Affidavit: A written statement made under oath.

Affirm: The act of an appellate body upholding a decision of a trial court, an adjudication committee, or a lower appellate court.

Against Actuals: A transaction generally used by two hedgers who want to exchange futures for cash positions. Also referred to as *exchange for physicals* or *versus cash.*

Aggregation: The policy under which all futures positions owned or controlled by one trader or group of traders are combined to determine reporting status and speculative limit compliance.

Aid and Abet: To actively, knowingly, intentionally, or purposefully facilitate or assist another individual in the commission or attempted commission of a crime.

ALJ: *See* Administrative Law Judge.

Allowances: The discounts (or premiums) allowed for grades or locations of a commodity lower (or higher) than the par (or basis) grade or location specified in the futures contract. (*See also* Differential.)

Answer: A written response to a demand or a third party claim. A written submission filed by a respondent named in a complaint which answers each allegation in the complaint by admitting, denying, or averring lack of sufficient knowledge to admit or deny the allegation.

AP: *See* Associated Person.

Appeal: A request to an appellate body to review a lower court's or an adjudication committee's decision.

Appeals Committee: A committee empowered by a self-regulatory organization for the purpose of hearing and deciding appeals from and reviews of decisions by hearing committees.

Appellant: The party bringing an appeal.

Appellate: About appeals; an appellate court has the power to review the judgment of a lower court or tribunal.

Appellee: The party against whom an appeal is brought.

Approved Delivery Facility: Any bank, stockyard, mill, storehouse, plant, elevator, or other depository that is authorized by an exchange for the delivery of commodities tendered on futures contracts.

ARA: *See* Associate Responsibility Action.

Arbitrage: The simultaneous purchase and sale of similar commodities in different markets to take advantage of a price discrepancy.

Arbitration: A process for settling disputes between parties. For example, the NFA's arbitration program provides a forum for resolving futures-related disputes between members or between members and customers.

Arbitration Panel: The arbitrators (one or three) appointed by the NFA to hear and decide disputes brought to the NFA for arbitration.

Arbitrator: A person chosen to decide disputes between parties in an arbitration proceeding.

Asian Option: An option whose payoff depends on the average price of the underlying asset during some portion of the life of the option.

Ask: Also called *offer.* Indicates a willingness to sell a futures contract at a given price. (*See also* Bid.)

Assignable Contract: A contract which allows the holder to convey his rights to a third party. Exchange-traded commodities are not assignable.

Associate: A person who is associated with an NFA member within the meaning of the term *associated* and who is required to be registered as an associated person with the Commodity Futures Trading Commission.

Associate Responsibility Action (ARA): An action whereby an NFA associate member may be suspended from membership or may otherwise be directed to take remedial action when the president of the NFA, with the concurrence of the executive committee, has reason to believe that the action is necessary to protect the commodity futures markets, customers, or other members or associates of the NFA. This may be a summary action.

Associated Person (AP): An individual who solicits orders, customers, or customer funds on behalf of a futures commission merchant, an introducing broker, a commodity trading advisor, or a commodity pool operator, and who is registered with the CFTC.

At the Market: An order to buy or sell a futures contract at whatever price is obtainable when the order reaches the trading floor. (*See also* Market Order.)

At the Money: An option with a strike price which is equal to—or approximately equal to—the current market price of the underlying futures contract.

Audit Trail: The record of trading information identifying, for example, the brokers participating in each transaction, the firms clearing the trade, the terms and time of the trade, and ultimately and when applicable, the customers involved.

Award: The written decision of arbitrators in a dispute.

Back Months: Those futures delivery months with expiration or delivery dates farthest into the future; futures delivery months other than the spot or nearby delivery month.

Backwardation: A market in which futures prices are progressively lower in the distant delivery months; the opposite of Contango. (*See also* Inverted Market.)

Bad Faith: Dishonesty or fraud in a transaction, such as entering into an agreement with no intention of ever living up to its terms, or knowingly misrepresenting the quality of something that is being bought or sold.

Banker's Acceptance: A draft or bill of exchange accepted by a bank where the accepting institution guarantees payment. Used extensively in foreign trade transactions.

Bar Chart: A chart that graphs the high, low, and settlement prices for a specific trading session over a given period of time.

Basis: The difference between the current cash price of a commodity and the futures price of the same commodity.

Basis Grade: The grade of a commodity used as the standard or par grade of a futures contract.

Basis Point: The measurement of a change in the yield of a debt security. One basis point equals ¹⁄₁₀₀ of a percent.

Basis Quote: Offer or sale of a cash commodity in terms of the difference above or below a futures price, e.g., 10 cents over December corn.

Basis Risk: The risk associated with an unexpected widening or narrowing of basis between the time a hedge position is established and the time that it is lifted.

Bear: One who expects a decline in prices. The opposite of a bull. A news item is considered bearish if it is expected to result in lower prices.

Bear Market: A market in which prices are declining.

Bear Spread: The simultaneous purchase and sale of two futures contracts in the same or related commodities with the intention of profiting from a decline in prices, but at the same time limiting the potential loss if this expectation does not materialize. In agricultural products, this is accomplished by selling a nearby delivery and buying a deferred delivery.

Bear Vertical Spread: A strategy employed when an investor expects a decline in a commodity price, but at the same time seeks to limit the potential loss if this expectation is not realized. This spread requires the simultaneous purchase and sale of options of the same class and expiration date but with different strike prices. For example, if call options are spread, the purchased option must have a higher exercise price than the option that is sold.

Beta: A measure of the variability of rate of return or value of a stock portfolio compared to that of the overall market.

Bid: An expression indicating a desire to buy a commodity at a given price; the opposite of *offer.*

Black Scholes Model: An option pricing formula initially developed by F. Black and M. Scholes for securities options and later refined by Black for options on futures.

Block Order: A futures or option order placed at the same time for more than one account.

Board of Trade: *See* Contract Market.

Board of Trade Clearing Corporation (BOTCC): An independent corporation that settles all trades made at the Chicago Board of Trade. The BOTCC acts as a guarantor for all trades cleared by it, reconciles all clearing member firm accounts each day to ensure that all gains have been credited and all losses have been collected, and sets and adjusts clearing member firm margins for changing market conditions. (*See also* Clearinghouse.)

Board Order: Also known as a *market-if-touched (MIT) order.* An order that becomes a market order when a particular price is reached. A sell MIT is placed above the market; a buy MIT is placed below the market.

Boiler Room: An enterprise which often is operated out of inexpensive, low-rent quarters (hence the term "boiler room") and uses high-pressure sales tactics (usually over the telephone) and possibly false or misleading information to solicit generally unsophisticated investors.

Book Entry Securities: Electronically recorded securities that include each creditor's name, address, social security or tax identification number, and dollar amount loaned (i.e., no certificates are issued to bondholders; instead, the transfer agent electronically credits interest payments to each creditor's bank account on a designated date).

Booking the Basis: A forward pricing sales arrangement in which the cash price is determined either by the buyer or the seller within a specified time. At that time, the previously agreed basis is applied to the then-current futures quotation.

BOTCC: Board of Trade Clearing Corporation.

Box Transaction: An option position in which the holder establishes a long call and a short put at one strike price and a short call and a long put at another strike price, all of which are in the same contract month in the same commodity.

Branch Office: Any location, other than the main business address of a registrant, at which the registrant employs persons engaged in activities requiring registration as an associated person.

Branch Office Manager: The person at a branch office designated to supervise the activities of that office.

Break: A rapid and sharp price decline.

Break-Even Point: The trading profit that a commodity pool must realize in the first year of a participant's investment to equal all fees and expenses so that the participant will recoup his initial investment.

Brief: A written document that outlines a party's legal arguments in a case.

Broker: A person paid a fee or commission for acting as an agent in making contracts, sales, or purchases. In futures trading, the term may refer to (1) a floor broker—a person who actually executes orders on the trading floor of an exchange; (2) an account executive or associated person—the person who deals with customers in the offices of a futures commission merchant or introducing broker; or (3) a futures commission merchant or introducing broker.

Broker Association: Two or more exchange members who (1) share responsibility for executing customer orders; (2) have access to each other's unfilled customer orders as a result of common employment or other types of relationships; or (3) share profits or losses associated with their brokerage or trading activity.

Brokerage Fee: Also known as a *commission fee.* A fee charged by a broker for executing a transaction.

Brokerage House: Also known as a *futures commission merchant,* as *commission house,* or a *wire house.* An individual or organization that solicits or accepts orders to buy or sell futures contracts or options on futures and accepts money or other assets from customers to support such orders.

Bucket Shop: A brokerage enterprise that "books" (i.e., takes the opposite side of) a customer's order without actually having it executed on an exchange.

Bucketing: Directly or indirectly taking the opposite side of a customer's order into the broker's own account or into an account in which the broker has an interest without open and competitive execution of the order on an exchange.

Bull: One who expects a rise in prices. The opposite of bear. A news item is considered bullish if it is expected to raise prices.

Bull Market: A market in which prices are rising.

Bull Spread: The simultaneous purchase and sale of two futures contracts in the same or related commodities with the intention of profiting from a rise in prices, but at the same time limiting the potential loss if this expectation is wrong. In agricultural commodities, this is accomplished by buying the nearby delivery and selling the deferred.

Bull Vertical Spread: A strategy used when an investor expects that the price of a commodity will go up but at the same time seeks to limit the potential loss should this judgment be in error. This strategy involves the simultaneous purchase and sale of options of the same class and expiration date but with different strike prices. For example, if call options are spread, the purchased option must have a lower exercise or strike price than the sold option.

Business Conduct Committee: A committee empowered by a self-regulatory organization to supervise the business conduct of the organization's members and, at some self-regulatory organizations, conduct investigations. A business conduct committee may also issue formal complaints, review settlement offers, conduct hearings, and issue decisions.

Butterfly Spread: A three-legged spread in futures or options. In the option spread, the options have the same expiration date but differ in strike prices. For example, a butterfly spread in soybean call options might consist of two short calls at a $6.00 strike price, one long call at a $6.50 strike price, and one long call at a $5.50 strike price.

Buy on Close: To buy at the end of the trading session within the closing price range.

Buy on Opening: To buy at the beginning of a trading session within the open price range.

Buyer: A market participant who takes a long futures position or buys an option. An option buyer is also called a *taker, holder,* or *owner.*

Buyer's Market: A condition of the market in which there is an abundance of goods available and in which buyers can afford to be selective and may be able to buy at less than the prices that previously prevailed.

Buying Hedge: Hedging transaction in which futures contracts are bought to protect against possible increases in the cost of commodities. (*See also* Long Hedge.)

Cabinet Trade: A trade that allows options traders to liquidate deep out-of-the-money options by trading the option at a price equal to one-half tick.

CACE: Citrus Associates of the Cotton Exchange

Calendar Spread: *See* Horizontal Spread.

Call Option: The buyer of a call option acquires the right, but not the obligation, to purchase a particular futures contract at a stated price on or before a particular date.

Call Rule: An exchange regulation under which an official bid price for a cash commodity is competitively established at the close of each day's trading. It holds until the next opening of the exchange.

Capital Gain: The profit made from the sale of a capital asset, such as real estate, a house, jewelry, or stocks and bonds.

Capping: Effecting commodity or security transactions shortly prior to an option's expiration date; depressing or preventing a rise in the price of the commodity or security so that previously written call options will expire worthless and the premium the writer received will be protected.

Carrying Broker: A member of a futures exchange—usually a clearinghouse member—through whom another broker or customer chooses to clear all or some trades.

Carrying Charge: The cost of storing a physical commodity, such as grain or metals, over a period of time. Includes insurance, storage, and interest on the invested funds, as well as other incidental costs. In interest rate futures markets, it refers to the differential between the yield on a cash instrument and the cost of the funds necessary to buy the instrument.

Carryover: Grain and oilseed commodities not consumed during the marketing year and remaining in storage at year's end. These surpluses are "carried over" into the next marketing year and added to the quantities produced during that crop year.

Cash Commodity: The actual physical commodity as distinguished from the futures contract based on the physical commodity. Also known as *actuals.*

Cash Contract: A sales agreement for either immediate or future delivery of the actual product.

Cash Forward Sale: A cash transaction common in many industries, including commodity merchandising, in which a commercial buyer and seller agree upon delivery of a specified quality and quantity of goods at a specified future date. A price may be agreed upon in advance, or there may be agreement that the price will be determined at the time of delivery.

Cash Market: A place where people buy and sell the actual commodities. Also known as *forward cash contract.* (*See also* Spot Market.)

Cash Price: The price in the marketplace for actual cash or spot commodities to be delivered via customary market channels.

Cash Settlement: A method of settling certain futures or options contracts wherein the seller pays the buyer the cash value of the commodity traded according to a procedure specified in the contract.

CBOT: Chicago Board of Trade.

CEI: Commodity Exchange, Inc. Also known as COMEX.

CFFE: Cantor Financial Futures Exchange.

CFTC: Commodity Futures Trading Commission.

CFTC Administrative Action: An action taken by the Commodity Futures Trading Commission to enforce the provisions of the Commodity Exchange Act and other regulations.

CFTC Injunctive Action: An action brought by the Commodity Futures Trading Commission in federal court to obtain an order requiring a party to refrain from doing or continuing to do a particular act or activity.

Charting: The use of graphs and charts in the technical analysis of futures markets to plot price movements, volume, open interest, or other statistical indicators of price movement. (*See also* Technical Analysis.)

Cheapest to Deliver: Usually refers to the selection of bonds deliverable against an expiring bond futures contract.

Chooser Option: An option which is transacted in the present, but which at some prespecified future date is chosen to be either a put or call option.

Churning: Excessive trading that results in the broker deriving a profit from commissions while disregarding the best interests of the customers.

Circuit Breaker: A system of trading halts and price limits on equities and derivatives markets designed to provide a cooling-off period during large, intraday market declines.

Civil Action: An action to protect a private, civil right, or to compel a civil remedy, as distinguished from a criminal prosecution.

Civil Monetary Penalty: A fine imposed by the Commodity Futures Trading Commission as a sanction for wrongdoing.

Claim: A demand for money or other relief.

Claimant: A party who asserts a right to money or property.

Clearing: The procedure through which the clearinghouse or association becomes the buyer to each seller of a futures contract, and the seller to each buyer, and assumes responsibility for protecting buyers and sellers from financial loss by assuring performance on each contract.

Clearinghouse: An agency or separate corporation of a futures exchange that is responsible for settling trading accounts, collecting and maintaining margin monies, regulating delivery, and reporting trade data.

Clearing Margin: Financial safeguards to ensure that clearing members (usually companies or corporations) perform on their customers' open futures and options contracts. Clearing margins are distinct from customer margins that individual buyers and sellers of futures and options contracts are required to deposit with brokers. (*See also* Customer Margin.)

Clearing Member: A member of an exchange clearinghouse. All trades of a nonclearing member must be registered and eventually settled through a clearing member.

Clearing Procedures Action Type: A violation arising from the failure to abide by clearing procedures.

Close: The period at the end of the trading session, officially designated by the exchange, during which all transactions are considered made "at the close."

Closing Price: The price (or price range) recorded during trading that takes place in the final moments of a day's activity that is officially designated as the "close."

Closing Range: A high and low range of prices at which futures transactions took place during the close of the market.

CME: Chicago Mercantile Exchange.

Co-Respondent: Other individuals or firms named in a disciplinary, reparation, or arbitration action.

COM Membership: A Chicago Board of Trade membership that allows an individual to trade contracts listed in the commodity options market category.

COMEX: Commodity Exchange, Inc. Also known as CEI.

Commission: A fee charged by a broker to a customer for performance of a specific duty, such as buying or selling futures contracts.

Commission House: *See* Futures Commission Merchant.

Commitments: *See* Open Interest.

Commodity: An article of commerce or a product that can be used for commerce. In a narrow sense, products traded on authorized commodity exchanges. The types of commodities include agricultural products, metals, petroleum, foreign currencies, and financial instruments and indexes, to name a few.

Commodity Credit Corporation: A government-owned corporation established in 1933 to assist American agriculture. Major operations include price support programs, foreign sales, and export credit programs for agricultural commodities.

Commodity Exchange Act: The federal act that provides for federal regulation of futures trading.

Commodity Exchange Authority: A regulatory agency of the U.S. Department of Agriculture established to administer the Commodity Exchange Act prior to 1975; the predecessor of the Commodity Futures Trading Commission.

Commodity Futures Trading Commission (CFTC):   The 1974-established federal regulatory agency that administers the Commodity Exchange Act. The federal oversight agency that monitors the futures and options on futures markets to detect and prevent price distortion and market manipulation, and to protect the rights of customers who use the markets for either commercial or investment purposes.

Commodity Option: An option to buy or sell a specific physical commodity or commodity futures contract at a given strike price within a specified time. Less frequently, an option on a financial futures contract. (*See also* Call Option, Put Option.)

Commodity Pool: An enterprise in which funds contributed by a number of persons are combined for the purpose of trading futures or options contracts.

Commodity Pool Operator (CPO):   An individual or organization which operates or solicits funds for a pool. Generally required to be registered with the Commodity Futures Trading Commission.

Commodity Trading Advisor (CTA):   An individual or organization which, for compensation or profit, directly or indirectly advises others as to the value of or the advisability of buying or selling futures or options contracts. Providing advice indirectly includes exercising trading authority over a customer's account. Registration with the Commodity Futures Trading Commission is generally required.

Complaint: Formal, written charges brought by a regulatory or self-regulatory organization which set forth the rules or requirements alleged to have been violated and describe each act or omission that constituted the alleged violations. Also, the initial document filed in a court to initiate a civil action.

Computerized Trading Reconstruction System: A Chicago Board of Trade computerized surveillance program that pinpoints in any trade, the traders, the contract, the quantity, the price, and the time of execution to the nearest minute.

Confirmation Statement: A statement sent by a futures commission merchant to a customer when a futures or options position has been initiated. The statement shows the number of contracts bought or sold and the prices at which the contracts were bought or sold. Sometimes combined with a purchase and sale statement.

Congestion: (1) A market situation in which shorts attempting to cover their positions are unable to find an adequate supply of contracts provided by longs willing to liquidate or by new sellers willing to enter the market, except at sharply higher prices. (2) In technical analysis, a period of time characterized by repetitious and limited price fluctuations.

Consent Order: Generally, any order to which all parties agree.

Contango: A market situation in which prices in succeeding delivery months are progressively higher than in the nearest delivery months; opposite of *backwardation*.

Contract: A term of reference describing a unit of trading for a commodity future or option.

Contract Grades: Those grades of a commodity which have been officially approved by an exchange as deliverable in settlement of a futures contract.

Contract Market: A board of trade designated by the Commodity Futures Trading Commission to trade futures or option contracts on a particular commodity. Commonly used to mean any exchange on which futures are traded.

Contract Month: The month in which delivery is to be made in accordance with a futures contract.

Contract Unit: The actual amount of a commodity represented in a contract.

Contributor: The Commodity Futures Trading Commission, National Futures Association, and any U.S. futures exchange which includes its disciplinary actions in the NFA's BASIC system.

Controlled Account: Any account for which trading is directed by someone other than the owner. Also called a *managed account* or a *discretionary account.*

Convergence: The tendency for prices of physical commodities and futures to approach one another, usually during the delivery month.

Conversion Factor: A factor used to equate the price of T-bond and T-note futures contracts with the various cash T-bonds and T-notes eligible for delivery. This factor is based on the relationship of the cash-instrument coupon to the required 8 percent deliverable grade of a futures contract and takes into account the cash instrument's maturity or call.

Corner: (1) Securing such relative control of a commodity or security that its price can be manipulated. (2) In the extreme situation, obtaining contracts requiring the delivery of more commodities or securities than are available for delivery.

Cost of Carry: *See* Carrying Charge.

Counterclaim: A claim by a respondent against a claimant.

Cover: (1) To buy back futures previously sold. Typically used to describe the closing of a short position. (2) To have in hand the physical commodity when a short futures or leverage sale is made, or to acquire the commodity that might be deliverable on a short sale. (*See also* Short Covering, Short Sale.)

Covered Option: A short call or put option position which is covered by the sale or purchase of the underlying futures contract or physical commodity.

CPO: Commodity Pool Operator.

Crop Year: The time period from one harvest to the next, which varies according to the commodity (e.g., July 1 to June 30 for wheat; September 1 to August 31 for soybeans).

Cross Claim: A claim filed by one respondent against a correspondent.

Cross Hedge: Hedging a cash market position in a futures contract for a different, but price-related commodity.

Cross Margining: A procedure for margining related securities, options, and futures contracts jointly when different clearinghouses clear each side of the position.

Cross Trading: Offsetting or noncompetitive matching of the buy order of one customer against the sell order of another customer, a practice permissible only when executed in accordance with the Commodity Exchange Act, CFTC regulations, and the rules of the contract market.

Crush Spread: In the soybean futures market, the simultaneous purchase of soybean futures and the sale of soybean meal and soybean oil futures to establish a processing margin. (*See also* Gross Processing Margin.)

CSCE: Coffee, Sugar & Cocoa Exchange, Inc.

CTA: Commodity Trading Advisor.

Curb Trading: Trading—by telephone or other means—that takes place after the official market has closed. Originally, curb trading took place on the curb of the street outside the market. Under CFTC rules, curb trading is illegal. Also known as *kerb trading.*

Current Assets: Cash and other assets or resources which can be reasonably expected to be realized in cash or sold during the next 12 months.

Current Delivery Month: The futures contract which matures and becomes deliverable during the present month. Also called *spot month.*

Customer Margin: Within the futures industry, financial guarantees required of both buyers and sellers of futures contracts and sellers of options contracts to ensure that contract obligations are fulfilled. FCMs are responsible for overseeing customer margin accounts. Margins are determined on the basis of market risk and contract value. (*See also* Clearing Margin.)

Customer Segregated Accounts: A special account used to hold and separate customers' assets from those of the brokerage house or firm.

Daily Price Limit: The maximum price advance or decline from the previous day's settlement price permitted during one trading session, as fixed by the rules of an exchange.

Day Order: An order which, if not executed, expires automatically at the end of the trading session on the day it was entered.

Day Trader: A speculator who will normally initiate and offset a position within a single trading session.

Day Trading: Establishing and offsetting the same futures market position within one day.

Dealer Option: A put or call on a physical commodity, not originating on or subject to the rules of an exchange, in which the obligation for performance rests with the writer of the option. Dealer options are normally written by firms handling the underlying commodity and offered to public customers, although the reverse may also be true.

Decision: A formal, written judgment or verdict.

Deck: The orders for purchase or sale of futures or option contracts held by a floor broker.

Decorum and Attire Action Type: A violation arising from an individual's demeanor or attire on an exchange floor.

Default: The failure to perform on a futures contract as required by exchange rules, such as a failure to meet a margin call or to make or take a delivery.

Deferred Delivery: The distant delivery months in which futures trading is taking place, as distinguished from the nearby futures delivery month.

Deferred Futures: The futures contracts that expire during the most distant months. Also called *back months.* (*See also* Forward Purchase or Sale.)

Deliverable Grades: The standard grades of commodities or instruments listed in the rules of the exchanges that must be met when delivering cash commodities against futures contracts. Grades are often accompanied by a schedule of discounts and premiums allowable for delivery of commodities of lesser or greater quality than the standard called for by the exchange. Also referred to as *contract grades.*

Deliverable Stocks: Stocks of commodities located in exchange-approved storage for which receipts may be used in making delivery on futures contracts. In the cotton trade, the term refers to cotton certified for delivery.

Delivery: The tender and receipt of an actual commodity or warehouse receipt or other negotiable instrument covering such commodity, in settlement of a futures contract.

Delivery Date: The date on which the commodity or instrument of delivery must be delivered to fulfill the terms of a contract.

Delivery Instrument: A document used to effect delivery on a futures contract, such as a warehouse receipt or shipping certificate.

Delivery Month: The specified month within which a futures contract matures and can be settled by delivery.

Delivery Notice: The written notice given by the seller of his intention to make a delivery against an open short futures position on a particular date. This notice, delivered through the clearinghouse, is separate and distinct from the warehouse receipt or other instrument that will be used to transfer title.

Delivery Option: A provision of a futures contract which provides the short with flexibility in regard to timing, location, quantity, or quality in the delivery process.

Delivery Points: Those locations designated by commodity exchanges where stocks of a commodity represented by a futures contract may be delivered in fulfillment of the contract.

Delivery Price: The price fixed by the clearinghouse at which deliveries on futures are invoiced, generally the price at which the futures contract is settled when deliveries are made.

Delta: A measure of how much an option premium changes, given a unit change in the underlying futures price. Delta often is interpreted as the probability that the option will be in-the-money by expiration.

Delta Margining: An option margining system used by some exchanges for exchange members and/or floor traders which equates the changes in option premiums with the changes in the price of the underlying futures contract or physical commodity.

Delta Value: The expected change in an option's price, given a one-unit change in the price of the underlying futures contract.

Demand: A claim filed by a claimant against a respondent on the form provided by the NFA.

Deposit: The initial outlay required by a broker of a client to open a futures position, returnable upon liquidation of that position.

Deposition: The pretrial testimony of a witness, given out of court with no judge present. The witness is placed under oath to tell the truth, and lawyers for each party may ask questions.

Derivative: A financial instrument, traded on or off an exchange, the price of which is directly dependent upon the value of one or more of the underlying securities, commodities, other derivative instruments, or any agreed-upon pricing index or arrangement.

Designated Self-Regulatory Organization (DSRO): When a futures commission merchant (FCM) is a member of more than one self-regulatory organization (SRO), the SROs may decide among themselves which of them will be primarily responsible for enforcing minimum financial and sales practice requirements. With approval, the SRO will be appointed DSRO for that particular FCM.

Diagonal Spread: A spread between two call options or two put options with different strike prices and different expiration dates.

Differential: The discount (or premium) allowed for grades or locations of a commodity lower (or higher) than the par of basis grade or location specified in the futures contract. (*See also* Allowances.)

Disclosure Document: A document that must be provided to and signed by prospective customers of CPOs and CTAs which describes fees, performance, etc.

Discount: (1) The amount a price would be reduced to purchase a commodity of lesser grade. (2) Sometimes used to refer to the price difference between futures of different delivery months, as in the phrase, "July is trading at a discount to May," indicating that the price of the July futures contract is lower than that of May. (3) Applied to cash grain prices that are below the futures price.

Discount Basis: Method of quoting securities where the price is expressed as an annualized discount from maturity value.

Discount Method: A method of paying interest by issuing a security at less than par and repaying par value at maturity. The difference between the higher par value and the lower purchase price is the interest.

Discount Rate: The interest rate charged on loans by the Federal Reserve Bank.

Discretionary Account: An arrangement by which the owner of the account gives written power of attorney to someone else, usually a broker or a commodity trading advisor, to buy and sell without prior approval of the account owner. Often referred to as a *managed account.*

Dismissal: In a legal context, the termination or removal of a case from the court without a complete trial.

Dismissal With Prejudice: Usually considered an adjudication upon the merits and operates as a bar to future action.

Dismissal Without Prejudice: Usually an indication that the dismissal affects no right or remedy of the parties, i.e., is not on the merits and does not bar a subsequent suit on the same cause of action.

Double Hedging: As used by the CFTC, this implies a situation in which a trader holds a long position in the futures market in excess of the speculative limit as an offset to a fixed-price sale, even though the trader has an ample supply of the commodity on hand to fill all sales commitments.

DSRO: *See* Designated Self-Regulatory Organization.

Dual Trading: Dual trading occurs when (1) a floor broker executes customer orders and on the same day trades for his own account or an account in which he has an interest, or (2) a futures commission merchant carries customer accounts and also trades, or permits its employees to trade, in accounts in which it has a proprietary interest, also on the same day.

Efficient Market: A market in which new information is immediately available to all investors and potential investors. A market in which all information is instantaneously assimilated and therefore has no distortions.

Elliot Wave Theory: (1) A theory named after Ralph Elliot, who contended that the stock market tends to move in discernible and predictable patterns reflecting the basic harmony of nature. (2) In technical analysis, a charting method based on the belief that all prices act as wavers, rising and falling rhythmically.

Enjoin: To command or instruct with authority; to abate, suspend, or restrain. For example, one may be *enjoined,* or commanded, by a court with equitable powers either to do a specific act or to refrain from doing a certain act.

Equity: The dollar value of a futures trading account if all open positions were offset at the going market price.

Escrow Account: A special account in which a lawyer or escrow agent deposits money or documents that do not belong to him or his firm.

Estoppel: A bar which precludes someone from denying the truth of a fact which has been determined in an official proceeding or by an authoritative body.

Eurodollar: U.S. dollar deposits placed with banks outside the U.S. Holders may include individuals, companies, banks, and central banks.

European Currency Unit: The official unit of account of the European Monetary System. It is a combination or basket of the currencies from the 12 European Community countries: the Deutsche mark, French franc, British pound sterling, Irish pound, Italian lira, Belgian franc, Dutch guilder, Luxembourg franc, Greek drachma, Spanish peseta, Portugese escudo, and the Danish krona.

Even Lot: A unit of trading in a commodity established by an exchange to which official price quotations apply.

Ex Parte: A Latin term that means "by or for one party." Refers to situations in which only one party (and not the adversary) appears before an adjudicating body. Such meetings are often forbidden.

Ex Pit Transaction: A transaction in which the buyer of a cash commodity transfers to the seller a corresponding amount of long futures contracts, or receives from the seller a corresponding amount of short futures, at a price difference mutually agreed upon. In this way, the opposite hedges in futures of both parties are closed out simultaneously. Also called *exchange for physicals, against actuals,* or *exchange of futures for cash.*

Exchange: *See* Contract Market.

Exchange for Physicals: A transaction generally used by two hedgers who want to exchange futures for cash positions. Also referred to as *against actuals* or *versus cash.*

Exchange of Futures for Cash: A transaction in which the buyer of a cash commodity transfers to the seller a corresponding amount of long futures contracts, or receives from the seller a corresponding amount of short futures, at a price difference mutually agreed upon. In this way, the opposite hedges in futures of both parties are closed out simultaneously. Also called *exchange for physicals, against actuals,* or *ex-pit transactions.*

Exchange Rate: The price of one currency stated in terms of another currency.

Exchange Risk Factor: The delta value of an option as computed daily by the exchange on which it is traded.

Exempt Foreign Firm: A foreign firm that does business with U.S. customers only on foreign exchanges and is exempt from registration under CFTC regulations.

Exercise: Exercising a call means that you elect to purchase the underlying futures contract at the option strike price. Exercising a put means that you elect to sell the underlying futures contract at the option strike price.

Exercise Price: The price specified in the option contract at which the buyer of a call can purchase the commodity during the life of the option, and the price specified in the option contract at which the buyer of a put can sell the commodity during the life of the option.

Expiration Date: Generally, the last date on which an option may be exercised. It is not uncommon for an option to expire on a specified date during the month prior to the delivery month for the underlying futures contracts.

Extrinsic Value: *See* Time Value.

FB: Floor broker.

FCM: Futures commission merchant.

Feed Ratio: The relationship of the cost of feed to the sale price of animals, expressed as a ratio, such as the corn-hog ratio. These serve as indicators of the profit margin or lack of profit in feeding animals to market weight.

Fictitious Trading: Wash trading, bucketing, cross trading, or other schemes which give the appearance of trading when actually, no bona fide, competitive trade has occurred.

Fiduciary Duty: An obligation to act solely in the best interest of another party. For instance, a corporation's board member has a fiduciary duty to the shareholders, a trustee has a fiduciary duty to the trust's beneficiaries, and an attorney has a fiduciary duty to a client.

Fill or Kill Order: A customer order which demands immediate execution or cancellation.

Final Injunction: An order of the court requiring a party to do something or refrain from doing or continuing to do a particular act or activity.

Final Order: In a registration disqualification proceeding, a final order is issued upon resolution of the matter. A final order will condition or deny an applicant's registration, or revoke, restrict, or suspend a registrant's registration.

Financial Action Type: A violation arising from failure to meet financial requirements.

Financial and Position Reporting Action Type: A violation arising from failure to meet financial reporting requirements or contract position reporting requirements.

Financial Instrument: As used by the CFTC, this term generally refers to any futures or option contract that is not based on an agricultural commodity or a natural resource. It includes currencies, securities, mortgages, commercial paper, and stock indexes of various kinds.

First Notice Day: The first day on which the notice of intent to deliver a commodity in fulfillment of an expiring futures contract can be given by the clearinghouse to a buyer. Varies from contract to contract.

Fix, or Fixing: The settling of the gold price at 10:30 a.m. (first fixing) and 3:00 p.m. (second fixing) in London by five representatives of the London Gold Market.

Fixed-Income Security: A security whose nominal (or current dollar) yield is fixed or determined with certainty at the time of purchase.

Floor Broker (FB): An individual who executes orders on the trading floor of an exchange for any other person.

Floor Committee: A committee empowered by an exchange for the purpose of resolving disputes and supervising the conduct and practices of members and others on the floor of an exchange. The committee may also conduct investigations and hearings and impose fines and other sanctions.

Floor Record-Keeping Action Type: A violation arising from failure to make or preserve any record required to be made on the floor of an exchange in connection with the disposition of an order or the execution of a trade.

Floor Trader (FT): Member of an exchange who is personally present on the trading floor of the exchange to make trades for himself or herself. Sometimes called *locals*.

FOB: Free on board. Indicates that all delivery, inspection, and elevation or loading costs involved in putting commodities on board a carrier have been paid.

Forced Liquidation: The situation in which a customer's account is liquidated (open positions are offset) by the brokerage firm holding the account, usually after notification that the account is undercapitalized. A margin call.

Foreign Exchange: Foreign currency. On the foreign exchange market, foreign currency is bought and sold for immediate or future delivery.

Foreign Exchange Market: Forex market. An over-the-counter market where buyers and sellers conduct foreign exchange business by telephone and other means of communication.

Foreign Futures or Foreign Options Secured Amount: The amount of money, securities, and property that an FCM must maintain in a separate account to cover or satisfy all of its current obligations to foreign futures or foreign options customers. Such money, securities, or property may not be commingled with the money, securities, and property of the FCM.

Foreign Terminal: Computer terminals placed in the United States by foreign boards of trade. These terminals are used for the purpose of facilitating the trading of products available through those boards of trade.

Forward Contract: A contract on which a seller agrees to deliver a specified cash commodity to a buyer sometime in the future. In contrast to futures contracts, the terms of forward contracts are not standardized. Forward contracts are not traded on federally designated exchanges.

Forward Market: Refers to informal (nonexchange) trading of commodities to be delivered at a future date. Contracts for forward delivery are personalized, i.e., the delivery time and amount are as determined between seller and customer.

Forward Purchase or Sale: A purchase or sale between commercial parties of an actual commodity for deferred delivery.

Forwardation: *See* Contango.

Frontrunning: A practice whereby a futures or options position is taken based on nonpublic information about an impending transaction in the same or related futures or options contracts.

FT: Floor trader.

Full Carrying Charge: Full carry. (*See also* Carrying Charge.)

Fully Disclosed Account: An account carried by a futures commission merchant in the name of the individual customer; the opposite of an *omnibus account.*

Fund of Funds: A commodity pool that invests in other commodity pools rather than directly in futures and options contracts.

Fundamental Analysis: The study of basic, underlying factors which will affect the supply and demand, and hence the price of a futures contract.

Futures Commission Merchant (FCM): An individual or organization which solicits or accepts orders to buy or sell futures or options contracts and accepts money or other assets from customers in connection with such orders. Must be registered with the Commodity Futures Trading Commission.

Futures Contract: A legally binding agreement to buy or sell a commodity or financial instrument at a later date. Futures contracts are standardized according to the quality, quantity, and delivery time and location for each commodity.

Futures Exchange: A central marketplace with established rules and regulations where buyers and sellers meet to trade futures and options on futures contracts.

Futures Industry Association (FIA): The national trade association for futures commission merchants.

Futures Price: (1) Commonly held to mean the price of a commodity for future delivery that is traded on a futures exchange. (2) The price of any futures contract.

Gamma: A measurement of how fast delta changes, given a unit of change in the underlying futures price.

General Conduct Action Type: A violation arising from conduct not described by any other action type violation.

Ginzy Trading: A trade practice in which a floor broker, in executing an order, particularly a large order, fills a portion of the order at one price and the remainder of the order at another price to avoid an exchange's rule against trading at fractional increments or split ticks.

Give Up: A contract executed by one broker for the client of another broker that the client orders to be turned over to the second broker. The broker accepting the order from the customer collects a wire toll from the carrying broker for the use of the facilities. Often used to consolidate many small orders or to disperse large ones.

Gold-Silver Ratio: The number of ounces of silver required to buy one ounce of gold at current spot prices.

Good This Week Order: Order which is valid only for the week in which it is placed.

Good 'til Canceled Order: Order which is valid at any time during market hours until executed or canceled.

Grades: Various qualities of a commodity.

Grain Terminal: A large grain elevator facility with the capacity to ship grain by rail and/or barge to domestic or foreign markets.

Grantor: A person who sells an option and assumes the obligation, but not the right, to sell (in the case of a call) or buy (in the case of a put) the underlying futures contract at the exercise price.

Gross Processing Margin: Refers to the difference between the cost of a commodity and the combined sales income of the finished products which results from processing the commodity. Various industries have formulas to express the relationship of raw material costs to sales income from finished products.

Guaranteed Introducing Broker: An introducing broker whose operations are guaranteed by an FCM. This type of IB has no minimum capital or financial reporting requirements. All of the accounts of a guaranteed introducing broker must be carried by the guaranteeing FCM. (*See also* Independent Introducing Broker.)

Guarantor: A secondary party who becomes obligated to repay a debt for the party primarily responsible if that party fails to repay the obligation. The guarantor of an introducing broker is a futures commission merchant, which is subject to discipline under NFA rules for violations committed by the introducing broker.

Haircut: (1) In determining whether assets meet capital requirements, a percentage reduction in the stated value of assets. (2) In computing the worth of assets deposited as collateral or margin, a reduction from market value.

Handheld Terminal: A small computer terminal used by floor brokers or traders on a board of trade to record trade information and transmit that information to the clearing organization.

Hearing: A proceeding wherein evidence is taken for the purpose of determining an issue of fact and reaching a decision on the basis of that evidence. An *administrative hearing* may take place outside the judicial process before officials who have been granted judicial authority expressly for the purpose of conducting such hearings.

Hearing Committee: A committee empowered by a self-regulatory organization to review settlement offers, conduct hearings, and issue decisions.

Hedge Ratio: Ratio of the value of futures contracts purchased or sold to the value of the cash commodity being hedged, a computation necessary to minimize basis risk.

Hedger: An individual or company owning or planning to own, or selling or planning to sell, a cash commodity, and which is concerned that the cost of the commodity may change before either buying or selling it in the cash market. A hedger achieves protection against changing cash prices by purchasing (or selling) futures contracts of the same or similar commodity and later offsetting that position by selling (or purchasing) futures contracts of the same quantity and type as the initial transaction.

Hedging: The practice of offsetting the price inherent in any cash market position by taking the opposite position in the futures market. Hedgers use the market to protect their businesses from adverse price changes.

Hog-Corn Ratio: *See* Feed Ratio.

Holder: The party who purchased an option.

Horizontal Spread: The purchase of either a call or put option and the simultaneous sale of the same type of option, typically with the same strike price but with a different expiration month. Also referred to as a *calendar spread.*

Hypothetical Disclaimer: Results of trading that was not actually executed in any account. For example, the results of proposed trades generated by a trading system but not actually entered for execution.

IB: Introducing broker.

Immunity: Exemption from a legal duty, penalty, or prosecution.

In-the-Money Option: An option having intrinsic value. A call is in-the-money if its strike price is below the current price of the underlying futures contract. A put is in-the-money if its strike price is above the current price of the underlying futures contract.

Independent Introducing Broker: An introducing broker who is subject to minimum capital and financial reporting requirements. This type of IB may introduce accounts to any FCM. (*See also* Guaranteed Introducing Broker.)

Index Arbitrage: The simultaneous purchase (or sale) of stock index futures and the sale (or purchase) of some or all of the component stocks which make up the particular stock index to profit from sufficiently large intermarket spreads between the futures contract and the index itself.

Indictment: The formal accusation of a felony, issued by a grand jury after considering evidence presented by a prosecutor.

Inelasticity: A characteristic that describes the interdependence of the supply, demand, and price of a commodity. A commodity is inelastic when a price change does not create an increase or decrease in consumption.

Initial Decision: A decision setting forth findings of fact and conclusions of law and the imposition of a penalty. An initial decision becomes a final decision within a specified time period unless it is appealed or stayed.

Initial Deposit: *See* Initial Margin.

Initial Margin: Customers' funds put up at the time a futures market position is established to serve as security for a guarantee of contract fulfillment.

Initial Performance Bond: The funds required when a futures position (or a short options on futures position) is opened.

Injunction: A prohibitive, equitable order, either permanent or temporary, issued by a court forbidding a person to commit some action that he is attempting to commit, or restraining him in the continuance of some action.

Intercommodity Spread: A spread in which the long and short legs are in two different but generally related commodity markets. Also called an *intermarket spread*.

Interdelivery Spread: A spread involving two different months of the same commodity. Also called an *intracommodity spread*.

Interest Rate Futures: Futures contracts traded on fixed-income securities, such as U.S. Treasury issues or CDs. Currencies are excluded from this category, even though interest rates are a factor in currency values.

Interim Order: A formal, written document stating that it is determined that a registrant is disqualified from CFTC registration under the Commodity Exchange Act. The issuance of an interim order suspends the registrant's registration and orders the registrant to show cause why his registration should not be revoked.

Intermarket Spread: *See* Spread, Intercommodity Spread.

International Commodities Clearinghouse: An independent organization that serves as a clearinghouse for most futures markets in London, Bermuda, Singapore, Australia, and New Zealand.

International Swaps and Derivatives Association: A New York-based group of major international swaps dealers, which has published the Code of Standard Wording, Assumptions, and Provisions for Swaps, or Swaps Code, for U.S. dollar interest rate swaps, as well as standard master interest rate and currency swap agreements and definitions for use in connection with the creation and trading of swaps.

Intracommodity Spread: *See* Interdelivery Spread.

Intrinsic Value: The absolute value of the in-the-money amount; that is, the amount that would be realized if an in-the-money option were exercised.

Introducing Broker (IB):   A firm or individual that solicits and accepts futures orders from customers but does not accept money, securities, or property from the customer. An IB must be registered with the Commodity Futures Trading Commission and must carry all of its accounts through a futures commission merchant on a fully disclosed basis.

Inverted Market: A futures market in which the nearer months are selling at premiums over the more distant months; characteristically, a market in which supplies are currently in shortage.

Invisible Supply: Uncounted stocks of a commodity in the hands of wholesalers, manufacturers, and producers which cannot be identified accurately; stocks outside commercial channels, but theoretically available to the market.

Jointly and Severally: Refers to the sharing of rights and liabilities among a group of people, collectively and also individually.

KCBOT: Kansas City Board of Trade.

KCBT: Kansas City Board of Trade.

Kerb Trading: *See* Curb Trading.

Lagging Indicators: Market indicators showing the general direction of the economy and confirming or denying the trend implied by the leading indicators. Also referred to as *concurrent indicators*.

Large Trader: One who holds or controls a position in any one future or in any one option expiration series of a commodity on any one contract market equaling or exceeding the exchange- or CFTC-specified reporting level.

Last Notice Day: The final day on which notices of intent to deliver on futures contracts may be issued.

Last Trading Day: The last day on which trading may occur in a given futures or options contract.

Leading Indicators: Market indicators that signal the state of the economy for the coming months. Some of the leading indicators include average manufacturing workweek, initial claims for unemployment insurance, orders for consumer goods and material, percentage of companies reporting slower deliveries, changes in manufacturers' unfilled orders for durable goods, plant and equipment orders, new building permits, index of consumer expectations, change in material prices, prices of stocks, and change in money supply.

Leaps: Long-dated, exchange-traded options.

Leverage: The ability to control large dollar amounts of a commodity with a comparatively small amount of capital.

Licensed Warehouse: An exchange-approved warehouse from which a commodity may be delivered on a futures contract.

Life of Contract: Period between the beginning of trading in a particular futures contract and the expiration of trading. In some cases, this phrase denotes a period already passed for which trading has already occurred.

Limit Down: The maximum price decline allowed from the previous day's settlement price permitted during one trading session, as fixed by the rules of an exchange. (*See also* Daily Price Limit.)

Limit Move: A price that has advanced to or declined to the limit permitted during one trading session as fixed by the rules of a contract market.

Limit Only: The definite price stated by a customer to a broker restricting the execution of an order to buy for not more than, or to sell for not less than, the stated price.

Limit Order: An order in which the customer specifies a price limit or other condition, such as the time of an order, as compared to a market order, which implies that the order should be filled as soon as possible.

Limit Price: *See* Limit Move.

Limit Up: The maximum price advance allowed from the previous day's settlement price permitted during one trading session, as fixed by the rules of an exchange. (*See also* Daily Price Limit.)

Limited Partnership: A partnership with two kinds of partners: limited partners, who provide financial backing and have little role in management and no personal liability; and general partners, who are responsible for managing the entity and have unlimited personal liability for its debts.

Liquidate: To sell (or purchase) futures contracts of the same delivery month purchased (or sold) during an earlier transaction, or to make (or take) delivery of the cash commodity represented by the futures contract.

Liquidity: Characteristic of a broadly traded market in which buying and selling can be accomplished with small price changes and bid and offer price spreads are narrow.

Local: A member of an exchange who trades for his own account. (*See also* Floor Trader.)

Locked In: A hedged position that cannot be lifted without offsetting both sides of the hedge (spread). Also refers to being caught in a limit move.

Long: Having bought futures contracts or owning a cash commodity. Opposite of *short*.

Long Hedge: Buying futures contracts to protect against possible increasing prices of commodities. Opposite of *short hedge*.

Long the Basis: Having bought the spot commodity and hedged with a sale of futures.

Lookback Option: An option whose payoff depends on the minimum or maximum price of the underlying asset during some portion of the life of the option.

Low: The lowest price of the day for a particular futures contract.

MACE: MidAmerica Commodity Exchange.

Maintenance Margin: A set minimum margin (per outstanding futures contract) that a customer must maintain.

Maintenance Performance Bond: A sum, usually smaller than but part of the initial performance bond, which must be maintained on deposit in the customer's account at all times. If a customer's equity in any futures position drops to or under the maintenance performance bond level, a "performance bond call" is issued for the amount of money required to restore the customer's equity in the account to the initial margin level.

Managed Account: *See* Discretionary Account.

Managed Funds Association: The trade association for the managed funds industry.

Managed Futures: Represents an industry comprised of professional money managers who manage client assets on a discretionary basis, using global futures markets as an investment medium.

Margin: An amount of money deposited by both buyers and sellers of futures contracts and by sellers of option contracts to ensure performance of the terms of the contract (the making or taking delivery of the commodity or the cancellation of the position by a subsequent offsetting trade). Margin in futures is not a down payment, as in securities, but rather a performance bond.

Margin Call: A call from a clearinghouse to a clearing member, or from a broker or firm to a customer, to bring margin deposits up to a required minimum level.

Mark to Market: To debit or credit on a daily basis a margin account, based on the close of that day's trading session.

Market Correction: In technical analysis, a small reversal in prices following a significant trending period.

Market If Touched (MIT):   An order that becomes a market order when a particular price is reached. A sell MIT is placed above the market; a buy MIT is placed below the market. Also referred to as a *board order.*

Market Maker: A professional securities dealer who has an obligation to buy when there is an excess of sell orders and to sell when there is an excess of buy orders. By maintaining an offering price sufficiently higher than their buying price, these firms are compensated for the risk involved in allowing their inventory of securities to act as a buffer against temporary order imbalances. In the commodities industry, this term is sometimes loosely used to refer to a floor trader, or local, who, in speculating for his own account, provides a market for commercial users of the market. (*See also* Specialist System.)

Market Order: An order to buy or sell a futures or options contract at whatever price is obtainable when the order reaches the trading floor.

Market Reporter: A person employed by the exchange and located in or near the trading pit who records prices as they occur during trading.

Material Fact: A fact that would be important to a reasonable person in deciding whether to engage in a particular transaction; an important fact, as distinguished from some unimportant or trivial detail.

Maximum Price Fluctuation: *See* Limit Move.

Mediation: A method of alternative dispute resolution in which a neutral third party helps resolve a dispute. The mediator does not have the power to impose a decision on the parties. If a satisfactory resolution cannot be reached, the parties can pursue a lawsuit.

Member Responsibility Action (MRA):   An action whereby an NFA member may be summarily suspended from membership, may be required to restrict its operations, or may otherwise be directed to take remedial action when the president of the NFA, with the concurrence of the executive committee, has reason to believe that the action is necessary to protect the commodity futures markets, customers, or other members or associates of the NFA.

Membership Committee: A committee empowered by a self-regulatory organization to review and make judgments on matters pertaining to membership qualification issues. At the NFA, the committee that also reviews and makes judgments on matters pertaining to CFTC registration issues.

Membership Denial: When a nonmember is denied exchange or NFA membership, a suspended or expelled member is denied reinstatement of membership privileges, or an explicit limitation is imposed upon the membership rights of a specific exchange or NFA member or group of members.

Membership Denial Action Type: The statutory denial of exchange or NFA membership.

MGE: Minneapolis Grain Exchange.

MIDAM: MidAmerica Commodity Exchange.

Minimum Price Fluctuation: The smallest increment of price movement possible in trading a given contract.

Misdemeanor: Crime that is punishable by less than one year in jail, such as minor theft or simple assault that does not result in substantial bodily injury.

MIT: Market If Touched.

Mitigating Factors: Information about a defendant or the circumstances of a crime that might tend to lessen the sentence for the crime with which the person is charged.

Money Laundering: Conduct or acts designed in whole or in part to conceal or disguise the nature, location, source, ownership, or control of money (can be currency or equivalents, e.g., checks, electronic transfers, etc.) to avoid a transaction reporting requirement under state or federal law, or to disguise the fact that the money was acquired by illegal means.

Motion: A request asking a judge to issue a ruling or order on a legal matter.

Motion for Summary Judgment: A request made by either party in a civil case asserting that the opposing party has raised no genuine issue of fact necessitating a hearing and asking the judge to rule in favor of the moving party based on the law. Typically made before trial.

Motion to Dismiss: In a civil case, a request to a judge by the defendant asserting that even if all the allegations are true, the plaintiff is not entitled to any legal relief and thus the case should be dismissed.

Moving Average Charts: A statistical price analysis method of recognizing different price trends. A moving average is calculated by adding the prices for a predetermined number of days and then dividing by the number of days.

MRA: Member Responsibility Action.

Naked Call: *See* Naked Option.

Naked Option: The sale of a call or put option without holding an offsetting position in the underlying commodity.

Naked Put: *See* Naked Option.

National Futures Association (NFA):   Authorized by Congress in 1974 and designated by the CFTC in 1982 as a registered futures association, the NFA is the industrywide self-regulatory organization of the futures industry.

National Introducing Brokers Association: The trade association for the introducing broker community.

NAV: Net Asset Value.

Nearby Delivery Month: The futures contract month closest to expiration.

Negative Carry: The cost of financing a financial instrument (the short-term rate of interest), when the cost is above the current return of the financial instrument. Opposite of *positive carry.* (*See also* Carrying Charge.)

Negative Yield Curve: *See* Yield Curve.

Net Asset Value (NAV):   The value of each unit of participation in a commodity pool. Basically, a calculation of assets minus liabilities, plus or minus the value of open positions when marked to the market, divided by the number of units.

Net Capital: The amount by which the current assets of an FCM or independent IB exceed its liabilities.

Net Performance: An increase or decrease in net asset value exclusive of additions, withdrawals, and redemptions.

Net Position: The difference between the open long contracts and the open short contracts held by a trader in any one commodity.

NFA: National Futures Association.

Nolo Contendere: A Latin phrase meaning, "I will not contest it." It is a type of plea which may be entered with leave of court to a criminal complaint or indictment by which the defendant does not admit or deny the charges, though a fine or a sentence may be imposed.

Nominal Price: Computed price quotation on futures for a period in which no actual trading took place, usually an average of bid and asked prices.

Nonmember Panel: A panel in which a majority of the arbitrators are not connected with an NFA member or the NFA.

Notice Day: Any day on which notices of intent to deliver on futures contracts may be issued.

Notice of Appeal: The document a person must file with an adjudicating body in order to pursue an appeal.

Notice of Intent: The first formal pleading issued to begin a registration disqualification proceeding. It states the allegations which will be proven to show that an applicant or registrant is disqualified from CFTC registration.

Notional Amount: The amount (in an interest rate swap, forward rate agreement, or other derivative instrument) or each of the amounts (in a currency swap) to which interest rates are applied (whether or not expressed as a rate or stated on a coupon basis) in order to calculate periodic payment obligations.

NYBOT: New York Board of Trade.

NYCE: New York Cotton Exchange.

NYFE: New York Futures Exchange.

NYME: New York Mercantile Exchange.

NYMEX: New York Mercantile Exchange.

Par: The face value of a security.

Pardon: A remission of punishment or penalty without indicating exoneration from guilt.

Partnership: An association of two or more people who agree to share in the profits and losses of a business venture.

Party: A claimant or respondent.

PBOT: Philadelphia Board of Trade.

Pegged Price: The price at which a commodity has been fixed by agreement.

Pegging: Effecting commodity transactions to offset a decline in the price of the commodity so that previously written put options will expire worthless, thus protecting premiums previously received.

Performance Bond: Funds to guarantee performance that must be deposited by a customer with his or her broker, by a broker with a clearing member, or by a clearing member with the clearinghouse. The performance bond helps to ensure the financial integrity of brokers, clearing members, and the exchange as a whole.

Performance Bond Call: A demand for additional funds because of an adverse price movement.

Permanent Injunction: A final order of the court requiring a party to do something or to refrain from doing or continuing to do a particular act or activity.

Petition: A written application to a court asking for specific action to be taken.

Petition for Review: A formal written request for review by an appellate body of the proceedings of a lower court or other adjudicative body.

Pit: The area on the trading floor of some exchanges where trading in futures or options contracts is conducted by open outcry.

Point: A measure of price change equal to $\frac{1}{100}$ of one cent in most futures traded in decimal units. In grains, it is one cent; in T-bonds, it is 1 percent of par. (*See also* Tick.)

Point and Figure Charting: A method of charting which uses prices to form patterns of movement without regard to time. It defines a price trend as a continued movement in one direction until it reverses when a predetermined criterion is met.

Point Balance: A statement prepared by futures commission merchants to show profit or loss on all open contracts by computing them to an official closing or settlement price, usually at calendar month end.

Pool: *See* Commodity Pool.

Pool Operator: *See* Commodity Pool Operator.

Position: A commitment in the market, either long or short.

Position Day: According to the Chicago Board of Trade rules, the first day in the process of making or taking delivery of the actual commodity on a futures contract. The clearing firm representing the seller notifies the Board of Trade Clearing Corporation that its short customers want to deliver on a futures contract.

Position Limit: The maximum number of speculative futures contracts one can hold as determined by the Commodity Futures Trading Commission and/or by the exchange where the contract is traded.

Position Trader: A trader who either buys or sells contracts and holds them for an extended period of time, as distinguished from a day trader.

Positive Carry: The cost of financing a financial instrument (the short-term rate of interest) when the cost is less than the current return of the financial instrument.

Positive Yield Curve: *See* Yield Curve.

Power of Attorney: The authority to act legally for another person.

Prearranged Trading: Trading between brokers in accordance with an expressed or implied agreement or understanding, which is a violation of the Commodity Exchange Act.

Preliminary Hearing: In criminal law, a legal proceeding in which a prosecutor presents evidence to a judge in an attempt to show that there is probable cause that a person committed a crime. If the judge is convinced probable cause exists to charge the person, then the prosecution proceeds to the next phase. If not, the charges are dropped.

Preliminary Injunction: A judicial remedy to prevent threatened injury, maintain the status quo, or preserve the subject matter of the litigation during trial.

Premium: Refers to (1) the amount a price would be increased to purchase a better quality commodity; (2) a future delivery month selling at a higher price than another; (3) cash prices that are above the futures price; or (4) the price paid for an option.

Price Discovery: The process of determining the price level of a commodity based on supply and demand factors.

Price Limit: The maximum advance or decline from the previous day's settlement price permitted for a futures contract in one trading session.

Price Limit Order: A customer order that specifies the price at which a trade can be executed.

Primary Dealer: A designation given by the Federal Reserve System to commercial banks or broker/dealers who meet specific criteria. Among the criteria are capital requirements and meaningful participation in Treasury auctions.

Primary Market: (1) For producers, their major purchaser of commodities. (2) In commercial marketing channels, an important center at which spot commodities are concentrated for shipment to terminal markets. (3) To processors, the market that is the major supplier of their commodity needs.

Program Trading: The purchase (or sale) of a large number of stocks contained in or comprising a portfolio. Originally designated this way when index funds and other institutional investors began to embark on large-scale buying or selling campaigns, or "programs," to invest in a manner which replicated a target stock index, the term now also commonly includes computer-aided stock market buying or selling programs, portfolio insurance, and index arbitrage.

Project A: An electronic trading system for futures and options developed by the Chicago Board of Trade.

Promotional Material: Any text of a standardized oral presentation, or any communication for publication in any newspaper, magazine, or similar medium, or for broadcast over television, radio, or other electronic medium, which is disseminated or directed to the public concerning a futures account, agreement, or transaction; any standardized form of report, letter, circular, memorandum, publication, or any other written material disseminated or directed to the public for the purpose of soliciting a futures account, agreement, or transaction.

Proof of Service: A court paper filed as evidence that the witness or party to a lawsuit was served with the papers.

Purchase and Sale Statement (P&S):   A statement sent by a futures commission merchant to a customer when a futures or options position has been liquidated or offset. The statement shows the number of contracts bought or sold, the prices at which the contracts were bought or sold, the gross profit or loss, the commission charges, and the net profit or loss on the transaction. Sometimes combined with a *confirmation statement.*

Put Option: An option that gives the option buyer the right, but not the obligation, to sell the underlying futures contract at a particular price on or before a particular date.

Pyramiding: The use of unrealized profits on existing futures positions as margin to increase the size of the position, normally in successively smaller increments.

Quick Order: *See* Fill or Kill Order.

Quotation: The actual price or the bid or ask price of either cash commodities or futures or options contracts at a particular time.

Rally: An upward movement of prices.

Random Walk: An economic theory that price movements in the commodity futures markets and in the securities markets are completely random in character, therefore, past prices are not a reliable indicator of future prices.

Range: The difference between the high and low price of a commodity during a given trading session, week, month, year, etc.

Ratio Hedge: The number of options compared to the number of futures contracts bought or sold in order to establish a hedge that is risk neutral.

Ratio Spread: A strategy, which applies to both puts and calls and involves buying or selling options at one strike price in greater number than those bought or sold at another strike price.

Reaction: The downward price movement tendency of a commodity after a price advance.

Receiver: A person appointed by the court to receive and preserve the property or funds that are the subject of litigation.

Recovery: An upward price movement after a decline.

Registered Representative: A person employed by and soliciting business for a commission house or futures commission merchant. (*See also* Associated Person.)

Registrant: A person or firm who has properly applied for and received approval to operate in one or more of the following capacities: futures commission merchant, introducing broker, commodity trading advisor, commodity pool operator, leverage transaction merchant, agricultural trade option merchant, floor broker, floor trader, or associate person.

Registration Action Type: A violation arising from failing to properly register with a regulatory body or being statutorily disqualified from registration.

Regulatory Action: A disciplinary or remedial action taken by a regulatory body, such as the exchanges, the NFA, or the CFTC, in enforcing its rules and the requirements of the Commodity Exchange Act.

Remand: When an appellate body sends a case back to a lower body for further proceedings.

Reparations: Compensation payable to a wronged party in a futures or options transaction. The term is used in conjunction with the CFTC's customer claims procedure to recover civil damages.

Reply: A written response to a counterclaim or a cross-claim.

Reportable Position: The number of open contracts specified by the CFTC at which one must begin reporting total positions by delivery month to the authorized exchange and/or the CFTC.

Reporting Level: Sizes of positions set by the exchanges and/or the CFTC at or above which commodity traders or brokers who carry these accounts must make daily reports about the size of the position by commodity, by delivery month, and whether or not the position is controlled by a commercial or noncommercial trader.

Resistance: In technical trading, a price area where new selling will emerge to dampen a continued rise.

Respondent: A person or firm named in a disciplinary or remedial action; a person or firm alleged to have been the cause of rule violations; a person or firm against whom a claim is asserted in an arbitration or reparations matter.

Response to Notice of Intent: A written response to a notice of intent submitted by the named applicant or registrant.

Resting Order: An order, held by a floor broker, to buy at a price below or to sell at a price above the prevailing market. Such orders may be either day orders or open orders.

Restitution: The act of making good, or of giving the equivalent, for any loss, damage, or injury.

Restraining Order: An order, often granted without notice or hearing, requiring the preservation of the status quo until a hearing can be held to determine the propriety of any injunctive relief, temporary or permanent. A restraining order is always temporary in nature and thus is often called a TRO, for *temporary restraining order.*

Resumption: The reopening the following day of specific futures and options markets that also trade during the evening session.

Retender: In specific circumstances, some contract markets permit holders of futures contracts who have received a delivery notice through the clearinghouse to sell a futures contract and return the notice to the clearinghouse to be reissued to another long. Others permit transfer of notices to another buyer. In either case, the trader is said to have *retendered* the notice.

Reversal: (1) A change of direction in prices. (2) In a legal context, when an appellate body sets aside the decision of another deciding body because of an error. A reversal is often followed by a remand.

Reverse Conversion: With regard to options, a position created by buying a call option, selling a put option, and selling the underlying futures contract. Also referred to as *reversal*.

Reverse Crush Spread: The sale of soybean futures and the simultaneous purchase of soybean oil and meal futures.

Revoke: To recall a power or authority previously conferred, or to annul, repeal, rescind, or cancel privileges or registration. In the case of Commodity Futures Trading Commission registration proceedings, to take away a previously granted registration.

Riding the Yield Curve: Trading in interest rate futures according to the expectations of change in the yield curve.

Ring: A circular area on the trading floor of an exchange where floor traders and floor brokers stand while executing futures trades.

Risk/Reward Ratio: The relationship between the probability of loss and profit. This ratio is often used as a basis for trade selection or comparison.

Roll-Over: The process of lifting a futures or options position and reestablishing it in a more deferred delivery month.

Round Lot: A quantity of a commodity equal in size to the corresponding futures contract for the commodity.

Round Turn: A completed futures transaction involving both a purchase and a liquidating sale, or a sale followed by a covering purchase.

Runners: Messengers who rush orders they receive from phone clerks to floor brokers for execution in the pit or ring.

Sales Practice Action Type: A violation arising from the solicitation and servicing of customer accounts, but not including trade practice or record-keeping matters.

Satisfactorily Subordinated Liabilities: Liabilities of an FCM or IB which are subordinated to the claims of all general creditors of the FCM or independent IB, pursuant to subordination agreements which meet certain standards.

Scalper: A floor trader who trades for small, short-term profits during the course of a trading session, rarely carrying a position overnight.

Secondary Market: Market where previously issued securities are bought and sold.

Security: Common or preferred stock; a bond of a corporation, government, or quasi-government body.

Segregated Account: A special account used to hold and separate customers' assets from those of a broker or firm.

Segregated Funds: The amount of money, securities, and property due to commodity futures or options customers which is held in segregated accounts in compliance with Section 4d of the Commodity Exchange Act and CFTC regulations. Such money, securities, or property may not be commingled with the money, securities, and property of the FCM.

Self-Regulatory Organization (SRO): Self-regulatory organizations (in this case, the futures exchanges and the National Futures Association) enforce minimum financial and sales practice requirements for their members. (*See also* Designated Self-Regulatory Organization.)

Sell on Close: To sell at the end of the trading session within the closing price range.

Sell on Opening: To sell at the beginning of a trading session within the open price range.

Seller's Market: A condition of the market in which there is a scarcity of goods available; hence sellers can obtain better conditions of sale or higher prices.

Seller's Option: The right of a seller to select, within the limits prescribed by a contract, the quality of the commodity delivered and the time and place of delivery.

Selling Hedge: Selling futures contracts to protect against possible decreased prices of commodities.

Settlement: Parties resolving their differences without a trial, commonly without any determination of the merits of the case.

Settlement Agreement: A document that spells out the terms of a resolution by the parties, without an adjudication.

Settlement Price: The daily price at which a clearinghouse settles all accounts between clearing members for each contract month. Settlement prices are used to determine both margin calls and invoice prices for deliveries. The term also refers to a price established by the clearing organization to calculate account values and determine margins for those positions still held and not yet liquidated.

Short: One who has sold futures contracts or the cash commodity. Opposite of *long*.

Short Covering: Purchasing futures to offset a short position.

Short Hedge: Selling futures contracts to protect against possible declining prices of commodities. Opposite of *long hedge*.

Short Selling: Selling a futures contract with the intention of delivering on it or offsetting it at a later date.

Short Squeeze: A market situation in which the lack of supplies tends to force shorts to cover their positions by offseting at higher prices.

Short the Basis: The purchase of futures as a hedge against a commitment to sell in the cash or spot markets. Opposite of *long the basis*.

Soft: A description of a price which is gradually weakening. Also refers to commodities such as sugar, cocoa, and coffee.

Sold Out Market: When liquidation of a weakly held position has been completed and offerings become scarce, the market is said to be sold out.

Sole Proprietorship: A form of business organization in which an individual is fully and personally liable for all the obligations (including debts) of the business, is entitled to all of its profits, and exercises complete managerial control.

SPAN: The Standard Portfolio Analysis of Risk Performance bond system. A portfolio-based method of computing margin requirements on futures and options. SPAN has been adopted by all major U.S. exchanges, many foreign boards of trade, and other participants in the futures industry.

Specialist System: A type of trading commonly used for the exchange trading of securities in which one individual or firm acts as a market maker in a particular security, and carries the obligation to see that trading in that security is fair and orderly by offsetting temporary imbalances in supply and demand by trading for his own account.

Speculative Position Limit: The maximum position, either net long or net short, in one commodity future (or option), or in all futures (or options) of one commodity combined, which may be held or controlled by one person as prescribed by an exchange or by the CFTC. Also called *speculative limit*.

Speculative Position Limit Action Type: A violation arising from exceeding limitations placed upon the number of contracts that may be held by a party at one time.

Speculator: One who tries to profit from buying and selling futures and/or options contracts by anticipating future price movements.

Spot Commodity: Usually refers to a cash market price for a physical commodity that is available for immediate delivery.

Spot Market: *See* Cash Market.

Spot Month: The futures contract which matures and becomes deliverable during the present month.

Spot Price: The price at which a physical commodity for immediate delivery is selling at a given time and place.

Spread: The purchase of one futures delivery month against the sale of another futures delivery month of the same commodity; the purchase of one delivery month of one commodity against the sale of that same delivery month of a different commodity; or the purchase of one commodity in one market against the sale of the commodity in another market, to take advantage of a profit from a change in price relationships. The term *spread* is also used to refer to the difference between the price of a futures month and the price of another month of the same commodity. A spread can also apply to options.

Spreading: The simultaneous buying and selling of two related markets in the expectation that a profit will be made when the position is offset.

Squeeze: A market situation in which the lack of supplies tends to force shorts to cover their positions by offseting at higher prices.

Stay: An order whereby some action is forbidden or held in abeyance until some event occurs or the issuing body lifts its order. Frequently, an order preventing the enforcement of a decision or order in a matter while it is on appeal.

Stock Index: An indicator used to measure and report value changes in a selected group of stocks. How a particular stock index tracks the market depends on its composition; the sampling of stocks, the weighting of individual stocks, and the method of averaging used to establish an index.

Stock Market: A market in which shares of stock are bought and sold.

Stop Close Only Order: A stop order which can only be executed, if possible, during the closing period of the market.

Stop Limit Order: A stop limit order is an order that goes into force as soon as there is a trade at the specified price. However, the order can only be filled at the stop limit price or better.

Stop Order: An order that becomes a market order when the futures contract reaches a particular price level. A sell stop is placed below the market; a buy stop is placed above the market.

Straddle: *See* Spread.

Strangle: An option position consisting of the purchase or sale of put and call options having the same expiration but different strike prices.

Strike Price: The price at which the buyer of a call (or put) option may choose to exercise his right to purchase (or sell) the underlying futures contract.

Summary Action: An action that is taken quickly and without a hearing beforehand.

Summary Judgment: A decision made on the basis of statements and evidence presented for the record without a trial. It is used when there is no dispute as to the facts of a case, and one party is entitled to judgment as a matter of law.

Summary Proceeding: A form of adjudication in which ordinary legal procedures are disregarded so that the issue at hand may be resolved in a timely fashion. Usually, a summary proceeding is limited to a single issue.

Support: The place on a chart where the buying of futures contracts is sufficient to halt a price decline.

Swap: In general, the exchange of one asset or liability for a similar asset or liability for the purpose of lengthening or shortening maturities, or raising or lowering coupon rates, to maximize revenue or minimize financing costs.

Swaption: An option to enter into a swap, i.e., the right, but not the obligation, to enter into a specified type of swap at a specified future date.

Switch: Offsetting a position in one delivery month of a commodity and simultaneously initiating a similar position in another delivery month of the same commodity.

Systemic Risk: Risk that the financial markets as a whole will cease to operate or will operate inefficiently.

Technical Analysis: An approach to forecasting commodity prices which examines patterns of price change, rates of change, and changes in volume of trading and open interest, without regard to underlying fundamental market factors.

Telemarketing: Use of the telephone to solicit or otherwise communicate with futures and options customers or potential customers.

Temporary Injunction: A prohibitive, equitable remedy issued by a court forbidding a person to commit some action that he is attempting to commit, or restraining him in the continuance of some action. It is intended to last only until a hearing can be held.

Temporary License: If certain conditions are met, an applicant for registration as an associated person, floor broker, floor trader, or introducing broker may be granted a temporary license (TL), which allows the applicant to conduct business in that capacity while the application is being considered.

Temporary Restraining Order (TRO):   Prohibits a person from an action that is likely to cause irreparable harm. This differs from an injunction in that it may be granted immediately, without notice to the opposing party and without a hearing. It is intended to last only until a hearing can be held.

Tender: To give notice to the clearinghouse of the intention to initiate delivery of a physical commodity in satisfaction of a futures contract.

Tenderable Grades: Those grades of a commodity which have been officially approved by an exchange as deliverable in settlement of a futures contract.

Terminal Elevator: An elevator located at a point of greatest accumulation in the movement of agricultural products which stores the commodity or moves it to processors.

Terminal Market: Usually synonymous with commodity exchange or futures market, specifically in the United Kingdom.

Theta: The derivative of the option price equation with respect to the remaining time to expiration of the option. A measure of the sensitivity of the value of the option to the passage of time.

Third Party Claim: A claim filed by a respondent against a person not a party to the action.

Tick: The smallest allowable increment of price movement for a contract. Also referred to as *minimum price fluctuation.*

Time Limit Order: A customer order that designates the time during which it can be executed.

Time of Day Order: This is an order which is to be executed at a given minute in the session.

Time Spread: The selling of a nearby option and buying of a more deferred option with the same strike price.

Time Stamp: Part of the order-routing process in which the time of day is stamped on an order. An order is time-stamped when it is (1) received on the trading floor and (2) completed.

Time Value: The amount of money options buyers are willing to pay for an option anticipating that over time, a change in the underlying futures price will cause the option to increase in value. In general, an option premium is the sum of time value and intrinsic value. Any amount by which an option premium exceeds the option's intrinsic value can be considered time value. Also referred to as *extrinsic value.*

To Arrive Contract: A transaction providing for subsequent delivery within a stipulated time limit of a specific grade of a commodity.

Trade Option: A commodity option transaction in which the taker is reasonably believed by the writer to be engaged in business involving use of that commodity or a related commodity.

Trade Practice Action Type: A violation arising from the manner of execution of trades on the floor of an exchange but not including decorum or record-keeping matters.

Traders: In general, people who trade for their own accounts or employees or institutions who trade for their employers' accounts.

Trading Advisor: *See* Commodity Trading Advisor.

Trading Limit: The maximum number of speculative futures contracts one can hold as determined by the CFTC and/or the exchange upon which the contract is traded. Also referred to as *position limit.*

Transfer Notice: A term used on some exchanges to describe a notice of delivery.

Transfer Trades: Entries made upon the books of futures commission merchants for the purpose of (1) transferring existing trades from one account to another within the same office where no change in ownership is involved, or (2) transferring existing trades from the books of one futures commission merchant to the books of another futures commission merchant where no change in ownership is involved. Also called *ex-pit transactions.*

Transferable Option: A contract which permits a position in the option market to be offset by a transaction on the opposite side of the market in the same contract. Also called *transferable contract.*

Trend: The general direction, either upward or downward, in which prices have been moving.

Trendline: In charting, a line drawn across the bottom or top of a price chart indicating the direction or trend of price movement. If up, the trendline is called *bullish;* if down, it is called *bearish.*

TRO: Temporary restraining order.

Uncovered Option: A short call or put option position which is not covered by the purchase or sale of the underlying futures contract or physical commodity.

Underlying Futures Contract: The specific futures contract that the option conveys the right to buy (in case of a call) or sell (in the case of a put).

Up-Front Fees: Fees charged to a pool or a managed account prior to commencement of trading for the pool or account.

Variable Price Limit: A price limit schedule, determined by an exchange, that permits variations above or below the normally allowable price movement for any one trading day.

Variation Margin: Additional margin deposited by a clearing member firm to an exchange clearinghouse during periods of great market volatility or in the case of high-risk accounts.

Versus Cash: A transaction generally used by two hedgers who want to exchange futures for cash positions. Also referred to as *against actuals* or *exchange for physicals*.

Vertical Spread: Buying and selling puts or calls of the same expiration month but which have different strike prices.

Volatility: A measurement of the change in price over a given time period.

Volume: The number of purchases and sales of futures or options on futures contracts made during a specified period of time.

Warehouse Receipt: Document guaranteeing the existence and availability of a given quantity and quality of a commodity in storage; commonly used as the instrument of transfer of ownership in both cash and futures transactions.

Wash Sale: Transactions that give the appearance of purchases and sales, but which are initiated without the intent to make a bona fide transaction and which generally do not result in any actual change in ownership. Such sales are prohibited by the Commodity Exchange Act.

Wash Trading: Entering into or purporting to enter into transactions to give the appearance that purchases and sales have been made, but without any actual change in the trader's market position.

Wire House: *See* Futures Commission Merchant.

Writer: The issuer, grantor, or maker of an option contract.

Yield: A measure of the annual return on an investment.

Yield Curve: A chart in which yield level is plotted on the vertical axis and the term to maturity of debt instruments of similar creditworthiness is plotted on the horizontal axis.

Yield to Maturity: The rate of return an investor receives if a fixed-income security is held to maturity.

A Glossary of the Bond Markets

Accrued Interest: Interest deemed to have been earned on a security but not yet paid to the investor.

Ask Price: Price being sought for the security by the seller.

Basis Point: One one-hundredth of 1 percent. Yield differences among fixed-income securities are stated in basis points.

Bearer Security: A security that has no identification as to owner. It is presumed to be owned by the person who holds it. Bearer securities are freely negotiable, since ownership can be quickly transferred from seller to buyer by delivery of the instrument. In the United States, however, it has not been legal to issue bearer bonds in the municipal or corporate markets since 1982. As a result, bearer bonds available in the secondary market are long-dated maturities issued before this date and are becoming increasingly scarce. Among the disadvantages of bearer securities are that you must clip the coupons and present them to the trustee in order to receive your interest. Also, if the bonds are called, you are not automatically alerted by the issuer or trustee.

Bid: The price at which a buyer will purchase a security.

Bond Insurers and Reinsurers: A partial list of bond insurers includes American Municipal Bond Assurance Corp: (AMBAC), ACA Financial Guaranty, Asset Guaranty Insurance Co., AXA Re Finance, Capital Guaranty Insurance Co., Capital Markets Assurance Corp. (CapMAC), Capital Reinsurance Co. (Capital Re), Enhance Reinsurance Co. (Enhance Re), Financial Guaranty Insurance Co. (FGIC), Financial Security Assurance (FSA), and Municipal Bond Insurance Association (MBIA).

Book-Entry: A method of recording and transferring ownership of securities electronically, eliminating the need for physical certificates.

Callable Bonds: Bonds which are redeemable by the issuer prior to the maturity date at a specified price at or above par.

Call Premium: A dollar amount, usually stated as a percent of the principal amount called, paid by the issuer as a "penalty" for the exercise of a call provision.

Cap: The top interest rate that can be paid on a floating-rate security.

Closed-End Investment Company: An investment company created with a fixed number of shares which are then traded as listed securities on a stock exchange. After the initial offering, existing shares can only be bought from existing shareholders.

Collar: Upper and lower limits (cap and floor, respectively) on the interest rate of a floating-rate security.

Collateralized Mortgage Obligation (CMO): A bond backed by a pool of mortgage pass-through securities or mortgage loans, which generally supports several classes of obligations. (*See* Real Estate Mortgage Investment Conduit.)

Coupon: This part of a bearer bond denotes the amount of interest due and on what date and where payment will be made. Bearer coupons are presented to the issuer's designated paying agent for collection. With registered bonds, physical coupons don't exist. (*See* Registered Bond.) The payment is mailed directly to the registered holder. Note that while bearer bonds are no longer issued in the United States and, hence, physical coupons are increasingly scarce, dealers and investors often still refer to the stated interest rate on a registered or book-entry bond as the *coupon.*

Current Yield: The ratio of interest to the actual market price of the bond, stated as a percentage. For example, a bond with a current market price of $1,000 that pays $80 per year in interest would have a current yield of 8%.

CUSIP: The Committee on Uniform Security Identification Procedures, established under the auspices of the American Bankers Association to develop a uniform method of identifying securities. CUSIP numbers are unique nine-digit numbers assigned to each series of securities.

Dated Date: The date of a bond issue from which the first owner of a bond is entitled to receive interest. Issue date.

Default: Failure to pay principal or interest when due. Defaults can also occur for failure to meet nonpayment obligations, such as reporting requirements, or when a material problem occurs for the issuer, such as a bankruptcy.

Debenture: An unsecured debt obligation issued against the general credit of a corporation rather than against a specific asset.

Discount: The amount by which the purchase price of a security is less than the principal amount, or par value.

Discount Note: A short-term obligation issued at discount from face value with maturity ranging from overnight to 360 days. There are no periodic interest payments; the investor receives the note's face value at maturity.

Discount Rate: The rate the Federal Reserve charges on loans to member banks.

Duration: The weighted maturity of a fixed-income investment's cash flows; used in the estimation of the price sensitivity of fixed-income securities for a given change in interest rates.

Embedded Option: A provision within a bond giving either the issuer or the bondholder an option to take some action against the other party. The most common embedded option is a *call option,* which gives the issuer the right to call, or retire, the debt before the scheduled maturity date.

Extension Risk: The risk that rising interest rates will slow the anticipated rate at which mortgages or other loans in a pool will be repaid, causing investors to find their principal committed longer than expected. As a result, they may miss the opportunity to earn a higher rate of interest on their money.

Face Amount: Par value (principal or maturity value) of a security appearing on the face of the instrument.

Federal Funds Rate: The interest rate charged by banks on loans of their excess reserve funds to other banks. The Federal Reserve's ability to add or withdraw reserves from the banking system gives it close control over this rate. Changes in the federal funds rate are sometimes studied by economists and investors for clues to Federal Reserve intentions.

Floating-Rate Bond: A bond for which the interest rate is adjusted periodically according to a predetermined formula, usually linked to an index.

Floor: The lower limit for the interest rate on a floating-rate bond.

General Obligation Bond: A municipal bond secured by the pledge of the issuer's full faith, credit, and taxing power.

Hedge: An investment made with the intention of minimizing the impact of adverse movements in interest rates or securities prices.

High-Yield Bonds: Bonds issued by lower-rated corporations, sovereign countries, and other entities rated Ba or BB or below and offering a higher yield than more creditworthy securities. Sometimes known as *junk bonds.*

Investment-Grade: Bonds considered suitable for preservation of invested capital by the rating agencies and rated Baa or BBB or above.

Issuer: An entity which issues and is obligated to pay principal and interest on securities.

Interest: Compensation paid or to be paid for the use of money. Interest is generally expressed as an annual percentage rate.

Junk Bond: A debt obligation with a rating of Ba or BB or lower, generally paying interest above the return on more highly rated bonds. Sometimes known as *high-yield bonds.*

Leverage: The use of borrowed money to increase investing power.

LIBOR (London Interbank Offered Rate):   The rate banks charge each other for short-term Eurodollar loans. LIBOR is frequently used as the base for resetting rates on floating-rate securities.

Marketability: A measure of the ease with which a security can be sold in the secondary market.

Maturity: The date when the principal amount of a security is payable.

Mortgage Pass-Through: A security representing a direct interest in a pool of mortgage loans. The pass-through issuer or servicer collects payments on the loans in the pool and "passes through" the principal and interest to the security holders on a pro rata basis.

Mutual Fund: Also known as an *open-end investment company,* to differentiate it from a *closed-end investment company.* Mutual funds invest the pooled cash of many investors to meet the fund's stated investment objectives. Mutual funds stand ready to sell and redeem their shares at any time at the fund's current net asset value, which is total fund assets divided by shares outstanding.

Noncallable Bond: A bond that cannot be called for redemption by the issuer before its specified maturity date.

Offer: The price at which a seller will sell a security.

Offering Price: The price at which members of an underwriting syndicate for a new issue will offer securities to investors.

Par Value: The principal amount of a bond or note, which is due at maturity.

Paying Agent: Place where principal and interest are payable, usually a designated bank or the office of the treasurer of the issuer.

Premium: The amount by which the price of a security exceeds its principal amount.

Prepayment: The unscheduled partial or complete payment of the principal amount outstanding on a mortgage or other debt before it is due.

Prepayment Risk: The risk that falling interest rates will lead to heavy prepayments of mortgage or other loans, forcing the investor to have to reinvest at lower prevailing rates.

Primary Market: The market for new issues.

Principal: The face amount of a bond, payable at maturity.

Ratings: Designations used by credit rating agencies to give relative indications of credit quality.

Registered Bond: A bond whose owner is registered with the issuer or its agent. Transfer of ownership can only be accomplished when the securities are properly endorsed by the registered owner.

Reinvestment Risk: The risk that interest income or principal repayments will have to be reinvested at lower rates in a declining rate environment.

Real Estate Mortgage Investment Conduit (REMIC): Because of changes in the 1986 Tax Reform Act, most CMOs are now issued in REMIC form to create certain tax advantages for the issuer. The terms REMIC and CMO are now used interchangeably.

Revenue Bond: A municipal bond payable from revenues derived from tolls, charges, or rents paid by users of the facility constructed with the proceeds of the bond issue.

Secondary Market: Market for issues previously offered or sold.

Settlement Date: The date for the delivery of securities and payment of funds.

Sinker: A bond with a sinking fund.

Sinking Fund: Money set aside by an issuer of bonds on a regular basis for the specific purpose of redeeming debt.

Swap: The sale of a block of bonds and the purchase of another block of similar market value. Swaps may be made to establish a tax loss, upgrade credit quality, extend or shorten maturity, etc.

Trade Date: The date when the purchase or sale of a bond is executed.

Transfer Agent: A party appointed by an issuer to maintain records of securities owners, to cancel and issue certificates, and to address issues arising from lost, destroyed, or stolen certificates.

Trustee: A bank designated by the issuer as the custodian of funds and official representative of bondholders.

Unit Investment Trust: Investment funds created with a fixed portfolio of investments that never changes over the life of the trust. They are created by brokerage houses and are liquidated as investments within the trust are paid off. They provide a steady, periodic flow of income to investors.

Yield: The annual percentage rate of return earned on a security. Yield is a function of a security's purchase price and coupon interest rate.

Yield Curve: A line tracing relative yields on a type of security over a spectrum of maturities ranging from three months to 30 years.

Yield to Call: A yield on a security calculated by assuming that interest payments will be paid until the call date, when the security will be redeemed at the call price.

Yield to Maturity: A yield based on the assumption that the security remains outstanding to maturity. It represents the total of coupon payments until maturity, plus interest on interest and whatever gain or loss is realized from the security at maturity.

Zero-Coupon Bond: A bond where no periodic interest payments are made. The investor receives one payment, which includes principal and interest, at redemption (call or maturity). (*See* Discount Note.)

SOURCE: The Bond Market Association. *An Investor's Guide to Bond Basics.* Copyright 1998. Reprinted with permission.